# Posttraumatic Growth

*Posttraumatic Growth* reworks and overhauls the seminal 2006 *Handbook of Posttraumatic Growth*. It provides a wide range of answers to questions concerning knowledge of posttraumatic growth (PTG) theory, its synthesis and contrast with other theories and models, and its applications in diverse settings. The book starts with an overview of the history, components, and outcomes of PTG. Next, chapters review quantitative, qualitative, and cross-cultural research on PTG, including in relation to cognitive function, identity formation, cross-national and gender differences, and similarities and differences between adults and children. The final section shows readers how to facilitate optimal outcomes with PTG at the level of the individual, the group, the community, and society.

**Richard G. Tedeschi, PhD,** is a professor of psychological science at the University of North Carolina at Charlotte, where he conducts research on posttraumatic growth and serves as core faculty for the health psychology doctoral program.

**Jane Shakespeare-Finch, PhD,** is a professor in psychology and counseling at Queensland University of Technology in Brisbane, Australia, and president of the Australasian Society for Traumatic Stress Studies. Dr. Shakespeare-Finch has conducted PTG research for 20 years and published widely.

**Kanako Taku, PhD,** is an associate professor in the Department of Psychology at Oakland University in Michigan. She has conducted PTG research cross-culturally and authored articles and books in English and Japanese.

**Lawrence G. Calhoun, PhD,** is a professor emeritus of psychological science at the University of North Carolina at Charlotte. Along with Dr. Tedeschi, he is one of the pioneers in research and applications of posttraumatic growth.

"It has been over twenty years since the term 'posttraumatic growth' was coined by Richard Tedeschi and Lawrence Calhoun. In that time, these authors' pioneering and inspirational work have helped posttraumatic growth become a flagship theme of positive psychology, one that has garnered interest from personality, social, and clinical psychologists across the world. This is a milestone book written by the leaders in the field, and it will surely set the agenda for theory, research, and practice for the next twenty years. It is a must read for all students, academics, and practitioners interested in the study of traumatic stress and how to help people overcome adversity."

**Stephen Joseph, PhD**, author of *What Doesn't Kill Us:*
*The New Psychology of Posttraumatic Growth*

"This new book is a plentiful harvest of more than twenty years of international research and applied practice on posttraumatic growth. The two world-leading originators of the concept are joined by the two leading experts in international research on posttraumatic growth. What a stupendous work of diligence and scholarship!"

**Andreas Maercker, PhD MD**, chair and professor
of psychology, Division of Psychopathology and
Clinical Intervention, University of Zurich

"*Posttraumatic Growth* is the definitive and up to date guide on trauma and positive change written by the world's leading researchers on the subject. The remarkable depth and global reach of the book shows just how far Richard Tedeschi and Lawrence Calhoun's pioneering work has come in just a few decades. *Posttraumatic Growth* is required reading for anyone hoping to understand this fundamental human response to struggle."

**Jim Rendon**, author of *Upside: The New*
*Science of Post-Traumatic Growth*

# Posttraumatic Growth

*Theory, Research, and Applications*

Richard G. Tedeschi, Jane Shakespeare-Finch, Kanako Taku, and Lawrence G. Calhoun

Routledge
Taylor & Francis Group

NEW YORK AND LONDON

First published 2018
by Routledge
711 Third Avenue, New York, NY 10017

and by Routledge
2 Park Square, Milton Park, Abingdon, Oxon, OX14 4RN

*Routledge is an imprint of the Taylor & Francis Group, an informa business*

*Library of Congress Cataloging-in-Publication Data*
Names: Tedeschi, Richard G., author.
Title: Posttraumatic growth : theory, research and applications / Richard G.
   Tedeschi [and three others].
Description: New York, NY : Routledge, 2018.
Identifiers: LCCN 2017058579 | ISBN 9781138675018 (hardcover : alk. paper) |
   ISBN 9781138675049 (pbk. : alk. paper) | ISBN 9781315527451 (e-book)
Subjects: LCSH: Suffering. | Posttraumatic growth. | Life change events—
   Psychological aspects.
Classification: LCC BF789.S8 T4295 2018 | DDC 616.85/21—dc23
LC record available at https://lccn.loc.gov/2017058579

ISBN: 978-1-138-67501-8 (hbk)
ISBN: 978-1-138-67504-9 (pbk)
ISBN: 978-1-315-52745-1 (ebk)

Typeset in Minion
by Apex CoVantage, LLC

# Contents

# Preface

The idea that challenges and struggles can lead to positive personal or societal change, even if they leave indelible scars and permanent wounds, is not new. The hero-journey, for example, where a quest leads to hardships and suffering, but where triumph eventually is achieved, has been part of human art and literature for thousands of years. However, it was not until the term *posttraumatic growth* first appeared in print in the mid-1990s that the systematic investigation of this phenomenon began in earnest. There had, of course, been pioneers who had suggested, and even studied, this possibility of positive post-trauma transformations. However, perhaps simply because of the accident of timing, the term, *posttraumatic growth*, and the scale designed to assess the construct, encouraged clinicians and researchers to closely examine the possibility of good coming out of the struggle with something bad—of growth emerging from the struggle with highly stressful events.

No doubt aided by the emphasis on positive psychology, a term coined by Martin Seligman a few years later (1998), posttraumatic growth is now known and investigated throughout the world. Posttraumatic growth does not deny the distress associated with highly challenging experiences at the time, and at certain times after. The evidence supporting posttraumatic growth does, however, demonstrate the unique capacity for many people to learn and grow from extreme adversity.

This book is itself a reflection of how far the idea has spread: the four authors represent, in one way or another, experiences and research from four continents. The goal of this volume is to provide a comprehensive overview of *posttraumatic growth* so that those both already familiar with this area and brand new to it will find answers to questions they may have.

In order not to break up the rhythm of reading, we have not been exhaustive with our in-text citations. However, we have also tried to be thorough and comprehensive in our description of the full literature on posttraumatic growth that is currently available. We have grouped our coverage of the PTG literature according to topics, but it is clear that some studies and writings fit into more than one topic. We avoided redundancy in citing these works, so for example, the reader may need to find works on cancer in places other than the specific section on cancer.

We hope that this volume will encourage a further examination of posttraumatic growth by researchers, and an application of the concepts of posttraumatic growth more broadly in clinical work. We also hope that the material will assist organizations and individuals to engage in best practice to support staff and volunteers in times of difficulties.

We are indebted to our students and colleagues who have contributed to our work, and to the many researchers and clinicians across the world who have advanced knowledge and interest in this field. We are especially grateful to all the people who have experienced traumatic events and devoted time and effort explaining to us what their experiences have been like, and how they have been changed by the struggle.

# PART I

# Posttraumatic Growth Theory

# CHAPTER 1

# What Is Posttraumatic Growth?

Tedeschi and Calhoun have given the same definition of *posttraumatic growth* (PTG) since coining the term in the mid-1990s, that is, positive psychological changes experienced as a result of the struggle with traumatic or highly challenging life circumstances. These changes occur in response to the challenge to what people assumed to be true about the lives they lived. Foundational to the concept of PTG is the constructivist perspective that people create individual versions of basic cognitive categories used to understand experience, and core beliefs about the self, their future, and their world. Personal construct theory (Kelly, 1955), schema theory (Epstein, 1990), and assumptive world models (Janoff-Bulman, 1992) provide ways to understand the PTG process in this constructivist tradition. In addition, the PTG concept has benefited from the broad existentialist tradition in philosophy and psychology, which provided a perspective on the problem of suffering and general life philosophies that guide meaning ascribed to events and initiatives taken (Frankl, 1963; Nietzsche, 1889/1990). We begin here with a careful consideration of the meaning of the term PTG, because its meaning is crucial in theory development and in how we choose to measure this construct. We will consider what we mean by *trauma*, *posttraumatic*, and *growth*.

There is disagreement about the definition of trauma (e.g., Weathers & Keane, 2007). Some of the reasons for this stem from the Criterion A definitions provided in the DSM-III and DSM-IV (Diagnostic and Statistical Manual of Mental Disorders, 1980, 1994), which include both a situational (i.e., nature of the event) and a response requirement for a diagnosis of posttraumatic stress disorder (PTSD). The former manual describes an event that is "generally outside the range of usual human experience" that would "evoke significant symptoms of distress in most people" (APA, 1980, p. 236). The later edition extended this definition to anyone who

> experienced, witnessed, or was confronted with an event . . . that involved actual or threatened death or serious injury, or a threat to the physical integrity of self or others . . . [that in adults was responded to with] intense fear, helplessness or horror.
>
> (APA, 1994, pp. 427–428)

Controversies have not diminished with the DSM-5 (APA, 2013; Wakefield, 2016). Trauma, when discussed in the classification systems devoted to psychiatric disorders (DSM; ICD), is currently defined in relation to events and to the presence of symptoms of PTSD.

However, our focus on growth led to a broader definition of what constitutes a traumatic event. As Calhoun and Tedeschi said (2004, p. 100), "it is not the event itself that defines trauma, but its effect on schemas, exposing them to reconstruction." In this book we will use the terms trauma, crisis, and major stressor, as well as related terms, as essentially synonymous expressions to describe circumstances that significantly challenge or invalidate important components of the individual's assumptive world (Calhoun & Tedeschi, 2006). From this perspective, to be considered traumatic events do not necessarily have to be life-threatening or narrowly defined as a cause for PTSD symptoms. We focus on both subjective and objective qualities when defining trauma, unlike the DSM-5, in which assessment of subjective responses following a traumatic event are no longer required when diagnosing PTSD. In addition, DSM-5 defines trauma as an aversive event involving actual or threatened death that must be violent or accidental, whereas we define trauma as a highly stressful and challenging *life-altering* event. It is not possible to determine in advance what events will be traumatic and which will set in motion substantial personal changes. This is why researchers may find no differences between DSM-defined traumatic events and others in terms of PTG outcomes (e.g., Silverstein, Lee, Witte, & Weathers, 2017). When Shakespeare-Finch and Armstrong (2010) examined PTG and symptoms of PTSD in people who had experienced (1) sexual abuse, (2) serious motor vehicle accidents, and (3) people who had been bereaved, all participants viewed their experiences as traumatic, even, for example, when their experience of bereavement was not violent or accidental. Tedeschi and Calhoun (2004b) reviewed PTG in the context of a variety of events, including HIV infection, cancer, and combat. The definition of what constitutes a traumatic event may change over time and may be different across cultures, which is another reason to take an extended view when defining an event as traumatic for a particular person. In some ways, whether or not an event is traumatic is in the eye of the beholder.

It is important to distinguish what constitutes a traumatic event from daily stressors or minor hassles. We are interested in how people change "in the aftermath of events that are undesirable in the extreme" (Tedeschi, Park, & Calhoun, 1998, p. 3)—events that are likely to cause fundamental and transformative changes. Our perspective is on traumatic events that are "seismic" (Calhoun & Tedeschi, 1999). Just as earthquakes can shake or shatter the foundations of buildings, some events are so psychologically seismic that they will seriously challenge or shatter an individual's assumptive world. The event needs to be significant enough to challenge

> the basic assumptions about one's future and how to move toward that future, and therefore produce massive anxiety and psychic pain that is difficult to manage. Inherent in these traumatic experiences are losses such as the loss of loved ones, of cherished roles or capabilities, or of fundamental, accepted ways of understanding life.
>
> (Tedeschi et al., 1998, p. 2)

Finally, we need to carefully consider what we mean by a traumatic, stressful, or challenging *event*. In many cases, people experience life-changing circumstances that are not easily described in terms of a single event. Some circumstances may occur over a period of time and include many events; this is usually the case with the aftermath of a traumatic event. In combat, it may not be a single battle that is the catalyst for change, but an entire deployment into a combat zone. A natural disaster may include a variety of specific components, including the disaster itself, finding help in the immediate aftermath, and what is sometimes a long process of rebuilding physically and psychologically. The terminal illness of a loved one may extend over days or months and include many interactions with that person and with others. Later we will consider the question of PTG for people who live in families or communities where traumatic events are an everyday fact of life. In such cases it can be difficult to identify a single traumatic event, or what is post-traumatic, and the degree to which there may be challenges to ways of thinking.

## What Is "Posttraumatic"?

The construct of PTG is focused on changes in people *after* an event rather than their responses during an event. In addition, posttraumatic growth does not focus on changes in the immediate aftermath of the event, when people may be reacting without any careful consideration, but almost instinctively. Instead, PTG is focused on longer-term changes that come about after more careful reflection. Post-trauma is usually an extended time period, from days to years, where people develop new ways of thinking, feeling, and behaving, because the events they have experienced do not permit a return to baseline functioning. This is a crucial way that PTG is also distinguished from "resilience," a return to baseline or resistance to trauma, and "recovery," which has similar connotations.

## What Is "Growth"?

One important feature of PTG is that the change is transformative. It involves positive changes in cognitive and emotional life that are likely to have behavioral implications; the changes can be profound and may be truly transformative (Tedeschi & Calhoun, 1995). Since 1995, research has provided evidence of positive changes in all of these domains: cognitive (Calhoun, Cann, Tedeschi, & McMillan, 2000), emotional (Park, Aldwin, Fenster, & Snyder, 2008), and behavioral (Shakespeare-Finch & Enders, 2008; Shakespeare-Finch & Barrington, 2012).

Personal development, change, increasing maturity, and growth are normative and occur throughout various developmental periods. This type of change is not PTG (Tedeschi & Calhoun, 2012). The changes characteristic of PTG may be similar to those seen in normative development, or may occur in the context of normative development as well as trauma. How the changes occur defines the difference. PTG occurs as a result of a *struggle* with the aftermath of a major life crisis. The struggle that leads to PTG is not usually at first a struggle to grow or change, but rather to survive or cope. The growth tends to be unplanned and unexpected, although we will discuss later that it may be facilitated by certain interventions.

The term "growth" rather than "benefits" is used in referring to PTG. In their earlier work in the 1980s and early 1990s, Tedeschi and Calhoun described the reports of growth in trauma survivors as "perceived benefits." However, they came to appreciate that this term might indicate that reports of growth might be untrustworthy, and that the changes might be beneficial without representing growth or transformation. Although there are different degrees of personal growth that can be seen in the aftermath of trauma, and there are different trajectories of PTG, we also prefer the term "growth" because the changes people report are experienced by them as indicating positive, transformative development.

The terms "perceived benefits" and "benefit-finding" are most often seen in the literature that examines physical health and illness (e.g., Antoni et al., 2001), and these perceived benefits are sometimes described as equivalent to PTG. However, they include changes such as improved health behaviors (e.g., stopping tobacco use), which for most people are beneficial but not experienced as personally transformative. In the health-related benefits literature, we might see true PTG or other less transformational change.

> Some pathways may involve profound changes in perspectives on living that will promote changes in health and social behavior that yield better health outcomes. Others may involve changed life perspectives that reduce stress responses and have effects on immune system functioning. Other pathways to better health outcomes might proceed from more specific changes in health or social behavior that yield health benefits, without more general personal transformation.
>
> (Aspinwall & Tedeschi, 2010, p. 7)

Changes analogous to PTG have also been investigated in the context of changes that occur in the aftermath of positive events, as well as those resulting from self-initiated challenging experiences. For example, Suedfeld, Kjærgaard, and Leon reported on the personal changes that occur in the aftermath of space travel (Suedfeld, Legkaia, & Brcic, 2010), solo circumnavigations by sailing (Kjærgaard, Leon, & Venables, 2015), and arctic exploration (Kjærgaard, Leon, Venables, & Fink, 2013). These scholars used the concept of PTG and found that persons who choose to endure such challenging environments can be changed in ways that are very much like those changes reported by people who are forced to endure traumatic events. These findings suggest that changes analogous to PTG can happen in people who have not been exposed to events defined as traumatic. However, by definition, PTG is a result of processes initiated by a significant challenge to a person's assumptive world—a challenge to their core beliefs.

# CHAPTER 2

# A History of the Concept of Posttraumatic Growth in Psychology and Related Disciplines

The specific term *posttraumatic growth* is relatively new. It was first published in 1995 in an early version of the PTGI in the appendix of *Trauma and Transformation* (Tedeschi & Calhoun, 1995) and measured using the PTGI in 1996 (Tedeschi & Calhoun, 1996). However, PTG as a phenomenon is not new. The history of mankind is the history of trauma and the history of PTG. As Tedeschi and Calhoun (2004b) have discussed, for thousands of years there have been stories of positive changes in individuals and societies in general as a result of suffering and distress. The potential for transformative positive change from the experience of great challenge and despair is referred to in the texts and teachings of all major religions and is reflected in the writings of ancient philosophers and scholars of other disciplines. Drawing on this wisdom, old and new, and combined with contemporary knowledge gained through empirical evidence of various types, it is clear that a majority of people who experience trauma recover, are resilient to the impact of potential trauma, or experience growth.

Philosophical and theoretical positions from scholars in more recent decades have articulated their thoughts about processes that parallel PTG. For example, Maslow's humanistic stance about human life has been made clear. He wrote:

> human life will never be understood unless its highest aspirations are taken into account. Growth, self-actualization, the striving toward health, the quest for identity and autonomy, the yearning for excellence (and other ways of phrasing the striving "upward") must by now be accepted beyond question as a widespread and perhaps universal human tendency . . . growth is often a painful process.
>
> (Maslow, 1970, pp. xii–xiii)

Similarly, Rogers repeatedly wrote about how painful personal growth is, "even though in the long run rewarding" (Rogers, 1961, p. 14). Dabrowski (1964) described a process of personality development called "positive disintegration," where dissolving mechanisms challenge a mediocre life cycle that may then give way to a more creative emotional and intellectual development. Existential theorists such as Frankl (1963, 1965) have clearly focused on the theme of creating meaning in the midst of trauma, and PTG theory owes much to this theoretical perspective and the reports in the existential literature of how people not only survive trauma but are transformed by it. The historical roots of PTG theory in religion, philosophy, and literature are explored in detail in Tedeschi and Calhoun (1995).

## PTG—the Beginnings

Although reports on *posttraumatic growth*, under that rubric, were first published in the 1990s when Tedeschi and Calhoun introduced the term, their previous studies of the potential positive impact of the struggle with stressful events appeared in the 1980s. The book *Trauma and Transformation: Growing in the Aftermath of Suffering* (Tedeschi & Calhoun, 1995) provides an overview of the studies of PTG that had been performed to that point using different terms, such as perceived benefits (which these authors used themselves in previous work; e.g., Calhoun & Tedeschi, 1991). Tedeschi, Park, and Calhoun (1998) also examined the development of the PTG concept, and conceptually related ones that predate it, with a chapter by O'Leary, Alday, and Ickovics in that volume particularly relevant. Some terms conceptually related to PTG include stren conversion (Finkel, 1974, 1975), positive psychological changes (Yalom & Lieberman, 1991), construing benefits (McMillen, Zuravin, & Rideout, 1995; Tennen, Affleck, Urrows, Higgins, & Mendola, 1992), stress-related growth (Park, Cohen, & Murch, 1996), adversarial growth (Linley & Joseph, 2004), flourishing (Ryff & Singer, 1998), positive by-products (McMillen, Howard, Nower, & Chung, 2001), discovery of meaning (Bower, Kemeny, Taylor, & Fahey, 1998), thriving (O'Leary & Ickovics, 1995), positive illusions (Taylor & Brown (1988), positive reinterpretation (Scheier, Weintraub, & Carver, 1986), drawing strength from adversity (McCrae, 1984), and transformational coping (Aldwin, 1994; Pargament, 1996). Tedeschi and Calhoun first used the term posttraumatic growth (PTG) in print in 1995 and in an article in 1996 describing the development of the Posttraumatic Growth Inventory (PTGI).

## Interdisciplinary PTG

Before systematic research examining PTG began, the theme of personal growth from life crises had been addressed in the arts, literature, philosophy, history, sociology, economics, biology, and psychology. Philosophical inquiry, as well as the work of novelists, dramatists, and poets, has focused on understanding and discovering the meaning of human suffering (Tedeschi & Calhoun, 1995, 2004b). Since the term PTG was coined in 1995, this phenomenon has become recognized as a powerful aspect of human nature, and it has been studied in various disciplines interested in the phenomenon of trauma response, including psychology, gender and sexuality studies, cultural studies, medicine, military studies, nursing, and social work.

As more studies have been conducted, it has become clear that PTG research can benefit from an interdisciplinary perspective. Interdisciplinary research is based on a conceptual model that links or integrates theoretical frameworks from two or more disciplines, uses study design and methodology that is not limited to any one field, and requires the use of perspectives and skills of the involved disciplines throughout multiple phases of the research process (Aboelela et al., 2007). As also encouraged by grant agencies, such as NIH (National Institutes of Health) or NSF (National Science Foundation), more studies are being conducted under the name of interdisciplinarity.

PTG is, and should be, an area of interdisciplinary interest, because it has clear links to a variety of disciplines. PTG researchers, theoreticians, and clinicians will better understand this human experience and ways in which to facilitate its application to clinical settings and everyday lives by considering PTG from the perspective of other disciplines. PTG is also better understood when taking holistic views of knowledge. For example, the combination of researchers and practitioners from psychology and creative industries may approach interventions for trauma survivors that are verbal or non-verbal, such as art therapy and art groups, performance art, music, and/or drama.

Interdisciplinary research on PTG can focus, for example, on how experiences are affected by the use of language with trauma survivors by working with researchers who have backgrounds in linguistics and anthropology. Considering PTG within a bio-psycho-social-spiritual framework requires familiarity with several disciplines. As demonstrated in this book, the possibility that people can change in a positive way from their struggle with a traumatic event can generate questions that may be better approached within one discipline or another. Instead of relying on one specific discipline, it is ideal to study this complex experience from interdisciplinary perspectives.

Cacciatore and Flint (2012), for example, reported a case study supporting the PTG framework in the bereaved by using an interdisciplinary paradigm for health-care professionals, including physicians, social workers, therapists, nursing staff, and other providers. As they indicated, many mental health providers face the reality of patients' requests, which often include alleviation of symptoms; this forces them to take pharmacologically based approaches, but at the same time, they see the hope and possibility in patients who are experiencing psychological growth. Even in patients who are dying, it is possible to see a glimpse of PTG, which may not make sense if we assume PTG and recovery are synonymous. PTG is better understood when the traditional biomedical model is combined with other models such as existential models, social-personality models, spiritual-philosophical models, and so on.

One thing we have noticed is that, although PTG research may be best studied in an interdisciplinary way, it has predominantly been conducted by psychologists and clinicians such as social workers, nurses, oncologists, psychiatrists, and other mental health specialists. So far, there has been almost no study of PTG in the humanities other than references to the concept of growth as noted above.

Another emerging approach in this area is transdisciplinary research. Rather than drawing on experts with different discipline orientations, theories, methods, etcetera, transdisciplinary research reflects the creation of a new holistic way of approaching a question—an approach that transcends traditional disciplines by creating a new subdiscipline in itself. Such approaches are understandably challenging as members of a research team learn about each other's disciplines on the road to creating new ways of thinking and approaching important research questions of the time.

## PTG and Psychology

PTG research is found in a variety of psychology subdisciplines and is rooted in a variety of theoretical perspectives in psychology, including cognitive, developmental, existential, health, humanistic, narrative/constructivist, personality, trauma studies, social, and clinical psychology.

### Cognitive Psychology

PTG can take the form of changes in a person's cognition. Historically, the cognitive tradition emerged in contrast to the objective tradition. PTG research fits within cognitive psychology well because it emphasizes how the structure of one's cognitive framework can be challenged or shattered through confrontation with extreme adversity and rebuilt as a result of the psychological struggle with life crises. Ultimately, because there is no "objective" scale to universally assess personal growth (PTG is not like height or weight), the experiences of PTG are essentially "cognitive," as reflected in the PTG model (Calhoun & Tedeschi, 2006) with key words such as cognitive challenges and cognitive processing. Notions of transformation through effortful rumination embody the idea of cognitively engaging with unhelpful or distressing thought processes.

### Developmental Psychology

PTG is consistent with the notion that any developmental change includes the joint occurrence of gain (growth) and loss (decline) in adaptive capacity (Baltes, 1987). Developmental psychology aims to obtain knowledge about principles of life-long development from conception to death, and about the patterns of positive and negative changes throughout a person's life. PTG is an example of these positive changes under one condition: They occurred due to the psychological struggle with some highly stressful life event/s. As we will discuss later in Part II, Chapter 12, findings have been accumulating in this area.

### Existential and Humanistic Psychology

The primary concern of existential psychologists is to understand human beings' lives from the broad perspective of meaning in life and the inevitable reality of death. This viewpoint can be traced back to philosophers Kierkegaard, Nietzsche, and Sartre. Perhaps the most relevant discussion to PTG can be seen in Victor Frankl's work (1946/1965, 1963). The work of Irving Yalom has also been greatly influential in the developments in this area. The existential perspective tends to focus on questions of life's meaning, and how meaningful living allows for suffering to be meaningful as well. Meaningful suffering becomes survivable. The humanistic approach to psychology is often viewed as close to existential psychology because it has roots in phenomenology. As Abraham Maslow and Carl Rogers, two main founders of humanistic psychology, described, human beings have the potential to set goals, seek meaning and values, and, for a minority, experience self-actualization. If this occurred with trauma, the goals and meaning and values concepts would be understood as the PTG process and self-actualization as an outcome.

### Health Psychology

Trauma is found in health psychology when studies are focused on health conditions that involved great suffering, personal challenge, and changed life circumstances. Highly stressful and traumatic life events can have detrimental health effects. And yet, PTG studies have demonstrated that one can change in a positive way and grow psychologically even while still experiencing extreme difficulties. Much of research on PTG in health psychology has been conducted with cancer patients and has shown positive health behavior changes a significant positive cognitive restructuring in many patients.

### Narrative and Constructivist Psychology

A significant contribution has been made in PTG research from researchers studying narrative psychology or those subscribing to a constructivist view of reality. Neimeyer (2006), for instance, proposed the PTG experience as a form of meaningful reconstruction in the wake of crisis and loss. He suggested that human beings develop personal narratives on three levels: personal, interpersonal, and social, which fit to the PTG theoretical model. "I hope that others who share a fascination with the growth often engendered by great suffering will find in a narrative framework a set of conceptual and practical tools with which to understand, study, and foster this life-enhancing process" (Neimeyer, 2006, p. 78). Researchers who focus on narratives have described how the form of narratives is challenged and disrupted in the face of highly stressful life events, as well as how the new, revised narratives are reconstructed, developed, created, and maintained.

### Personality Psychology

Because PTG can be seen as personality change or personality transformation, it has been of great interest to personality psychologists. Recently, for example, Jayawickreme and Blackie (2014) outlined the ways in which personality psychology can be enriched by studying PTG and vice versa, by rephrasing PTG as positive personality change. Perhaps the most challenging part is the notion that it is difficult to arrive at a universally agreed upon set of "positive" personality traits (Trull & Widiger, 2015) that would indicate that PTG has produced a lasting change in personality. Further, conceptualizing PTG as personality change is contentious within the broader personality psychology literature, much of which proposes fundamental personality traits as robust and consistent in adulthood (e.g., McAdams,

1993; McCrae, 1984). PTG can also be considered from the point of view that certain personalities may be better equipped to experience it; indeed, there is research that demonstrates relationships between personality dimensions and PTG (e.g., Tedeschi & Calhoun, 1996; Shakespeare-Finch, Gow, & Smith, 2005).

### Trauma Psychology

Historically, systematic research on PTG was developed based on a thorough review of the literature on crisis and trauma available at the time (1980s and 1990s), and on clinical and qualitative work with people who had experienced major stressful events; thus, it has a close relationship with trauma psychology. PTG research aims to further understanding those who experience a highly stressful or traumatic event, and identify ways to help people move through the difficulties associated with such experiences; this aligns with the aim of trauma psychology. With an accumulating number of texts, trauma psychologists now have a growing set of resources to inform their practice (e.g., Calhoun & Tedeschi, 1999, 2006, 2013; Tedeschi & Calhoun, 1995, 2004a, 2006; Tedeschi & Moore, 2016a).

### Social Psychology

As reflected in the model, PTG has an important interpersonal aspect, and the PTG phenomenon can only be fully understood when the surrounding contexts are fully recognized. The relationship between dyads and larger systems and groups in a person's life can exert significant influence over the potential for PTG: for example, social support networks, peer support, and responses of loved ones to disclosure of the experience. PTG can also be experienced at a societal level, which we will discuss in Chapter 17. PTG research has been advanced in the past two decades using research methodologies common to social psychology.

### Clinical Psychology

PTG has a close relationship with the area of clinical psychology, because it targets those who may be distressed in reaction to an encounter with highly challenging and traumatic life events. Research in clinical psychology involves developing ways to measure the outcome of clinical interventions—that is, assessment of changes in symptoms of clinical disorder, along with ways to develop more effective interventions. The psychological processes observed and shared by clinical psychologists and their clients often parallel PTG processes. Many clinicians, including psychologists, social workers, psychiatrists, dieticians, counselors, and general practitioners, understand that if the difficulty for which a client or patient has sought assistance is not explicitly about a traumatic experience, there is often a history of trauma beneath the presenting problem. Clinical interventions that are strengths-based, and therefore mindful of the potential for PTG, are an extremely important resource for those struggling with a spectrum of manifestations of their distress (e.g., somatic or emotional).

## PTG and Positive Psychology

PTG first appeared in the literature as a named construct in 1995 (Tedeschi & Calhoun, 1995), whereas positive psychology was not explicitly defined until 2000 (Seligman & Csikszentmihalyi, 2000); thus, research on PTG *predates* the positive psychology movement. The call for researchers to focus on positive aspects of human behavior could be traced as far back as the work William James, Abraham Maslow, and Carl Rogers (Froh, 2004)—long before Seligman introduced the phrase "positive psychology" at the American Psychological Association in 1998. In other words, PTG and positive psychology are related constructs but are not the same.

Because PTG and positive psychology have both been developed partly with the assumption that in the past researchers and clinicians focused too much on deprivation and the mental ill-health of human beings (e.g., how we could repair damage, rather than how we could support each other to grow as human beings or to live meaningfully), they have much common ground.

It is very clear, however, that the scope of PTG goes beyond that of positive psychology and can be better understood with a broader perspective that does not rely solely on ideas within the scope of positive psychology. One reason is that the process of PTG contains psychological struggle initiated by major life crises, which are, in themselves, unpleasant and negative aspects of life, but the key is that people often report both positive and negative experiences when reflecting on experiences of PTG.

PTG is not the same as concentrating only on positive aspects of the human condition. In other words, although positive psychology shares a strengths-based approach to research and understanding the human condition, it does not retain the inevitable distress and difficulty that is inherent in life (Antonovsky & Sagy, 1986; Antonovsky, 1987) and that brings many people to see mental health professionals. Unlike the theory and research on PTG, the emphasis on positive psychology may lead some to artificially dichotomize the study of behavior and of the human condition as either only positive or only negative.

Aspinwall and Tedeschi (2010) raised concerns about the creation of a subdiscipline of positive psychology. They asserted that understanding how people respond to highly challenging experiences, and helping people to negotiate their path through them, has been a core focus of psychology as a discipline. Such a focus includes the investigation of concepts such as growth, resilience, and adaptation more broadly because these impact psychological and physical health. As they suggested:

> We caution that we should not conceptualize these variables that have a "positive flavor" as contained within something we call positive psychology. If we divide the world into positive psychology and not and designate specific concepts as "positive" or "negative," we may create artificial barriers in our communications, the development of our theoretical models, and our decisions about variables to include in our research and interventions.
>
> (Aspinwall & Tedeschi, 2010, p. 4)

As we have indicated, research on PTG should not be confined within the domain of an exclusively "positive" psychology—PTG fits better when examined under the umbrella of a variety of theories and subdisciplines of psychology, including humanistic, existential, clinical, trauma, cognitive, social, personality, developmental, health, and narrative psychology, as well as other social sciences and humanities disciplines.

It is important to note that PTG research does not neglect what are dichotomously termed either positive or negative components of the human condition. As we will describe later in the process depicted in the model of the development of PTG, the current model does not explicitly include the role of positive emotions. However, Calhoun and Tedeschi (2006) considered that the appropriate place to include positive emotions might be in the characteristics of the person's pre-trauma. While neuroticism, or negative emotionality, has not been found to be correlated with PTG (Tedeschi & Calhoun, 1996), positive emotions might be an indicator of success that allows for reflection in the presence of psychological discomfort.

The emergence of PTG requires a complex interaction between intrapersonal processes and interpersonal processes, following exposure to highly stressful and traumatic life events. Positive psychology alone, although a positive influence, is not a sufficiently comprehensive framework within which to understand the phenomenon of PTG.

# CHAPTER 3

# Religion, Philosophy, and Posttraumatic Growth

Religion can play an important role in PTG in multiple ways. A number of studies have examined the role of religion and spiritual beliefs in PTG. Religious participation may prime people for PTG. People who are involved in religious organizations are likely to report greater PTG than those who do not identify with a religious doctrine (Currier, Mallot, Martinez, Sandy, & Neimeyer, 2013). Longitudinal studies have demonstrated that baseline faith predicted an increase in PTG (Yanez et al., 2009). Even with adolescents, identification with a religion has been associated with PTG (Milam, Ritt-Olson, Tan, Unger, & Nezami, 2005). However, other studies showed that openness to religious change, rather than the mere amount of religious participation, is more likely to predict PTG (Calhoun, Cann, Tedeschi, & McMillan, 2000).

A second way religion is involved in PTG is when religion acts as a trigger for PTG. One key element that provides the foundation for PTG is a challenge to one's fundamental core beliefs. Religious beliefs can be one such core belief framework. A highly stressful event, especially an unexpected one, may shatter or shake one's religious beliefs. Serious challenge to one's central religious beliefs may lead to emotional distress, which in turn activates the cognitive processing that may foster PTG. Indirectly, religion may also play a critical role as a distal cultural element. As a distal element, religion can create an environment and culture to develop PTG by affecting the narratives, definitions, and meanings of PTG.

A third connection between PTG and religion is when religion is viewed as an outcome. As illustrated by one of the five factors of the PTGI, profound religious or spiritual changes are sometimes reported as part of the experience of PTG (Tedeschi & Calhoun, 1996). Yanez et al. (2009), for example, measured faith among cancer survivors twice with one year between measurement points, and found that an increase in faith over time predicted an increase in a person's reports of growth. There are, however, differences in the extent to which people endorse religious or spiritual change, both at an individual level and at the level of broader cultural contexts. For example, this dimension of the PTGI is the least endorsed change in Australian populations (Shakespeare-Finch & Morris, 2010).

For those with an existing religious commitment, beliefs inherent in that religious doctrine can provide a way of coping and creating meaning around the challenging experience/s. Religiosity affects PTG processes through the discovery of meaning, coping strategies and resources such as social support, and the development of new or revised narratives (Ai, Hall, Pargament, & Tice, 2013; Shaw, Joseph, & Linley, 2005). Chan and Rhodes (2013) found that positive religious coping strategies, such as seeking spiritual support (e.g., "looked for God's strength, support, and guidance"), benevolent religious reappraisals (e.g., "God might be trying to strengthen me in this situation"), and religious forgiveness (e.g., "asked God to help me overcome my bitterness"), were associated with greater PTG.

Religion can also be viewed as a mediator between demographic variables, such as gender or race, and PTG (Gerber, Boals, & Schuettler, 2011). Bellizzi et al. (2009) provided support that religiousness can be an indirect indicator of greater social support from religious organizations, which could provide means of talking through the experience, leading to PTG. Religiousness can also influence how people respond to a traumatic experience. Religion may encourage forgiveness, for instance, through espousing worldviews that value forgiveness (Schultz, Tallman, & Altmaier, 2010) or maintaining a belief that whatever the experience they have endured, it was part of God's plan for them.

Some religions view pain as necessary for purification, holiness, or preparation for life to come (Calhoun & Tedeschi, 2006). It may be the case that persons in those specific religious cultural contexts find PTG processes and concepts more familiar and cognitively accessible, compared to people who are not participants in those religious cultures. However, the focus exclusively on organized religious institutions does not include the possibilities that spirituality is distinct from religion or that there are helpful strategies and resources that can be drawn on by atheists and agnostics, who can also discover deep meaning in their experience with trauma without reference to religion or a higher power called God. Indeed, some authors have questioned religion as a component of PTG, suggesting it may be confounded when measured as part of PTG (Joseph, 2012).

## PTG and Christianity

Approximately 84% of the world's population subscribes to a religious belief system; Christianity is still the largest religion (Emerson, Mirola, & Monahan, 2016). Although each of the sub-branches of Christianity, such as Roman Catholicism, Orthodox, and Protestantism, have some differing values, practices, and beliefs, in general, Jesus's suffering for human beings is described as something with the power to transform pain for greater growth. Indeed, Christianity was born in the aftermath of trauma: the execution of Jesus. John 16: 20–21 reflects on the crucifixion and says: "Very truly, I tell you, you will weep and mourn . . . you will have pain, but your pain will turn to joy" (see Collicutt McGrath, 2006 for a detailed discussion of PTG and early Christianity).

As discussed by Collicutt McGrath (2006) and by Tedeschi and Calhoun (2004a), the crucifixion of Jesus is a major transformative theme in Christian traditions. Through pain and suffering, Jesus became a symbol for change as his followers rapidly expanded in number and reach throughout the world. According to Tan (2013), the Bible has much to say about suffering and how one can grow through the trials and tribulations of life. God promises that one day, in Heaven to come, there will be no more suffering or pain, which indicates that the Bible does not glorify suffering. A biblical perspective on posttraumatic growth will emphasize the outcomes of brokenness, humility, and deeper Christ-likeness, rather than greater strength and self-confidence. This perspective focuses on God's strength or power being made perfect in human beings' vulnerability and weakness. Weakness is see as the way or the key to a Christian spiritual life, rather than strength and self-sufficiency, which can lead to pride (Tan, 2013). Tan (2013) indicated that "benefit-finding is not the ultimate meaning or end of human suffering" and that "God is doing his deeper work of grace in our hearts and lives through redemptive and sanctified suffering, and in so doing reveals his greater glory in and through us" (p. 363).

One interesting study, conducted by Proffitt, Cann, Calhoun, and Tedeschi (2007), showed that Judeo-Christian clergy experienced PTG out of their own personal traumatic life events. As these researchers said, clergy are people who would typically be expected to have a strong foundation and a secure relationship with God that enabled them to cope with traumatic experiences. But what they found was not only greater use of positive beliefs in coping, such as "I tried to put my plans into action together with God," but also that greater use of negative beliefs, such as "I wondered whether God had abandoned me," further predicted PTG.

Empirical studies, such as that by Harris et al. (2010) targeting non-clergy in Midwestern American Christian churches who experienced traumatic events, also revealed that the use of prayer for calm and focus fostered PTG. Thus, Christians (if not clergy) who can find peace within, or keep themselves focused by having a religious faith, are more likely to experience PTG.

Experiencing PTG does not seem to cause conflict in Christians. The case reports presented by Proffitt et al. (2007) indicated that "to achieve well-being clergy apparently must somehow overcome the social constraints they perceive to be operating that prevent them from sharing their thoughts and insights with others" (p. 229). The degree to which Christians report PTG following core belief challenge may also depend on which type of Christianity people are affiliated with. As is the case with other religions, there are many specific differences in individual interpretations of doctrine intentions and ways that people's lives are shaped, despite a universal overarching belief—in this case, in Jesus as the son of God.

## PTG and Buddhism

Considering PTG in the context of Buddhism, it is useful to consider the following metaphor. Lotus, the flower that blossoms above the surface of the water, is often used in Buddhist art and literature. This may be seen as an image of PTG:

> Because the lotus flower blooms above the muddy waters of stagnant ponds, the lotus is used as a symbol for the purity of mind that develops out of the pollution that is SAMSARA but remains unsullied by it. In addition, the lotus is said to be the only plant that produces its flower and fruit simultaneously,

indicating in some interpretations that the cause (the Buddha's teaching) and its effect (enlightenment) are not separate.

(Buswell & Lopez, 2013, p. 606)

SAMSARA refers to a cycle of birth, aging, death, and rebirth but does not include transmigration of the soul.

A well-known Buddhist folk tale about the plight of a young woman named Kisa Gotami is another example of a PTG-like story in Buddhism.

> Such was the experience of the young woman Kisa Gotami, who had found in her newborn son the full measure of life's joy and fulfillment, until the infant suddenly died. Deranged by grief, she continued to carry the child on her hip as she went from house to house asking for medicine to cure him. Someone took pity and sent her to the Buddha. "O Exalted One," she said, "give me medicine for my son!" The Buddha replied that she had done well to come to him for medicine. He told her to return to town to fetch a few mustard seeds from each household where no one had died and to bring the collection back to him. Relieved that a magical ritual for her son's resurrection was under way, she set out eagerly. An exhaustive canvass, however, yielded not a single grain. At every door in town the reply was the same: "O, Gotami, many have died here!" Finally Kisa Gotami realized the nature of the medicine Buddha had dispensed. Her insane grief was now replaced by gratitude for the Buddha's compassionate wisdom, she took her son to the cremation grounds.
>
> (Novak & Smith, 2003, pp. 15–16)

In the story, the Buddha teaches Gotami two lessons:

> that all human beings are similarly situated in this universe, no matter what their particular differences might be, as death is every human's inevitability; and that one's individual interests, projects and passions are not inherently more valuable than those of others.
>
> (Bhushan, 2008, p. 63)

The lessons of suffering in this story are about its universality and how narcissism contributes to it. Out of the grief that appeared to be inconsolable, the woman in the story achieves an enlightenment that might only have been possible through her experience of tragedy. Note also that the grieving woman does not initially seek enlightenment, but relief from her suffering. This seems to be the case with people who report PTG: The growth is a by-product of the attempt made to cope with suffering and subsequent transformative changes.

In Buddhism, people try to live their lives by following the teaching of the Buddha, Siddhartha Gotama, without necessarily believing in Buddha. Unlike many other religions, Buddhism does not encourage people to espouse faith in a higher power or supernatural being but rather to explore the nature of human experience, including suffering (Wallace & Shapiro, 2006). It is important to note that just as there are differences in the forms Christianity takes, there are many different forms of Buddhism in the world today. Buddhism in Tibet, such as Vajrayana, for example, is very different from Buddhism in China, such as Mahayana, which is also different from Buddhism in Burma or Thailand, that is, Theravada. But because all schools of Buddhism emphasize enlightenment, interconnectedness, realization of emptiness and non-attachment, suffering, and wisdom, in this section, we will discuss how PTG-like themes have been described in Buddhism's context.

First, in Buddhism, life is defined as being full of suffering, and suffering is not only caused by environmental stimuli, but caused by an imbalance of the mind. If one is too happy, he or she is suffering. If one is not happy, he or she is suffering. Thus, people are encouraged to reflect on what desires they have, because whatever desires they have, including becoming happier, can potentially create suffering. This leads to a "middle way" approach advocated in Buddhism. Freedom from suffering can be achieved by letting go of attachments to desire. Buddhists therefore may practice not elevating the desire to experience greater growth, because the desire to change in a better way creates further suffering. To end suffering or reach Nirvana (the ideal goal for Buddhists), the person follows the path of self-improvement by following the spiritual path that contains correct action, speech, and mindfulness (Holt & Austad, 2013). This path means cultivating wisdom, ethics, and meditative absorption or concentration. PTG can be described as a process and an outcome of this path when experiencing suffering, without necessarily labeling it as PTG. But because Buddhists think nothing can stay the same (impermanence) and life is full of suffering, PTG is also a part of life for Buddhists.

Second, connectedness is essential in Buddhism. PTG is likely to be recognized when growth occurs at an inter-relationship level. Even when one is suffering from his or her personal desire,

> the reflection is carried further, focusing not only on the desire and goal itself but also on the cause and effect of specific desires. For example, "if I continue on this track and I try to fulfill this desire, what are the consequences for my own and others' well-being?" In such ways, the right intention implies an altruistic devotion to meaningful desires that are conducive not only to one's own well-being but to the flourishing of others as well.
>
> (Wallace & Shapiro, 2006, p. 694)

Therefore, interpersonal growth, rather than intrapersonal growth, may have been emphasized as a PTG-like theme in Buddhism, which also supports the notion of inter-subjectivity or "no-self." There is a connection here with the view that the ultimate phase of the PTG process can involve finding an altruistic motive or devoting oneself to the service to others (Tedeschi & McNally, 2011).

As more people in Western cultures practice Buddhism, especially Zen Buddhism, the positive role of mindfulness training or Buddhist meditation on PTG has been recognized. However, as Tedeschi and Blevins (2015) cautioned, "the current Western understanding of mindfulness practice appears to be largely informed by the Theravadin Buddhist tradition, a lineage that emphasizes mindful engagement in the goal of developing three primary types of insight: impermanence, suffering, and no-self" (p. 376); this may encourage a different form of human growth than the form we consider as posttraumatic growth. One example of this different form of PTG is to better appreciate negatives rather than to overcome negatives. Zheng and Gray pointed out that Confucianism and Buddhism teach the value of fully experiencing all emotions, both positive and negative in a balanced way. "Western approaches to the treatment of psychological problems have the explicit goal of eliminating or minimizing distress, whereas Chinese approaches tend to be more appreciative of the value of negative emotion provided that emotions are balanced" (Zheng & Gray, 2015, p. 729).

Although the majority of the studies examining the role of religion in PTG has been primarily conducted with samples of people who identify as Christians, a few studies have looked at the PTG in a Buddhist context. Falb and Pargament (2013) examined the relationships between Buddhist coping and PTG among American caregivers who self-identified as practitioners of Buddhism. Of the different types of Buddhist coping strategies, morality (e.g., "practiced right speech") and impermanence (e.g., "recognized that all things change") positively predicted PTG. Another study of contemplative practices derived from Buddhism found that non-reactivity to emotion and judgment of emotion together predicted enhanced cognitive processing, or deliberate rumination, which was associated with PTG (Hanley, Garland & Tedeschi, 2017). Judgment rather than the nonjudging stance encouraged in mindfulness approaches was related to PTG, perhaps because growth is dependent on a motivation to change negative post-trauma experience, and to reflect on how that can be accomplished.

There appears to be more commonality than difference between Buddhists' view of suffering/growth and PTG. Calhoun and Tedeschi (2006) underscored that PTG does not mean ignoring or downplaying the impact of pain caused by traumatic events; Buddhism views constant growth processes that are full of attending to the suffering of others or of the self, implying a coexistence between suffering and growth. Buddhist psychology and PTG theory also share attitudes toward people who are grieving. Wada and Park (2009), for example, discussed how Buddhist psychology may be integrated into grief therapy. They discussed the loss of power a person experiences when they are bereaved. Rather than pathologizing grief, Wade and Park encouraged people to see grieving individuals as undergoing a process of growth, focusing on the power they have to decide their way forward, thereby empowering them.

## PTG and Judaism

Judaism dates back to around 2000 BCE and is probably the world's oldest monotheistic religion. The one G*d worshipped in Judaism is the same G*d worshipped by Christians and Muslims: Abraham's G*d. In most English written accounts, the title "Yahweh" is used to denote G*d. Like other religions, there are various forms of Judaism, with the predominant branches being Orthodox (the largest and only until approximately 300 years ago), Reform, and Conservative. The Jewish sacred text is the Hebrew Bible, which dates back to approximately 800 BCE, and the first five books of the Hebrew Bible (i.e., the Christian Old Testament), called the

Torah. Judaism emphasizes that actions are more important than beliefs and holds to following 613 commandments (*mitzvot*) rather than only the ten best known that were delivered to Moses on Mount Sinai. The stories recounted in the Torah are filled with themes of the Israelites' triumph through great suffering; themes that continue today, and are analogous to PTG themes. Certainly the trials of Job are well known beyond the Jewish tradition, representing the lengths to which humans must endure suffering in life, and how difficult it is to understand the purpose of it. Yet, at the end of his suffering, Job encounters the divine response to his suffering and loss and the role he has played in a spiritual battle

Jewish people observe many special days in which their focus is turned to G\*d and his *mitzvot*, including the sharing of narratives about ancestors to keep memories of suffering and survival alive for current and future generations. A number of studies about PTG have been conducted in Israel. For example, Laufer and Solomon (2006) examined PTSD and PTG in nearly 3,000 adolescents, most of whom had been exposed to at least one experience of terror. While approximately 40% of the participants reported mild to severe symptoms of PTSD, nearly 75% also reported at least some PTG. Religiosity was not associated with symptoms of PTSD but was a strong predictor of growth.

## PTG and Hinduism

Hinduism is the oldest of the world's five major religions and dates back to around 4000 BCE. Hinduism is characterized by the drive toward the realization of the innermost nature of an individual's being and achieving unity of one's spirit with the Supreme Being. With an emphasis on karma and the doctrine of reincarnation, one's present condition is viewed as the result of the past, which affects not only the future in this life but also in the next life. Hinduism considers spiritual liberation as the ultimate purpose of earthly life and offers the choice of four different paths to achieve the goal: path of devotion, path of ethical action, path of knowledge, and path of mental concentration (Tarakeshwar, Pargament, & Mahoney, 2003). Thus, one can speculate that PTG may overlap the multiple pathways described in Hinduism. Perhaps some domains of PTG, such as spiritual change, may be more encouraged than other domains, such as new possibilities, because spiritually good deeds are believed to be passed to the next through reincarnation. In addition, *Anasakti*, a Sanskrit term for personality traits like non-attachment, equipoise, and effort in the absence of concern for the outcome, is considered to be ideal in Hinduism. This state of mind involves being able to keep one's mind above any turmoil and trials created by the environment (Banth & Talwar, 2012), because non-attachment is believed to produce equanimity. In this sense, PTG may be experienced in Hinduism as "remains unaffected" when facing trauma, rather than "changes in a positive way." Thombre, Sherman, and Simonton (2010), for example, examined the relationships between PTG and four different types of religious coping (i.e., benevolent religious reappraisal, spiritual connection, punishing God reappraisal, and spiritual discontent) among family caregivers of cancer patients in India, whose religious affiliation is mostly Hindu (84.5%). Religious responses to illness such as cancer often include making offerings at a family shrine, chanting mantras, singing hymns, or quiet reflection. Researchers found that the caregivers who made greater use of benevolent religious reappraisal (e.g., "saw my situation as part of God's plan") and less use of punishing reappraisal (e.g., "decided that God was punishing me for my sins") were more likely to report a higher level of PTG.

## PTG and Islam

Muslims, those who follow Islam, comprise the second largest group of religious followers in the world, with a trajectory that suggests it will be the largest world religion by 2070 (Pew Research Center). "In some Islamic traditions, suffering is seen as instrumental to the purposes of Allah" (Tedeschi & Calhoun, 2004b, p. 2). The famous stories of *One Thousand and One Nights*, for example, include PTG-like themes. For example, a triggering event for struggle is the King's discovery of his wife's infidelity. Psychological struggle may be the process for him to accept his curiosity about the tale a new bride was reading; even though he wanted to kill her, he could not. PTG can be found in this process as the King learns to acquire wisdom and acceptance. Islam is a religion that strongly affects everyday life—praying, fasting in the holy month of Ramadan, and the importance of the cadence of the moon and sun in daily activities. In Islam, PTG may be described in more collectivistic or religious group-based changes. Punamäki (2010) identified three elements in Arab-Islamic culture that can enhance PTG: emphasis on narrative, poetic, and emotional expression with social cohesion; appreciation of sharing and feeling of belonging; and a strong presence of religion in everyday life. For example, "the life of the Prophet Muhammad, poetically documented in the Qur'an, brings solace and strengths as well as helps reconstruct experiences in life-endangering conditions" (Punamäki, 2010, pp. 33–34). According to Sahih al-Bukhari, one of the six major hadith collections of Islam, "If Allah wants to do good to somebody, He afflicts him with trials" (Sahih al-Bukhari, Vol. 7, Book 70, Hadith No. 548). Although Islam also consoles its followers in the Quran as "Verily, after hardship there will come ease. After hardship there will come ease" (Quran, 94:5–6), people are generally taught to see crisis as a gift or chance to develop a deeper understanding of the Quran. Islam teaches that every believer will be examined by hardships. The stronger the iman (i.e., one's faith, belief, and reason in Islam), the harder the trial.

Underlying themes might come from the knowledge that the Prophet Muhammad is known to have experienced great loss when his beloved wife and uncle died in the same year. His sadness was recognized with that year recorded as "the year of sorrow" in Islamic history. Following the loss and subsequent hardships, Muhammad took spiritual journey, known as Isra or Mi'raj. This journey, a process of struggle triggered by life crises, is one of the most important events in Islam; during this journey, Allah is said to have given the Prophet Muhammad special worship as a gift—the prayer, five times a day, which serves as the direct communication between Muslim and Allah. In addition, believers are said to be like a single body in their mutual love, mercy, and sympathy, emphasizing the empathy and connectedness among families, friends, and communities.

One of the few studies that specifically measured the extent to which belief in Islam predicted PTG was conducted in Indonesia (Subandi, Achmad, Kurniati, & Febri, 2014). Subandi and colleagues individually administered surveys to 90 people who had survived the 2010 eruption of Mount Merapi in Java. They had all experienced significant losses, including family members, cattle, houses, and/or farms, and were living in temporary housing not far from where the eruption damaged or destroyed areas where their villages once stood. In addition to completing an Indonesian version of the PTGI, participants completed measures of gratitude, hope, and spirituality as well as some open-ended questions. Participants' spiritual beliefs were the only one of the three predictor variables to significantly influence PTG scores. Qualitative responses indicated increases in daily prayers and attending mosque and a "return to the path of God" (p. 23). Qualitative comments also indicated positive changes in relationships, new possibilities, appreciation of life, and a feeling of harmony (*rukun*) with others.

Through all of these religious belief systems one thing is constant: Religion provides a means of making sense of the world and a person's place in it. Such doctrines provide a structure for meaning, pathways to understanding, and a higher being to defer to when sense is not apparent. It may be tempting to believe that people who do not hold to a religious doctrine struggle more in the face of adversity than those who do. It appears this is no more true for the atheist or the gnostic than it is for the religious or spiritual person. For example, some people make sense of the world using science to explain phenomena, and others may rely of the teachings of secular philosophy.

## PTG and Philosophy

The most cited philosophical work in PTG research is probably that of Friedrich Nietzsche, perhaps because of his very well-known quote: "That which does not kill us makes us stronger." Stephen Joseph, for example, used this quote in the title of his book on PTG (Joseph, 2011b). However, not just this, but the very nature of PTG being so paradoxical, coupled with the fact that it reflects a philosophical shift from a pathogenic to a salutogenic paradigm in trauma literature (Morris, Shakespeare-Finch, Rieck, & Newbery, 2005), invites us to face questions that may be more philosophical than empirical. Such questions may include: Is PTG different from other forms of growth, such as normative maturation? Is PTG irreversible (i.e., once one has achieved a new perspective based on PTG is it impossible to view life from the old perspective again)? Do we all grow? We can say that humans are in the process of dying as long as they live. And if so, can we say living, dying, and growing all share the same connotations? If changes occur constantly as we live and die, then should we assume everyone is potentially in the midst of PTG? Is PTG a matter of the degree to which individuals are aware of their changes and how they connect their changes with their suffering? And if PTG is a valued outcome of suffering, we might consider the question Hall, Lunger, and McMartin (2010) asked—"should alleviating suffering always be the primary goal in treatment?"—as they considered that in some traditions, suffering is something to be sought rather than avoided. Philosophical shifts are part of PTG.

When people change the way they view the world and/or their place in it post-trauma, they are making a philosophical shift from the views they held prior to experiencing trauma. Aloni (1989) asserted that despite being known for his views about nihilism, Nietzsche had a second and related central concern with the elevation of people: in identifying how people could enhance their existence, grow, and find meaning in their existence. This view is not unlike Frankl's (1963). Indeed, Frankl drew on Nietzsche's work around the notion that suffering is alleviated when meaning is imposed upon the catalyst or consequences for that suffering. The answer to the question of relationships between PTG and philosophy is clear—there are many—these ideas and observations are intertwined.

# CHAPTER 4

# Posttraumatic Growth as Process and Outcome

PTG can be both a process and an outcome. Whether it is considered one or the other may simply depend on where a person is standing in time. For example, positive reappraisals may be a component of PTG as a process, whereas an assertion that a person's life has changed in a lasting and positive way may be more accurately conceptualized as an outcome. PTG as a process is initiated by an encounter with highly challenging life events, prompted by an initial challenge to one's assumptive world or core beliefs; experiencing psychological struggle; coping with emotional distress and intrusive ruminations; moving to deliberate or effortful ruminating about what has happened; and eventually realizing the experience of PTG. This realization of PTG, that is the outcome, can be understood to refer, broadly, to a cluster of positive changes that result from a complex combination of cognitive, emotional, and social processes (Tedeschi & Blevins, 2015). PTG is an outcome of these processes, reflected in the permanency of changes that have occurred. A sense of strength, for example, may not be identified during the initial process of psychological struggle, even though this process is a part of PTG; only later may it be recognized as a consequence of struggle and integrated into the new self. Thus, PTG as process and PTG as outcome may be sequential, as people engage in such processes as positive reinterpretation, positive reframing, interpretive control, or reconstruction of the narrative related to the event/s (Tedeschi & Calhoun, 1996).

Another consideration in this discussion of the processes involved in PTG, and of what outcomes are to be considered PTG, is that different researchers may focus on different indicators of growth. Some have insisted on observable behavioral changes as the only criterion for PTG (e.g., action-focused growth: Hobfoll et al., 2007), whereas others focus on cognitive elements such as reorganization of one's beliefs or assumptive world (Tedeschi & Calhoun, 2004b). Still others focus on changes in personality (e.g., positive personality changes: Jayawickreme & Blackie, 2014). PTG can be seen in all of these ways—cognitive, emotional, behavioral, and, more recently, biological.

Although the conceptual model of PTG is sometimes categorized as a focusing on outcome (e.g., Zoellner & Maercker, 2006), it is still "an ongoing process, not a static outcome" (Tedeschi & Calhoun, 2004b, p. 1). The process may take various shapes, such as a spiral, going back and forth in interactions with other systems. PTG as an outcome, in some cases, may be quite sudden and may not involve an extended process. For example, consider patients who have experienced a severe

heart attack. They may engage in a prolonged period of adjustment and reconstruction of their lives following this threat, or positive changes may come about
quite suddenly, akin to an epiphany about life and what the future may hold. In
that way, it may sometimes be difficult to neatly separate PTG as process from
PTG as outcome. Having established a new path in life or made a career change
that never would have otherwise been considered may sound like an outcome;
however, starting to explore a new path or career that one did not consider before
may sound like a process. It is important, then, to pay attention to the overall
context rather than focusing on a single statement in order to capture both process and outcome elements of PTG (e.g., Hefferon, Grealy, & Mutrie, 2010; Shakespeare-Finch & Barrington, 2012).

## PTG Outcomes

Early studies of PTG focused on an examination of outcomes (Calhoun & Tedeschi, 1989–1990; Tedeschi & Calhoun, 1988; Tedeschi, Calhoun, Morrell, & Johnson, 1984). Based on these early studies, a quantitative measure, the Posttraumatic
Growth Inventory (PTGI), was developed (Tedeschi & Calhoun, 1996). The items
for the new measure represent outcomes and were based on quotations from
recorded interviews and from a thorough review of the literature available at the
time. A number of qualitative studies have since been published that demonstrate
a high degree of consistency in the kinds of positive post-trauma outcomes that
are measured by the PTGI; at the very least, these are broadly representative of the
construct (Kampman, Hefferon, Wilson, & Beale, 2015).

Some studies have considered whether different types of events may lead to
different patterns of PTG. For example, circumstances that involve disability or
illness may lead to a new way of relating to one's own body and engagement in
health-promoting behavior (Hefferon, 2013). We will consider the role of trauma
type later, but in keeping with the more general theme of PTG as a transformative experience that has common themes, we can describe PTG outcomes in a
few different ways. Prior to the development of the PTGI, growth outcomes were
described in three general areas: changes in relationships with others, philosophy
of life, and views of the self (Tedeschi & Calhoun, 1995). Later, with the development of the PTGI, factor analysis yielded five empirically derived PTG domains:
appreciation of life, personal strength, new opportunities, relating with others, and
spiritual change (Tedeschi & Calhoun, 1996). A more detailed discussion of the
measurement of PTG will focus on these five domains and the degree to which
they have been supported in subsequent work. However, there is enough support
that we can illustrate the concept of PTG outcomes using these five dimensions
here (e.g., Cohen, Cimbolie, Armeli, & Hettler, 1998; Morris, Shakespeare-Finch,
Rieck, & Newbery, 2005; Taku, Cann, Calhoun, & Tedeschi, 2008).

### *Personal Strength*

This domain can be summarized with the phrase—"I am more vulnerable than
I thought, but much stronger than I ever imagined" (Calhoun & Tedeschi,

2006, p. 5). PTG can be experienced by an increased sense of self-reliance, a sense of strength and confidence, and a perception of self as survivor or victor rather than "victim." It can also involve the idea of having survived the traumatic event—a sense that there's nothing a person feels they cannot do. This can then lead to behavioral changes, such as a newfound engagement in the challenges of learning something completely new (Shakespeare-Finch & Barrington, 2012).

### Relating to Others

This domain reflects the experience of positive changes in relationships (e.g., PTGI items "being more compassionate"; "feeling a greater connection with others"). Not only the relationship itself, but one's attitudes or behaviors in relationships may be changed in positive ways (e.g., PTGI items "more willing to express emotions"; "more willing to accept help from others") or reflect a conscious decision to spend more time with family and friends and tell them how much you love and value them (Shakespeare-Finch & Barrington, 2012). Changes in relationships are also evident in accounts of PTG that include decisions to move on from relationships no longer seen as positive or beneficial. Changes in this way may also be connected to changes in personal strength. For example, following a stillbirth, a mother said that the experience acted as a catalyst for her to reevaluate her life and her relationships in order to include only those people that she perceived as giving her the support she needed and deserved (Krosch & Shakespeare-Finch, 2016). Such decisions about relationships have also been found in survivors of natural disasters. For example, following devastating bushfires that killed 173 people, one woman, nodding toward her husband conversing with a neighbor at their fenceline said: "We never really spoke [to the neighbor] before the fires, in fact he was quite rude—that's all changed now" (Shakespeare-Finch, 2009).

### New Possibilities

This domain can be seen in the individual's identification of new possibilities for one's life or of the possibility of taking a new and different path in life (Tedeschi & Calhoun, 2004b). It also can be experienced through developing new interests, activities, or habits, or by building a new career that would not have been a part of one's life if there had been no triggering event in the first place. For example, those who have faced a life-threatening illness often report positive changes in health behavior (Costa & Pakenham, 2012; Morris, Campbell, Dwyer, Dunn, & Chambers, 2011), and people who have been bereaved may decide not to wait until retirement to embark on the travel they have always wanted to do. Others have reported changes in career path and greater involvement in community groups (Shakespeare-Finch & Barrington, 2012). The aftermath of trauma may provide people with a sense that they are called to address the kinds of circumstances they have gone through by making changes in their personal and work lives so that they can be of service.

### Appreciation of Life

This domain includes a greater appreciation for all the things that life has to offer, whether small things previously taken for granted or a greater appreciation for things that people still have in their lives. Because of what has happened, some people may see life as the gift of a second chance that should be cherished. People may report, for example, that having to deal with a major stressor has made them realize that it is important to spend more time on their intimate relationships, to appreciate each day and its small pleasures more, to take life easier, and simply be more aware and appreciative of their environment. Thousands of conversations with people who have experienced traumatic events clearly indicate that a common PTG theme is about noticing things that, for most people, are simply incidental to daily existence—a sunset, a clear blue sky, a beautiful flower, or other things always in a person's landscape that they simply had not taken the time to deeply appreciate before.

### Spiritual and Existential Change

This domain reflects the experience of people who are religious, but also the experience of people who are not, including agnostics and atheists. In the original PTGI, only two questions reflected this area—one asked about spiritual changes and one about religious changes. The extent to which people endorsed such changes varied across cultures (Weiss & Berger, 2010), and subsequent research around the world indicated a need to increase and broaden the items assessing this domain to reflect a broader concept of spiritual and existential changes. The PTGI has been recently expanded to sample a more extensive and cross-culturally applicable set of items relevant to this factor. Items now include the measurement of existential aspects of these changes, and it also includes items that ask about reflections on interconnections with others, harmony, and mortality (Tedeschi, Cann, Taku, Senol-Durak, & Calhoun, 2017). This factor of the PTGI now reflects an engagement with matters related to religious beliefs, spiritual matters, and existential/philosophical questions.

## Pathways to PTG

The term "pathways" can refer to the results of model testing found in path analysis or structured equation modeling, but the term may also refer to possible avenues to PTG suggested in the model. Here we will focus on the latter. The model of PTG that has evolved since 1995 (Calhoun, Cann, & Tedeschi, 2010; Calhoun & Tedeschi, 1998a, 2006; Tedeschi & Calhoun, 1995, 2004b) emphasizes how PTG originates from psychological struggle with a highly stressful or traumatic event. Circumstances that are precursors to PTG are those that challenge one's assumptive world or core beliefs. The emotional and cognitive challenges that emanate from such disruption of core beliefs give rise to a path with multiple specific aspects through which intra-individual (emotional or cognitive processing) and inter-individual (social or contextual) factors are likely to influence PTG.

As suggested in the PTG model, there are specific factors that can operate within the general pathway. For example, PTG progress is assumed to be influenced by the characteristics of events as well as pre-trauma individual differences. The PTG model also indicates that the way one experiences a traumatic event is critical. This involves whether the event is challenging or seismic enough to challenge schemas; how relevant or central the event might be to the person's core beliefs; how emotional distress is managed in the initial time post-trauma; what kind of characteristics people or the triggering event itself contain; how ruminative thinking occurred and how the characteristics of rumination were changed over time; how self-disclosure through writing or talking was activated; which socio-cultural contexts affect this whole process; and how life narratives have been developed— which, in turn, all affect PTG. These aspects of the general pathway to PTG will be fully described in Chapter 7.

Because the model of PTG is comprehensive, multiple factors exist within it. For example, the model shows parallel relationships between PTG development and narrative development. Although this relationship is common, multiple specific pathways can exist depending on whether a person is introverted or extraverted; whether the damage is caused intentionally or not; whether or not the person engages in disclosures about the events to other people; the kinds of responses others give to such disclosures; and how cognitive processing is activated. For example, persons with different personality dispositions may respond to traumatic events in ways that lead to different effects on core beliefs. Persons with different sets of core beliefs may be more or less likely to have such beliefs challenged, decimated, reconstructed, modified, or strengthened.

Evidence supporting the influence of the elements included in the model of PTG can be found in several studies. For example, Cann et al. (2011) found strong support for the proposed pathway to PTG through challenges to core beliefs, intrusive rumination, and deliberate rumination. Similarly, the pathway to PTG through deliberate rumination and social support has also been supported (Morris & Shakespeare-Finch, 2011). Pathways to PTG through positive coping, such as problem-focused coping and emotion regulation strategies (including accessing instrumental and emotional social support, prayer, positive reinterpretation, and acceptance) has also been found (Park, Aldwin, Fenster, & Snyder, 2008). A pathway to PTG after events that include a significant interpersonal transgression, such as infidelity, physical harm, or betrayal, has been found to occur through forgiveness, religiosity, and spirituality (Schultz, Tallman, & Altmaier, 2010). Meta-analytical findings that time since the event does not seem to significantly affect PTG may also support the possibility of multiple versions of the process that leads to PTG (Prati & Pietrantoni, 2009); some people may show signs of PTG very early following a traumatic or highly challenging experience, whereas the road to PTG may take years for others to traverse.

Other researchers have also looked at factors that are key to the PTG model and considered them in relation to both PTG and posttraumatic stress. For example, deliberate and intrusive rumination, the centrality of the events, and controllability were examined as predictors of PTG and posttraumatic stress (PTS) symptoms in a sample of 250 people who had experienced various kinds of traumatic experiences (Brooks, Graham-Kevan, Lowe, & Robinson, 2017). Using SEM, results showed significant pathways of all predictor variables on PTG and distress. The model accounted for 68% of variance in distress and 30% in PTG. Intrusive rumination had the strongest relationship with PTS (.66), whereas a sense of control in the present (.41) and event centrality (.44) had the strongest relationship with PTGI short-form scores. It is interesting to note that although PTG research has been undertaken across the globe for more than 20 years now, there are still many parts of the puzzle that are unclear. Just as Brooks and colleagues were able to account for more than double the variance in posttraumatic stress systems than PTG, Gul and Karanci (2017) accounted for 64% of variance in PTS scores and only 40% in PTG scores using multiple predictors, including coping, rumination, social support, extraversion, openness, conscientiousness, neuroticism, agreeableness, previous history of psychiatric problems, and various demographic variables. There was a significant correlation between PTS and PTG scores in this study of 740 community participants in Turkey, but the coefficient between the two factors of .14 indicated a negligible to weak relationship accounting for very little variance. The differential predictors of PTG and PTS symptoms further support the relative independence of these constructs in many studies and varying cultural contexts. It is important to remember that the pathways to PTG are *not* the same as the pathways to recovery from posttraumatic stress symptoms. Although these pathways may overlap with one another, experiencing PTG and alleviating posttraumatic symptoms of distress do not necessarily have parallel processes.

# CHAPTER 5

# Posttraumatic Growth as Common and Universal Experience

The phenomenon of personal growth, resulting from a struggle with major life crises, has been reported throughout history and around the world. There is ample evidence that people and communities can dramatically change in positive ways as a result of the struggle with highly challenging, traumatic life events (Tedeschi & Calhoun, 1995; Calhoun & Tedeschi, 1999). From Greek philosophy to the Bible to playwrights and poets, trauma is not only viewed as potentially devastating but also as a catalyst for positive change. For example, over four centuries ago, William Shakespeare wrote in *As You Like It*: "Sweet are the uses of adversity which, like the toad, ugly and venomous, wears yet a precious jewel in his head." Wole Soyinka, poet, playwright, and Nobel Prize winner, remarked following the horrors and genocide that took place in Rwanda: "Rwanda, which is one of the younger independent states in Africa, must be regarded as a model of how great human trauma can be transformed to commence true reconstruction of people" (Mugisha, 2012).

## Reports of PTG Across Cultures

PTG has been reported across many different cultures and geographical locations. Matsumoto and Juang (2008) defined culture as "a unique meaning and information system, shared by a group and transmitted across generations, that allows the group to meet basic needs of survival, pursue happiness, well-being, and derive meaning from life" (p. 12). Culture may contain a variety of social groups. For instance, groups that contain cultures include age and generations, disability, religion, ethnicity, social status, sexual orientation, indigenous heritage, national origin, and gender, which are depicted in the ADRESSING framework model (Hays, 1996). Since the introduction of PTG (Tedeschi & Calhoun, 1995), numerous studies have demonstrated that PTG is found in many cultural groups and is likely to show cultural differences, such as gender differences (Vishnevsky, Cann, Calhoun, Tedeschi, & Demakis, 2010), age differences (Meyerson, Grant, Carter, & Kilmer, 2011), ethnic differences or racial differences (Kent et al., 2013; Siegel, Schrimshaw, & Pretter, 2005), and cross-national differences (Kehl, Knuth, Hulse, & Schmidt, 2015; Taku & Cann, 2014). Clearly, PTG is not tied to one specific culture but is observed in many cultures (Weiss & Berger, 2010), albeit with subtle differences.

Weiss and Berger (2010) suggested that culture plays a major role in many aspects of PTG processes, including the nature of the traumatic events, meanings of trauma, images of personal growth, and philosophy of life. The model of PTG includes both proximal and distal cultural elements. Proximate cultural elements include an individual's immediate social systems (e.g., family and neighborhood) and various communities such as workplaces, schools, and worship spaces. Distal cultural elements, on the other hand, involve a broader cultural framework that may indirectly affect individuals' PTG experiences, and may also include PTG stories embedded in religion, myth, and art. These include broader themes that are common to larger society. Although referring to "individualistic" as opposed to "collective" societies paints a broad stroke and may not be applicable to all individuals who live in a society classified as either individualistic or collective, some PTG differences can be seen. In Western or individualistic societies, for example, there is value attributed to being independent and autonomous. Most people who experience PTG find themselves moving toward a collective orientation. That is, people learn to value the collective: the importance of good relationships and the value of not "going it alone." Studies with people from collectivist nations, however, tend show that such individuals assert that their survival following trauma was because they are part of a collective—a strong, unified sense of community and shared experiences (e.g., Kayser, Wind, & Shanker, 2008; Shakespeare-Finch, Schweitzer, King, & Brough, 2014).

Beginning with the work of Tedeschi and Calhoun in the 1980s, research specifically focused on PTG using systematic methods of inquiry, and has now been conducted in many countries and cultural contexts. Stories of growth and scores on inventories such as the PTGI (Tedeschi & Calhoun, 1996) have provided convincing evidence of PTG as a universal phenomenon. However, although PTG does indeed appear to be universal, it can also have culture-specific aspects (Splevins, Cohen, Bowley, & Joseph, 2010). The way PTG is experienced and expressed, what forms of positive changes are identified as PTG (and labeled as personal growth), or which mechanisms promote or hinder PTG have been investigated in different ways among people in many different places. For example, a meta-analytic review conducted by (Sawyer, Ayers, & Field, 2010) included 38 studies with diverse samples, including African American, Caucasian, Chinese, Hispanic, Indian, Latina, Malay, Maori, Native American, and Puerto Rican ($N = 7,927$) who were diagnosed with cancer or HIV/AIDS. The results demonstrated that people who reported PTG also reported enhanced well-being and reduced levels of negative or pathological psychological symptoms. Interestingly, results with samples comprised of more than 25% non-White participants demonstrated an even stronger relationship between PTG and positive psychological adjustment, leading Sawyer et al. (p. 443) to suggest that "PTG is associated with positive adaptive consequences, and is therefore an important construct to be studied in clinical and health research."

The mechanisms that promote PTG may also include factors that are specific to particular cultural groups. This conclusion is supported by studies conducted with culturally diverse samples, including in Australia, China, France, Germany, India, Japan, Spain, Turkey, the United Kingdom, and the United States. Weiss and

Berger (2010) pointed out that there are indeed universal aspects of PTG, but also that there can also be culturally specific characteristics. Although recognizing that PTG can have culturally specific elements,

> researchers and clinicians from diverse cultures and subcultures on four continents documented that PTG exists in all the societies that were explored, from survivors of earthquakes in Turkey and Japan to Israelis and Palestinians exposed to terror and imprisonment related to conflict in the Middle East; from Latina immigrants in the United States to Chinese international students in Australia; from survivors of World War II in Germany to those who experienced the war in the former Yugoslavia.
>
> (pp. 189–190)

The conclusion that PTG is indeed universal is supported by the available data, but there are certainly places where PTG has not been studied. Although it has been studied as an outcome in many cultures, the processes that may lead to PTG have not been studied as often. Where they have, however, predictions of the processes based on the PTG model have been supported, for example in Turkey, Australia, and Japan (Kilic & Ulsoy, 2003; Shakespeare-Finch & Morris, 2010; Taku, 2010).

## Measurement Thresholds and Cut-Off Scores for PTG

Despite assertions from a handful of researchers (discussed later in this volume), PTG is not rare. Studies have shown that PTG occurs in a very wide range of people (see Tedeschi & Calhoun, 2004b, for review). The prevalence of PTG, however, varies across samples and as a result of the research methods used. One standard method of assessing PTG is the use of self-report scales, such as the PTGI (Tedeschi & Calhoun, 1996). Using the PTGI, as well as other measures that have some similarities to the PTGI such as the Stress-Related Growth Scale (SRGS: Park, Cohen, & Murch, 1996), Changes in Outlook Questionnaire (CiOQ: Joseph, Williams, & Yule, 1993), Thriving Scale (TS: Abraído-Lanza, Guier, & Colón, 1998), and Perceived Benefit Scale (PBS: McMillen & Fisher, 1998), a meta-analytic study indicated that the prevalence rate for PTG ranged from 3% for bereaved persons to 98% for women with breast cancer (Linley & Joseph, 2004, p. 14). A main reason the quantitative data on PTG can vary so dramatically is the different cut-off values researchers use to determine whether or not growth has occurred. Although perhaps obvious, it bears saying that when cut-off criteria are set very low—for example, if a respondent endorses at least one item on the PTGI indicating a high level of positive change—then the prevalence will be judged as quite high. If, on the other hand, a very stringent criterion is set—for example, requiring that a respondent endorse every item indicating high levels of positive change—then the prevalence would be judged to be very low. Our view is that if people regard change in even one specific domain—for example, greater compassion for others—as significant and important for them, then researchers and clinicians should regard those persons as having experienced growth.

Following are examples of studies that illustrate how rates of PTG can vary. A study with women, 5 to 15 years after a diagnosis of breast cancer, showed that on average they endorsed 15 of the 21 areas of growth represented by PTGI items at a moderate to a very strong degree. Items such as "I have more compassion for others" were reported by 87.3% of the participants (Lelorain, Bonnaud-Antignac, & Florin, 2010). A study with American veterans of Operations Enduring Freedom and Iraqi Freedom (OEF/OIF)—the wars in Afghanistan and Iraq, respectively—showed that 72% of the participants endorsed one or more of the PTGI 21 items to a great or very great degree. The most frequently endorsed item was "I changed my priorities about what is important in life," which was reported by 52.2% of participants (Pietrzak et al., 2010). A study conducted with survivors of a major earthquake in China showed a PTG prevalence rate of 51.1% (Xu & Liao, 2011) when the criterion was a raw score of at least 57 on the Chinese version of the PTGI. It should be noted, however, that the score ranged from zero to 95 in this study, because the researchers eliminated the two spiritual change items from the PTGI. A study following the tsunami in Thailand found that approximately 34% of participants reported moderate levels of PTG (Tang, 2006) when a PTGI item mean score was above 3 (the range of options is 0 to 5); this is equivalent to a total score of 63 as the cutoff point (possible range of 0 to 105 in this study). In a study with adolescents (Vloet et al., 2014), PTG was reported by 92.8% using mean item ratings greater than 1 (indicating a little change) on at least two of the ten items on a childhood version of the PTGI called the PTGI-C-R (Kilmer et al., 2009). These studies show how the rate of PTG judged to be present can vary significantly from study to study. However, as we have argued, even the endorsement of a great deal of growth on only one item of the PTGI can indicate significant change for an individual, even if the total score is low. In addition, a moderate total score that is the result of the sum of many relatively low scores on individual items may not indicate much significant growth.

In spite of issues around thresholds and cutoffs, these studies, as well as studies using qualitative research methods, have shown that PTG is not rare. As an example of a qualitative study, adolescent survivors of childhood cancer took part in a semi-structured interview in which the majority of participants (84.7%) reported at least one positive outcome of having had to deal with cancer; nearly one third reported four or more positive changes (Barakat, Alderfer, & Kazak, 2006). Even before the PTGI was developed, a relatively high rate of positive personal changes following adversity had been reported in the literature. Collins, Taylor, and Skokan (1990), for example, reported their sample of cancer patients derived more benefit (i.e., positive changes in priorities and relationships) than harm, even though their participants were only asked how they were changed after a diagnosis of cancer (i.e., they were not primed by the specific questions containing "positive" changes or "personal growth").

However, the finding that PTG is common does not mean that PTG occurs in everyone who experiences trauma. This is important to emphasize, especially for practicing clinicians. Growth may not occur in all dimensions; for some people, PTG may not occur at all. The intensity of the traumatic event is likely to impact outcomes of both growth and distress. If the intensity of a traumatic experience surpasses a certain threshold of traumatic intensity—for example, extreme, prolonged torture—people may be less likely to report outcomes of growth and more likely to report only negative psychosocial consequences. Tedeschi and Calhoun (1995) pointed out that there might be a relationship between psychological fitness and reports of PTG, such that persons who are particularly vulnerable or who are highly invulnerable to the impact of highly stressful events may report less PTG than those with moderate levels of vulnerability.

# CHAPTER 6

# The Validity of Reports of Posttraumatic Growth

One controversial argument, proposed by a few, centers around whether or not PTG is merely an illusion—a self-deceptive way of coping with highly negative circumstances. This view is based on the assumption that self-reported PTG does not always reflect "authentic" personal growth. This idea can be found in assumptions of self-perception that pre-date the introduction of systematic investigations of PTG.

The psychoanalytic idea of ego defense mechanisms suggested that it is virtually impossible for people to have an accurate view of themselves, and that people have a general tendency to protect the self against anxiety by creating favorable self-images. Taylor (1983), for example, described a theory of cognitive adaptation to threatening events that included attempts to restore self-esteem through self-enhancing biases. The idea that not all self-reported growth is "real" is also reflected in the Janus-faced model described by Maercker and Zoellner (2004). This model was inspired by a series of studies on self-enhancement and positive illusions (i.e., distorted positive perceptions of self, holding unrealistically optimistic beliefs) in the face of highly stressful or threatening situation (Taylor, Lerner, Sherman, Sage, & McDowell, 2003), and by studies about the distinction between benefit-finding as a coping outcome and benefit-reminding as a coping strategy (Affleck & Tennen, 1996). This position is not inconsistent with Calhoun and Tedeschi's (2004) assertion that PTG is both a process and an outcome. The process usually begins with an effort to cope, manage, and survive a traumatic event without the intention to benefit from the struggle; after some period of time, personal growth and transformation become more evident. Seldom do people initially respond to traumatic events with a motive to grow or to find benefit, but these outcomes can be identified at some later time. The degree to which personal growth is maintained over a trauma survivor's life may depend on other factors that affect the person over time.

Because the form of personal growth varies from person to person and from culture to culture, it is understandably difficult to reach a homogeneous consensus as to what precisely constitutes PTG. People experience and express their own personal growth for various reasons, in various forms, and at various levels. Perhaps for the same reason, no consensus has been reached as to what illusory PTG may be. For example, different researchers have addressed this as "illusory growth versus constructive growth" (Maercker & Zoellner, 2004), an "illusion versus PTG as a reality" (Sumalla, Ochoa, & Blanco, 2009), "perceived growth versus actual growth" (Frazier et al., 2009), and "PTG versus quantifiable change" (Johnson & Boals, 2015). The methods used to "test" if someone has experienced *real* PTG or *illusory* PTG have varied in their rigor, and when scrutinizing methods, quite often conclusions drawn regarding the authenticity of a person's PTG are questionable.

The approach offered by Maercker and Zoellner (2004) focuses on PTG as an outcome. They propose that illusory PTG is self-perceived PTG that is self-deceptive and used to avoid a painful reality; thus, it makes one feel temporarily good but is maladaptive in the long run because the person is avoiding dealing with their new reality. On the other hand, constructive PTG is an outcome of successfully dealing with the aftermath of trauma and is self-transcending. So, from this proposed perspective, constructive PTG contains *real* growth, and thus has a lasting effect (Maercker & Zoellner, 2004; Lahav, Solomon, & Levin, 2016). If people report experiencing PTG, it could reflect successfully coping with their experience—a state of being that transcends their functioning prior to the experience that created core belief disruption. It is a transformative positive change in one or more areas of a person's life. This is the form that both Maercker and Zoellner, and Tedeschi and Calhoun, have described as PTG when conceptualized as an outcome. However, these scholars differ in their explanations of PTG as a process. Maercker and Zoellner maintain that perceptions of PTG are more common and that such perceptions may not be long-lasting as they are self-deceptive or illusory attempts to manage, through avoidance, the distress that results from highly challenging and traumatic experiences. Such perceptions are hypothesized to be functional in the short term, but not likely sustainable as a long-lasting transformative change. However, Tedeschi and Calhoun would view positive reinterpretation as an aspect of effortful and deliberate rumination and therefore reflective of PTG as a process.

One study operationally defined constructive PTG as an improvement in coping in addition to an increase in PTG, and illusory PTG as an increase in PTG only without showing any improvement in coping (Pat-Horenczyk et al., 2015). The researchers compared breast cancer survivors who participated in an eight-session group intervention with breast cancer survivors in the control group and found that a higher proportion of constructive PTG as opposed to illusory PTG was observed in those in the intervention. As they also indicated, it is still challenging to establish external criteria to define illusory PTG.

The distinction between PTG as a means to avoid reality and PTG as a result of struggle with reality may be key; however, it is often difficult to identify what perceptions were intentionally or unconsciously taken to avoid reality or were elicited by the struggle with traumatic circumstances, because they are inevitably intertwined. Similarly, a few researchers claim some, or perhaps most, experiences of growth are illusory because the goal, conscious or otherwise, is to reduce the negative emotions resulting from the traumatic event. This would be a short-term palliative coping strategy. However, an attempt to reduce negative emotions, or, stated somewhat differently, the management of and coping with emotional distress, is included in the model of PTG as an important element; it is predicted to trigger the cognitive processing that provides impetus for what may ultimately result in PTG (Calhoun & Tedeschi, 2006; Tedeschi & Calhoun, 2004b). It may require more discussion, and certainly better designed empirical investigation, to determine whether any experiences that traumatized persons report are indeed "illusory PTG." Our position, however, is that if such "illusory" PTG occurs, it is likely to be in the minority rather than the majority of cases. And an admonition that will be reiterated throughout this book is that clinicians should attempt to work within the framework of understanding traumatic events in which their clients operate, regardless of the possibility that some degree of positive illusions may be operating.

Sumalla et al. (2009)'s concept of PTG as an "illusion" versus PTG as a "reality" follows a similar logic. However, they proposed identity change or identity transformation as the criterion for "real" PTG. They assumed that PTG should be understood

> as the unexpected or unintentional result of the struggle against the adverse event . . . and in contrast with those models that present PTG as an illusory process or a coping strategy, it is the accommodation processes, rather than the assimilation processes
>
> (p. 27)

that should lead to important identity change. The argument is based on the assumption that some people express PTG with the aim of keeping their own identity intact and free from any significant change in order to protect themselves. However, such a motive seems to be counter to experiencing transformational and significant changes in identity. How people can be initially motivated to preserve their identity and then find it transformed is unclear. Furthermore, if PTG is understood as a positive identity change or transformation, there are at least two questions unresolved. PTG can be understood as multi-dimensional. Thus, "positive identity change" may be reflected in PTG in one domain, such as personal strength, while other forms of PTG, such as appreciation of life, may well be experienced without being directly connected to identity transformation. There is no consensus as to what positive identity change or transformation should be or how to distinguish positive identity changes from negative or even from neutrally valenced identity changes.

Some researchers suggest that PTG should only be considered authentic if it involves positive personality changes (e.g., Jayawickreme & Blackie, 2014). There is some evidence for a relationship between positive personality characteristics and PTG (Peterson, Park, Pole, D'Andrea, & Seligman, 2008). A large cross-sectional sample correlating the VIA Inventory of Strengths with the PTGI showed positive relationships between character strengths and reported growth. However, demonstrating a relationship between PTG and positive personality change is not the same as demonstrating they are the same thing.

A few researchers who emphasize the illusory aspects of PTG (e.g., Sumalla et al., 2009; Zoellner & Maercker, 2006) define "actual" PTG as unintentional and illusory PTG as voluntary. Others (e.g., Kastenmüller, Greitemeyer, Epp, Frey, &

Fischer, 2012) define actual PTG as voluntary and illusory PTG as unintentional. This type of debate (i.e., authenticity of self-perceived construct, labeling of positive-negative dimension) seems to be repeating some of the history of psychology, such as the debate of prosocial behaviors versus pure altruism, obedience versus cooperation, and authentic versus illusory happiness. In the end, it may simply be impossible to clearly separate the experiences a person has into two clear distinct categories of real and illusory experiences.

Nolen-Hoeksema and Davis (2004) asserted that when personal changes are measured with a self-report inventory, there may be reason to question the validity of some reports. However, they suggest that bearing witness to the detailed narratives of people explaining their experiences of trauma and how they have grown from the struggle they engaged in post-trauma can be compelling. They do not propose that such accounts necessarily demonstrate real change, as there are other potential explanations for narratives about PTG. Clinicians and researchers who work with trauma survivors have some hunches or experiences that clients are usually quite clear about in their descriptions of the growth they have perceived, but clients may sometimes express PTG-like perceptions to at least temporarily maintain pride, feel better, or make their significant others not too worried about them, or to deeply want to believe that they have changed in a better way, and so on. Attention to individual trajectories of change over time may be the only way to disentangle these competing perspectives. It should also be acknowledged that the life narrative continues with various subsequent experiences that determine the longevity of the personal changes initiated by traumatic events.

Claims about "actual" PTG versus illusory PTG should also be considered in light of the methodologies that have been used to address this supposed distinction. One common approach focuses on the measurable and longitudinal differences between two time points (e.g., pre- and post-trauma). For example, Frazier et al. (2009) used subtraction of scores on self-report inventories of Time 2 from Time 1 and examined its relationship with self-perceived PTG that is often assessed at Time 2. These researchers assumed that if self-perceived PTG at Time 2 is real, it should be correlated with the large differences between the two time points in the status of PTG-relevant elements such as spiritual understanding, satisfaction with life, and relationship quality. Although similar research designs have been used in a few studies (e.g., Johnson & Boals, 2015), this method is quite problematic for a variety of reasons, including due to cognitive or response shifts that may occur over time, ceiling or floor effects, failure of some of the measures to have actually measured PTG, and the selection of problematic external criteria against which reports of growth are considered to be "real." Aspinwall and Tedeschi (2010) provide a helpful critical perspective on this methodology.

Much of the debate about PTG's authenticity is based on the questionable assumption that self-perceived PTG, without having evidence of observable, external change, must be illusory. For example, Kastenmüller et al. (2012) claimed "no evidence was found that real PTG took place" (p. 477). But the question arises: What evidence can indicate real PTG? One study (Blackie, Jayawickreme, Helzer, Forgeard, & Roepke, 2015) investigated the veracity of self-reported PTG by examining how the participants and their informants, such as family members, friends, or coworkers, would agree on the changes in the participants' overall profile across five domains of PTG. By using a profile analysis procedure, the researchers found a good participant-informant agreement on the domains that the participants experienced as relatively high or low, suggesting that at least some proportion in the PTGI can be attributed to an observable and verifiable phenomenon. Although the informants' reports are affected not only by themselves but also their relationships with the target participants, using the third person's observation has been used as a way to test the authenticity of PTG reports.

A third approach to this question is to view PTG as synonymous with recovery. The assumption here is that if one experienced "authentic" PTG, one should also be free from negative symptoms. However, PTG and recovery are most assuredly *not* the same thing. Evidence shows that PTG and reduced symptoms of distress or pathology do not always co-occur at the same time, and that PTG and symptoms can co-occur (Shakespeare-Finch & Lurie-Beck, 2014), perhaps because the traumatic event can both create symptoms and initiate the PTG process. Understanding that symptoms of distress or disorder and PTG are not mutually exclusive requires dialectical thinking and appreciation of paradox. This is at the core of the PTG concept: that loss can produce gain.

To a degree, the debate over the "authenticity" of PTG is based in both methodological concerns and conceptualization or philosophical standpoints. It is important to reiterate that PTG is a process, and not just an outcome. Only over long periods of time can we discern the effect of traumatic experiences in individual lives that are also affected by many other factors. Although there is limited longitudinal research in this area to date, it should not be overlooked that there have been many longitudinal clinical relationships with traumatized clients that led to the development of PTG as a construct and informed early ideas reflected in the PTGI.

As meta-analytic studies (e.g., Sawyer, Ayers, & Field, 2010) have revealed, PTG tends to be related to increased positive mental health, reduced negative mental health, and better subjective physical health. Overwhelmingly, reports of PTG support its positive impact. However, it has been claimed that PTG can make a negative impact if it is "linked to dysfunctional coping strategies, such as denial, wishful thinking, or cognitive avoidance. In those cases, the perception of PTG might be detrimental for long-term adjustment because it hinders the cognitive emotional processing of the trauma" (Zoellner & Maercker, 2006, p. 348). Lahav et al. (2016) have also suggested that adhering to beliefs that one has grown, as a means by which to avoid dealing with painful thoughts and feelings, has a detrimental impact on the body as a result of the demand such thought and its accompanying behavior have on the autonomic nervous system. However, PTG has been conceptualized as positive change as a result of "struggle" with stressful life events, which should follow active cognitive engagement (Calhoun & Tedeschi, 2006); thus, reports of positive changes with practically no cognitive struggle may not automatically be experienced as PTG. An important component of the model of PTG is not to deny adverse or negative impacts of experiencing trauma while still recognizing that transformative changes are possible as a consequence of the same experience and that these may be concurrent for some people (Shakespeare-Finch & de Dassel, 2009).

# CHAPTER 7

# Components of the Theoretical Model of Posttraumatic Growth

A theoretical model was first introduced by Tedeschi and Calhoun in 1995 in order to outline the general psychological processes that lead to growth, and that were considered to be useful targets for research and clinical application. In this early model, a variety of theoretical conceptions of coping (Lazarus & Folkman, 1984; Scheier, Weintraub, & Carver, 1986), creativity (Strickland, 1989), and change (Janoff-Bulman, 1992; McCann & Pearlman, 1990; Schaefer & Moos, 1992) were incorporated. Tedeschi and Calhoun laid out a series of principles in developing an essentially cognitive framework for describing the process of growth. The first three principles establish schema change as the basis for growth using Kelly (1955), Neimeyer (1993), and Janoff-Bulman (1992) as starting points for theory development. These principles emphasize how reconstrual with positive evaluations of trauma and its outcome are the foundation for growth. Antonovsky's (1987) model of salutogenesis, comprising meaningfulness, comprehensibility, and manageability, was used to organize ideas about what positive evaluations can produce for a trauma survivor in order for growth to be perceived and realized. Principle four posits that different types of traumas may produce different growth outcomes. Principle five emphasizes that growth is dependent on personality characteristics and suggests that self-efficacy, locus of control, hardiness, optimism, creativity, and cognitive flexibility may be the sort of characteristics that position individuals to respond to traumas in ways that lead to growth. The sixth principle states that "growth occurs when trauma assumes a central place in the life story" (Tedeschi & Calhoun, 1995, p. 85). This principle used the narrative approach (McAdams, 1993) to explain how traumas are reworked cognitively, and foreshadowed the work on centrality of events that has been shown to be important in determining PTG (Berntsen & Rubin, 2006; Johnson & Boals, 2015). Finally, the seventh principle suggests that wisdom is a product of growth. Tedeschi and Calhoun (1995) recommend research into PTG that uses measures of positive characteristics of people in order to tap the increased maturity or wisdom that may accrue from engaging in the process of confronting trauma.

In the 1995 model introduced by Tedeschi and Calhoun, "Initial Growth" represented the influence of support from others, or personality characteristics, and of schema revision that had taken place on the acceptance of the unchangeable aspects of the situation. It also involved the setting of new, more realistic goals and the development of a new understanding of what happened. This is success-ful coping, where the situation is understood, emotional distress decreases, and action is taken to successfully obtain revised goals. The individual also finds that personal resources are sufficient to be able to assist others. As a result of this pro-cess, the situation is perceived to be more manageable and comprehensible, and some initial growth is possible. Growth in this case takes the form of a sense or personal strength, a recognition that others can be helpful in ways not previously experienced, and an understanding of the vicissitudes of life. The degree of growth in turn may contribute to positive change in the personality (Jayawickreme & Blackie, 2014).

In the 1995 Tedeschi and Calhoun model,

> more growth occurs after additional cognitive processing by a particularly creative personality. This rumination is a somewhat more reflective, expan-sive version because the situation has become more manageable and compre-hensible, and there is less emotional distress. This growth is the wisdom to which we have previously referred. There is emotional serenity together with an acute appreciation for life, as well as exhilaration that can come from a recognition that the self is vulnerable, yet strong. Cognitive changes are char-acterized by a review and revision of the life narrative and development of dialectical thinking . . . This leads to new creativity in behavior that is reflected in enhanced personal relationships, which are deepened because of lessons in empathy and the experience of support and caring . . . There is likely a recipro-cal relationship between wisdom and meaningfulness as well. The meaning-fulness of life is deepened when the preciousness of what remains is enhanced by the losses.
>
> (Tedeschi & Calhoun, 1995, p. 91)

Revisions of this model have since appeared and refer explicitly to PTG. How-ever, the central ideas have remained constant, with different schematics offered as illustrations. The second version of the schematic can be found in Calhoun and Tedeschi (1998b), a third revision in Calhoun and Tedeschi (2006) and Tedeschi and Calhoun (2004b), and the most recent version, prior to the one presented here, can be found in Calhoun, Cann, and Tedeschi (2010) and Calhoun and Tede-schi (2013). These models include the following nine components.

1. The person pre-trauma (moderate well-being; nascent schema for develop-ment posttrauma; complex, active, open, hopeful cognitive style as character-istics that allow more efficient movement toward PTG)
2. Seismic traumatic event (what is traumatic varies in individual circumstances)
3. Challenges (to higher-order goals, higher-order beliefs, and ability to manage emotional distress, therefore defining what "seismic" is for an individual)
4. Rumination (more automatic and intrusive than deliberate)
5. Coping success (disengagement from unreachable goals and untenable beliefs; decreased emotional distress through effective emotion regulation strategies)
6. Rumination (more deliberate than automatic and intrusive)

7. Social support (sources of comfort, new schemas, adaptive coping behaviors represented in "expert companionship" rather than general support)
8. Posttraumatic growth (relating to others, new possibilities, personal strength, spiritual change, appreciation of life), narrative development, and wisdom
9. Some enduring distress from trauma (that can keep the focus on change and growth)

In this model, characteristics of the person pre-trauma are expected to affect how the person experiences the traumatic event/s, which challenge one's core beliefs and lead to inevitable cognitive processing such as automatic rumination. In the case that this automatic rumination leads to coping success, it would also lead to more deliberate rumination, which interacts with PTG and distress. Social support is assumed to explain coping success and both types of rumination. Posttraumatic growth is experienced from interactions between deliberate rumination, narrative development, wisdom, and some enduring distress from trauma. Thus, this PTG theoretical model assumes a coexistent relationship between growth and distress that varies depending on the level of either growth and/or distress.

The model was then refined based on empirical tests of some components included in the earlier models as well as on the authors' further experiences as practicing psychologists (Calhoun & Tedeschi, 1999). This version (Calhoun & Tedeschi, 2006; Tedeschi & Calhoun, 2004b) included 11 components. Eight are the same as the ones in the previous model. For the remaining three, one is split (i.e., PTG is distinguished from narrative and wisdom), one is differently labeled (i.e., social support), and one is added (i.e., culture). This model suggests that although they are inter-correlated and overlapping, PTG and development of a revised narrative or wisdom are not identical. Second, social support in this model has been relabeled as self-disclosure. The earlier models included the key role of social support affecting both types of rumination and coping; however, the third version of the model specifically suggested a role of "self-disclosure" through writing (or other creative expression) or talking about PTG experiences. This clarification, based on data, indicated that self-disclosure about emotions and about one's perspective on current life crises, as well as on how others responded to their self-disclosure, are likely to influence PTG. In addition, socio-cultural elements, both distal and proximate, were added to the third version.

The most current version, as seen in Figure 7.1, was developed based on earlier iterations of the PTG model (Calhoun et al., 2010; Calhoun & Tedeschi, 2013). Similar to the previous models, this one describes the antecedents of PTG and the ways in which people experience it. However, there are some changes. First, unlike the versions from 2004/2006, this model includes the effects or outcomes of PTG, that is, an indirect effect of PTG and a direct effect of acceptance or narrative/wisdom on well-being. This most recent model suggests that PTG and distress coexist, but that a sense of well-being can also arise from PTG even though some distress remains. This latest version illustrates that an event may challenge and disrupt some people's core beliefs or life goals, leading to intrusive rumination that in turn may lead to deliberate rumination (left-hand side), while the same event may not threaten other people's core beliefs and thus may not trigger the PTG processes.

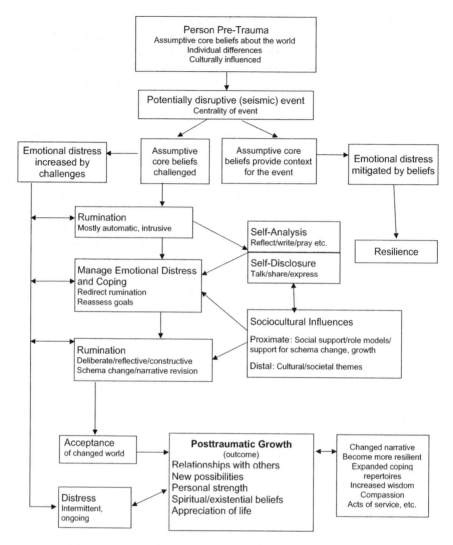

*Figure 7.1* A Revised Model of Posttraumatic Growth

This model also clarifies the multiple roles of emotional distress on PTG and well-being. As we describe below, intrusive rumination soon after the event is likely to reflect the emotional distress caused by the disruption of core beliefs. However, once the more intrusive ruminative thoughts change to more constructive and deliberate thoughts, emotional distress may still continue but with potentially different meaning attributed to the experience, or the experience of stress. This complex interaction between challenged core beliefs, rumination, and distress is key to experiencing PTG.

Finally, the most recent model that we have included in this volume makes more explicit that there is a pathway through the assumptive beliefs that provide context for the event; this pathway leads through emotional distress in a way that produces resilience, where the effects of the event lead not to PTG but to a sense of well-being without great personal change or growth.

## The Person Pre-Trauma and PTG

Pre-existing characteristics easily can affect the likelihood of PTG (Calhoun & Tedeschi, 1998b). Person pre-trauma factors include (1) demographic character-istics such as age, gender, and religiousness, (2) individual differences, personal-ity traits, or cognitive tendencies, including hope, extraversion, and openness to experience, (3) pre-trauma mental health status, and (4) assumptive worlds built before the event happened. Many of these factors have been found to differentiate scores on the PTGI.

### *(1) Age or Developmental Stage When the Event Happened May Influence PTG*

Although findings of the age differences in PTG, especially in childhood, are mixed (Meyerson, Grant, Carter, & Kilmer, 2011), children may not have fully developed world assumptions to be challenged if a traumatic event happened dur-ing an early developmental period and may or may not be able to recognize PTG because of cognitive and expressive capabilities. It may be that traumatic experi-ences shape, rather than change, early schematic charts. The way PTG is currently conceptualized requires an ability to appreciate and think dialectically, since the fundamental paradox of PTG is that out of loss can come gain. There is evidence that children must be at least 9, or a bit older, in order to hold conflicting ideas in relation to the same target (Harter & Buddin, 1987). A study of a wide age range of adults (20- to 70-year-olds) showed an inverse relationship between age and PTG (Manne et al., 2004). Sex differences are mostly consistent, but small, in that women are more likely to report PTG than men (Vishnevsky, Cann, Calhoun, Tedeschi, & Demakis, 2010). Although gender can be seen as a pre-trauma factor, gender differences might be due to the fact that gender also affects post-trauma factors such as self-disclosure and religiosity.

### *(2) Personality Pre-Trauma Is Likely to Affect PTG in a Variety of Ways*

Hope, for example, allows an open response to the distress caused by stressful life event/s while revising goals, perspectives and behaviors, which may lead to PTG (Calhoun & Tedeschi, 1998b). Of the "big five" personality factors, extraversion and openness to experience or new ideas may be related to PTG (Shakespeare-Finch, Gow, & Smith, 2005; Sheikh, 2004; Tedeschi & Calhoun, 2004b), although these relationships may depend on the severity of distress or the coping strategies employed (Shakespeare-Finch et al., 2005; Zoellner, Rabe, Karl, & Maercker, 2008). Another example of pre-trauma person variables possibly related to PTG is creativ-ity, because highly creative people are able to channel their stressful life experiences as sources of inspiration and motivation for their lives and work (Forgeard, 2013). Attachment style may also be related to PTG. In an American study of 54 adult survivors of various types of cancer, secure attachment was related to PTG but not to avoidant, ambivalent-worry, or ambivalent-merger attachment styles (Schmidt, Blank, Bellizzi, & Park, 2012). Secure attachment was also the only style related to active coping, positive reappraisals, or religious coping; the authors suggested these variables are mediators between secure attachment and PTG. Schmidt and colleagues more recently (Schmidt, Blank, Bellizzi, & Park, 2017) examined the relationship between attachment and PTG and the mediating role of social support and coping strategies in 546 college students, 359 of whom had experienced a traumatic event in adolescence. Results indicated that attachment was not directly related to PTG, but rather was mediated by intrapersonal coping and social support. Spiritual changes were not included in the structural equation model as they did not load highly enough in the measurement model. These results may have been different in this regard if the PTGI-X, which includes more existential items than the original PTGI, had been used. Intrapersonal coping accounted for most variance, and that variable was comprised of active coping, positive reframing, and planning in both the trauma and comparison groups. There is some confounding of PTG in this study as the comparison group reported on changes they attributed to the transition from school to college, whereas the trauma group reported on changes as a result of the trauma they had experienced in adolescence. Of course, the trauma group had also experienced the transition from school to college. The most notable difference between the groups was that the new possibilities domain of the PTGI was significantly higher in the comparison group.

Dekel (2007) examined avoidant and anxious attachment styles in a controlled design of the wives of men who had been prisoners of war (POWs) compared to wives of non-POW veterans in Israel. The ex-POW wives had higher levels of distress and PTG than the control group, and both anxious and avoidant attachment styles were significantly related to distress and to PTG. Arikan, Stopa, Carnelley, and Karl (2016) measured PTG, PTSD, and attachment in 393 Turkish people who had experienced various kinds of trauma. They used structural equation modeling to test attachment anxiety and attachment avoidance of posttraumatic stress and growth. There was a significant relationship between distress and growth ($r = .38$) and a direct negative pathway between attachment avoidance and PTG ($r = -.28$). Clearly, there is more work needed to clarify the inconsistent findings regarding attachment and PTG.

### (3) Pre-Trauma Mental Health and Stress Exposure

Because a curvilinear relationship between posttraumatic stress symptoms and PTG has been suggested (Shakespeare-Finch & Lurie-Beck, 2014), and because posttraumatic stress symptoms are likely to be predicted by trait anxiety (Ristvedt & Trinkaus, 2009), prior stress exposure (Doron-LaMarca, Vogt, King, King, & Saxe, 2010), and pre-trauma mental health status (Gil, 2005), these pre-trauma factors are also likely to affect PTG. Persons who show particularly poor mental health status before a traumatic event might be more likely to be too overwhelmed to even initiate cognitive processing or to be effective at managing the initial emotional distress, and then may experience intrusive rumination without the ability to convert it to a more constructive deliberate rumination. They may also cope with their distress using strategies such as avoidance, which in turn may hinder PTG development. On the other hand, people who maintain better pre-trauma mental health status will be more likely to be able to more effectively cognitively process new information generated by the triggering event.

### (4) Pre-Trauma Assumptive World and Core Beliefs

The final component of the person pre-trauma is the assumptive world: the general set of core beliefs a person held before the event happened. "Under typical circumstances, this broad set of beliefs helps individuals maintain a sense of how events in the world should unfold, and how they can influence events" (Calhoun, Tedeschi, Cann, & Hanks, 2010, p. 131). One efficient measure of the challenge to core beliefs includes the following as examples of central beliefs that can be affected by trauma. Trauma can bring into question notions of the world being a fair place—where good things happen to good people. Ideas about the extent to which a person has control over what happens to them, their personal motivations, relationships, capabilities, and expectations of the future may be challenged as well as a person's sense of their own worth. Experiences perceived to be traumatic can also lead to questioning the meaning of life and previously held spiritual or religious beliefs (Cann, Calhoun, Tedeschi, Kilmer, Gil-Rivas, Vishnevsky, & Danhauer, 2010).

## Challenges to Core Beliefs, Rumination, and PTG

Cognitive struggle with traumatic circumstances plays a key role in PTG. This struggle is initiated by a person's core beliefs being challenged by a traumatic event. Events that challenge core beliefs, no matter how traumatic these events may appear to observers, are traumatic to the person struggling to understand what to believe about the world and their place in it in the aftermath of these events.

Just as an earthquake can occur in an unexpected place and at an unexpected time, shaking, damaging, or destroying everything that has been built over the years, a highly stressful life event can challenge or disrupt one's core beliefs (Calhoun & Tedeschi, 2013). Just as damage and disorganization to the infrastructure of a city is disruptive, so too is a challenge to the core belief system. The person must rebuild this system, just as a city after an earthquake, must rebuild its infrastructure out of what remains.

Challenges to core beliefs are often stressful, and such challenges generally lead to initial emotional distress. Both challenges and emotional distress interactively initiate ruminative thoughts. Two different types of rumination are often activated in this process; one is intrusive and automatic in nature, and the other is more reflective, deliberate and a vehicle for an individual's attempts to understand what has happened and what is left in the aftermath (Calhoun & Tedeschi, 2006; Cann et al., 2011). Intrusive rumination is a normal part of initial responses to trauma;

images may be stuck in the forefront of a person's mind, unwanted thoughts of the experience intrude during waking hours, and for some people nightmares about the experience disrupt their nights and sleep. For most people, these intrusive thoughts and images fade with time, and intrusive rumination may be replaced, or may at least begin to be accompanied, by more deliberate and effortful rumination.

Deliberate rumination occurs when an individual is trying to understand why or how the event happened and engages in conscious, sometimes effortful, cognitive work to do so. In addition, and crucially to PTG, deliberate rumination is also an attempt to adapt to the changed circumstances of life and develop a revised core belief structure that accounts for them. Through deliberate rumination, a survivor of a traumatic event seeks to integrate these experiences into the life narrative. It should be noted that deliberate rumination is not the same as coping appraisals that include positive reframing.

> Appraisal reflects the tendency to assess a given stressor relative to its context and resource availability, [while] deliberate rumination reflects the ability to think in-depth or engage in repetitive thoughts with relation to psychological or emotional topics. Deliberate rumination is an effortful strategy enacted with the intention of reconceptualizing (i.e., reappraising) highly stressful circumstances in such a way that meaning or growth become potential outcomes.
>
> (Tedeschi & Blevins, 2015, p. 374)

Empirical studies have consistently demonstrated positive associations between deliberate rumination and PTG (Cann et al., 2011; Morris & Shakespeare-Finch, 2011), although the strength of this association can vary depending on the target and timing of the study. In the PTG model, deliberate rumination may involve what has been termed a search for meaning or meaning-making. It should be noted that a "search for" meaning, rather than recognizing the presence of meaning, may be temporarily associated with negative changes, even though deliberate rumination constitutes the necessary cognitive process through which people are able to accept or make meaning (Linley & Joseph, 2011). Intrusive rumination is a precursor to deliberate rumination, although painful and stressful, and deliberate rumination ultimately allows for a more meaningful perspective on life in the aftermath of trauma and PTG. In sum, "growth is not an inevitable outcome of this cognitive work, but it is quite common under conditions that encourage growth" (Calhoun et al., 2010, p. 7).

## Disclosure, Social Support, and PTG

Disclosure (also called self-disclosure) about the person's traumatic or highly challenging experience, and the response of others in the social network to such disclosures, can have a significant impact on the discloser's journey. Disclosure can take many forms, most commonly through talking to others about stressful or traumatic events. But this form of disclosure is not the only way in which a person may "tell their story." Some people write about their experiences in journals and books or on blogs and social media, etc. Although it may not be what some would think of precisely as self-disclosure, trauma survivors also may draw, create music, dance, or use a number of other creative ways of communicating their experience and the impact it has had on them. Disclosure has been studied by investigating its effect on psychological and physiological health, as well as its the potential to promote PTG. For example, in a study of people who had experienced a serious accident, those who disclosed about the event reported higher levels of PTG than those who had not (Dong, Gong, Jiang, Deng, & Lui, 2015). Self-disclosure is relevant to PTG for a number of reasons; it can (1) alleviate the initial emotional distress associated with the experience, (2) foster cognitive processing, (3) be achieved as a form of PTG, (4) bring unconscious thoughts and feelings to the fore, and/or (5) establish supportive others as there for the person who has disclosed. Of course, the latter may also highlight a lack of support if the person being disclosed to does not provide validation of a person's experience and the responses they are having as a result of that experience.

Self-disclosure can be an effective way to manage emotional distress, which in turn can affect PTG. There are a variety of coping behaviors that help manage responses to a highly stressful event, such as analyzing the situation (i.e., problem focused coping strategy) and enjoying leisure (i.e., emotion-focused coping strategy); self-disclosure is a strategy that can serve both of these purposes. Talking about the situation may directly solve the problem, or it may simply provide comfort in a situation that cannot be changed. Early studies (e.g., Pennebaker, 1999; Petrie, Booth, Pennebaker, Davison, & Thomas, 1995) found overall support for the beneficial impact of self-disclosure on health. More recent studies with meta-analytical approaches have provided mixed results regarding the effect of written disclosure on physical health and psychological health (Riddle, Smith, & Jones, 2016). Although the effect is rather small (Frattaroli, 2006; Frisina, Borod, & Lepore, 2004), self-disclosure generally can help alleviate distress, which in turn will affect the PTG processes. It is important to distinguish in the disclosure literature between studies of written disclosure and those that involve personal disclosure to another. Small effects may be due to only measuring if a person disclosed to another rather than also including the response to that disclosure. For example, in two conversations with two different survivors of childhood sexual assault, the role of response to disclosure was clear. For one woman, her mother embraced her, reinforced that she would be there no matter what, sought professional counseling immediately, and helped her negotiate the court system in charging the perpetrator when she reached adulthood. The other told her mother about her stepfather, who had been raping her for some years. Her mother's first response was to ask if he had mentioned a preference for the daughter over the mother. There was no support at the time of disclosure for this victim or later when she too reached adulthood and charged her perpetrator. Both cases had a guilty verdict. One woman still has a strong bond with her mother, and the other has no family of origin in her life. The latter is related to what Laura Brown (2015) refers to as *the price of admission* and S. Caroline Taylor (2011) refers to as *social death*.

Disclosure can also affect the cognitive processing that plays a major role in PTG. Because there are individual differences as to which coping strategies are more effective (e.g., talking with others may be helpful for some people, whereas playing sports or listening to music may be more helpful to reduce stress for others), disclosure may not directly decrease the stress level for some people. However, disclosure is likely to affect cognitive processing that can produce more meaningful outcomes even when distress still exists, especially when social responses to that disclosure are supportive. Traumatic events often force people to ruminate about what has happened. In this process, disclosing one's thoughts, emotions, and feelings about the traumatic experience, through talking or writing, is likely to foster qualitative changes in cognitive processing.

As the model of PTG suggests, self-disclosure can shift the characteristics of ruminative thought from mostly automatic and intrusive to more deliberate and reflective rumination, thereby providing a chance to reassess life goals or create a meaningful narrative. Although the journey post-disclosure depends on how those being disclosed to react, the act of disclosing alone can help people to reflect; make sense of what happened and what they have recognized about themselves, their relationships, and their world; accept the reality of their experience; and gain insight (Pennebaker, 1999; Tedeschi & Calhoun, 2006).

These two aspects of disclosure—self-disclosure as a coping mechanism and self-disclosure as a stimulus that fosters cognitive processing—focus on the role of self-disclosure as an antecedent of PTG. These ideas have been tested and supported by studies investigating the effects of disclosure on PTG. For example, Hemenover (2003) asked one group of study participants to write about a traumatic life event and another group to write about their daily plans (i.e., control group) to examine the impact of disclosure on self-perceptions. Results showed that disclosures about traumatic events changed self-perception and led to a more resilient self-concept, reflected in higher levels of psychological well-being. Perhaps some may wonder if self-reported PTG measured immediately following the completion of an expressive writing task is just an illusory coping response. However, this hypothesis has been empirically tested and has not been supported (Lancaster, Klein, & Heifner, 2015). Lancaster and colleagues compared levels of PTG immediately before and after a disclosure task and revealed that there were no significant increases in PTG. Unfortunately, long-term follow-up data were not available in this study, and this methodology assumes an immediate effect of self-disclosure on PTG.

However, disclosure may affect other factors that can possibly lead to growth, such as cognitive processing or perceptions of support. It is possible, then, that self-disclosure may be more likely to have a long-term, rather than a short-term, effect on the experience of PTG. Some people may not experience PTG right after they talk or write about their traumatic experiences. Instead, after a while, they may ruminate about what they talked or wrote about, which in the long run is likely to help in making sense of what had happened—more constructive rumination—leading to PTG. In a study that included an eight-week follow-up after participating in an internet-based expressive writing session, PTG did indeed increase, especially with a greater use of insight words, such as *understand, realize,* or *knew* (Stockton, Joseph, & Hunt, 2014). Available research collectively suggests that self-disclosure, especially when it includes a deeper level of self-analysis, self-reflection, or insight, is likely to foster PTG.

### Disclosure Itself May Reflect a Form of PTG

In addition to its role as a mediating or predictor variable, disclosure can also be viewed as an outcome. A traumatic event can sometimes help people to interact with others in a more intimate way and may provide an impetus for disclosure about aspects of themselves in ways that had never happened before. Disclosure may then foster narrative development when the person is in the presence of a good listener. As Calhoun and Tedeschi (2013) described, it is not "the simple fact of self-disclosure that is likely to be important, but the combination of such self-disclosure, with accepting and supportive responses to the disclosure by members of primary reference groups" (p. 46). This effort at disclosure may also elicit social support from others. Within this framework, disclosure and social support are connected.

### Social Support Can Play a Significant Role in PTG

Social support can influence PTG in a number of ways, including (1) as a pre-trauma context factor and predictor variable, (2) as a mediator, and (3) as an outcome.

### (1) Social Support May Affect PTG as a Pre-Trauma Factor or Predictor Variable

Having a strong social support network pre-trauma is likely to help people to cope effectively with the traumatic event, and thus may or may not directly increase PTG; regardless, it can affect the PTG process. For example, Sattler, Boyd, and Kirsch (2014) found that the perception of network availability was a significant predictor of growth in firefighters who had been exposed to a potentially traumatizing event. Further, Yu and colleagues (2014) found that perceptions of social support were correlated with PTG in women who were struggling with infertility. In a study where social support was placed as a predictor variable investigating PTG in 164 colorectal cancer survivors, results demonstrated that although there were moderate to strong correlations between social support and PTG and between resilience and PTG, resilience mediated the relationship between social support and PTG (Dong et al., 2017).

### (2) Social Support as a Mediator Between Individual Difference Variables and PTG

Having someone who can provide constructive support may assist in the development of new schemas. When people engage in automatic intrusive rumination, sharing those thoughts with someone they trust may help them to look at things in a different and more hopeful or adaptive way. The listeners may be able to offer different perspectives or serve as role models, especially if they have also experienced a similar event. For example, in a study of people who had survived various types of cancer, results demonstrated the positive adaptive capacity of having someone model positive post-cancer outcomes (Morris, Shakespeare-Finch, & Scott, 2012). Morris et al. found that PTG was higher in breast cancer survivors than other types of cancer and that being exposed to campaigns for survival championed by well-known personalities was a key resource for drawing strength for these women. However, such role models are not readily seen in the public eye promoting survival and growth following anal or colorectal cancers. Some studies have also demonstrated the significant impact of receiving emotional support on PTG (e.g., Dirik & Karanci, 2008; Tallman, Shaw, Schultz, & Altmaier, 2010), especially in the domain of relating to others (Cieslak et al., 2009). This positive relationship between social support and PTG has also been found in emergency medical dispatchers (Shakespeare-Finch, Rees, & Armstrong, 2015). However, it should be noted that other studies have provided mixed results. For example, a study conducted with hematopoietic stem cell transplant survivors revealed that instrumental support, rather than emotional support, significantly affected PTG (Nenova, DuHamel, Zemon, Rini, & Redd, 2013), whereas a study with cardiovascular disease patients did not find any significant effect of social support satisfaction on PTG (Sheikh, 2004).

The source and nature of support are also important in PTG. Schroevers, Helgeson, Sanderman, and Ranchor (2010) conducted a longitudinal multiple methods study with 206 people who were long-term survivors of various types of cancer. The emotional support received at three months post-diagnosis significantly predicted positive changes attributed to their battle with cancer eight years later, controlling for support reported at the eight-year time point. An interesting aspect of this research was that received social support measured at the eight-year time point was not correlated with PTG, so the important role provided by support three months post-diagnosis would have been missed using a cross-sectional design many years later. The source of support is also an important variable in predicting PTG. For example, Armstrong, Shakespeare-Finch, and Shochet (2016) examined sense of belonging in 250 firefighters using the Psychological Sense of Organizational Membership scale (PSOM; Cockshaw & Shochet, 2010). This scale measures the extent to which a person feels that they belong in an organization and are respected and valued by their peers and supervisors—in other words, how supported a person feels in their work environment. The results demonstrated that there was no significant direct relationship between organizational stress and PTG; however, there was a significant pathway to PTG through the extent to which a person felt supported by peers and supervisors. The importance of the source of support in the workplace was also demonstrated in a study of 740 paramedics (Shakespeare-Finch & Daley, 2017). Controlling for common factors explored in emergency services research, such as severity of trauma exposure and length of service, the sense of belonging and of being supported by colleagues and superiors was the most influential variable in buffering symptoms of PTSD and in promoting resilience. Prati and Pietrantoni (2009) conducted a meta-analysis that included examining the relationship between social support and PTG. They found a moderate relationship between the two and argued that seeking social support reflects an active coping strategy to deal with either the problem issue at hand or the emotional consequences of it.

Calhoun and Tedeschi (2006) argued that the relationship of PTG to social factors is highly specific and that certain types of responses to certain kinds of behaviors, including supportive ones, on the part of the person in crisis will have a relationship with the degree of growth reported. The exclusive use of broad gauge, general measures of social support, however, seems a less fruitful approach to utilize than previously anticipated.

## (3) Developing a Support Network or Utilizing Social Support and PTG

After experiencing a major life crisis, a person may get involved with a support group or be able to meet new people whom they would not have encountered had they not experienced the crisis. Qualitative research has been useful in exploring experiences of a changing social support system. For example, successfully negotiating a post-trauma journey can lead to people becoming positive role models (Morris et al., 2012), or it can provide motivation to support others through a newly found sense of compassion (Shakespeare-Finch & Copping, 2006). Social support can help to develop a stronger sense of connectedness to others and with the community, which can, in turn, be interpreted as an example of PTG. Taku, Tedeschi, Cann, and Calhoun (2009) demonstrated that those who not only disclosed their stressful experiences but also perceived their recipients' reactions as involving mutual disclosure reported a higher level of PTG than those who experienced negative reactions to their disclosures. Social support can be reciprocal. For example, people who receive emotional or instrumental support from others may also use the opportunity to reflect on their own experiences and may even share them with the person whom they have supported. This mutuality may foster a deeper understanding of self, relationships, and life in general. Positive changes in relationships is a factor of the PTGI that is frequently endorsed, and social support is intricately involved in positive relationships.

## Wisdom, Narrative Development, and PTG

People who report significant levels of PTG can be identified by many of the same characteristics as those who are seen as wise (Calhoun & Tedeschi, 1998b). Wisdom has been seen as an ultimate goal of human development (Erikson, 1984). Although there is no consensus as to the definition of wisdom, generally those definitions that exist include good decision-making, wide and deep knowledge of life, holding prosocial values, better self-reflection, and being able to acknowledge uncertainty (Bangen, Meeks, & Jeste, 2013). Because PTG is paradoxical, dialectical, and profound (Calhoun & Tedeschi, 1998a), it can closely relate to wisdom. Thus, wisdom can be seen as an outcome, but in reality, PTG and wisdom are reciprocally related, co-occur, and interact (Webster & Deng, 2015). However, it is inaccurate to assume that all people who report PTG are also wiser. The degree to which this may be true would depend on the particular definition of wisdom and the particular type of PTG involved.

One way to consider the effects of a traumatic event is on a person's ability to better manage future life difficulties; the ability to manage life's difficulties can be considered an aspect of wisdom. This connection between PTG experiences and responses to future stressful events has been described as psychological preparedness by Janoff-Bulman (2004). "Survivors are not only better prepared for subsequent tragedies, but, as a consequence, are apt to be less traumatized by them as well" (p. 31). Walsh (2015) suggested that recognizing our existential challenges is necessary but not sufficient for full wisdom, and defined "practical wisdom" as skillful benevolent responsiveness to the central existential issues of life.

Wisdom does not necessarily come from a struggle with traumatic events. There are many other routes to wisdom. Weststrate and Glück (2017), for example, proposed that self-reflection may be the significant source of wisdom and the reason why not all people with life experience are wise, even though wisdom is believed to be cultivated through a diverse range of life experience. They defined wisdom as a body of experience-based knowledge about the fundamental issues of human life that is both broad and deep, and implicit and explicit, and assessed it using three different approaches (self-report, performance, and nomination approaches). They then looked at why people reflect on the past (i.e., reasons for reminiscence) and how they do it (i.e., autobiographical reasoning) by conducting interviews about what participants considered to be the most difficult events in their lives. Narratives were then coded as either exploratory processing (i.e., interpretive approach to self-reflection on life events, which emphasizes meaning making, complexity, and personal growth from the past) or redemptive processing (i.e., the tendency to redeem life experiences by transforming an initially negative event into an emotionally positive one, which provides the narrator with a sense of emotional closure and event resolution). They found that across the three different methods for assessing wisdom, wisdom was positively associated with exploratory processing of difficult life experiences, but not with redemptive processing. Redemptive processing, on the other hand, was positively associated with adjustment. This study suggested how and why people self-reflect matters more for wisdom than how much they reflect, and that the "exploratory" type of reflection is more associated with wisdom and growth. If growth is experienced as resulting from psychological struggle involving challenged core beliefs and intrusive and deliberate rumination as depicted in the PTG theoretical model, then this growth is likely to lead to wisdom because wisdom is likely to be fostered by exploratory processing rather than redemptive processing (Weststrate & Glück, 2017). However, the "redemptive" processing may be more akin to a coping strategy, a defense mechanism, or self-enhancement motivation (possibly illusory growth) by reframing the negative experience in a way that may foster adjustment but not wisdom or growth.

In sum, traumatic, "seismic" experiences are likely to force people to explore existential issues such as the meaning of life, meaning of death, purpose of life, eternity, and reality; the PTG model indicates that true PTG experiences are expected to connect to wisdom for some people. As the ancient Greek playwright Aeschylus penned in Agamemnon, "Wisdom comes through suffering." Wiser people process life challenges in an exploratory manner that emphasizes meaning and growth, even if that process may sometimes be unpleasant (Weststrate & Glück, 2017).

Likewise, narrative development may also co-occur with PTG. This growth narrative reflects the wisdom that recognizes the complexity of the life rather than simple notions of general happiness or depression (Calhoun et al., 2010). As studies using narratives have indicated (Adams, 2015; Chun & Lee, 2008), PTG can enhance the life story and narratives can include a theme of PTG, so that PTG and the changed narrative are intertwined and co-occurring. Neimeyer (2006) suggested that "narrative is more than just a post hoc accounting for the changes that we undergo in response to life disruption—though it also serves that vital, meaning attribution function" (p. 78). Changed narratives can initiate and foster the PTG processes but also be fostered by the realization of PTG experiences. In a study of 30 sex offenders, Vanhooren, Leijssen, and Dezutter (2015) found that new life narratives were an important component in offenders' experiences of PTG, developed through therapy, which encouraged reflection and re-narration of life stories. Participants described a better understanding of who they were as people, bringing a new perspective and meaning to their lives and a new sense of purpose and direction.

## Type of Trauma and PTG

There is sparse research examining the effect of type of traumatic event and the form PTG takes. Further, the impact of different types of events on PTG may not be separated from a number of potentially confounding factors. For example, the level of perceived severity or stressfulness associated with the event is likely to impact PTG. It could also be that causal attribution for the trauma influences PTG, such as if the experience was preventable or predictable and who was primarily responsible—man-made versus natural cause. Geography may also be a factor; for example, people living in a certain area may be more likely to be assaulted than those in another area or experience some type of natural disaster such as a hurricane or an earthquake. Women are more likely to be victimized by sexual assault, whereas men are more likely to be involved in other forms of violence, and time since the event or developmental period (childhood trauma; adolescent-specific trauma) may impact PTG.

PTG has been reported as an outcome following many different types of events. Some studies have focused on PTG resulting from one specific event, such as cancer (Danhauer et al., 2013; Holtmaat, van der Spek, Cuijpers, Leemans, & Leeuw, 2016; Morris & Shakespeare-Finch, 2011), war (Powell, Rosner, Butollo, Tedeschi, & Calhoun, 2003), or natural disaster (Siqveland, Hafstad, & Tedeschi, 2012; Taku, Cann, Tedeschi, & Calhoun, 2015). Of the limited research aimed at examining PTG as a function of type of event, Shakespeare-Finch and Armstrong (2010) found that people who experienced bereavement reported higher levels of PTG than those who experienced a motor vehicle accident or sexual assault. In this research, different event types resulted in differences in the domains in which growth was reported. Those who lost a family member reported a higher level of PTG in appreciation of life compared to the survivors of sexual abuse. Results of this study also indicated that those who had lost a close family member reported more PTG in the relating to others domain than those who experienced sexual assault. There were no clear differences in the domains of personal strength, new possibilities, and spiritual change between the three trauma type groups.

Ickovics et al. (2006) found that adolescents who experienced pregnancy and motherhood, death of a loved one, or physical threat reported more PTG than those who experienced relationship problems, sexual abuse, harassment, or secondary trauma. They confirmed that these differences were not affected by the time since the trauma. Similar to Shakespeare-Finch and Armstrong's findings (2010), Ickovics et al. showed that PTG in the appreciation of life domain was higher in those who experienced the death of a loved one, as well as pregnancy and motherhood, than those who experienced interpersonal problems. Moreover, PTG in the domain of relating to others was also higher in those who experienced the death of a loved one than those who experienced interpersonal problems. Taku et al. (2007) reported that Japanese participants who lost friends and family reported a higher level of spiritual change and appreciation of life than any other people. Karanci and colleagues (2012) examined PTG as a function of three types of trauma in a sample of 969 Turkish adults who had experienced a natural disaster, an accident, or the loss of a loved one. Those who had experienced a natural disaster had significantly higher scores on the relating to other dimensions than those who had been bereaved. Another report from earthquake survivors in New Zealand also highlighted that growth in the relating to others domain is more likely to occur than growth in the personal strength domain (Marshall, Frazier, Frankfurt, & Kuijer, 2015).

Even within a sample of people who lost family members, differences have been observed in PTG depending on the manner of death. One study examined the levels of PTG among three groups of families whose Marine fathers died by suicide, compared to families whose fathers died by accident and in combat (Aronson, Kyler, Morgan, Perkins, & Love, 2017). Oftentimes, combat deaths are more likely to be recognized as being heroic and selfless, thus leading to a feeling of pride, whereas deaths by suicide can be stigmatized and thus lead to feelings of guilt and shame. These researchers in fact found that spouses of those who died by suicide were more likely to feel isolated, rejected, and without support than those whose spouses died by other means; however, they also found that PTG was possible. Spouses of those bereaved by suicide reported greater growth in new possibilities than the other groups. Clearly, differences in these studies are not easily comparable because of the different kinds of traumatic experiences represented.

An innovative way to address the relationship between PTG and different kinds of traumatic events has been offered by Kira and colleagues (Kira et al., 2013). This research group classified traumas into four types: (1) events that happened once and stopped, (2) events that happened several times and stopped, (3) events that continue to happen, and (4) an accumulation of different traumatic events. Cumulative trauma was positively related to PTG, and events that continue to happen were negatively associated with PTG. It appears that the sample was highly traumatized, and few participants fell into the first two categories. The researchers also considered the relationship between PTG and specific traumatic events. For example, war and combat experiences were positively related to appreciation of life; life-threatening illness was positively related to appreciation of life and spiritual change; being physically attacked was associated with appreciation of life, personal strength, new possibilities, and relationships with others; refugee experiences were positively related to appreciation of life and new possibilities. Shuwiekh, Kira, and Ashby (2017) also found that the experience of a life-threatening single event such as car accident or secondary traumas led a greater PTG, whereas the experience of a continuous chronic trauma such as discrimination, or sexual and physical abuse, abandonment by parent, or neglect had an indirect negative impact on PTG. These studies argue for the utility of analyzing PTG using the various PTG domains that may have differential relationships with varying trauma types.

In summary, the type of event a person experiences is likely to affect PTG. However, it is likely that these differences are due to the influence of other factors such as the severity of the event or causal attribution, rather than purely to the types of events. Because types of events are confounded with other variables, it is challenging to make conclusions that hold across various populations exposed to differing contexts. Helgeson, Reynolds, and Tomich (2006), for example, proposed that the severity and perceived stressfulness of events were more likely to be associated with PTG than the objective characteristics of the event itself.

## Time Since the Event and PTG

The relation between time since the triggering event and PTG is perhaps one of the interesting themes that has elicited inconsistent findings in literature. It may be easy to assume growth takes time to emerge, but this is not necessarily the case. Many studies have provided non-significant direct relationships between PTG and time since the event, making it reasonable to assume that there are many different temporal courses that PTG can take.

Su and Chen (2015) used a two-month longitudinal research design and analyzed data from participants who had experienced a traumatic event between Time 1 baseline survey and Time 2 survey. Although the average length of time since trauma was rather short (i.e., approximately three weeks), 68.2% of the participants reported some degree of positive change. The most common theme was growth in the relating to others domain (e.g., "I feel a greater sense of closeness with family members"), suggesting that growth could occur in a short period of time. In fact, Miller (2004) has investigated "quantum change," where a very rapid transformational experience occurs that is perceived to be the result of a mystical experience or insight more characteristic of psychotherapeutic change. These are abrupt and enduring changes in personal values. Another type of change mechanism was noted by Carver (1998) in the cusp catastrophe model. This approach describes how high importance (i.e., traumatic) events can produce efforts toward personal change in those who have high self-confidence, as if a person moves from one plane of understanding to another. In quantum change and catastrophic change, the person may experience quite sudden, rather than drawn-out, processes of growth. They may also find it difficult to go back to previous perspectives as they have now shifted into a new level of understanding living that does not permit a reversion to old ways of experiencing.

Zernicke and colleagues (2016) examined PTG in 62 people with cancer. Using a wait-list control design, participants completed an eight-week mindfulness intervention. Remembering that participants were undergoing treatment for cancer at various stages of progression, PTG was evident prior to the intervention and was higher in women than men. Following the intervention, PTG increased, and the increase was significantly different for men than women, with men's scores on the PTGI increasing across time more than women's scores. However, women's scores were still higher than men's—the change between pre- and post-intervention was simply greater for men.

Some studies have suggested that there are moderating effects of time since the event. For example, a meta-analytic study suggested that when the time since the traumatic event was more than two years, then PTG or benefit finding was more strongly related to less depression and greater positive affect (Helgeson et al., 2006). Similar findings were found in a meta-analytic study of PTG among those with cancer or HIV/AIDS (Sawyer, Ayers, & Field, 2010). These authors reported that the longer the time since the event, the stronger the relationship between PTG and positive mental health, and the shorter the time since the event, the stronger the relationships between PTG and negative adjustment. These relationships suggest that in the early time following a traumatic event, PTG may reduce the negative effects of trauma, but as time elapses, PTG is likely to enhance well-being. There may also be an indication that in the time directly after traumatic events, PTG is being catalyzed by the negative experience, and the negative aspects of the experience are important drivers of growth. After time, PTG may consolidate and have more robust impacts on a person's sense of well-being, purpose, meaning, or related constructs.

Another moderating effect of time since the event in PTG was examined regarding its relationship with cognitive processing among stroke survivors (Gangstad, Norma, & Barton, 2009). These researchers found that the relationship between anxiety and PTG became negative as time since the stroke increased. They also found that cognitive processing is important for PTG due to the moderating effect of time on these relationships. Thus, even though the direct relationships between PTG and time since the event appears to be inconsistent, time matters for the processes and consequences of PTG experiences.

The role of time since the event in PTG was also examined in a study comparing people who had sustained spinal cord injuries in childhood (pediatric-onset) and those who experienced spinal cord injuries later in life (adult-onset). Since the researchers only had data from the pediatric-onset group, they used two published studies to obtain the mean scores for adult-onset (January, Zebracki, Chlan, & Vogel, 2015). They found that overall PTG and all PTG domains were greater in those with pediatric-onset; however, they revealed that PTG was not related to either age at injury or injury duration (January et al., 2015). If younger people are more likely to experience PTG, it may be because they have more potential to change their lives (e.g., shifting their life goals, building another career path, more chances to meet new people); in that case, not only will the time since the event be important, but also the age when it happened. Because PTG is generally understudied with elderly populations, future research may target a wider range of people to examine the interactive effects of age and time since the event.

In a longitudinal study, Tsai, Sippel, Mota, Southwick, and Pietrzak (2015) examined PTG in 1838 veterans at two time points two years apart. Using cluster analyses, five distinct groups of veterans emerged: (1) those with consistently low PTG scores, (2) consistently high PTG, (3) moderately declining PTG, (4) dramatically declining PTG, and (5) increasing PTG. There were a large number of variables examined in this research—the major results included that when compared to the consistently low PTG group, the consistently high and increasing PTG groups had endured more traumatic experiences and had higher post-traumatic stress scores. The consistently high PTG group also had more physical health conditions than the consistently low group, but greater levels of gratitude and purpose in life. Nearly 60% of those who reported moderate or greater PTG at Time 1 maintained growth across the two years. The results demonstrated that there are many pathways to growth, to maintaining and increasing PTG, as well as declining PTG scores.

The apparently inconsistent results for the relation between time since the stressful event and PTG may be due to at least two factors. First, there is individual variability in the trajectories of PTG over time. Second, measurement of time since the event may sometimes not be long enough to reveal changes. For some persons, PTG may emerge over long periods of time, and some research designs may truncate the time measure and mislead us about how time and PTG are related.

A question that is related to time since the event is the degree to which PTG is maintained over time: Does PTG taper off, increase, or maintain stability? Morgan and Desmarais (2017) studied a military sample and discerned four groups related to time since event. There were a low PTG group and a high PTG group regardless of time, and two moderate growth groups, one associated with short time frames and another with longer time frames of up to three years. However, this was a cross-sectional study. In contrast, a longitudinal study by Danhauer and colleagues (2013, 2015), which examined PTG in 653 breast cancer patients, showed that PTG increased rapidly after a breast cancer diagnosis and remained stable or increased over almost two years. The researchers were able to discern six trajectories of PTG in this sample. Another study with adolescents and young adults with cancer revealed four trajectories over two years (Husson et al., 2017). By using a longitudinal prospective study (6, 12, and 24 months after baseline, which was conducted within the first four months of diagnosis), the researchers examined the PTGI scores at each follow-up point. Although no significant mean differences in the PTGI scores were found over time within the sample as a whole, they identified four trajectories of individual change or stability by using a cut-off of 63 of the total PTGI 105 to classify low versus high PTG levels. They found that 14.1 % showed increasing PTG, 44.8 % remained at a stable high PTG level, 14.1 % showed decreasing PTG, and 27.0 % remained at a stable low PTG level. Pat-Horenczyk et al. (2016) also studied breast cancer patients and concluded that there were transitions over a two-year period among different forms of PTG and that the six to twelve month period was especially important for the patients as they struggled to consolidate their perspectives about growth.

# CHAPTER 8

# Theories Related to Posttraumatic Growth

## Conservation of Resources Theory and PTG

Conservation of resources theory (COR: Hobfoll, 1989) was originally developed to bridge the gap between environmental and cognitive viewpoints of stressful circumstances. "The model's basic tenet is that people strive to retain, protect, and build resources and that what is threatening to them is the potential or actual loss of these valued resources" (Hobfoll, 1989, p. 516). Unlike the transactional stress model (Lazarus & Folkman, 1984), in COR theory, "resources are seen as largely observable, objectively quantifiable, and experienced in a generally common manner regarding their importance among people in a shared culture, rather than subjectively determined" (Hall, Rattigan, Walter, & Hobfoll, 2006, p. 230). COR theory states that stress will occur following the actual or threat of loss of resources, or failure to gain resources following significant resource investment. Four general categories of resources are: objective resources (e.g., car, house), condition resources (e.g., relationships, marriage, tenure, employment, status), personal characteristic resources (e.g., self-esteem, self-efficacy, optimism), and energy resources (e.g., time, credit, knowledge, money).

Both COR theory and PTG theory address the way people live as a result of experiencing a highly traumatic life event. However, these two theories also have some differences. One difference is the way to see the impact of losing resources. COR theory emphasizes the attempts to protect resource loss, which is more salient than resource gain, and explains people's behaviors as an attempt to regain resources. On the other hand, PTG theory emphasizes how one's assumptive world or core beliefs are shaken by a traumatic event. Loss of resources is likely to affect the degree to which core beliefs are shattered; however, they are not identical. Thus, instead of assessing what or how many resources have been lost or threatened to be lost, researchers are trying to investigate the subjective impact of the experience in PTG theory.

In relation to subjectivity versus objectivity, COR theory focuses on objective changes (i.e., action-focused growth: Hobfoll et al., 2007), whereas PTG focuses on subjective changes. This difference may affect the way to identify people at risk. COR theory suggests people with greater resources are less vulnerable to resource loss and more capable of resource gain, whereas PTG theory suggests people with little challenge to core beliefs (e.g., highly resilient) are less vulnerable regardless of the amount of loss of resources. It should also be noted that in the PTG facilitation or intervention framework, turning growth to missions of service to others is viewed as a final phase in the PTG process (Calhoun & Tedeschi, 2013; Tedeschi & McNally, 2011), and in this way action based on new perspectives on living is an expression of PTG.

Although few studies have directly tested the validity of COR and PTG theory in a single study, one claim repeatedly proposed by some researchers utilizing a COR framework is that PTG demonstrates the pathogenic rather than salutogenic function, because PTG reflects cognitive biases such as outgroup bias. One study, with a very limited and specific group of participants, for example, analyzed data from Jews and Arabs in Israel and found that PTG was related to increasing support for political violence, and that PTG did not have an effect on either symptoms of depression or PTS, although in looking at the weightings on the cross-lagged panel design, the relationship was very weak (Johnson, Thompson, & Downs, 2009). The authors concluded that in the case of terrorism and political violence, PTG is a defensive illusion. However, a reliance on PTG theory would lead to a different interpretation of these results. The reason for the positive correlations between PTG and increasing support for political violence may be that when participants held cultural beliefs unique to their very specific situation, violence should be understandable to foster their survival. This variable was assessed by asking participants if they believed that "when *taking into account the bad political situation in our country* [italics added], physical violence toward civilians is understandable." However, stating that use of violence is "understandable" is very different from condoning or committing to it. Wagner, Forstmeier, and Maercker (2007) also pointed out that the participants referred to included Israeli settlers, who have very strong political beliefs and are strongly politically committed. Wagner et al. suggest that such political commitment could actually be a protective factor against negative psychological sequelae following a traumatic experience.

The experience and type of growth, and its outcomes, can also vary from culture to culture, and the research Hobfoll and colleagues conducted was in a very specific cultural context with strong and ongoing clashes of culture. In addition, what was called PTG in that report was assessed by only six items developed by the research team, rather than by an inventory with demonstrated reliability and validity such as the PTGI. In their measurement of "growth," participants were asked the degree to which they had gained (1) hope, (2) sense of confidence, (3) feeling that my life has purpose, (4) intimacy with one or more family members, (5) feeling closer to at least one person, and (6) intimacy with at least one friend, in the past three months. Clearly these items do not reflect the way PTG had been understood and measured in the larger literature on PTG. Furthermore, the lack of a significant relationship between PTG and reduced symptoms was interpreted as a negative quality of PTG; however, this is a clear misunderstanding of PTG, and the result contradicts the claim that PTG is a defensive illusion, because if so, it should lead to reduced distress. Essentially, the lack of a validated measure of growth, the weak and non-significant relationships, and the unique cultural and geographic context in which the research was conducted clearly may have influenced the results, and the limited context certainly restricts the potential generalizability of these findings.

Some researchers, using a COR theory framework, have also suggested that PTG is a rare phenomenon and that it should be viewed as a path for offsetting the negative impact of trauma. Again, this is a misunderstanding of PTG theory and of the larger empirical literature in this area. PTG theory assumes growth can occur to anyone—under certain conditions (e.g., core beliefs shaken, rumination, disclosure, etc.). PTG theory also suggests that growth and distress can coexist and that they are probably best viewed as independent dimensions. See Tedeschi, Calhoun, and Cann (2007) for a more extensive discussion of PTG and COR.

## Terror Management Theory and PTG

Terror management theory (TMT: Greenberg, Pyszczynski, & Solomon, 1986) is a theoretical explanation for how humans manage the terror engendered by the inevitable realization that we are mortal and will all face death. TMT assumes that death is terrifying, because humans are aware that death is inevitable. TMT posits that this terror is managed by a cultural anxiety buffer that consists of a cultural worldview and self-esteem. That is, a great deal of individual and social behavior is assumed to be directed toward preserving faith in a cultural worldview (e.g., achieve symbolic immortality by living up to the standards of cultural values, such as writing books) and in self-esteem (e.g., put the importance of how well one is living up to the standards of value prescribed by the worldview) as a way to manage the fear of death.

TMT includes two distinct hypotheses (Harmon-Jones et al., 1997). The anxiety-buffer hypothesis states that if a psychological structure (worldview faith or self-esteem) provides protection against anxiety or terror, weakening the structure should make one more prone to exhibit anxiety in response to threats. The mortality salience hypothesis states that reminding individuals of death should increase the need for that structure. If an individual experienced greater self-esteem as a result of psychological struggle with a traumatic event, from a TMT perspective this may be the result of a defense mechanism in the face of the fear of death, whereas from a PTG perspective the increase in self-esteem might be derived from the personal strength domain of PTG experiences.

TMT and PTG may share the importance of considering the subjective impact of highly traumatic life events. TMT assumes that humans are the only animals that recognize they will die one day, and that this leads to existential terror or anxiety. The PTG perspective also involves the understanding that certain types of events can lead to spiritual and existential questions and growth. They both also grant importance to a cultural worldview. The differences, on the other hand, may be that TMT claims that people try to defend their worldview by increasing self-esteem or matching their behaviors to their society to reduce the terror. So, from a TMT perspective, PTG can be a form of defensive mechanism, which some researchers define as illusory PTG or PTG as a coping mechanism. In PTG theory, people experience PTG because they are forced by circumstances to struggle with challenged or shattered core beliefs; PTG is not merely a result of motivation to reduce anxiety, although the challenge to core beliefs does create emotional distress. The solution to this in the PTG approach is reconstructing a more resilient system of core beliefs, not merely finding an anxiety-reducing mechanism. In PTG, managing the emotional distress of core belief challenge is, for the ultimate purpose of core belief reconstruction, accomplished through deliberate rumination that becomes possible in calmer emotional states.

One study examined both TMT and PTG (Lykins, Segerstrom, Averill, Evans, & Kemeny, 2013). They suggested that in the face of an event that includes reminders of, or the potential for, personal mortality, TMT supports extrinsic shifts (e.g., making more money, being more attractive to boost self-esteem, materialism), whereas PTG supports intrinsic shifts (e.g., building closer relationships, helping the world be a better place). The authors conducted a series of studies and concluded that the key is the influence of time. If a threat is short-term, reminders of death are likely to make people defensive. However, when people encounter death over a longer period of time or in a manner consistent with their goal structure, they move to transcend their defensiveness and maintain or become more intrinsically oriented, supporting findings related to PTG as an outcome.

## Mortality Salience, Mortality Reminders, and PTG

According to TMT (Greenberg et al., 1986), humans are the only animals that know they are going to die. Reminders of death are predicted to trigger anxiety. TMT theorists explain people's behaviors, such as physical activities and risky behaviors (e.g., skydiving), as something they do to reduce the feelings of terror associated with death. In TMT studies, death awareness is activated through an experimental manipulation called *mortality salience*. Mortality salience has been activated in research by asking the participants to write about their own mortality; being primed with death-related imagery or words, such as standing in front of a funeral home; engaging in death-related health screenings; or responding to inventories measuring a fear of death (Cozzolino, Staples, Meyers, & Samboceti, 2004; Routledge et al., 2010). Research on TMT has been designed to test, in addition to the anxiety-buffer hypothesis, the *mortality salience hypothesis*. This hypothesis proposes that a person's faith in their culturally bound worldview is increased in the presence of reminders about one's own mortality. As a result of these essentially ethnocentric worldviews, due to the enhanced positive evaluations that people make of others who share their worldview, and increasingly negative evaluations of people who dissent from their views, the behavior, values, beliefs, and even the existence of people in the world who challenge those views increases or maintains said worldviews. The idea of mortality salience then is that people who perceive some others to share their worldviews prefer them over those who do not. Harmon-Jones et al. (1997) referred to these preferences as worldview defenses. Leippe, Bergold, and Eisenstadt (2017) examined a control prime or mortality salience in a mock juror scenario in which judgments were made about guilt or otherwise in murder or carjacking trials with three ethnic groups in the US (White, Hispanic, Black). Their results suggested that mortality salience is more pronounced when making judgments about people not belonging to a person's in-group, but only when the case was extremely serious (murder), and only if the hypothesized defendant was in an ethnic group deemed as non-threatening.

A series of TMT studies have compared the effects of mortality salience inductions with those of other threat inductions (e.g., uncertainty, failure, public speaking, social exclusion, and so on) on a variety of cognitive and emotional variables, and found that death-related cognition decreased satisfaction with life, subjective vitality (i.e., aliveness and energy about living), and meaning in life (Routledge et al., 2010). Death-related cognition increased hostility and aggression toward those perceived as threats to important cultural beliefs, negative affect, state anxiety, and beliefs in the divine and supernatural; these relationships are affected by self-esteem and cultural beliefs. It was proposed that mortality salience is about efforts to enhance a person's self-perception that they are a significantly worthy member of society, which distances or protects a person from the terror associated with death. From the TMT perspective, a one-time self-report of PTG may be interpreted as a self-defensive mechanism: i.e., by experiencing PTG one can temporarily increase self-esteem or closely connect with in-group members so that mortality salience will be reduced to a level that is no longer threatening. Davis and McKearney (2003), for example, demonstrated that people are more likely to exaggerate the extent to which their life is meaningful and seek positives or gains in order to defend against mortality threats, suggesting the possible coping aspects of PTG. However, Luszczynska et al. (2012) pointed out that TMT studies are usually conducted with healthy individuals who have not necessarily had a traumatic experience. They studied people living with HIV, breast cancer survivors, and caregivers of people living with HIV, and found that they reported a lower level of PTG or finding benefits when reminded of their own mortality. But the time elapsed since diagnosis was a significant moderator, indicating that PTG reports may represent a palliative defensive response to a life threat among survivors with a more recent diagnosis.

Cozzolino et al. (2004) also suggested that PTG studies have indicated that coming face to face with mortality (e.g., near-death experience) is in fact likely to leave individuals striving for intrinsic rewards (i.e., becoming more selfless) as a result of psychological struggle, unlike the conclusion made by TMT studies (i.e., reminders of one's own mortality are likely to lead people to further embrace their worldview and actually be more narrow-minded). They distinguished mortality salience ("what do you think of death?") from mortality awareness, which involves self-reflection, by asking the participants to read a scenario in which they were asked how they anticipated dealing with their final moments if they were to die in a particular way. Cozzolino and colleagues reported that mortality salience led highly extrinsic people to manifest greed, whereas death reflection generated more intrinsic and unselfish behavior, which was thought to be an indicator of PTG.

One thing that should be noted, in comparing TMT predictions from those derived from the model of PTG, is that the outcome is often assessed right after the mortality salience induction in TMT studies, whereas in studies of PTG the outcome is often assessed weeks, months, or sometimes years after the highly stressful life event. This makes it even more difficult to compare the effects of predictions from the two perspectives. A study considering the duration of death processing has suggested that a longer duration of processing was related to outcomes that are consistent with PTG (Lykins et al., 2007). When the researchers longitudinally tested the impact of mortality reminder, participants were more likely to maintain or become more intrinsically oriented, rather than extrinsically oriented. Finally, the methodology of mortality salience inductions may not present a good analogue to PTG experiences. Compared to actually living through life-threatening or other circumstances that may challenge core beliefs, lab-based mortality salience inductions would seem to have a much smaller impact on how people think and live, especially over an extended period of time. The laboratory manipulations found in TMT studies may not be particularly relevant to the PTG experience. In other words, they may lack external validity when specifically discussing responses to people's actual lived traumatic experiences.

## The Recovery Concept and PTG

"The concept of recovery is significantly different from 'cure' or 'remission'" (Webb, 2011, p. 732). According to Resnick and Rosenheck (2006), the origins of the recovery model lie in the psychiatric survivor movement in the US. It originated in the liberating experiences of those who struggled with symptoms of mental illness (Fardella, 2008). The recovery model focuses on helping people lead more fulfilling lives, even in the presence of symptoms of mental illness. It encourages people to avoid simplified forms of understanding mental illness and urges professionals to be more mindful of seeing their patients as persons and not merely a sum of psychiatric symptoms. The recovery model emphasizes the development of a new sense of purpose and meaning in life through changes in attitudes, values, and skills as well as shifts in role identity. A core component of the model is the empowerment of clients to take responsibility for their own healing journey. The idea is to avoid being overly dependent on others for a person's sense of self, achievement of goals, healing, and social connectedness (Frese III, Stanley, Kress, & Vogel-Scibilia, 2001).

However, the model is not without its critics—especially by those who subscribe to the notion of reality being objective, and that modes of therapeutic intervention need to be scientific and evidence-based, relying on a form of the medical model of mental illness where the treating therapist (e.g., psychiatrist) is the expert. Munetz and Frese (2001) suggest that this medical model puts limitations on a client's capacity for growth through an emphasis on weakness, illness, and limitations. Frese III and colleagues (2001) also suggest that there is a need to embrace the recovery model, which is popular with consumer advocacy groups, and synthesize the strengths-based approach of the recovery model with evidence-based practice. Perhaps the extent to which the recovery model can be effective is dependent on other factors, such as the extent of cognitive impairment associated with a person's mental illness and the client's preference for a particular treatment approach.

There are also significant differences between the recovery model and PTG given that the recovery model was designed specifically to assist those people who have a diagnosable psychiatric disorder. PTG studies and treatment frameworks tend to focus on the experiences and healing processes that result from experiencing traumatic life events that challenge core beliefs. Those who have experienced a traumatic event may have assumed, or indeed had generally peaceful lives, until they experienced a particular event (e.g., "my life was OK until I was diagnosed"; "I thought my life was wonderful until I lost my child"). But because of their experience, assumptive world or core beliefs are challenged, which in turn leads to cognitive processing that can foster PTG. On the other hand, in the recovery model, the main targets are those who deal with more chronic conditions, such as schizophrenia or mental disorder, and so, the two theories are distinct, even though they overlap in some ways. This is not to suggest that some people who experience traumatic circumstances do not go on to develop psychiatric disorders—for example, posttraumatic stress disorder. Perhaps studies on benefit finding rather than PTG may have a closer connection with the recovery model.

## Empowerment Theory and PTG

The concept of empowerment incorporates both a process of becoming empowered and an outcome, or a state of being empowered (Schulz, Israel, Zimmerman, & Checkoway, 1995). Empowerment is a multi-level construct (i.e., individual, organizational, and community). Psychological empowerment—the individual level of empowerment—includes an ability to set achievable goals with self-knowledge about the scope of personal resources available and factors that may impinge on the capacity to fulfill set goals (Zimmerman, 1995). There are three qualities of psychological empowerment: the intrapersonal component (perceived control, self-efficacy, motivation control, perceived competence), the interactional component (critical awareness, understanding causal agents, skill development, skill transfer across life domains, resource mobilization), and the behavioral component (community involvement, organizational participation, coping behaviors).

Efforts to gain control, access to resources, and a critical understanding of one's sociopolitical context are fundamental aspects of the empowering processes. Empowerment processes may overlap with PTG processes. For example, in PTG, people cognitively experience psychological struggle to try to make sense of what happened, which may include some elements of making efforts found in the empowerment model to gain control. Utilizing social support, for example, by disclosing what happened (part of the PTG model), may involve accessing resources (as described in empowerment theory). Enhanced wisdom, resulting from PTG, may be similar to the critical understanding of one's context emphasized in empowerment theory.

Empowerment theory has often been discussed with reference to people who are marginalized or oppressed in some way. The idea of empowerment is to increase the personal, political, and interpersonal power of people in a transformative way at both individual and collective levels. Turner and Maschi (2015) discuss empowerment as a theory as a process that starts with recognition that a person or group are subordinate to others in some way, and moves through stages to raise awareness of power differentials, including at individual and systems levels, that result in the oppression of others. Trauma can sometimes lead a person to feel powerless, for example, as can be the case for victims of childhood sexual assault.

Empowerment is an important component of a person's journey to healing and/or growth. For example, the recognition that a child does not have equal power to an adult perpetrator of sexual assault may begin to shift feelings of guilt (Vilenica & Shakespeare-Finch, 2012) by raising awareness of the power differential at play at the time of the abuse.

People's feelings of being empowered can be seen in their behavior. For example, a long term unemployed person may start to seek employment or enroll in a course to increase their chances of gaining employment. A person who has experienced trauma and is on a road of recovery may seek to assist others in difficult situations by volunteering to participate in community service. Many support and advocacy groups are started by people who have endured specific challenges and seek to help those who have had these same experiences.

Hipolito-Delgado and Lee (2007) proposed three ways to facilitate personal empowerment in a school setting. Their target audience was children who were oppressed due to belonging to particular minority communities. Their approach to empowerment was to foster critical consciousness—for example, create consciousness-raising groups for students of marginalized communities. Second, they suggested ways to develop positive identity such as helping students to develop a sense of pride in their cultural heritage. Encouraging social action through participation in community groups, social advocacy groups, and political rallies also facilitates school children's personal empowerment in much the same way it does for an adult. For many years, Ian Shochet and colleagues have investigated factors important in helping adolescents to find a sense of their own personal strength and empowerment, and they have assessed their interventions using randomized control trials and other longitudinal designs. Consistent with the suggestions above, a sense of connection to the school community, often through extra-curricular activities, accounted for more variance than anything else (e.g., Shochet, Dadds, Ham, & Montague, 2006). The empowerment is related to being connected or part of something bigger than yourself. If participants who experienced these program approaches then had experienced a traumatic or another highly challenging life event, it is likely that such approaches would have helped adolescents to experience PTG. This type of social action may align with the action-focused growth Hobfoll et al. (2007) discuss, the altruism born of suffering that Vollhardt and Staub (2011) propose, and the mission or service-oriented aspect of PTG suggested by Tedeschi and McNally (2011).

## Mindfulness to Meaning Theory and PTG

Garland and colleagues (Garland, Farb, Goldin, & Fredrickson, 2015) have proposed that the contemplative practice of mindfulness can contribute to the reappraisal of trauma by a distancing or "decentering" from the intrusive stress responses that accrue from the event. These intrusions narrow the focus of cognition and contribute to inflexibility in behavior. In contrast, mindful awareness broadens the scope of cognition, producing a pathway toward reappraisal and the overcoming of habitual avoidance responses in thinking and behavior. There is much in this model that overlaps with the model of PTG described in this volume, especially as mindfulness may play a central role in helping trauma survivors move from intrusive rumination to deliberate rumination that yields positive reappraisals found in PTG (Tedeschi & Blevins, 2015).

Mindfulness has been described as having five facets: observing, describing, acting with awareness, nonjudging, and nonreacting (Baer, Smith, Hopkins, Krietemeyer, & Toney, 2006). Not all these aspects of mindfulness have been associated with the facilitation of PTG. It appears that in order to engage in the reconstruction of beliefs and personal narratives that is the hallmark of the PTG process, an evaluative process is necessary. Therefore, the nonjudging facet of mindfulness has been found to be negatively related to the facilitation of this process. At the same time, nonreacting appears to be helpful in this facilitation, perhaps because this is involved in the calming of emotions (Hanley, Garland, & Tedeschi, 2017). To date, the work of Garland and colleagues in mindfulness to meaning theory appears to be compatible at the theoretical and empirical level with the PTG model of Tedeschi and Calhoun.

## Is PTG the Opposite of PTSD?

The concise answer is—no. The assumption that PTG must be the opposite of PTSD may have been based on the idea that if PTG has been defined as positive psychological changes people experienced as a result of struggle with a highly stressful or traumatic life event, then it is the opposite of negative changes represented by PTSD symptoms. To place PTG and PTSD at opposing ends of a continuum is simplistic, erroneous, and does not account for the complexities of human response to trauma.

People who experience posttraumatic symptoms report PTG-like changes simultaneously (Devine, Reed-Knight, Loiselle, Fenton, & Blount, 2010; Shakespeare-Finch & de Dassel, 2009). Likewise, the opposite of PTSD should be the lack of PTSD symptoms, and there are people who have recovered from PTSD and yet do not necessarily report PTG. Zoellner and Maercker (2006) argued that PTG and PTSD can both be plotted on separate continuums because they are independent constructs. This assertion of independence does not necessarily suggest that there is no relationship between these constructs, just that PTG is not the opposite of PTSD and vice versa.

Both PTG and PTSD have been observed in those who have experienced the most stressful of life's events, although such studies have not produced completely consistent results. A positive linear relationship between PTSD symptoms and PTG has been found in studies in the USA (e.g., Kilmer et al., 2009), China (Jin, Xu, & Liu, 2014), and in Japan (Taku, Calhoun, Cann, & Tedeschi, 2008). Other researchers have found a negative relationship (e.g., Kilic & Ulsoy, 2003), or that the constructs are independent (Krosch & Shakespeare-Finch, 2016). A number of authors have also suggested a curvilinear solution best explains the relationship (Kleim & Ehlers, 2009). Shakespeare-Finch and Lurie-Beck (2014) conducted a meta-analytical review that included 42 studies to clarify the relationship between PTG and the symptoms of PTSD. They concluded that PTG and PTSD symptoms are positively and linearly correlated, indicating they are not on opposite ends of a single dimension. Moreover, they also demonstrated a stronger curvilinear relationship between PTG and PTSD symptoms, with PTG being higher when moderate levels of PTSD symptoms presented; but that pattern varied with age and type of event.

Research has conceptually and empirically demonstrated that PTG and PTSD symptoms do not sit on opposite ends of the same dimension. For instance, trauma-related guilt often has been described as a negative cognitive-affective state due to its relationship with psycho-pathology, such as suicidal ideation (Bryan, Ray-Sannerud, Morrow, & Etienne, 2013). However, guilt is also a psychologically adaptive conscious emotion because it promotes a sense of regret, which in turn motivates reparative action and possibly changes the future behaviors in a positive way (Tangney, Stuewig, & Martinez, 2014). The negative and positive role of guilt is evident in a study of the differences between PTG and PTSD (Dekel, Mamon, Solomon, Lanman, & Dishy, 2016). Results indicated that a sense of guilt was positively correlated with both PTSD symptoms and PTG. Moreover, the longitudinal research design indicated that initial guilt predicted subsequent PTG among combat veteran, after controlling for initial PTSD levels, which is another indicator showing PTG and PTSD are not the opposite ends of a single spectrum.

It is important to remember that PTG is conceptualized as positive but transformational change that may be driven by the same set of factors leading to PTSD symptoms (e.g., guilt, intrusive rumination), but that it is not the same as a decrease in PTSD symptoms (Tedeschi & Calhoun, 2004b). Decreasing the level of guilt often plays an important role in reducing PTSD symptoms. However, initial experience of guilt might initiate a process of rumination that could eventually lead to PTG, and eventual resolution of trauma-related guilt may foster PTG. Therefore, reducing stress and experiencing growth may involve different processes and are two different outcomes. Enduring distress has been part of the model of PTG since first proposed because persons who experience trauma do not get over their experience as much as they weave it into their lives with the experience as part of their new reality. Experiencing PTG does not necessarily completely diminish the pain that inevitably accompanies trauma.

## Stress-Related Growth, Benefit Finding, Thriving, Flourishing, and Other Related Terms

Some of these terms have been used interchangeably, particularly when there was no single term that described this phenomenon of positive change (Tedeschi, Park, & Calhoun, 1998). Until Calhoun and Tedeschi coined the term PTG in 1995, the phenomenon had been variously referred to in the research literature as, for instance, "positive psychological changes" (Yalom & Lieberman, 1991) or "drawing strength from adversity" (McCrae, 1984). In this section, we will discuss how PTG is different from similar concepts such as stress-related growth, benefit finding, thriving, and flourishing.

Research on stress-related growth (SRG) was influenced by Schaefer and Moos's (1992) theoretical model for life crises and personal growth, which shares a common background with PTG. Similar to research on PTG, studies on SRG were derived from a self-report inventory called the Stress-Related Growth Scale (SRGS: Park, Cohen, & Murch, 1996). Several studies have used the SRGS and labeled the positive changes detected as PTG (Park, Aldwin, Fenster, & Snyder, 2008), used the PTGI and labeled it as SRG (Spielman & Taubman-Ben-Ari, 2009; Weinrib, Rothrock, Johnsen, & Lutgendorf, 2006), and used both the SRGS and the PTGI but labeled it as PTG (Cadell, Regehr, & Hemsworth, 2003). Despite these inter-changeable uses of terms, there are a number of differences between stress-related growth and PTG.

First, SRG has not been conceptualized as something that requires challenge to core beliefs. Second, SRG has been mostly tested in general populations such as college students who experienced a stressful, but not necessarily a traumatic, life event (e.g., not getting the grades you wanted). It appears that even though the PTGI and the SRGS may be correlated, SRG is not related to trauma as much as non-traumatic events (Kira et al., 2013), whereas research on PTG includes both student and community samples and traumatized populations from many coun-tries around the world. Third, the SRGS is used as a single dimension by comput-ing a total score of the 50 items (e.g., Park & Fenster, 2004) because in developing the scale (Park et al., 1996), principal component analyses did not support the hypothesis that the scale would be multi-dimensional. However, there is now a 15-item short version and a 43-item version that Armeli, Gunthert, and Cohen (2001) suggest has eight dimensions. Fourth, the SRGS includes items that assess coping skills or emotional regulation (e.g., "I learned not to let hassles bother me the way they used to"; "I learned not to freak out when a bad thing happens"; "I learned to get less angry about things"), which are not elements of the PTGI.

Benefit finding, although it refers to phenomena similar to PTG, also refers to changes that are not as transformational as those that can be found in PTG. The origin of research in this domain is also somewhat different. For example, one scale assessing benefit finding (Tomich & Helgeson, 2004) adapted items from Behr's Positive Contributions Scale used with parents of disabled children (Behr, Murphy, & Summers, 1991). As Tomich and Helgeson (2004) asserted, the items included to assess personal growth had been identified in previous research, and the authors might have not have distinguished the psychological construct assessed by their scale from PTG. When developing the items assessing benefit finding, the authors prepared eight positive growth domains. Therefore, some items seem to overlap (e.g., personal priorities, world views). However, others seem to be different from personal growth (e.g., daily activities, career). In fact, as implied by the differences between the words, growth, and benefits, certain types of benefits that may not be labeled as personal growth have been reported. For example, Sears, Stanton, and Danoff-Burg (2003) qualitatively assessed benefit finding among early-stage breast cancer patients and found the theme of health-related benefits (e.g., "Now that I'm being monitored for cancer, any recurrences may be detected earlier and involve less invasive treatment," p. 491). This is clearly a benefit and does not reflect the transformative changes mea-sured by the PTGI. Sears and colleagues also utilized the PTGI in the same study and found no correlations between perceived benefits and PTG, indicating that these two constructs are distinct.

Thriving is also a term used to describe PTG-like experiences. For example, Norlander, Von Schedvin, and Archer (2005) used the PTGI to assess what they called thriving. Conceptually, thriving could apply to healthy living in any circumstance that might not be relevant to a highly stressful or traumatic life event. Indeed, most of the literature that uses the term thriving refers to thriving in a complex work environment (e.g., Britt & Jex, 2015; Ren, Yunlu, Shaffer, & Fodchuk, 2015). It has been suggested that thriving may occur in the face of a cancer diagnosis and treatment. For example, Sheldon (2016) provides a personal narrative of his battle with cancer and associated treatments where he reports his sense of thriving was due to drawing on the works of Viktor Frankl, his relationship with his wife, and the support he felt from medical professionals. Sarkar and Fletcher (2014) sought to understand resilience and thriving in high achievers. They examined the characteristics common to 13 professionals who were extremely successful and concluded that thriving was related to factors such as a positive personality, balance in perspectives, experience, flexibility, and social support. The term thriving is not necessarily used in relationship to a traumatic event, and the current literature does not define the term in the context of trauma or explain mechanisms for change. Thriving, as the term is typically used, currently refers to doing well in stressful situations.

Flourishing is a word that has been used primarily in the area of well-being. It describes the desirable state whereby both hedonistic and eudemonistic components of well-being are simultaneously present within an individual (Huppert & So, 2013). Ryff (1989, 2013) suggests the term is more suited to studies of hedonic rather than eudemonic well-being. Like the term thriving, flourishing is a broad term applicable to measurement of well-being rather than specifically to adjustment following a highly stressful or traumatic event. Barrington and Shakespeare-Finch (2013) examined the relationship between PTG, posttraumatic depreciation (PTD), well-being, distress, and flourishing. Results indicated that there was no relationship between psychological flourishing, life satisfaction, depression, anxiety, or stress with any PTGI factor or the total score. However, there were moderate to strong negative correlations between PTD and all other measures, including flourishing. These results provide further evidence that terms like PTG, flourishing, and thriving should not be used interchangeably. For example, Sarkar and Fletcher (2014) examined resilience and thriving in high achievers, and in 2017 claimed that adversity-related experiences are crucial to being a successful Olympian. There are other terms that sometimes have been used to refer to the kinds of changes described in PTG theory (O'Leary, Alday, & Ickovics, 1998), such as perceived benefits (McMillen & Fisher, 1998) and adversarial growth (Linley & Joseph, 2004). Adversarial growth refers to growth in the aftermath of "adversity," which appears to be identical to PTG, but it is a term infrequently used in the current literature. Perceived benefits was a term originally used by Tedeschi and Calhoun (1994), but was superseded by PTG in recognizing that the changes reported by trauma survivors were not only perceived but were significant personal changes "beyond their previous level of adaptation, psychological functioning, or life awareness" (Tedeschi et al., 1998, p. 3). Unlike the terms we reviewed in this section, PTG involves significant changes that would not have happened without the struggle with a major life crisis. Researchers should take some care about using the terms interchangeably, and understand that there are differences in these constructs to the extent that results from studies that use a particular term to describe a construct are not necessarily transferable to another (Aspinwall & Tedeschi, 2010).

## The Relationship Between Resilience and PTG

PTG has been featured on the American Psychological Association's Road to Resilience website, and some have viewed PTG and resilience as synonymous (Sattler, Boyd, & Kirsch, 2014). However, the two are different constructs. Resilience is the personal attribute or ability to bounce back from difficulty, or to resist the effects of difficulties without experiencing prolonged negative effects (Rutter, 1985). Others refer to this as bouncing forward (Haas, 2015). PTG is a process and outcome resulting from "struggle" with difficult circumstances. PTG is conceptually different from resilience because resilience describes the characteristics of people who can adjust quickly and successfully, even under the most stressful circumstances. Highly resilient people are expected to be less likely to experience challenged assumptions or cognitive struggle, so may be less likely to experience profound transformational changes such as PTG. Bonanno and colleagues have conducted a number of trajectory studies with various traumatized populations over the past decade (e.g., Bonanno et al., 2012). Results from these studies clearly demonstrate that resilience is the most common outcome following stressful events, and that positive transformative changes following trauma, such as PTG, are distinct from resilience.

Cross-sectional designs have provided mixed findings about the relationship between resilience and PTG. Several studies supported a positive association between resilience and PTG (Bensimon, 2012; Hooper, Marotta, & Lanthier, 2008; Ogińska-Bulik, 2015; Yu et al., 2014), but others showed negative correlations, especially when assessing resilience as an absence of PTSD symptoms (Levine, Laufer, Stein, Hamama-Raz, & Solomon, 2009; Zerach, Solomon, Cohen, & Ein-Dor, 2013). Yet other studies have found no relationship between resilience and PTG (Wilson, Morris, & Chambers, 2014). These mixed findings may be due to inconsistent definitions of resilience (personal trait, ability, or lack of symptoms) or the timing of data collection. If data are collected early post-trauma, the relationship between PTG and resilience may be negative, while later, PTG may have yielded changes that enhance resilience, producing a positive relationship with PTG. If a person has experienced PTG, that same person may be more resilient in the future. The journey to PTG requires effortful rumination, reflection, a newfound understanding of self and effective ways to deal with difficulty. A common finding in PTG research is a newfound sense of one's own personal strength—"if I have survived this, I can survive anything." Changes such as those may enhance resilience to future difficulties (Tedeschi & Blevins, 2017). For example, following a natural disaster that claimed lives and left thousands of people homeless, a regional doctor was concerned for those she called her vulnerable patients. One of those patients was a woman who two years earlier had lost her adult daughter and, understandably, struggled immensely in her grief. The doctor asked the patient to come in for an appointment and explained that she was concerned for her mental health because she had lost her home and everything in it. The patient replied that she was absolutely fine as no loss would ever be as great as the loss of her child. Through her struggle, she had become more resilient. For further consideration of this issue, see Tedeschi and Blevins (2017), who provide a discussion of the relationship between the constructs of resilience and PTG.

## Happiness, Positive Emotions, and PTG

The concept of happiness is an elusive one (Oishi, Graham, Kesebir, & Galinha, 2013). In most cultures, happiness is associated with positive events. If we take this external view of happiness, experiencing a traumatic event is the opposite of happiness, even though dealing with the event can later lead to personal growth. For example, a young couple may have experienced PTG (e.g., appreciating people's warm support or finding a new opportunity) after experiencing an unexpected stillbirth. The loss of their baby is not likely to become a "happy" event, regardless of PTG experiences. A study with women who had experienced a miscarriage or stillbirth demonstrated that pregnancy loss could lead to PTG but, importantly, PTG occurred in the context of significant grief and symptoms of PTSD for most of the participants (Krosch & Shakespeare-Finch, 2016).

As Lyubomirsky and Lepper (1999) have indicated, most people are capable of reporting on the extent to which they are a happy person or an unhappy one. If so, women who have lost their babies, as well as those who have experienced other tragedies, are not likely to say "I am a happy person," even if they have experienced PTG. They instead might say "I've learned something valuable," "I've changed because of that," or "This became a turning point." It is unlikely that we would find many people who would look to experience trauma so that they can experience PTG and feel happy about it.

Although many common human experiences are regarded as events that make people happy, the definition of happiness is different from culture to culture. For example, Oishi et al. (2013) discuss the common pairing of the words happiness and pursuit in the United States, which suggests that achieving happiness is in the control of the individual. They compare this idea of happiness with an ancient Greek concept of happiness as fragile and external. Delle Fave et al. (2016) concur that in the US happiness has come to mean a positive inner state that is achieved through the attainment of goals and aspirations. If happiness is defined this way, it is understandable why PTG can be perceived as something that might coincide with becoming happier, because people in individualistic societies such as the US seem to believe happiness can be gained through one's cognitive effort. For example, Carlson (2006) proposed that you can achieve happiness through understanding how your mind works. This viewpoint has been applied in some of the empirical studies of happiness and PTG. January and her colleagues, for example, investigated PTG reports among people who had sustained spinal cord injuries in childhood, hypothesizing that their PTG should be associated with happiness (January, Zebracki, Chlan, & Vogel, 2015). Their hypotheses were supported, but it should be noted that happiness was inferred from scores on Diener, Emmons, Larsen, and Griffin's (1985) Satisfaction with Life Scale, which according to Diener, is not a complete measure of happiness. Diener is an international leader in research about happiness, and he claims the one consistent factor shared by happy people is that they care for others and feel cared for themselves.

The mindset of "the pursuit of happiness" seems to have spread to Eastern cultures as well. One study in Korea found that certain domains of PTG were associated with happiness in people with physical disabilities (Kim, Kim, & Park, 2016), just like the study conducted in the US (January et al., 2015). The majority of people with physical disabilities experience ongoing discrimination or prejudice in Korea; the authors expected that PTG would lead to a higher level of happiness. Results showed that happiness was predicted by at least two PTG domains, new possibilities and personal strength; those who were able to take new paths in their lives or gain strength reported higher levels of happiness. These researchers also operationalized happiness as scores on the five-item Satisfaction with Life Scale (Diener et al., 1985). So, even though experiencing PTG does not necessarily make people happier, empirical findings have revealed some positive relationships between them in Western and Eastern cultures when happiness is operationalized as satisfaction with life in general.

Understanding how PTG and happiness may be related becomes more complicated if PTG is viewed as a set of coping strategies to manage stress and to become happier. For example, the authors of the abovementioned study (Kim et al., 2016) interpreted their findings as the new possibilities dimension of PTG being related to coping strategies, which in turn promoted happiness. If we take this approach, PTG may be replaced with the idea of positive reframing or reinterpretation, with PTG only a process rather than PTG's key quality of transformation when viewed as an outcome. It seems to make more sense to recognize that people do not use, or intentionally experience, PTG in order to be happier. PTG is not the means people use to achieve happiness; instead it is a result of the psychological and interpersonal processes used to manage the aftermath of traumatic events. PTG, then, is associated more with a eudemonic than an hedonic experience (Joseph & Hefferon, 2013).

Empirical data indicate that PTG is associated with happiness, but not strongly, supporting the argument that PTG and happiness are not synonymous. But then again, happiness can be defined in many different ways. The Chinese philosopher Zhuang Zhou, for example, said that happiness is the absence of the striving for happiness. Some people may experience PTG when they finally "forget" about how they are dealing with and changing as a result of trauma, which may be identified as ultimate resolution, including happiness.

Since emotions are sometimes fleeting states, equating PTG with such experiences may lead to the view that PTG is illusory or only a coping mechanism. However, there have been attempts to understand how PTG may be related to positive emotions. For instance, the thriver model suggests that positive emotions after traumatic experiences, in addition to supportive relationships and finding meaning, are the key to facilitating PTG (Mangelsdorf & Eid, 2015). This view is based on the broaden-and-build theory (Fredrickson, 2001), which suggests that positive emotions can support coping processes by broadening one's attention, thinking, and behavioral skills. Their data supports this argument by showing moderate relationships between PTG and positive emotions. The significant role of dispositional positive affectivity in PTG has been indicated by other studies as well (Lelorain, Bonnaud-Antignac, & Florin, 2010). Chun and Lee (2010) also suggested leisure, any activities that occur during free time, can foster PTG among people with spinal cord injury if these activities generate positive emotions, in addition to providing opportunities to find strengths, build meaningful relationships, and make sense of traumatic experiences. Even though PTG does not always lead people to feel good or have positive emotions, experiences of positive emotions seem to help people to recognize their own growth or vice versa (i.e., positive emotions seem to be the consequence of PTG)—or perhaps positive emotions may allow people to recognize pathways to growth. Fredrickson's (2001) "broaden and build theory" supports a relationship between positive emotion and the ability to perceive a wider range of possibilities for addressing challenges. There is certainly evidence that positive reappraisals as a coping strategy are a significant predictor of PTG (e.g., Shakespeare-Finch, Gow, & Smith, 2005).

In sum, people experience PTG without necessarily becoming happier or feeling better. Roepke (2013) suggested that people who experience PTG recognize benefits from the adversity they have experienced but could still be sad in the long term. She added that people may change in positive ways following positive experiences but not necessarily be happier in the long term. Roepke suggested the need to examine eudemonic well-being in relation to growth rather than the narrower focus on hedonic well-being. Happiness fits within the hedonic view of well-being. Because some researchers use happiness and well-being interchangeably, we will discuss the relationships between two types of well-being and PTG in the following section.

## Hedonic and Eudaimonic Well-Being and PTG

Well-being means different things to different people. It may mean physical, spiritual, or psychological wellness, which themselves are nebulous terms. It may be a sense of feeling happy and satisfied, or it may mean feeling as though one is achieving purpose in life through contributions to community, environmental mastery, or by the criterion of successful personal relationships. The concept of well-being has been dichotomized in psychological research, which is easy to understand given the etymology of the term. Aristotle conceptualized well-being as *Eudaimonia*, which has been translated to mean human striving or *the best good* (Kraut, 2016). *Eu* means well, and *daimonia* was linked to concepts like virtue; the focus is on living well and doing well, rather than on doing things that are personally beneficial or advantageous (Kraut, 2016). Plato's writing spoke of Eudaimonia as *to be successful* and Socrates suggested that well-being involved living a virtuous life (Brown, 2016). The word eudaimonia is commonly translated into English as "happiness." However, happiness can also be seen in the etymology of the word hedonic, in which notions of well-being relate to pleasure and satisfaction. The problem with equating hedonism to well-being is that it does not need to mean that one is living a virtuous life (O'Keefe, 2016).

In psychology, both of these terms have been used to define well-being. Psychological well-being is equated with eudaimonia, whereas subjective well-being reflects hedonic well-being. Hedonic well-being refers to an affective state and focuses on pleasure, feeling good, contentment, and life satisfaction. Ryff (1989) argued that most modern theories of well-being were atheoretical, and she adopted a theoretical position about the content of eudaimonic well-being based on the contours of positive functioning. Ryff's measure of well-being comprises six elements: self-acceptance, purpose in life, environmental mastery, positive relationships, personal growth, and autonomy (Ryff & Singer, 2008). The six dimensions of well-being suggest that eudaimonic well-being is conceptually closer to PTG than hedonic well-being. However, psychological and subjective well-being are often used interchangeably as well. For example, in a study of PTG and well-being in breast cancer patients, McDonough, Sabiston, and Wrosch (2014) found cancer specific support and distress were related to PTG, whereas general social support and general distress were related to subjective well-being. Although they refer to subjective (hedonic) well-being throughout their paper, they used Ryff's (1989) psychological (eudaimonic) well-being scale.

Some people have defined PTG as increased eudaimonic well-being caused by confrontation with a traumatic life event. Joseph (2014), for example, conceptualized PTG as a form of eudaimonic well-being. Empirical studies (e.g., Durkin & Joseph, 2009) have confirmed positive associations between PTG and eudaimonic well-being, and found no, or only weak, relationships between PTG and hedonic well-being. It is likely that the way eudaimonic well-being is measured in Western individualistic societies is not completely applicable to those who live in essentially collectivist cultures. For example, one of the six dimensions of eudaimonic well-being listed above is autonomy. Autonomy may be valued in the West but is unlikely to be viewed as a positive indication of well-being in a society where collective well-being includes reliance on each other—that the whole group is more important than the well-being of one person.

## PTG and Behavior Change

Some have argued that PTG should focus exclusively on observable changes in behavior. Hall et al. (2008) and Hobfoll et al. (2007), for example, proposed what they called action-focused growth. They claimed that the benefit of PTG would emerge only when people committed to action and translated PTG perceptions into behavior; from this point of view, only action should be considered growth. This may be true for some cases. If PTG reports do not align with what is occurring in everyday life, these reports may reflect defense mechanisms to avoid facing reality or accepting unavoidable changes. Fleeson (2014), for example, suggested that if someone claims they enjoy being with family more, but does not demonstrate it often in their behavior, this might call the report of PTG into question. However, Fleeson also acknowledged that there are certain areas of PTG that cannot be translated into physical action, such as maturity, wisdom, and self-transcendence. Yet, these changes are still valuable regardless of whether any specific observable behaviors follow. Overt behaviors are hard to evaluate because the same behaviors might have opposite meanings or exact opposite behaviors may be interpreted as positive changes depending on intentions and contexts (Roepke, Forgeard, & Elstein, 2014). For example, two people have experienced a traumatic event. Following the event, one person decides to enroll in a university course and the other decides to withdraw. The first person has not studied before and wants to get a degree to improve their career prospects for themselves and for their family. The second person has a busy and successful career and two university degrees. Following their traumatic experience, they realized that a third degree will not change their career prospects and that their career and university studies have meant they have had very little time to spend with family and friends. Seemingly opposite behaviors both reflect a form of growth for these two people that could not be identified without understanding the subjective changes surrounding the decisions.

Furthermore, the same behavioral changes may reflect PTG in one type of personality but not another. Being able to express emotions more freely may be a good indicator of PTG for introverted people, but may not be for extraverted people. In summary, it may seem valid to use behavioral observation to further understand PTG. However, redefining PTG as involving *only* behavioral changes, or asserting that PTG cannot occur in the absence of action or behavioral changes, misses the essence of PTG because there are significant internal changes that may not be observable or that may reflect a change from action to inaction. Although there is clear evidence that behavioral changes frequently accompany self-reported PTG, reflecting the internal shifts people reported making when completing the PTGI (Shakespeare-Finch & Barrington, 2012), behavioral changes may not occur in every instance of PTG.

## PTG and Personality Change

The definition of PTG as personality change can be seen in items from the Stress-Related Growth Scale (SRGS: Park et al., 1996), such as "I learned to be a more optimistic person" (optimism) or "I learned to be open to new information and ideas" (openness to experience). Jayawickreme and Blackie (2014) used the term positive personality change to define PTG, by which they meant enduring change in an individual's thoughts, feelings, and behaviors. Their idea seems to be derived from organismic valuing theory that states that traumatic events can cause changes in meaning, personality schemas, and relationships (Joseph & Linley, 2008). The organismic valuing process refers to "people's innate ability to know what is important to them and what is essential for a fulfilling life" (Joseph, 2009, p. 338). Joseph and Linley's theory, however, views personality as a predictor of PTG. Jayawickreme and Blackie, on the other hand, view personality as a marker to assess changes by suggesting that researchers need to focus on how traumatic life events can have transformative impacts on personality itself. Their view of PTG as positive personality change aligns with the definition in Affleck and Tennen (1996, p. 918) that "the possibility of profound changes in personality emanating from people's efforts to restructure their views of themselves, others, and the future." The suggestions to conceptualize PTG as positive personality change may depend on how "personality" is defined. Some researchers might reject the idea that experiencing a single traumatic event can change personality. Personality has traditionally been understood as having stability over time, but some studies have indicated possible changes in personality in adulthood (Caspi, Roberts, & Shiner, 2005). And yet, what is challenging is the difficulty of objectively defining, *a priori*, what constitutes *positive* personality change. If a person who used to have a low level of openness now exhibits a high level of openness after struggling with a trauma, does it mean this person experienced positive personality change? If a person who had a high level of conscientiousness is now less so, is that a positive personality change? Because the positive-negative aspects of each personality trait are the product of optimal interactions with people and their environments (i.e., goodness of fit), it would be challenging to identify and measure what constitutes positive personality changes. There is also the question of the definition of personality itself, which changes depending on what theory is used. Is personality viewed from a trait perspective, such as the Five-Factor Model, from a psychoanalytic viewpoint as a consistent cluster of motivations and defenses, or perhaps a humanistic view? If using a typology such as Hippocrates's four humors, personality is rooted in excesses of bodily fluids and so can be changed by things like diet, lifestyle, and even climate.

Personality may: (1) affect pre-trauma individual differences such as the content or strengths of world beliefs and the type and amount of resources, (2) affect post-trauma individual differences such as cognitive processes, social support, and the way to express the thoughts and emotions, and (3) be an outcome that may be manifested as a part of PTG. In order to understand all these roles, it is important to look at the profile or combinations of personality traits rather than separate individual traits. Although the concept of personality reflects a set of individual characteristics that are consistent across situations and time, researchers most often report the relationship of single personality dimensions to PTG, rather than on a person's unique personality profile that reflects several dimensions. For example, extraversion and openness to experience have been found to correlate with PTG in some studies (Shakespeare-Finch, Smith, Gow, Embelton, & Baird, 2003; Tedeschi & Calhoun, 1996). However, these relationships appear to be mediated by coping strategies (Shakespeare-Finch et al., 2005). So, the reason that extraversion and openness are related to growth is likely due to differences in the coping strategies employed by extraverts and people open to new experiences (e.g., self-disclosure, seeking social support, trying new ways of seeing things). But knowing scores on only one dimension of personality tells us nothing of what a person's personality profile is. For example, what strategies and resources to cope with adversity are used by a person with high levels of neuroticism, who is introverted, open, antagonistic, and conscientious? The coping strengths associated with conscientiousness and openness, and the stubbornness associated with antagonism, may counter the potentially maladaptive habits of a person who also tends to be both neurotic and introverted.

Another example of how individual differences may affect PTG comes from the literature on resilience. Westphal and Bonanno (2007) argued that people who are highly resilient are not likely to engage in the cognitive processing (challenged core beliefs, intrusive and deliberate rumination) that is associated with PTG, because these people tend not to struggle as much. They emphasized the importance of flexibility in the ways resilient people perceive highly aversive life events. As shown in some studies (DeViva et al., 2016; Rodríguez-Rey et al., 2017), resilience and PTG are not correlated. However, other studies (Bensimon, 2012) have demonstrated positive relationships between them. McGrath (2011) suggested two different paths that lead to PTG, depending on whether the attempt of cognitive assimilation is successful or not. Successfully assimilating what has happened, into the pre-existing assumptive world, can strengthen existing schemas, which can, in turn, promote PTG. This is an example of how some highly resilient people may still experience PTG. On the other hand, if assimilation is not successful, the assumptive world is likely to be severely challenged, and changing schemas and rebuilding a new worldview may achieve PTG. To better explain these different paths and empirically mixed findings, it may be useful to look at the combinations between baseline resilience, cognitive processing, and resilience level after PTG. Recent studies have used latent profile analyses (Tillery, Sharp, Okado, Long, & Phipps, 2016) and found three profiles based on the combinations of PTG and PTS, suggesting that the majority of their participants appeared to be highly resilient.

One personality trait that has been studied in relation to PTG is optimism. In general, optimism is linked to PTG (Prati & Pietrantoni, 2009) and is considered a positive and beneficial personality trait because optimistic people tend to hold to a positive outcome expectancy. Expecting generally positive outcomes could lead to persistence and striving toward goals in the face of adversity, which in turn makes them less likely to be bothered by stress symptoms (Scheier & Carver, 1985). However, there are some situations in which a pessimistic tendency seems more beneficial (Gibson & Sanbonmatsu, 2004). People who are concerned with safety and security (i.e., prevention) are likely to take a pessimistic approach and perform even better when adopting a pessimistic outlook, whereas people who are concerned with growth and advancement (i.e., promotion) are likely to take an optimistic approach and perform better when adopting an optimistic outlook (Hazlett, Molden, & Sackett, 2011). Becoming pessimistic, but also more realistic, may be more indicative of personal growth for some people who have experienced life crises and have now prioritized safety. Becoming optimistic can be still be indicative of growth for other people who experience PTG, perhaps in the domain of personal strength. This example highlights the importance of looking at personality traits in combination (realistic-unrealistic and optimistic-pessimistic) rather than separate traits. Glad, Jensen, Holt, and Ormhaug (2013) pointed out the contradictory nature of growth; learning to differentiate between safe and unsafe situations may be considered a positive change for traumatized youth, but excessive watchfulness and prudence in interpersonal relationships may also be reflective of anxiety and the lack of a sense of safety. Likewise, Joseph (2011a) suggested that it is wrong to assume that deepening of faith is the only spiritual way to experience PTG, because a lessening of faith can also be experienced as growth by some. This complex relationship depends on the nature of the person's faith and its strength and rigidity prior to trauma. Joseph emphasized the need for a nuanced and in-depth qualitative understanding of how people reconcile their spiritual beliefs with the reality of suffering. The content and the experience of personal growth depend on individual contexts, developmental stages, and cultural background. It is critical to study PTG in both quantitative and qualitative ways.

# PART II

# Posttraumatic Growth Research

# CHAPTER 9

# Qualitative Research on Posttraumatic Growth

Qualitative research has an important role in understanding PTG for a number of reasons. First, unlike quantitative research that is positivist in nature, the assumptions underlying qualitative research include social constructionism. Qualitative research asks questions rather than tests hypotheses in order to summarize the voices of people's lived experiences. Qualitative approaches are helpful to discover ways people may experience PTG that might not be captured in standardized scales used in quantitative research. Second, qualitative research can provide a richer collection of data that may assist in understanding the underlying mechanisms of growth, factors that are associated with growth not thought of *a priori*, and that can be used later to develop hypotheses to be tested in larger groups using quantitative analyses. Third, because qualitative research allows the collection of people's unique experiences, it helps researchers to learn about the individual, cross-cultural, and developmental differences in the way people perceive and express PTG. In addition, qualitative methods, especially using neutral questions (e.g., how have you changed since then? How have you been affected by the event?), can allow for discovery of spontaneous, as opposed to guided, reports of PTG.

## How Qualitative Methods Contribute to the Study of PTG

There are several different ways and reasons to study PTG qualitatively. The following methods of data collection illustrate some of the ways qualitative methods have been used in PTG research and the reasons for the approaches taken.

### Semi-Structured Interviews

As discussed in an earlier section, there have been some disagreements in the literature about what PTG is and what measures like the PTGI are actually measuring (i.e., validity). In order to provide evidence that the PTGI was indeed measuring what it assumed it was measuring, Shakespeare-Finch, Martinek, Tedeschi, and Calhoun (2013) conducted semi-structured interviews with people who had experienced trauma after the same people had completed the PTGI. They used thematic analyses to examine the content of the interviews to evaluate the content validity of the PTGI; the analyses revealed that PTGI items were indeed being understood in the way they were intended to be. Because the PTGI has been utilized in many quantitative studies, it was important for validity to learn how trauma survivors actually interpreted each item.

As PTG research started to gather momentum around the world, it became apparent that mean scores on the PTGI differed between some countries. For example, Australian reports indicated that mean PTGI scores were significantly lower (e.g., Morris, Shakespeare-Finch, Rieck, & Newbery, 2005) than those obtained using similar US samples (e.g., Tedeschi & Calhoun, 1996). What quantitative research could not answer was if these changes were an artifact of self-report or perhaps reflected cultural differences in the expression of the degree that growth had taken place. Using a grounded theory design and collecting data through semi-structured interviews, Shakespeare-Finch and Copping (2006) found that there were some subtle differences (as well as many more similarities) in the way an Australian population thought about and expressed PTG. Semi-structured interviews are also helpful in the study of PTG in younger populations. Glad, Jensen, Holt, and Ormhaug (2013), for example, focused on one question in a CAPS (Clinician Administered PTSD Scale for Children) interview: "How do you think (trauma event) has affected your life?" Their results revealed two sub-themes (maturity/wisdom and a desire to help/protect others) that may not be reflected in standardized questionnaires such as the PTGI-C (Kilmer et al., 2009).

### Open-Ended Responses

Although interview is the most widely used method to study PTG qualitatively, some researchers use open-ended responses to explore factors that are relevant to PTG. Open-ended questions are commonly included in a survey battery requesting that participants add any more information they think is relevant to the question at hand. Stutts, Bills, Erwin, and Good (2015) used open-ended responses about coping, social support, discrimination, support groups, acceptance, and also the PTGI in a group of women with limb amputations. Similarly, Taku, Cann, Tedeschi, and Calhoun (2009) used the PTGI and open-ended responses about the perceived social reactions people received when they disclosed their traumatic life events. Taku et al. (2009) found that people who experienced mutual disclosure reported a greater level of PTG than people who perceived their recipients' reactions to be one of confusion. Shakespeare-Finch and Barrington (2012) also used open-ended responses to assess positive behavioral changes. This was a useful way to use open-ended questions to assess the large individual differences in the type of positive behaviors described. Morris, Shakespeare-Finch, and Scott (2012) used an open-ended question at the end of their survey, which was administered to 209 people who had experienced cancer. Thematic Analysis (TA) of that data revealed that the experience of having cancer increased the participant's compassion for others and was a catalyst for positive health change behaviors (e.g., quitting smoking, improved diet, exercise).

### Focus Groups

The focus group has been also used to explore accounts of PTG. Usually people know why they are in a focus group, so their responses may be considered, rather than spontaneous. Kissil, Nino, Jacobs, Davey, and Tubbs (2010) used focus groups with African American adolescents who had a parent with breast cancer in order to discover which coping approaches they had taken to manage the experience. Hyatt-Burkhart (2014) held focus groups with mental health professionals who work with traumatized children and adolescents. Using this group discussion format is not only helpful for researchers to explore themes around PTG, but may also help foster PTG among participants because of their shared positive experiences.

## What We Know So Far From Qualitative Studies of PTG

First, it is important to understand that the PTGI was developed from qualitative research. The original PTGI items are quotes or adapted quotes from persons who had been interviewed because they seemed to represent particularly adaptive functioning in the aftermath of trauma, such as suffering a physical disability in adulthood (Tedeschi & Calhoun, 1988). Since then, the findings from other qualitative studies have helped us to learn about PTG characteristics that are specific to various populations. We know that different traumatic events may lead to different levels of PTG and also that some types of trauma may elicit differences in the type of PTG reported. Because most scales that have been used in quantitative studies to measure PTG are intended to capture rather general PTG for anyone who has experienced a life crisis, it is possible that there may be elements of event-specific or sample-specific PTG that are not captured in standardized PTG measurements. Qualitative studies do not need to rely on a pre-determined set of question items, so are helpful to explore these possibilities. The interest in this type of research is not in generating data that is generalizable but, rather, collecting data that captures the unique or ideographic experiences of people in a rich and meaningful way in order to understand the nuance of personally constructed lived experiences. We will consider some examples.

In a study of PTG among people with life-threatening illness, Kampman, Hefferon, Wilson, and Beale (2015) pointed out that the experience of being severely injured has elements that are unique from other traumas due to the corporeal nature of the experience: the direct and substantial impacts to the body. They reviewed 13 journal articles that used qualitative data to investigate PTG and identified key themes, such as existential reflection (e.g., acknowledging the unchanged and changed aspects of life, related to building a new relationships with the body), increased awareness of humanity, increased meaningful leisure engagement (e.g., sports, dance, playing an instrument, which can be a source of independence for patients), and new abilities (i.e., new awareness of physical and psychological potential). Although most themes seem to overlap with the five factors of the PTGI, qualitative studies are able to identify this kind of event-specific PTG, consider the more general domains of PTG represented in the PTGI, and understand these changes in more specific and personal ways. For example, the domain of new possibilities is reflected specifically in the development of new physical skills in order to manage disability. In the case of being severely injured, a sense of personal strength includes being able to endure more physical pain, being able to push physical abilities more, or having a strong sense of being in control of one's own body. Increased awareness of health issues was also suggested as a positive change in another qualitative study with patients who were diagnosed with a vascular brain injury (Kuenemund, Zwick, Rief, & Exner, 2016). Hefferon, Grealy, and Mutrie (2009) conducted a systematic review of qualitative research examining PTG and life-threatening illnesses. They found 57 articles at the time of their data collection and confirmed that positive changes in areas such as life priorities and appreciation of life are found in this population, as they are with people who have experienced other types of trauma. Development of the self was a third dimension that reflected perceptions of an increased sense of personal strength, meaning making, empathy, and concern for others. Another common finding across studies was the positive changes people reported in their relationships with others (e.g., family and friends). Consistent with other research in this area of health crisis, they also found that participants across studies had a new awareness of their bodies. Such awareness led to some people engaging in more health-promoting behaviors. Interestingly, only four of the studies reviewed had intentionally set out to examine PTG. But using qualitative methods, all studies reviewed were able to "discover" that many people who survive serious illness (mostly cancer in this review) report elements of PTG. In contrast, Morris and colleagues (2012) examined PTG in people who had been diagnosed with cancer. A strong theme that emerged from the qualitative data was an increased compassion for others. Five items were then developed to measure compassion and administered with the PTGI to a group of 514 men who had been diagnosed with prostate cancer (Morris, Wilson, & Chambers, 2013). The items, together with the PTGI items, were then subjected to both exploratory and confirmatory factor analysis, revealing that in addition to the original five factors of the PTGI, a sixth factor that they called compassion emerged that accounted for nearly 50% of the variance for these prostate cancer survivors.

Guse and Hudson (2014) conducted interviews with ex-offenders in South Africa. Their examples of growth, such as changing the gang culture within the prison or taking responsibility for their own actions, might not have been found without the interview data. Quotes taken from the interview data confirmed that some inmates saw their experience of incarceration as a catalyst for positive change. For example, "I can say that it was indeed good for me that I went to prison because that's where my life changed" and "as much as prison is a negative place for me . . . I really doubt if I would have changed the way I have changed if I had not gone to prison." Similar narratives have been recorded elsewhere, indicating the universality of some aspects of PTG.

Qualitative studies also have helped us to identify PTG that is specific to a particular culture. Johnson, Thompson, and Downs (2009) used Interpretive Phenomenological Analysis (IPA) to extract themes from interview data collected from non-Western interpreters who experienced trauma in their country of origin (e.g., Syria, Kosovo, Somalia, and Iraq). Findings showed the importance of the shared experience or collective traumatization. Johnson et al. reported that the participants believed they had been targeted because of their allegiance to their country and that that they were part of a collective. For example, one participant said: "I was one of the people, victims, in about eighteen million, nothing else.

What was happening to the people was happening to me the same." The interpreters spoke of collective traumatization but also of cultural protection and growth. Hashim said, "it learns us practice, courage," and Mehdi said, "I've learned to be grateful" (p. 415). PTG was also examined using IPA in recently arrived refugees from Myanmar (Shakespeare-Finch, Schweitzer, King, & Brough, 2014). Some participants reported growth at an individual level, such as feeling that they had become stronger or developed a newfound compassion. As one participant said, "I cannot delete my bad experiences in life . . . The thing I have learned is that I have to help people" (p. 326). There was also a significant element of collective growth and compassion for others. People spoke of the need to send money home and that in time they wanted to return to Myanmar to help change the political situation that caused them, as ethnic minorities, to flee. One woman explained, "I feel that I am learning something and I have something to give out to my people" (p. 325).

The idea that you are strong and able to deal with extreme hardship due to being part of a collectivist culture has also been demonstrated using qualitative methods with people who have refugee backgrounds from Africa. For example, "[we can cope] because we have in-built mechanisms, you're born in Africa, you're born into survival race, that's it" (Copping & Shakespeare-Finch, 2013, p. 108). The idea that an individual becomes strong following trauma was not as prolific in Copping's (2010) comprehensive work with refugees from Sudan, Sierra Leone, and Liberia. She found that rather than strength being a result of the struggle with trauma, collective strength was seen as the reason for survival.

Another culture-specific PTG theme is reflected in Confucian teachings. Woo, Chan, Chow, and Ho (2007) revealed that Chinese widowers in Hong Kong were likely to define growth as human learning, rather than "growth" per se. The concept of *person* in this context refers to the person within a relationship, and the learning coming from the loss of relationship. This notion of learning may bear some similarity to the *development of self* dimension that Hefferon et al. (2009) found in their systematic review of PTG in people with serious physical health diagnoses. In Woo and colleagues' research, narrative data were collected, from which three themes of growth were extracted using a grounded theory approach: intrapersonal growth (e.g., feeling more comfortable being a vulnerable human being, becoming more comfortable embracing negative emotions), interpersonal growth (e.g., adopt a more holistic view when perceiving human beings, greater appreciation of relationships with people), and transpersonal growth (e.g., better appreciation of life and death). These are similar to the three theoretical PTG domains that were suggested by Tedeschi and Calhoun before conducting a factor analysis on the PTGI (Tedeschi & Calhoun, 1996); however, the meanings are culturally specific. For example, from a Confucian perspective, emotions are neither positive nor negative; they function as tools to help people keep in harmony.

Another contribution from the findings of qualitative studies is that they have strengthened the findings that have been accumulated from quantitative studies, especially by providing evidence to confirm validity of the measures. Shakespeare-Finch et al. (2013) used a semi-structured interview format to investigate the content validity of the PTGI. Following completion of the PTGI, participants individually engaged in conversation with the researchers regarding what they understood specific items on the PTGI to be asking. Using thematic analyses to examine the interview transcripts, data confirmed that the PTGI items were interpreted in the way they were intended. The content validity of PTGI was also examined in a larger study of university students and community participants who had experienced trauma (Shakespeare-Finch & Barrington, 2012). Five open-ended questions about behavioral changes post-trauma reflected the five dimensions of cognitive changes assessed by the PTGI. Data confirmed that positive behavioral changes were consistent with changes in cognition. For example, where the PTGI asks if someone has developed new interests, using a behavioral question, participants wrote that they had taken up new interests such as traveling, guitar, study, or writing. Importantly, these changes were corroborated by a significant other who had known the person before, during, and after a traumatic experience. The factorial validity of the PTGI has also been supported in qualitative work. By using focus groups, Kissil et al. (2010) confirmed five domains of the PTGI among African American adolescents who were coping with parental breast cancer. All of the participants in this study described PTG. Content analysis revealed that PTG occurred in four of the five dimensions assessed with the PTGI (not in the religious or spiritual change dimension). Results also revealed health behavior changes and attitudinal changes—findings that may not have been evident using quantitative measures.

The qualitative study of PTG can also supplement quantitative findings by adding more details to our understanding of the multi-dimensionality of PTG. Denney, Aten, and Leavell (2011), for example, focused on the spiritual domain of growth. Due to the complexity and depth of the theme, there are often limits to quantifying spiritual and religious growth. Thus, these researchers aimed to investigate the phenomenological or lived experiences of spiritual growth among cancer survivors. Their reports, such as "ultimately I have no control over this. I can turn it over to God and let Him carry it" or "putting him [God] in charge of what I did instead of myself was probably how I grew the most," are something we cannot directly see in the quantitative research procedure. Shakespeare-Finch and de Dassel (2009) also used narratives to supplement their quantitative findings to understand PTG in survivors of childhood sexual abuse (CSA). By using a thematic analysis, they identified "positive themes," such as a realization that there was no need for self-blame; "negative themes," such as lack of support or coping through avoidance and dissociation; and other "event-specific themes," such as the feeling that the abuse was taboo. Another key finding in this research was that participants scored moderate levels of growth on the PTGI, yet 95% also recorded clinically significant levels of PTSD symptoms. The narratives helped to clarify what was happening for them, as it was concluded that some aspects of PTSD criteria (e.g., vigilance) are normal outcomes for those who had experienced CSA—to scan your environment becomes a useful part of who you are for people who have experienced CSA, rather than a symptom of pathology.

Content analysis using PTG domains as a starting point is another way to approach qualitative data. For example, narrative accounts of 31 people who were in or within a few of blocks of the World Trade Center during the 9/11 terrorist attacks were coded using content analysis (Dekel, Hankin, Pratt, Hackler, & Lanman, 2016). The analysis was guided by the 21 items and five factors of the PTGI.

At the first time point, which was seven months after the attacks, 64% of participants' transcripts contained themes of PTG and at Time 2, 18 months after, that rose to 71%. Only 10% of the sample narratives displayed no PTG like themes. All five factors were identified, as well as a proposed sixth construct the authors felt was not captured by the PTGI, which they labeled positivity. One male participant explained, "I benefited that it's brought me closer to my family," and another said, "I now feel like I can cope well." A female participant said as a result of her experience, "I just feel like my priorities are all lined up."

Qualitative studies are often necessary when we study PTG in younger populations or with people who are not comfortable using written languages. Glad et al. (2013) used one question from the CAPS interview—"how do you think (traumatic event) has affected your life?"—to examine PTG among children and adolescents in Norway. They identified three salient themes of PTG: personal growth such as maturity, wisdom, personal strength, and self-protection; relational growth such as improved relationships, empathy, compassion, and a desire to help others; and philosophy of life such as appreciation of life and making future plans. Later, we will discuss PTG in childhood.

## The Concept of Narrative in the Study of PTG

Narrative is a concept that is often studied using qualitative methods. It is an important way to study PTG for a number of reasons. PTG itself is a complex experience that may sometimes seem contradictory ("I feel pain whenever I think of it, but . . ." or "It was very sad and I still wish that did not happen, but at the same time . . ."); therefore, a narrative approach that can provide a rich description is useful for PTG studies. Narratives allow people to reflect on comprehensive experiences, rather than being forced to talk about specific aspects (e.g., positive or negative, instead of aspects that are neither positive nor negative). Furthermore, PTG is often manifested in life stories. PTG has been conceptualized as the process of reconstructing our disrupted core beliefs and integrating them into our lives. Narratives can demonstrate how the meaningful and coherent life story has been developed. Narrative revision or development has been included in the PTG theoretical model (Calhoun, Tedeschi, Cann, & Hanks, 2010).

PTG includes both outcome and processes, and yet, quantitative studies often focus on the "outcome" aspects of PTG (i.e., many studies use the PTGI scores as dependent variables). Narrative is a way to capture the processes involved in PTG and allow people to develop their thoughts about how their new reality or past events started making sense (or not make sense). Hall et al. (2009) indicated that "context" is another missing element in quantitative studies and thus investigated thriving and PTG among women with childhood maltreatment by using narrative analyses. They revealed a dynamic process of becoming "resolute," that is, a process of developing decisive agency and a steely willfulness in refusing to be defined by, or focused on, one's abuse history. This process is found to be characterized by the following six dimensions. (1) determined decisiveness in finding or creating PTG, (2) counter-framing perceptions (i.e., a realization that the world of abuse is limited and that there would be other ways of being in the world), (3) facing down death (i.e., overcoming the fright of abuse), (4) redefining abusers and family of origin (i.e., making strict boundaries with abusers and accomplices), (5) quest for learning (i.e., searches for inspiring and ethically clarifying experiences), and (6) moving beyond (i.e., rather than moving back to normal, drawing a line under the life story and moving forward).

Narratives can be so insightful that researchers and clinicians may be able to explore some understudied ideas that have been limited by quantitative research. For example, the five domains of PTG may be expressed in sequence (e.g., first, appreciation of life; then, second, personal strength). If we exclusively rely on the standardized measurements, this kind of potential sequence cannot be easily assessed. Also, qualitative studies are helpful to explore different patterns of PTG paths. One study with women living with a chronic illness, for example, suggested three pathways between a schema revision and changes in multiple components of PTG: (1) a single schema shift alters multiple areas of growth, (2) a single schema shift alters a single area of growth, and (3) multiple schema revisions contribute to alter a single area of growth (Adams, 2015). Adams suggested that researchers should pay more attention to the content of the schemas to understand the PTG mechanisms, rather than quantifying or categorizing them.

Like quantitative research, most qualitative research uses a cross-sectional approach to data collection. Of course, there are limitations with this method, which is essentially a snapshot of individuals or groups and relies on retrospective accounts of experiences. However, there is an emerging body of research that uses both a qualitative and longitudinal approach. For example, Barrington and Shakespeare-Finch (2014) conducted semi-structured interviews with mental health professionals who exclusively worked with victims of torture and trauma at two time points a year apart. Using interpretive phenomenological analysis, five superordinate themes and 19 constituent themes were identified, including a broad range of coping strategies, vicarious trauma, and vicarious PTG. One year later the same themes were found, as well as an additional two themes that were about policy changes that had made systems more difficult to negotiate for the clinicians and their clients (e.g., refugees not having visas granted for family members to join them) and intrapersonal challenges such as feeling ineffective or helpless in their work. It may be that the latter theme was present at time one but not acknowledged in the interview and that the building of rapport that took part over time encouraged a deeper level of disclosure about intrapersonal feelings.

## Grounded Theory in the Development of the PTG Concept

Grounded theory (GT) approaches to research are attempts to avoid preconceptions about what may be in the data, in order to allow patterns from the data to emerge naturally without premature interpretations by the researchers. PTG essentially derived from such a similar perspective (Tedeschi & Calhoun, 1988). Now that the concept of PTG is well-known, it may be more difficult for researchers to use a strict GT analysis. Shakespeare-Finch and Copping (2006) used GT to explore PTG dimensions in an Australian population and identified potentially culture-specific areas of PTG (i.e., spirituality, religiosity, and compassion). One intriguing finding was the meaning of compassion. They pointed out that having compassion for others for American people may be purposeful; therefore, it naturally leads to stronger bonds in existing relationships, whereas for Australian people, having compassion does not always relate to strengthening existing relationships. This kind of subtle but important culture-specific nuance can only be identified by using this type of research method. As was the case in a childhood maltreatment study by Hall et al. (2009), acceptance of the trauma, being resolute about it, or becoming resigned to it, was found to be a crucial step in recovery and in PTG. Another study using GT (Salick & Auerbach, 2006) with the narratives of people who had experienced a serious injury (e.g., amputation) suggested five stages to explain the PTG processes in three areas (self, connection, and meaning): (1) apprehension: This starts with the pre-diagnosis phase of having a vague feeling that something is wrong, and it continues until the time of diagnosis; (2) diagnosis and devastation: This is the stage at which the diagnosis is clarified and the participants realized how their body changed, which leads to withdrawal from the social world or community. It is akin to the shattering of assumptions; (3) choosing to go on: Participants talked about an inner strength, deciding not to miss out or refusing to let life pass them by, and finding other ways of getting around even under the difficult circumstances; (4) building a way to live as a coping mechanism. The participants had experienced a severe injury, including amputation; thus, this stage depicted how the participants reclaimed the physical body through sports or alternative physical expression, as well as finding a personal meaning, locating hope, and even using humor: "people talking to you like you're an idiot. It's like, my leg has the problem, not my brain! Carrying a crutch doesn't diminish my I.Q.!"; and (5) integration of the trauma and expansion of the self (integration of pre- and post-trauma lives). The final stage identified in this work involves not only moving forward but giving something back to the social or world community, like paying forward, as Tedeschi and McNally (2011) suggested in describing the ultimate benefits of PTG. Elder, Domino, Rentz, and Mata-Galán (2017) also used GT to formulate a comprehensive model explaining the journey following sexual trauma among veteran male survivors, and defined similar altruistic outcomes, including having developed a commitment to advocate for powerless individuals and developing a sense of respect for gay men.

# CHAPTER 10

# Quantitative Measures of Posttraumatic Growth

When PTSD was recognized in the DSM-III in 1980, there was a groundswell of work to measure the severity of the disorder, look for treatment options, and understand predictors and correlates of the disorder. As clinicians worked with people who had experienced traumatic events, they came to realize that symptoms of PTSD and other difficulties (e.g., depression, anxiety) were not the only outcomes of experiencing trauma. During the 1980s and 1990s a number of clinical academics around the world began to write about both the positive and negative sequelae of trauma, and designed scales that would tap either positive changes or both positive and negative changes.

## The Posttraumatic Growth Inventory

Since the introduction of the term PTG, it has been assessed primarily using the Posttraumatic Growth Inventory (PTGI: Tedeschi & Calhoun, 1996). The PTGI has been translated into many languages, which we detail later in this text (e.g., Japanese, Turkish, Spanish, Chinese, Thai, Nepali) and used in thousands of research projects. In this section, we briefly review the various measures of PTG-like changes, focusing on the PTGI because it is the most commonly used inventory and has been subjected to the most rigorous research about its psychometric qualities.

In creating the PTGI, a large set of items was first generated, based on a thorough review of the literature available at the time and on interviews with people who had lost a spouse and people who had become physically disabled as adults. Items focused on three broad areas (i.e., perceived changes in self, relationships with others, and philosophy of life). Based on results of exploratory factor analyses, the 21-item PTGI measure was developed. Factor analysis revealed five factors: personal strength, relating to others, new possibilities, spiritual change, and appreciation of life. Changes in these areas are measured as changes experienced in the aftermath of a highly stressful or traumatic life event. Instructions ask respondents to "Indicate for each of the statements below the degree to which this change occurred in your life as a result of your experience [or the researcher inserts a specific event]." Items are rated on a 6-point scale, ranging from 0 (*I did not experience this change as a result of my crisis*) to 5 (*I experienced this change to a very great degree as a result of my crisis*).

Reliability for the total scale and its subscales has been well established. Excellent internal consistency, α = .90, was originally reported (Tedeschi & Calhoun, 1996). Since then, strong reliability has been reported in numerous studies with diverse samples (e.g., Brunet, McDonough, Hadd, Crocker, & Sabiston, 2010; Moore et al., 2011; Morris, Shakespeare-Finch, Rieck, & Newbery, 2005). Data have also revealed a high level of test-retest reliability for the PTGI over two months (.71) with an American sample (Tedeschi & Calhoun, 1996), as well as over three months (.78) with an Australian sample (Bates, Trajstman, & Jackson, 2004).

Concurrent validity has been demonstrated by the correlations with the conceptually related constructs included in the PTG model such as disrupted core beliefs and intrusive and deliberate rumination (Calhoun, Cann, & Tedeschi, 2010; Taku & Oshio, 2015; Tedeschi, Cann, Taku, Senol-Durak, & Calhoun, 2017; Triplett et al., 2012). Construct validity has been further demonstrated by the relationship of the five PTGI factors with measures of positive behavioral changes in those same domains (Shakespeare-Finch & Barrington, 2012). Qualitative research with people who have experienced highly stressful events has also confirmed that the construct validity of the PTGI is actually measuring what it was designed to measure (Shakespeare-Finch, Martinek, Tedeschi, & Calhoun, 2013). Convergent validity has been confirmed by testing the relationships between existing measures such as PWB-PTCQ and PTGI scores (Joseph et al., 2012), and by testing the correlations between self-reports and the reports made by a third person who was close to the respondents before, during, and after their traumatic experience (Shakespeare-Finch & Barrington, 2012; Shakespeare-Finch & Enders, 2008; Taubman-Ben-Ari, Findler, & Sharon, 2011; Weiss, 2002). Factorial validity has been verified by confirmatory factor analysis of the PTGI (Brunet et al., 2010; Lee, Luxton, Reger, & Gahm, 2010; Taku, Cann, Calhoun, & Tedeschi, 2008) and by replicating the factor structure in other Western contexts such as Australia (Morris et al., 2005).

### The PTGI Short Form

A short form (PTGI-SF) of the PTGI was developed by Cann and colleagues (Cann, Calhoun, Tedeschi, Taku, Vishnevsky, Triplett, & Danhauer, 2010). The PTGI-SF includes ten items—two items from each of the five subscales of the original PTGI. Instructions and scale format are the same as the ones used for the PTGI. Empirical studies have confirmed the reliability and concurrent validity of the PTGI-SF with a sample of National Guard soldiers (Kaler, Erbes, Tedeschi, Arbisi, & Polusny, 2011).

### The PTGI Expanded

A 25-item expanded version of the PTGI (PTGI-X) has recently been developed (Tedeschi et al., 2017). The PTGI-X is designed to reflect a diversity of perspectives in spiritual-existential PTG experiences so that the scale can be useful in a broader range of cultural settings. Four items were added in the existential and spiritual domain. No changes were made to the other four subscales of the PTGI.

This expansion allows people who may not be affiliated in any religious group or who have non-traditional perspectives on religion to report PTG experiences. Good internal consistency for the newly created spiritual existential change factor (SEC) has been reported (α = .91), showing improvement from the original spiritual change factor (α = .83) in an American sample. The original five factors of the PTGI are retained in the PTGI-X, as well as the relationships with constructs that predict PTG (Tedeschi et al., 2017).

## Measures of PTG in Children

The first standardized instrument developed to assess PTG in children was the *Posttraumatic Growth Inventory for Children* (PTGI-C: Cryder, Kilmer, Tedeschi, & Calhoun, 2006), developed to assess PTG in children affected by Hurricane Floyd in North Carolina in the USA. The PTGI-C includes 21 items that are adapted from the adult version of the PTGI (Tedeschi & Calhoun, 1996). Like the PTGI, the PTGI-C also includes the same five domains: relating to others (e.g., "I can better understand other people's feelings"), personal strength (e.g., "I learned that I can count on myself"), new possibilities (e.g., "I have some new ideas about how I want things to be when I grow up"), spiritual change (e.g., "My religious beliefs are stronger now"), and appreciation of life (e.g., "I have learned what is most important to me"). Unlike the PTGI, the PTGI-C uses a 4-point rating scale for each item (1 = not at all true for me, 2 = a little true for me, 3 = mostly true for me, and 4 = very true for me). This inventory was originally developed for use with children (6 to 15 years old) who had experienced a hurricane in the US. The authors found that the PTGI-C has good internal consistency and there was considerable variability, ranging from 37 to 84, with a mean of 65.11 (*SD* = 11.87).

A short form of the PTGI-C, Posttraumatic Growth Inventory for Children-Revised (PTGI-C-R: Kilmer et al., 2009), is currently the most widely used measure assessing PTG among children. This ten-item scale is designed to assess the same five domains based on the original 21-item PTGI-C (Cryder et al., 2006). The PTGI-C-R can be used with children of elementary school age and up (roughly age 7 to adolescence). Items employ a 4-point scale for each item (1 = not at all true for me; 4 = very true for me). Instructions include two sections. Part 1 identifies the psychological impact of the focal event (i.e., "we are interested in understanding a little about the [event] and how you felt afterward. Which of these best describes how bad it was for you? Circle your answer: A—about the worst thing that could happen, B—very bad, but worse things happen to people, C—bad enough to upset me for a while, and D—not too bad"). Part 2 includes the ten-item PTGI-C-R.

The PTGI-C-R was developed for the study of children who experienced Hurricanes Katrina and Rita in the US. The PTGI-C-R demonstrates satisfactory internal consistency, with a mean of 20.0 (*SD* = 6.5), ranging from 0 to 30. The PTGI-C-R has been translated in multiple countries, including Chile (Andrades, García, Reyes-Reyes, Martínez-Arias, & Calonge, 2016), China (Yu et al., 2010), Germany (Vloet et al., 2014), Japan (Taku Kilmer, Cann, Tedeschi, & Calhoun,

2012), the Netherlands (Alisic, van der Schoot, van Ginkel, & Kleber, 2008), and Norway (Hafstad, Gil-Rivas, Kilmer, & Raeder, 2010). Some modifications have been made in the translated versions. In the Chinese version, for example, two items ("I understand how God works better than I used to" and "My faith/belief in God is stronger than it was before") have not been included because the majority of students in China have no religious beliefs. Although the culture of China is similar to that of Japan, the Japanese version keeps these two items, but the items have been modified: "I understand how nonhuman power [God, Buddha, or ancestors, etc.] works better" and "My faith in nonhuman power [God, Buddha, or ancestors, etc.] is stronger."

## Scoring and Interpretation of PTG Measures

Scoring of the various PTG measures is accomplished by simply adding item responses. There are no established "cut-offs" for growth, so the interpretation of degree of PTG can be estimated by referring to the anchors on the response scale and matching the mean item scores with the anchors. Subscales are useful in discerning whether there are patterns of PTG in a respondent, even though overall PTG may be fairly low. In fact, it could be argued that a single item showing endorsement of a high level of PTG is an indicator of PTG even if other items do not indicate very much PTG. Therefore, there are various ways of approaching the interpretation of responses to the PTGI and associated measures depending on the purposes of the research and how fine-grained an analysis is desired. For clinical purposes, consideration of individual item responses or domains may be useful.

## Other Measures Related to PTG

As discussed in the section on theory and terms used to describe concepts related to PTG, there are a number of concepts that overlap with PTG, and there are measures of these concepts that have been used at times to study PTG. Because the concepts, though related, are not identical to PTG, and because some items on these inventories are not strictly representative of PTG, use of these inventories in PTG research must be accompanied by careful interpretation of the results. We describe some of the more common measures that have been used to represent PTG or related concepts.

### *The Stress-Related Growth Scale*

The Stress-Related Growth Scale (SRGS) was developed to measure stress-related positive changes (Park, Cohen, & Murch, 1996). The original SRGS is a unidimensional 50-item scale that reflects positive changes in personal resources, social relationships, and coping skills. Examples include "I learned to communicate more honestly with others" or "I learned to take life more seriously." Each item is rated as 0 (I did not experience this at all), 1 (experienced somewhat), or 2 (experienced this a great deal). A short version that consists of

15 items has also been used (Park & Blumberg, 2002). Some items overlap with that of the PTGI (e.g., "I learned that I was stronger than I thought"; "I learned that it's OK to ask others for help"); however, most items are somewhat different, in that the SRGS includes a change in personality or attitude (e.g., "I learned to be a more optimistic person"; "I learned to get less angry about things"), relationships with parents specifically (e.g., "I became better able to view my parents as people, and not just as parents"; "I now better understand why, years ago, my parents said/did certain things"), and God (e.g., "I understand better how God allows things to happen"; "I developed/increased my trust in God"). There have been various versions of the SRGS used in research over the past 20+ years. A 43-item version used by Armeli, Gunthert, and Cohen (2001) contained only the original items that could be reworded to allow participants to indicate if a negative change had occurred as well as if a positive change had occurred. For example, the item "I learned that I was stronger than I thought I was" in the reworded version became "my belief in how strong I am." Items were responded to on a 7-point scale from strongly disagree to strongly agree with a neutral mid-point. More recently Vaughn, Roesch, and Aldridge (2009) found that only 19 items from the SRGS represented three different factors in a sample of adolescents ($N = 388$) from racial/ethnic minority backgrounds. The factors extracted through EFA were also subject to CFA and comprised cognitive/affective, religious, and social changes.

### Measures of "Benefit Finding"

A 36-item version of the Benefit Finding Scale (BFS) was developed to assess the ways a specific event such as cancer could have a positive impact on one's life. Examples include: "Having had breast cancer has made me more grateful for each day" or "Having had breast cancer has taught me how to adjust to things I cannot change." The items are rated using a 4-point scale (1 = not at all; 4 = very much) (Tomich & Helgeson, 2004). A 29-item version of the BFS that measures perceived benefits in the six domains (i.e., acceptance, family relations, personal growth, worldview, social relations, and health behaviors) has been used in some studies (Weaver, Llabre, Lechner, Penedo, & Antoni, 2008), as has a 17-item version (Kim, Schulz, & Carver, 2007). A more targeted measure of benefit-finding is the Benefit Finding in Multiple Sclerosis Scale (BFiMS) developed by Pakenham and Cox (2009). The 43-item BFiMS includes seven factors: compassion/empathy ("become more respectful of others"), spiritual growth ("become more spiritual"), mindfulness ("learned to slow down"), family relations growth ("My friends and family worry about me more"), lifestyle gains ("I re-evaluated my diet and physical activity"), personal growth ("I become more motivated to succeed"), and new opportunities ("New opportunities have become available"). Instruction for completion are: "Sometimes people who have an illness find something positive about the experience. Please rate how much you have experienced each item below as a result of having multiple sclerosis." Items are rated on a 3-point scale (1 = not at all to 3 = a great deal).

## The Benefit Finding Scale for Children

The Benefit Finding Scale for Children (BFSC: Phipps, Long, & Ogden, 2007) is a measure that has been used specifically to assess the potential benefits of dealing with illness in children. In contrast to scales assessing PTG, this measure does not require an assumption of prior experience of traumatic stress, nor does it explicitly require a positive change or growth experience. The authors suggested that there could be direct benefits associated with the child's illness, such as increases in social support, and that this may occur in the absence of changes in attitudes or beliefs, or having experienced an event as traumatic. Additionally, they asserted that using a framework of benefit finding is perhaps less cognitively demanding for children and more concrete, suitable to their stages of development. This ten-item BFSC has a 5-point Likert-type response format ranging from 1 (not at all true for me) to 5 (very true for me), and has been used by children who are 7 to 18 years old. Sample items include: "Having had my illness has helped me become a stronger person" or "Having had my illness has helped me learn who my real friends are." The BFSC is a unidimensional scale with excellent reliability (Michel, Taylor, Absolom, & Eiser, 2010).

## Benefit Finding/Burden Scale for Children

The Benefit Finding/Burden Scale for Children (BBSC: Currier, Hermes, & Phipps, 2009) has been used to assess children's perceptions of positive and negative effects of a cancer experience. This scale has a total of 20 items, with two subscales. The benefit subscale includes ten items, which were taken from the BFSC (Phipps et al., 2007) described above, and the burden subscale includes ten items. The burden subscale was added to avoid a socially desirable response and to better reflect negative aspects of the cancer experience that covers affect, relationships with peers, and family relationships. The authors reported there were no correlations between these two subscales of burden and benefit.

## The Psychological Well-Being–Posttraumatic Changes Questionnaire

The Psychological Well-Being–Posttraumatic Changes Questionnaire (PWB-PTCQ) was developed based on the six dimensions of psychological (eudaimonic) well-being proposed by Carol Ryff (1989; Ryff & Singer, 2008). The six subscales are: autonomy, environmental mastery, personal growth, positive relationships, purpose in life, and self-acceptance. The PWB-PTCQ consists of 18 items rather than the original versions, which were much longer (e.g., 42 items) so that there are only three items per domain. Examples are: "I like myself," "I have confidence in my opinions," and "I have a sense of purpose in life." Unlike the PTGI or the original SRGS, this questionnaire asks respondents to rate how much they perceive themselves to have changed on each item as a result of the trauma on a 5-point scale that includes both less and more changes perceived (i.e., 1 = much less so now, 2 = a bit less so now, 3 = I feel the same about this as before, 4 = a bit more so now, and 5 = much more so now). Although the items were prepared to reflect six dimensions, the scale is considered to be unidimensional (Joseph et al., 2012).

### The Changes in Outlook Questionnaire

During the same period Tedeschi, Calhoun, Park, Cohen, McMillan, and others were working in this area in the US, so too were Stephen Joseph and his colleagues in the UK. Preliminary work on the development of the Changes in Outlook Questionnaire (CiOQ: Joseph, Williams, & Yule, 1993) was conducted with 35 survivors of a disaster. The scale was designed to measure both positive and negative post-trauma changes. In 2005 Joseph and colleagues published evidence that the best solution for the 26-item CiOQ was a two-factor structure that measured positive (e.g., I live every day to the full now) and negative (e.g., I don't look forward to the future anymore) changes following highly adverse events, and that the questionnaire was a valid and reliable measure of such changes. They used four samples of adults and college students to conduct a PCA followed by CFA, and bivariate correlations with other measures, including the PTGI and the SRGS, to assess convergent and discriminant validity. Although the strength of relationships varied between the samples, correlations demonstrated that there were positive relationships between the positive dimension of the CiOQ with the PTGI, SRGS, the positive dimension of the PBS (McMillen & Fisher, 1998), and the Thriving Scale (TS; Abraído-Lanza, Guier, & Colón, 1998).

### The Perceived Benefit Scales

The Perceived Benefit Scales (PBS: McMillen & Fisher, 1998) were also designed to measure positive post-trauma changes. Thirty-six positively worded items were developed from responses to open-ended questions in a number of previous studies, and were initially sorted into 12 categories. To counter for response bias, an additional eight negative items were included but not analyzed. Using a convenience sample of 300 adults at a children's baseball game, an eight-factor structure was extracted: enhanced self-efficacy, increased community closeness, increased spirituality, increased compassion, increased faith in other people, increased family closeness, lifestyle changes, and financial gain. As can be seen by the labels of the eight-factor solution, there are some similarities with the PTGI but also quite distinct differences, in that they do not denote the same transformative changes that are assessed by the PTGI. For example, a strong correlation was found between the PTGI personal strength factor and the PBS self-efficacy factor but not with the PBS's material gain dimension.

### The Thriving Scale

The Thriving Scale (TS: Abraído-Lanza et al., 1998) was developed based on interview responses at two time points with Latino women ($N$ = 106 at T1 and 66 at T2) in New York who were suffering a variety of chronic physical health problems such as arthritis and fibromyalgia. The participants were asked what contributed to any growth they may have experienced as a result of their illness, if their philosophy of life had changed, or if they had learned a life lesson. However, the scale was comprised of only two questions from these interviews, three items from the

PTGI, and 15 items from the SRGS. It is likely the sample size lacked power for the PCA conducted; this may account for the reason the authors could not clearly identify an interpretable factor structure. Hence, all 20 items were totaled for an overall thriving score. A number of path analyses with other variables (e.g., self-esteem and self-efficacy) failed to produce an adequate goodness of fit for the data.

### Silver Lining Questionnaire

Using another sample of people with physical illnesses, Sodergren and Hyland (2000) developed the Silver Lining Questionnaire (SLQ) to assess if participants had experienced any positive benefits from their illness. The authors' proposed 38-item SLQ measures ten elements of growth, but the items were not subjected to the same rigorous analyses as many of the other scales discussed here. In 2008, McBride and colleagues examined the factor structure of the SLQ-38 with 504 people experiencing various illnesses. They found that the scale could be represented by a five-factor structure that looks very similar to the PTGI with the exception that there was no spiritual dimension extracted; instead, there appeared to be a dimension regarding influencing others.

## Validity of PTG Quantitative Measures

A few researchers have expressed skepticism about whether retrospectively self-reported PTG, especially assessed with the PTGI, correlates with "actual" changes between pre- and posttraumatic events. A study by Frazier and colleagues (2009), and a critique by Coyne and Tennen (2010), provide challenges to the concept and measurement of PTG; these, in turn, have been criticized themselves (e.g., Aspinwall & Tedeschi, 2010). We mentioned this issue in the section on theory, and will summarize some of this debate here, but refer readers to these original sources for more detail, especially to the serious methodological limitations of the Frazier et al. study.

The researchers who have questioned the validity of reports of PTG often use the qualifier "perceived" PTG to connote questions about the validity of those reports, and they have sometimes used the qualifiers "actual or genuine" (Frazier et al., 2009), "quantifiable" (Johnson & Boals, 2015) or "measured" growth (Yanez, Stanton, Hoyt, Tennen, & Lechner, 2011) to connote the validity of their numeric results. The "current standing" version of the PTGI (C-PTGI) was a modified version of the PTGI that was used to assess this "actual" PTG by asking participants to describe their feelings over the past two weeks for each of the original PTGI items (e.g., "I have had a strong religious faith" rather than "I have a stronger religious faith"). They used this method of assessment, which dispensed with asking about any change over time, because they questioned whether people are able to accurately discern changes in themselves from one point in time to another, and generally whether self-report is trustworthy.

There are many ways in which these arguments, and the study by Frazier et al. (2009), are flawed. If self-report of PTG cannot be accurately made, we might also question much of the psychological literature that relies on any self-report not directly connected with the present moment. PTG is not immune to bias, but other self-reports that form the basis for psychological research are prone to biases as well. There is little indication that retrospective self-reports of symptoms related to PTSD are suspect. It could be assumed that objective behavioral measures are more scientific than subjective measures of behavior. However, Sherman and colleagues pointed out that there tends to be misperception that objectively measured behavioral data is somehow better or more scientific but, typically, operational definitions must be created by the researchers with these measures as well (Sherman, Nave, & Funder, 2009).

What distinguishes PTG reporting is that the change people are asked to report occurs after a distinct marker event in a person's life, and so it may be easier to discern this change as a result. Furthermore, people can experience response shift; that is, they use a different perspective to assess themselves after the experience of events than they did before. For example, people might claim they are psychologically healthy at one point in time, but after navigating a trauma, their view of their own health has shifted, so that although they claim they are healthy, the meaning of this is quite different to them. Sometimes people refer to this as their "new normal." Another important consideration in PTG research is that group data inevitably masks individual differences in trajectories of change. A variety of differences in such trajectories can be expected (Danhauer et al., 2013), and it is better to understand these differences over long periods of time than to dismiss reports of change. People are also able to make distinctions among domains of PTG, and they are able to report PTD and other negative aspects of their experience at the same time they report PTG (e.g., Baker, Kelly, Calhoun, Cann, & Tedeschi, 2008; Barrington & Shakespeare-Finch, 2013; Cann, Calhoun, Tedeschi, & Solomon, 2010; Powell, Rosner, Butollo, Tedeschi, & Calhoun, 2003). This indicates some ability to discern the complexity of their experience, and not a tendency to whitewash it all with a naïve view of PTG. These people are generally not naïve, and they understand very well that they have been through demanding trials. Finally, the substantial evidence for the reliability and validity of the PTGI argues strongly for the general validity of reports of PTG.

## Posttraumatic Depreciation

As noted in the previous section, the CiOQ (Joseph et al., 2005) and the PBS (McMillen & Fisher, 1998) were designed to measure what is referred to as positive and negative post-trauma changes. People do experience both positive and negative changes in the aftermath of traumatic events. However, most inventories in the quantitative PTG literature have focused on measuring positive changes, such as the PTGI (Tedeschi & Calhoun, 1996) and the SRGS (Park et al., 1996), whereas negative posttraumatic changes have usually been assessed as posttraumatic stress symptoms (PTSS), and other negative states such as distress, depression, or anxiety. As more studies have examined both positive and negative changes simultaneously (Shakespeare-Finch & Lurie-Beck, 2014, for review), researchers have come to understand that the predictors of PTG are not the same as the predictors of negative changes. Also, researchers have learned that the outcomes related to PTG are not the same as the consequences of negative changes. These positive and negative changes can be considered as independent constructs. However, early studies failed to assess the negative changes in exactly the same domains in which people typically report growth.

### The PTGI-42

To remedy this earlier failure, the 42-item Paired Format Posttraumatic Growth Inventory (PTGI-42) was developed. The PTGI-42 captures both PTG and posttraumatic depreciation (PTD) in corresponding domains (Baker et al., 2008; Cann, Calhoun, Tedeschi, & Solomon, 2010). This effort was made partly because several researchers pointed out that scales such as the PTGI and SRGS have been designed to only allow respondents to report positive changes (Park & Lechner, 2006). The PTGI-42 includes the 21 items from the original PTGI and 21 matched, but negatively worded, items to measure PTD. The items are presented in pairs. Cann et al. explained that presenting the items as pairs permitted respondents to think about their post-event self more holistically—to consider growth and depreciation concurrently for each item. Thus, a researcher can gather a wider amount of information about a person's perceptions of their post-trauma outcomes with the one scale. The response format is the same as for the PTGI, from 0 (I did not experience this change as a result of my crisis) to 5 (I experienced this change to a very great degree as a result of my crisis). Researchers can use the sum of the 21 positive items (PTG composite score) and the 21 negative items (PTD composite score) separately, but of course the factors can be compared, too.

The ratings respondents give are usually higher for PTG than for PTD. Research has demonstrated that PTG and PTD are not correlated, and the relationships with influential variables, such as core belief disruption, are different for PTG compared to PTD (Baker et al., 2008; Cann, Calhoun, Tedeschi, & Solomon, 2010). The effects of rumination are also distinct in PTG and PTD. For example, Allbaugh, Wright, and Folger (2016) found that only deliberate rumination positively predicted PTG, whereas automatic or reflecting and brooding rumination, both predicted PTD. This finding suggests that event-specific constructive cognitive processing led to PTG, but more trait-like rumination, whether reflecting or brooding, affected PTD. All of these studies once again indicated that PTG and PTD are not correlated. As Cann, Calhoun, Tedeschi, and Solomon (2010) indicated, it might seem commonsensical to predict that as a positive element, PTG, goes up, a negative element, PTD, will go down commensurately; however, that has not been seen to be the case.

Research has also shown that PTG and PTD, as measured by the PTGI-42, are independent predictors of other psychological states. For example, Barrington and Shakespeare-Finch (2013) examined PTG and PTD total and factor scores in a series of regressions to assess their capacity to predict anxiety, depression, satisfaction with life and psychological flourishing, and the Scale of Positive and Negative Experience (Diener et al., 2010). Results showed that PTG total and factor scores were not related to any of the aforementioned variables, but that the PTD scores predicted anxiety, depression, stress, and negative experiences scores, and were inversely related to satisfaction with life. These findings may suggest the response format, such as -3 (very much negative way), -2 (moderately negative way), -1 (negative way), 0 (neutral), 1 (positive way), 2 (moderately positive way), and 3 (very much positive way), may lead to misunderstanding, because one seems to be able to experience both changes at the same time. There is, in fact, a multi-dimensional 43-item revised version of the SRGS (Armeli et al., 2001) that contains several domains (affect-regulation, religiousness, treatment of others, self-understanding, belongingness, personal strength, and optimism). Participants rate each item on a bipolar 7-point scale (1 = greatly decreased, 2 = moderately decreased, 3 = slightly decreased, 4 = neither increased nor decreased, 5 = slightly increased, 6 = moderately increased, 7 = greatly increased). These formats may have their own strengths; however, having two scales (instead of one scale with opposites) that can cover both positive and negative changes will better fit to the reality of humans, reflected by Tedeschi and Calhoun's concept of persons who experience PTG as stronger and yet more vulnerable. This style of response format does not permit a clear view of the ongoing difficulties that can be seen in many people who also see themselves as having changed in positively transformative ways.

Relying only on quantitative data analyses, independent relationships between negative changes and positive changes seem hard to digest; however, with qualitative approaches, this is not surprising. Relying on the narratives of two athletes with acquired permanent physical disability, Day and Wadey (2016) described the occurrence of synchronous positive and negative experiences, even within the same dimensions of growth. The narrative of one of the athletes highlighted the benefits of being around other athletes with a disability, because it afforded him a sense of belonging that he had not found since becoming disabled. However, he also said the newfound sense of belonging negatively affected his existing relationships. He said,

> I came home from [training camp] and I was buzzing. I just wouldn't shut up because there was so much to talk about. You know, I've got to work on this and do that. But she [wife] doesn't understand what I've got to work on and what I've got to do. I was buzzing and I wanted to tell her but she was so transfixed in her little bubble of understanding, it's very, very hard. It's so very strange, but it takes an immense toll on your personal life. You just wish that in your own personal life you had someone who understands.
>
> (p. 135)

### The PTGDI-50

As mentioned above, the original PTGI has only two items that tap religious or spiritual change, and the wording of those items does not reflect the potential for broader existential changes. Additionally, those two items may not be appropriate in other cultural contexts. For these reasons, the 25-item PTGI-X, an expanded version of the PTGI, has been developed recently (Tedeschi et al., 2017). A corresponding version of the PTGI-X has been developed as a revision of the PTGI-42 and is being tested in multiple cultural contexts. This new measure of PTG and

PTD is called the Posttraumatic Growth and Depreciation Inventory (PTGDI-50) and includes 25 items assessing PTG and a corresponding 25 items assessing PTD.

## Measures of Core Belief Challenge and Rumination

Measures have been developed to assess key factors included in the PTG model (Calhoun et al., 2010). Both the Core Beliefs Inventory (CBI) (Cann, Calhoun, Tedeschi, Kilmer, Gil-Rivas, Vishnevsky, & Danhauer, 2010) and Event Related Rumination Inventory (ERRI) (Cann et al., 2011) have demonstrated good reliability and validity and are good predictors of PTG, supporting the theoretical model that gives key roles to cognitive challenge and processing.

### *The Core Beliefs Inventory*

The Core Beliefs Inventory (Cann, Calhoun, Tedeschi, Kilmer, Gil-Rivas, Vishnevsky, & Danhauer, 2010) measures perceived challenges to the person's core beliefs or assumptive world. Exposure to a highly stressful life event is likely to cause core beliefs to be challenged, disrupted, or shattered. PTG tends to occur through the process of rebuilding or restructuring those beliefs.

The CBI was designed to assess the degree to which one's assumptive world is challenged or disrupted by a highly stressful or traumatic life event. This inventory includes nine items assessing a wide range of challenged beliefs, such as one's strengths and weaknesses, controllability of the event, religious/spiritual beliefs, or expectations for the future; for example, "Because of the event, I seriously examined my beliefs about my relationships with other people." Studies have demonstrated the scale has high internal consistency (Cann, Calhoun, Tedeschi, Kilmer, Gil-Rivas, Vishnevsky, & Danhauer, 2010; Losavio et al., 2011). Items are responded to on a rating scale from 0 (not at all) to 5 (to a very great degree). It is important to note that the challenge to core beliefs measured by the CBI is different from the degree to which an individual believes a negative event has become a core part of their identity, known as centrality of event (Boals, 2010). As Groleau, Calhoun, Cann, and Tedeschi clarified (2013), challenges to core beliefs represent the degree to which major components of one's understanding or beliefs of self, others, and the world are called into question by the event. On the other hand, centrality of event refers to the degree to which one's life story or narrative is defined by the traumatic experience. They reported moderate positive relationships between CBI scores and scores on the Centrality of Event Scale, as well as rumination, PTSD, and PTG.

### *The Event Related Rumination Inventory*

The Event Related Rumination Inventory (ERRI; Cann et al., 2011) assesses two distinct types of ruminative thoughts that may occur as a result of traumatic events: intrusive rumination and deliberate rumination. When people experience a highly stressful life event that potentially challenges their core beliefs, intrusive rumination is a typical response. Intrusive rumination is automatic, unwanted, repeated thinking about what happened. It may also include unwanted images of the experience. Deliberate rumination, on the other hand, refers to an intentional attempt to think about the event. As Calhoun, Cann, Tedeschi, and McMillan (2000) suggested, the more an individual ruminates—deliberately "chews the cud" about what happened, actively thinking about the circumstances and ways to make sense out of them—the more likely it is that PTG will occur.

The ERRI was developed to measure these two types of event-specific rumination, rather than the stable disposition to engage in rumination (e.g., the Ruminative Responses Scale (Nolen-Hoeksema & Morrow, 1991) or ruminations as symptoms (e.g., the Impact of Event Scale IES-R: Weiss & Marmar, 1997). The ERRI is a 20-item self-report inventory with ten items that assess intrusive rumination and ten items that assess deliberate rumination. It can be used to assess rumination retrospectively regarding the time of the event and at the survey point, with altered instructions regarding the timing and the type of rumination. Ratings are made on a 4-point scale, ranging from 0 (not at all) to 3 (often). Instructions for the intrusive rumination items at the time of the event are: After an experience like the one you reported, people sometimes, but not always, find themselves having thoughts about their experience even though they don't try to think about it. Indicate for the following items how often, if at all, you had the experiences described during the weeks immediately after the event. A sample item is "I thought about the event when I did not mean to (during the weeks immediately after the event)." Instructions for the intrusive rumination items at the survey point are the same as those above; however, the part "during the weeks immediately after the event" is replaced with "in the last few weeks." The instructions for the deliberate rumination items at the time of the event are: After an experience like the one you reported, people sometimes, but not always, deliberately and intentionally spend time thinking about their experience. Indicate for the following items how often, if at all, you deliberately spent time thinking about the issues indicated during the weeks immediately after the event. A sample item is "I thought about whether I could find meaning from my experience (during the weeks immediately after the event)." The instructions for the deliberate rumination items at the survey point are the same as above, except for the part "during the weeks immediately after the event" replaced with "in the last few weeks."

# CHAPTER 11

# Cross-Cultural Research on Posttraumatic Growth

Since the Posttraumatic Growth Inventory was published (PTGI: Tedeschi & Calhoun, 1996), it has been translated into many languages and has become the most widely used instrument in assessing PTG globally. We provide a summary of translations here, but realize that others may be published in journals that are not easily accessed in the databases available. This list is not likely to represent every language into which the PTGI has been translated. There are instances where more than one translation in a specific language is available, and there may be discrepancies between different versions. There is also some variability in how translations are accomplished, and there are likely to be shifts in meaning between the original content of PTGI items and the translated versions. Therefore, we do not consider the listing we provide here to be either a complete or an "official" endorsement of these measures as representing accurate measures of PTG in various languages.

## Translations of the PTGI

### Albanian

An Albanian version of the PTGI was developed using a standard back-translation process with a sample of Albanian people in Kosovo, seven years after the war (Arënliu & Landsman, 2010). This version demonstrated good internal consistency. The researchers reported the mean PTGI score as 47.33 for those who reported high levels of stress and 40.24 for those with low levels of stress.

### Arabic

An Arabic translation of the PTGI was developed using a standard back-translation process by Salo, Qouta, and Punamäki (2005) with a sample of Palestinian men who were imprisoned. They changed the response format and used a 4-point scale, from 1 (not at all) to 4 (to an extremely great degree). Kira et al. (2013) also translated the PTGI to the Arabic language by using a standard back-translation process with a Palestinian adult sample who experienced a variety of trauma. They reported the mean total PTGI score as 55.54 ($SD = 26.84$) and strong internal consistency. The same Arabic version was also used in a study with college students in Egypt (Shuwiekh, Kira, & Ashby, in press), with a mean total PTGI score of 64.24 ($SD = 19.62$).

## Bosnian

A Bosnian translation of the PTGI was developed using a standard back-translation process by Powell, Rosner, Butollo, Tedeschi, and Calhoun (2003), with a sample of adult former refugees and displaced people who lived anywhere in former Yugoslavia before the war and lived in Sarajevo, Bosnia and Herzegovina, after the war. The authors reported that the participants had difficulty understanding and adapting to the 6-point scale; therefore, they also changed the response format to a 4-point scale, ranging from 1 (not at all) to 4 (very strongly). Even after converting the scores from 21–84 to 0 to 105, the PTGI total score was very low, with a mean of 35.82 (*SD* = 18.09). This low score may reflect some cultural differences, but more likely it is due to the fact that these individuals experienced an unusual accumulation of severe traumatic events over a prolonged period of time and, thus, their core beliefs systems may have been shattered in ways that made PTG difficult to obtain. Perhaps this is the kind of sample on the upper end of the hypothesized curvilinear relationship between PTG and posttraumatic distress.

## Czech

A Czech version of the PTGI was translated by Krutiš, Mareš, and Ježek (2011). A modified Czech version has been also published by Mareš (2009).

## Chinese

Chinese versions of the PTGI have been developed by multiple researchers. The first translation was by Ho, Chan, and Ho (2004) with a sample of cancer patients in Hong Kong, using a standard back-translation process. It was later used with a bereaved sample (Ho, Chu, & Yiu, 2008), producing a mean for the PTGI total score of 45.02 (*SD* = 25.03). It has also been applied to cancer patients not only in Hong Kong but also in Taiwan (Ho et al., 2013), with a reduced number of items. The second translation was done by Gao and Qian (2010). Although the details of their research procedure, translation process, or results are unknown, the study using this Chinese version with a sample of cancer patients produced a mean of 60.07 (*SD* = 22.42), ranging from 0 to 105 (Li, Miao, Gan, Zhang, & Cheng, 2016). A third translation was made by Wang, Chen, Wang, and Liu (2011). Although the details of their methods or results are also unknown, the study using this Chinese version produced a mean of 42.55 (*SD* = 16.83), ranging from 0 to 105, with a sample of women with infertility in China (Yu et al., 2014).

## Dutch

A Dutch version of the PTGI has been developed using a standard back-translation process by Jaarsma, Pool, Sanderman, and Ranchor (2006), with a sample of cancer patients. They used the original 21 items in the same sequence, with the same response categories. They confirmed that the factor structure of their Dutch translated PTGI was comparable with the original five-factor structure generated in the US, and that the translated version had overall good reliability and construct validity. They reported the PTGI total score, ranging from 0 to 105, to have a mean of 47.87 ($SD$ = 24.04), and that women reported higher levels of PTG ($M$ = 50.75, $SD$ = 23.69) than men ($M$ = 39.94, $SD$ = 23.35). This finding is consistent with the findings from a meta-analytical study of differences between male and female scores on the PTGI (Vishnevsky, Cann, Calhoun, Tedeschi, & Demakis, 2010). The same Dutch version was also used in a study with victims of interpersonal violence, such as sexual or physical assault (Kunst, Winkel, & Bogaerts, 2010). They reported a mean of 40.58 ($SD$ = 10.77), and good internal consistency.

### French

Lelorain, Bonnaud-Antignac, and Florin (2010) translated the PTGI into French. These researchers examined PTG in 307 women who had recovered from breast cancer (disease free 5–15 years later). Confirmatory Factor Analysis did not show the factor structure in the translated version to fit the data well, but good reliability was found for the total score ($\alpha$ = .93) and all five factors ($\alpha$ = .79–.86). Scores ranged from 9–104 and the mean indicated a trend for moderate amounts of positive change ($M$ = 59.9, $SD$ = 20).

### Georgian

A Georgian version of the PTGI was developed by using the back-translation procedure (Khechuashvili, 2016) in a sample of adults living in Georgia. The authors modified four of the 21 items and reported that the inventory demonstrated good internal consistency (they did not report the total or mean score).

### German

A German translated version of the PTGI has been developed by Maercker and Langner (2001). There is some variability in response formats using the German version. The original German version (Maercker & Langner, 2001) used a 3-point scale. Another study using the German version used a 5-point scale "to retain the uneven rank number of the German scale and at the same time to allow for more differentiation within the range" (Zoellner, Rabe, Karl, & Maercker, 2008, p. 250). A more recent study using the German version used a 6-point scale (Kuenemund, Zwick, Rief, & Exner, 2016), the same as the original English version of the PTGI (Tedeschi & Calhoun, 1996). High internal consistency has been reported in these studies. A study with motor vehicle accident survivors reported an overall PTGI mean of 38.5 ($SD$ = 17.1) for those who did not show PTSD symptoms, a mean of 38.4 ($SD$ = 15.8) for those with subsyndromal PTSD, and a mean of 40.2 ($SD$ = 18.4) for those with full PTSD (Zoellner et al., 2008). This is an interesting trend that could indicate the important role of core belief disruption and rumination in PTG. In addition, the revised PTGI for Children (PTGI-C-R: Kilmer et al., 2009) has been also translated into German (Vloet et al., 2014). The authors reported that 92.8% of their sample of traumatized adolescents who had been referred to a specialized health service reported PTG (ratings ≥1 = a little change on at least two items). The mean PTGI-C-R score was 8.7, with a range of 0 to 30, indicating a relatively low level of PTG.

### Greek

A Greek version of the PTGI has been developed using a standard back-translation process with a sample of patients receiving palliative care due to having advanced cancer (Mystakidou, Tsilika, Parpa, Galanos, & Vlahos, 2008). The translated inventory showed a satisfactory internal consistency, test-retest reliability, and construct validity. The response format from the original measure was used ranging from 0 to 5 with the set of 21 items. They reported the mean of the total score as 42.47 ($SD$ = 16.91); however, these researchers removed four items (4, 6, 11, and 12) due to the poor model fit and double-loading, thus, the mean score may not be directly compared with other studies unless standardized.

### Hebrew

A Hebrew version was developed using a standard back-translation process with a sample of adolescents who faced at least one terror incident (Laufer & Solomon, 2006). In this version the researchers used a 4-point scale (1 = I didn't experience this change at all, to 4 = I experienced this change to a very great degree). It was later used in other studies (Bayer-Topilsky, Itzhaky, Dekel, & Marmor, 2013; Cohen & Numa, 2011), and a high level of internal consistency was confirmed. The latter study (Cohen & Numa) reported a relatively high level of PTG ($M$ = 70.22, $SD$ = 17.38), ranging from 0 to 105, with their sample of breast cancer survivors.

### Hungarian

A Hungarian version of the PTGI was used in a study by Tanyi, Szluha, Nemes, Kovács, and Bugán (2014) of cancer patients undergoing radiation therapy. Over a period of several weeks, these patients reported PTGI scores of 63 (at Time 1) to 67.5 (at Time 2) on the 21-item measure with the original response scale and standards deviations of 22.3 to 23.9 respectively. They also found that the spiritual change factor increased over time.

### Indian

Marathi is an Indo-Aryan language which is spoken by people who live in the Goa and Maharashtra states of Western India. Thrombre, Sherman, and Simonton (2010) translated the PTGI into Marathi to administer to 61 cancer patients in Pune, India. A pilot study indicated that the targeted population had difficulty with the usual 6-point rating scale, and therefore they used a 3-point scale: "did not experience this change," "not sure," "did experience this change." Means are thus not comparable to most literature unless converted. However, the authors reported that scores were in the mid-range and, interestingly, that patients who had experienced a reoccurrence of their cancer reported higher levels of PTG than those who had not had a reoccurrence.

### Italian

Italian versions of the PTGI have been developed by using the standard back-translation approach with a sample of Italian adults who experienced a variety of traumatic or life-altering events, such as illness and loss of a loved one (Prati & Pietrantoni, 2014). The original response format was used producing scores ranging from 0 to 105. The authors reported the mean PTGI total score was 44.98 ($SD$ = 24.59) with good internal consistency. These researchers also developed the Italian version of the PTGI-SF; however, instead of assuming the cross-cultural validity of the PTGI-SF, the authors used the same procedure as Cann et al. (2010) to select their own ten items (two items from each of the five domains). Therefore, there are some differences in the items included in PTGI-SF (i.e., Italian version includes items 4, 13, and 14, whereas the original English version does not and instead includes items 1, 7, and 19).

### Japanese

The Japanese version of the PTGI has been developed with a sample of college students who experienced a variety of stressful or traumatic life events (Taku et al., 2007), again employing the back-translation procedure. They used the same 21 items with the same response format from 0 to 5, and reported the overall mean of the PTGI as 38.9 ($SD$ = 20.8), with good reliability and content validity. The scale was later used to measure PTG among medical student volunteers after the earthquake in Japan (Anderson et al., 2016). They reported the mean of the PTGI as 36.38 ($SD$ = 18.18) for female volunteers and 44.19 for male volunteers.

### Korean

A Korean version of the PTGI-SF has been developed by using the back-translation procedure in a sample of individuals with acquired physical disabilities as well as individuals with congenital disabilities in Korea (Kim, Kim, & Park, 2016). They modified some of the items, and later excluded one item, thus using a total of nine items with a theory-driven five factors, given that one item does not comprise a factor. They also changed the scale format and used a 7-point scale ranging from 1 (strongly disagree) to 7 (strongly agree).

### Nepali

The PTGI has also been translated into Nepali, and again the back-translation approach was used. Although the translated version has been used with several different samples, including girls and women rescued from commercial sexual exploitation and earthquake survivors, results are not yet available, since the data collection is ongoing as of 2017 (R. Volgin, personal communication, August 5, 2017; Y. Honda, personal communication, August 6, 2017).

## Norwegian

A Norwegian version of the PTGI, with the original response format, was developed by Siqveland, Hafstad, and Tedeschi (2012) using standard translations and back-translation procedures for a study of people who had experienced the great Southeast Asian tsunami. PTG scores revealed a mean of 41 (*SD* = 26.4), and the scale yielded high internal reliability with a Cronbach's alpha of .96.

## Portuguese

A Portuguese version of the PTGI was developed by Teixeira and Pereira (2013) using a back-translation procedure, using all 21 items with the original response format. With a sample of cancer patients, they reported the mean of the total PTGI as 57.72 (*SD* = 21.92). Another translation was developed by Silva, Moreira, Pinto, and Canavarro (2009) using the original items and response format. Ramos, Leal, Marôco, and Tedeschi (2016) tested this version in a study of breast cancer patients and found that a CFA yielded the original five-factor solution with this instrument. Mean item scores were 3.09 with standard deviations of 1.09 on the 0 to 5-point scale. A Portuguese version of the PTGI-SF (Lamela, Figueiredo, Bastos, & Martins, 2014) has been also developed by using the back-translation procedure in a sample of divorced adults who ranged from 24 to 65 years of age. The original response format ranging from 0 to 5 was used. The authors reported the total score of the PTGI-SF as 29.01 (*SD* = 11.29), ranging from 0 to 50, with a high internal consistency as well as a satisfactory convergent and factorial validity.

## Spanish

A Spanish version of the PTGI has been developed with a sample of Latina immigrants (Weiss & Berger, 2006) using a systematic translation process. Although they excluded eight items based on the factor analytical results, they reported the mean of the remaining 13 items as 44.21 (*SD* = 15.14), ranging from 0 to 65, which is equivalent to 71.42 in a 21-item scale, according to the authors. There are full versions of the PTGI and the PTGI-X translated in Spanish available from Richard Tedeschi and Ana Orejuela-Davila of the PTG research lab at UNC Charlotte. Another Spanish version of the PTGI-Short Form was developed with a Chilean population (García & Wlodarczyk, 2016). It was developed with a sample of adults who experienced the 2010 earthquake in Chile, with the original response format ranging from 0 to 5. The authors reported the total score of the PTGI-SF as 26.25 (*SD* = 14.21), ranging from 0 to 50, with high internal consistency.

## Swedish

A Swedish version of the PTGI was developed with an adult sample of tsunami survivors in Stockholm (Michélsen, Therup-Svedenlöf, Backheden, & Schulman, 2017). The authors first translated to Swedish, back-translated into English by independent professional translators, and then reexamined. The mean of the total

PTGI score was 30.98 (*SD* = 24.63), ranging from 0 to 105, with high internal consistency (Cronbach's alpha was reported as .96).

## Thai

A Thai language version has been developed using a standard back-translation process (Tang, 2006), with a sample of adult survivors of the great Southeast Asian earthquake-tsunami. The original 6-point scale was used and reliability analysis showed excellent internal consistency. The authors reported a mean item score of 2.63 (*SD* = 1.06), ranging from 0 to 5, indicating moderate levels of PTG.

## Turkish

A Turkish translation of the PTGI used the original 6-point response format with the 21items (Dirik & Karanci, 2008) in a sample of rheumatoid arthritis patients. The mean of the total PTGI score was 51.86 (*SD* = 25.91), ranging from 0 to 105, and showed excellent internal consistency. This Turkish version was used in a sample of female breast cancer patients undergoing postoperative chemotherapy treatment or coming to the hospital for their routine controls (Bozo, Gündoğdu, & Büyükaşik-çolak, 2009), and they reported the overall mean as 21.39 (*SD* = 7.54). Using this translation, Şenol-Durak and Ayvaşik (2010) reported mean PTG scores in spouses of myocardial infarction patients as 59.2 with a standard deviation of 24.2.

## Urdu

The PTGI was translated into this Pakistani language by Kausar and Saghir (2010) to use in a study of breast cancer patients and their spouses. Translations were accomplished by a team who attempted to create items with the same conceptual meaning in Urdu rather than literal translation of words. The scale remained at 21 items with the original response format. The scores on the PTGI by patients were a mean of 42.7 (*SD* = 7.57), and for spouses the mean was 49.9 (*SD* = 8.38). Internal reliability on subscales were reported to range from .65 to .88.

## Cross-Cultural Research on the Factor Structure of the PTGI

The original five-factor structure of the PTGI (Tedeschi & Calhoun, 1996) has been replicated with a variety of samples (e.g., Brunet, McDonough, Hadd, Crocker, & Sabiston, 2010; Lee, Luxton, Reger, & Gahm, 2010; Taku, Cann, Calhoun, & Tedeschi, 2008), as well as the PTGI-SF (Cann et al., 2010; Kaler, Erbes, Tedeschi, Arbisi, & Polusny, 2011). The five-factor structure has been supported in other English-speaking countries such as Australia (Morris, Shakespeare-Finch, Rieck, & Newbery, 2005) and the UK (Linley, Andrews, & Joseph, 2007). Some translated versions of the PTGI have also been subjected to EFA and have supported the five-factor structure, including the Italian versions of the PTGI and PTGI-SF (Prati & Pietrantoni, 2014), the Spanish version of the PTGI-SF with a Chilean population (García & Wlodarczyk, 2016), Portuguese versions of the PTGI with cancer patients (Ramos et al., 2016; Teixeira & Pereira, 2013), and a Portuguese version of the PTGI-SF with divorced adults in Portugal (Lamela et al., 2014). However, different factor structures have been also reported.

### Single-Factor Structure

A one-factor solution was presented for the Italian version of the PTGI short form (Saccinto, Prati, Pietrantoni, & Pérez-Testor, 2013). It should be noted, however, that these authors did not use the same ten items of the original English version of the PTGI-SF. Rather, they selected two items from each of the five factors comprising the PTGI on their own, and conducted a factor analysis. One study that compared multiple factor structures (e.g., 1, 3, 5, and 7), in a context of DSM-defined traumatic events, suggested using the total score, because none of the factor models showed a good fit. Given that the majority of the studies have reported an excellent internal consistency for the overall scale, a one-factor or total score approach is often used with the PTGI.

### Two-Factor Structure

A higher order two-factor structure was identified for the Chinese version, based on a four- factor model (Ho et al., 2004). Because the original, theory-driven five-factor model did not fit their data set, Ho and colleagues conducted an exploratory factor analysis and found a four-factor solution comprised o: self, spiritual, life orientation, and interpersonal changes. Ho et al. then identified a second-order factor, named intrapersonal, that contains self, spiritual, and life orientation, which led to a second order, two broader categories (intrapersonal and interpersonal) model. This four-factor model (self, spiritual, life orientation, and interpersonal) with a higher-order two-factor structure (intrapersonal and interpersonal) has been supported by further confirmatory factor analyses with a sample of patients with chronic disease in Hong Kong (Cheng, Ho, & Rochelle, in press).

### Three-Factor Structure

There are multiple language versions that have found a three-factor solution for the PTGI items. One study of the Turkish version (Dirik & Karanci, 2008), for example, supported the three-factor structure: changes in relationships with others, changes in philosophy of life, and changes in self-perception. Using the Arabic version (Salo et al., 2005), a three-factor solution was also found: personal strength, affiliation to others, and spiritual change (two items from the appreciation of life scale loaded on their personal strength factor, and one item loaded on their spiritual change factor) with their Palestinian male ex-prisoners. Using the Bosnian version (Powell et al., 2003), a three-factor structure was also found: changes in self/positive life attitude, philosophy of life, and relating to others. There are only 20 items in this version, as the researchers removed Item 1 ("My aims in life changed in comparison with before the war") because the translation was problematic and had very low correlations with all other items. A Spanish translation of the PTGI also produced a three-factor solution (philosophy of life, self/positive life attitude, and interpersonal relationships) (Weiss & Berger, 2006), as does the Albanian PTGI (personal strength and new possibilities, relating to others, and appreciation of life) (Arënliu & Landsman, 2010).

### Four-Factor Structure

A four-factor structure was suggested as the best solution in the Japanese (Taku et al., 2007) and Georgian translations (Khechuashvili, 2016) of the PTGI. Both found the four-factor structure comprised of new possibilities, relating to others, personal strength, and a combined factor of spiritual change and appreciation of life. The original four-factor solution found by Ho and colleagues in Hong Kong (2004) has also been confirmed as a robust solution for cancer patients in both Hong Kong and Taiwan (Ho et al., 2013). Multi-sample Confirmatory Factor Analysis supported the solution that identified changes in self, spirituality, life orientation, and at an interpersonal level.

### Alternative Five-Factor Structure

The Greek version of the PTGI identified a five-factor structure after removing four items that showed complex loadings (Mystakidou et al., 2008). However, one of the five factors included items from the original personal strength, relating to others, and new possibilities; therefore, they named it "confrontation." Five factors of the Greek version therefore include: confrontation, relating to others, new possibilities, appreciation of life, and spiritual change.

It should be noted, however, that even though factor structures may appear to be identical, some cross-national differences in the "meaning" of the factors have been suggested. Shakespeare-Finch and Copping (2006), for example, pointed out that in the original PTGI, compassion is incorporated into the relating to others domain, assuming having more compassion can directly relate to the actual existing relationships with other people. However, for some people, compassion can reflect a personal philosophy and does not necessarily center around existing relationships. A study with an Australian sample found through an exploratory factor analysis that the single compassion item on the PTGI loaded more strongly on the appreciation of life factor, rather than the relating to others factor (Morris et al., 2005).

## Reports of Cross-Cultural Differences in PTG

As shown in the acronym ADRESSING (Hays, 1996), there are many cultures within cultures, such as age (e.g., young people have their own culture), disability, religion, ethnicity, social status, sexual orientation, Indigenous heritage, national origin, and gender. Each of these aspects of a person's identity can correspond to a distinct culture, with unique norms, values, and beliefs. Beliefs and the values associated with self, others, and the world are not only challenged when experiencing a life crisis but also affect what constitutes growth and its processes. Many researchers have pointed out the importance of taking culture into consideration in describing or explaining PTG (Calhoun, Cann, & Tedeschi, 2010; Splevins, Cohen, Bowley, & Joseph, 2010; Weiss & Berger, 2010). It should be noted that culture exists at multiple levels and can be subjective. Calhoun and Tedeschi (2013) point out that culture has both proximal and distal elements. Families, groups of friends, and workplaces have their own cultures that can be influential in how people think, feel, and respond to traumatic events.

In spite of differences in some aspects of PTG across cultures, available studies have shown the universality of PTG experiences (Weiss & Berger, 2010). It appears that people in very different cultural contexts recognize the possibility of growth after trauma. Some groups report a higher level of overall growth, and some groups report a specific domain of growth, but PTG has been found in all locations where it has been investigated. Variables that correlate with PTG seem to be consistent across cultures, too. For example, PTG is positively associated with intrusive rumination soon after the event and with deliberate rumination in different cultures (Taku et al., 2009). A number of international studies have also demonstrated positive relationships between PTG and social support or disclosure (Bozo et al., 2009; Taku, Tedeschi, Cann, & Calhoun, 2009; Yu et al., 2014), as well as relationships between PTG and positive coping, such as positive reframing (Schroevers & Teo, 2008) and problem solving coping (Dirik & Karanci, 2008). However, there are also some differences in PTG between cultural groups.

### Cross-National Differences

Compared to American scores on the PTGI, Japanese samples consistently report remarkably lower levels of PTG (Taku & Cann, 2014). Similarly, Americans report higher levels of PTG than people in Australia (Morris et al., 2005) or Spain (Steger, Frazier, & Zacchanini, 2008). Zoellner et al. (2008) suggested that this may be due to Americans' attitudes towards getting positives out of deteriorating events. They suggested that perhaps trauma survivors in the US might feel more social pressure to report PTG compared to trauma survivors in other countries. Steger et al. (2008) suggested that this finding might be due to American attitudes toward valuing self-enhancement. Other cross-national studies have also shown some differences between countries. A study comparing the level of PTG reported on the PTGI-SF, for example, showed that PTGI scores were higher in Colombia and Chile than in Spain (Wlodarczyk et al., 2016). The authors suggested that one reason may be religious background, because people in Colombia and Chile reported more frequent usage of spiritual coping than those in Spain. Another reason for cross-national differences in PTG is that different cultural groups may define PTG in different ways. Having a stronger religious belief can be an indicator of growth for those in more religious cultural settings. Having a greater feeling of self-reliance can be an indicator for those in individualistic cultural groups. And, being more willing to express emotions can be a good indicator of growth for those in cultures that emphasize expression and open communication. Without assuming all items on the PTGI equally represent personal growth for all people, Taku

(2011) assessed PTG defined from an individualistic perspective and PTG defined from a collectivist perspective using American and Japanese samples. PTGI items that were rated as most indicative of growth in both samples were "I know better that I can handle difficulties," "I can better appreciate each day," and "I have a greater appreciation for the value of my own life." However, some PTGI items (e.g., "I discovered that I'm stronger than I thought I was") were less indicative of growth for Japanese people than for Americans.

### Gender Differences

A meta-analytic study found that women report moderately higher PTG than men (Vishnevsky et al., 2010). Such differences have been reported in several studies, including in people from the Netherlands (Jaarsma et al., 2006), Italians (Prati & Pietrantoni, 2014), and Asian populations (Xu & Liao, 2011). This difference may be due to the use of different coping patterns (Gerber, Boals, & Schuettler, 2011) or the ability/willingness to express emotions (Jaarsma et al., 2006); however, further studies are needed to fully understand why gender differences are often observed in the level of PTG reported, because studies using translated PTGI versions have provided mixed results. A Georgian sample, for instance, showed no gender differences on new possibilities and personal strength domains (Khechuashvili, 2016) and Japanese samples showed men reported higher PTG than women (Anderson et al., 2016) or little differences between the sexes (Taku et al., 2015). Taku (2013) hypothesized that there may be cross-cultural differences as to what type of positive changes men consider as most indicative of psychological growth, because masculinity (e.g., emotional toughness) is affected by culture. Results indicated that for American men, "I know better that I can handle difficulties" was the most representative indicator of personal growth, whereas "I have more compassion for others" was the most representative indicator of personal growth for Japanese men. Because compassion has been traditionally characterized as a feminine trait, Japanese men might not be expected to be compassionate due to their male-dominant cultural background, but because of that, if they experience this type of change as a result of struggling with life crises, they may view it as an important indicator of psychological growth. On the other hand, for American men self-reliance and capabilities seem important, while, for example, "new opportunities are available which wouldn't have been otherwise" was the least commonly endorsed indicator of growth for American men.

It is also worth noting that studies have been limited by the binary terms that researchers tend to adopt when erroneously using the word gender. Male and female are categories of sex, not gender, and are not the only sexes (i.e., intersex). Gender is an infinitely more complex construct, and there are many more terms that a person may subscribe their gender to than simply being biologically intersex, male, or female. There are few studies that have explicitly sought to study PTG in people who identify as being in another category of gender. There are quite a few studies that have looked at stress-related growth as a result of *coming out* using the SRGS with people who identify as gay, lesbian, or bisexual (Solomon, McAbee, Åsberg, & McGee, 2015; Vaughan & Waehler, 2010; Wang, Rendina, & Pachankis,

2016; Cox, Dewaele, van Houtte, & Vincke, 2011). The focus on stress-related growth in these studies may indicate that coming out is not regarded as traumatic per se, but, rather, that it is a stressful experience. However, some people have regarded coming out as traumatic (Arnold, Calhoun, Tedeschi, & Cann, 2005). One study that did examine PTG using the PTGI was conducted in Hong Kong with 141 Chinese males with HIV who identified as homosexual (Yu et al., 2016). Positive and negative appraisals in the light of their disease were examined as predictors of PTSD, depression, and PTG, with resilience being placed as a covariate using structural equation modelling (SEM). As predicted, positive appraisals were significantly associated with PTG and negative appraisals were predictive of PTSD and depression.

## The Role of Religious Factors and Spirituality in Culture and PTG

As previously discussed, religious background and spirituality play a significant role in PTG for some people. There are many empirical studies examining which aspects of religiosity and spirituality are associated with PTG. Historically, religion has been defined in relation to observing doctrine such as the Bible or Quran. Such texts set conditions of practice through literal and symbolic means that explain how people can best connect with sacred beings. Spirituality is often conceptualized as a personal journey to understanding the world, the environment and a person's place in it. It reflects searching for meaning in life at a more individual level and notions of personal transcendence (Denney, Aten, & Leavell, 2011). As shown in qualitative and quantitative studies, people have reported spiritual or religious growth resulting from their crises, and at the same time they may develop narratives about their spirituality and religiosity that led them experience PTG.

One consistent empirical finding regarding religiosity and PTG is that positive religious coping is associated with PTG (Abu-Raiya, Pargament, & Mahoney, 2011; Gerber et al., 2011; Pargament, Magyar, Benore, & Mahoney, 2005). Positive religious coping reflects the perception of a secure relationship with God or higher powers and includes seeking spiritual support, benevolent religious reappraisals, and religious forgiveness. On the other hand, negative religious coping reflects the perception of a less secure relationship with God or higher powers and includes a tenuous and ominous view of the world, demonic or punitive religious reappraisals, spiritual discontent, and a religious struggle to find and conserve significance in life (Pargament, Smith, Koenig, & Perez, 1998). Similar results have been obtained in a study focusing on Buddhist coping (Falb & Pargament, 2013). Positive Buddhist coping, such as morality (e.g., used the five precepts or mindfulness training as guidelines for life; practiced right speech) and impermanence (e.g., reminded self the stress would pass; recognized that all things change), was associated with PTG.

Another way religiosity may play a role in PTG is through the support of a religious community. Participation in religious ceremonies and spending time with groups of people who share the same religious beliefs can foster a sense of belonging. López, Camilli, and Noriega (2015) indicated the support of a religious community is key for older people to experience PTG. Currier, Mallot, Martinez, Sandy, and Neimeyer (2013) indicated that involvement with a church or other formal religious group, in addition to religious coping, is associated with PTG in people who have been bereaved. According to the systematic review conducted by Shaw, Joseph, and Linley (2005), religious openness, readiness to face existential questions, and intrinsic religiousness are all associated with PTG.

## Individualistic-Collectivistic Characteristics of Cultures and PTG

Cross-national studies involving individualistic and collectivistic cultures have indicated that PTG, and the contents and the levels of PTG, may be influenced by this cultural dimension. Taku (2010), for example, discussed that some types of PTG (e.g., I developed new interests, I have a greater feeling of self-reliance, or I established a new path for my life) are somewhat intra-individual. A series of PTG studies in Japan consistently showed a low level of growth in the domain of personal strength, which often reflects the individualistic characteristics of Western cultures (Taku, Tedeschi, & Cann, 2015). Overall, in traditionally collectivistic cultures, such as Japan, whether or not a single individual experiences growth may be less salient than whether a group of people or community experience growth as a whole.

However, collectivistic cultures in East Asia and collectivistic cultures in South America have distinct characteristics. The former tends to suppress emotional expressivity to maintain harmony, whereas the latter tends to emphasize the expression and social sharing of positive emotions. Unlike the findings that have been obtained in cross-national studies comparing Japan and the US, researchers have found that PTG is higher in the relatively more collectivistic countries, such as Columbia and Chile, than in a relatively more individualistic country, such as Spain (Wlodarczyk et al., 2016). Similar results have been reported in a study comparing Guatemala, Spain, and the US (Vázquez & Páez, 2010). It is important to look at other dimensions, such as expressiveness and willingness to disclose, when we discuss the dimension of individualism versus collectivism.

There is also a growing body of research that has been conducted with people from Africa who have resettled in host countries following forced migration (i.e., refugees and asylum seekers). In order not to impose predetermined categories of growth that were essentially developed in Western cultures, much of the work with people from refugee backgrounds has been qualitative. PTG can be seen in data of this nature. For example, Shakespeare-Finch and Wickham (2010) sought to investigate helps and hindrances to adaptation in refugees that had fled South Sudan and resettled in Australia. Most participants discussed a newfound strength they attributed to the difficulties they had faced and that this sense of personal strength assisted them in negotiating challenges associated with resettlement. Likewise, Copping, Shakespeare-Finch, and Paton (2010) used a grounded theory method to examine post-migration well-being in a group of people that had fled Sudan. Four themes were extracted from the data: support, strength, new possibilities, and religion. Support and religion were the predominant coping strategies and resources reported, which have also been found in other qualitative studies conducted with refugees from Sudan (e.g., Khawaja, White, Schweitzer, & Greenslade, 2008). Participants spoke of sharing stories of distress with others in their social networks: that it was only when distressing intrusive thoughts were being experienced that they felt the need to talk through their feelings and thoughts with someone else. For example, one person explained "I will start with an event that happen, they will talk about it . . . then it [intrusions] will just disappear" (p. 56). Faith in God to protect them from further harm and guide them to safety was endorsed by all participants. In this sample strength and association with themes of hope and determination were seen as reasons for their survival rather than as a product of negotiating challenges. However, the recognition of new possibilities was regarded as an indication of PTG; most participants spoke about future goals and opportunities that they saw ahead. For example, one man said "we have wasted a lot of time there [in Sudan] not going to school, a lot of terrible things which we don't want to hear it. We should start thinking and plan our future properly" (p. 57).

Among other measures and qualitative data, Kroo and Nagy (2011) used the PTGI to measure positive changes in 53 Somali people who fled the war and violence in Somalia to resettle in Hungary. Results demonstrating moderate to high levels of PTG ($M$ = 68.92; $SD$ = 16.77) were reported. Acknowledging ongoing distress primarily around the separation from family, positive changes were also presented. For example, one participant said, "I must move forward, and I feel capable of doing it, I believe in myself now" (p. 448). Williamson (2014) wrote an interesting paper about collective PTG that she extracted from the testimonials of 18 female survivors of the genocide that took place in Rwanda. She explained that PTG changes at an individual level are largely cognitive in nature, but that socially shared ideological changes can be seen as collective PTG. Using discourse analysis, Williamson established that some of the testimonials included changes in philosophy of life and the making of new meaning, and that PTG at a collective level is about agency and communion.

# CHAPTER 12

# Developmental Research on Posttraumatic Growth

What are the differences between normative development and PTG? There may be many different ways to answer this question—one might focus on the differences, while assuming that PTG process and normative maturation processes co-occur in the same child. Some researchers have raised the question regarding whether or not PTG in children reflects normative maturation. Kilmer and Gil-Rivas (2010), for example, suggested examining the degree to which children's self-reported PTG reflects actual growth versus normative maturation. Cohen, Hettler, and Pane (1998) also suggested that longitudinal research on PTG in children would require the ability to distinguish PTG from changes that result from normal maturation processes. These viewpoints indicate that because typical development in children is a transformative process in itself, it may be difficult to determine if PTG has occurred in children who have experienced trauma, because of the trauma. If we take this perspective, then the differences between normative development and PTG could be observed by examining if the changes between pre-trauma and post-trauma in traumatized children are larger in the five domains of PTG (e.g., the degree to which children found new possibilities or are more able to deal with big problems) than the changes observed in a matched sample (e.g., age, sex, ethnicity) of non-traumatized children.

Another way to think about this question is to focus on the meaning of "normative" maturation. "Normative maturation" for children who have experienced a traumatic event is perhaps different from the "normative maturation" in children who have not yet experienced such an event. To distinguish PTG from normative maturation we could assume the child had two lives, with and without trauma; once they have experienced a traumatic event, their development is affected by the event and, thus, mostly automatically overlaps with PTG processes, which in turn now becomes "normative" development. The child might have experienced the exact same positive changes without having experienced the traumatic event; but we would not know. If researchers define the experience of a highly stressful event as "non-normative," then the option of "normative maturation" may not apply. If we take this approach, discussion will center on the way to integrate PTG and normative processes, rather than the way to distinguish PTG from normative maturation, because they are inseparable in those who have been traumatized. For example, sexual trauma in young childhood likely affects the development of schemas rather than the shattering and rebuilding of them. Survivors may develop negative schemas or core beliefs about themselves such as being fundamentally *wrong* or *damaged*, and because of the nature of development through childhood and adolescence, these beliefs are not reflected on or challenged until adulthood.

Tackling this question using empirical data, we can compare the reports of personal growth between those who have experienced a highly stressful event with the reports of those who have not. Taku, Kilmer, Cann, Tedeschi, and Calhoun (2012) assessed the capability of perceiving one's own growth among Japanese middle school students (mean age of 13.38, *SD* = .93). They included the question, "I don't know (if I have changed)" because of a traumatic event for traumatized youth and due to the passage of time for non-traumatized youth. Taku and colleagues found that those who had not experienced any traumatic event had greater difficulty in recognizing their own growth. Of those who did not report any traumatic experience, 43.6% were unable to perceive their own growth on at least one of the ten different changes listed in the Revised Posttraumatic Growth Inventory for Children (PTGI-C-R: Kilmer et al., 2009), compared to 11.8% of those who experienced a traumatic event. Traumatic experiences seemed to create a "before and after" reference point for those who experienced a highly stressful event; those with a traumatic experience seemed more able to assess their own growth than those who did not. In addition, the study showed that youth who reported traumatic events that met DSM criteria for a traumatic event were more likely to report a moderate or high level of personal growth compared to those who had experienced events that did not meet DSM criteria and those who had not experienced a traumatic event. This finding suggests that recognition of PTG and normative maturation are not identical.

## How Is the Experience of PTG Related to Cognitive and Emotional Maturation or Capability?

The findings on the relationship between age and PTG are not consistent (Meyerson, Grant, Carter, & Kilmer, 2011). Some studies have found that older children reported more PTG (Glad, Jensen, Holt, & Ormhaug, 2013; Milam, Ritt-Olson, & Unger, 2004), whereas others have found no correlation between age and reports of PTG (Hafstad, Gil-Rivas, Kilmer, & Raeder, 2010; Wilson et al., 2016). However, there is good consistency in the age at which reports of PTG appear. The youngest ages at which PTG has been reported is around 6 (Cryder, Kilmer, Tedeschi, & Calhoun, 2006; Hafstad et al., 2010) or 7 years old (Wilson et al., 2016). Quantitative studies, using standardized inventories, indicate that children at around age 7 are able to report their PTG experiences (Alisic, van der Schoot, van Ginkel, & Kleber, 2008; Exenberger, Ramalingam, & Höfer, 2016). A comprehensive review of the literature on PTG in children indicates that there is a lower age limit for PTG (Kilmer et al., 2014). This is likely due to the cognitive ability of children below age 6 or 7 to be able to engage in rumination about the stressful events, expressing their internal experiences, and integrating positive elements of their negative stressful experiences into new worldviews (Meyerson et al., 2011). Because PTG also demands an ability to appreciate the paradox that bad things can yield good outcomes, PTG may also depend on an ability to engage in some degree of dialectical thinking. Studies by Harter and colleagues have demonstrated that this ability may begin developing around age 8 (e.g., Harter & Buddin, 1987).

Qualitative studies also suggest children can express their PTG experiences. One study used a focus group with African American adolescents, ranging from 11 to 18 years old, who were coping with their parent's breast cancer (Ma, Niño, Jacobs, Davey, & Tubbs, 2010). Ma et al. found that the adolescents reported positive changes that can be categorized into the known five domains of PTG, with an additional domain referring to healthier attitudes and habits. Glad et al. (2013) used one of the open-ended questions in the CAPS (Clinician Administered PTSD Scale for Children): "How do you think (traumatic event) has affected your life?" with traumatized youth, aged 10 to 18, in Norway. Children in their study were able to articulate PTG-like experiences. Children's reports were categorized into three overarching areas. They described personal growth such as maturity, wisdom, personal strength, and self-protection: "I'm a bit more aware of who I am and I know myself a little better now, what I want and don't want; I set more boundaries before things happen" (p. 336). They described relational growth such as improved relationships, empathy, compassion, and desire to help others: "I can show more feelings, and I'm able to tell others that it's OK to be upset, that it's nothing to be ashamed of" (p. 337). They described a changed philosophy of life such as appreciation of life and future plans: "I believe I've begun to think more, become more aware of things, I don't take things for granted, I don't think that what's around me now is going to be there forever" (p. 337). These are clearly related to the PTG domains reflected in the quantitative measures.

## The Role of Posttraumatic Growth in Identity Formation

Erik Erikson's psycho-social theory has been one of the most important theories in developmental psychology. Erikson (1968) described the processes of adolescents' identity formation and how psycho-social strengths may be achieved at each of the eight developmental stages when the developmental tasks or crises are successfully addressed. His fifth stage is identity versus role confusion. Here, adolescents are faced with the task of developing a sense of self-continuity (Dunkel & Sefcek, 2009). Although Erikson's terms of "crises" or "developmental tasks" are different from the terms that have been used to indicate a trigger for PTG (e.g., life crises, highly challenging life events, traumatic events), his idea of development fostered by resolving the conflict seems to overlap with the concept of PTG. McLean and Pratt (2006), for example, conducted a longitudinal study to examine the relationships between narratives of turning points (e.g., relationships, achievement, autonomy, or mortality), meaning-making, and identity status. They found that low identity exploration (diffusion and foreclosure) was negatively related to story meaning and that mortality events (e.g., stories about accidents, death, or near death experiences) are most fertile for meaning-making, suggesting that a potentially traumatic event can trigger meaning-making cognitive processing, which may in turn contribute to PTG. Adolescence generally involves significant challenges and changes, with the theme of psycho-social development resulting from questioning identity, life purpose, and direction, and seems in part parallel with PTG processes caused by psychological and cognitive struggle.

A contrasting perspective is that identity formation is a less dynamic process than Erikson assumed and that many adolescents do not change identity status across a long period of time (Kroger, Martinussen, & Marcia, 2010; Meeus, 2011). Moreover, based on a meta-analytic review of longitudinal studies, Meeus concluded that there is no empirical proof for the assumption that "exploration," that is, the extent to which adolescents consider various alternative commitments, precedes "commitment," that is, the degree to which adolescents have made choices and committed to those choices, in the process of identity formation. PTG, on the other hand, is generally assumed to occur as a result of psychological struggle with life crises, and is thought to be more dynamic and transformational than identity formation processes. Erikson (1968) described the process of adolescent identity formation as slow, and so it may reflect the normative maturational process, while PTG may be a process that contains a more clearly transformative aspect. Because these reviews indicate that adolescents' identity status is rather stable, future research can examine whether PTG experiences may foster qualitative changes in identity status where, for example, youth in foreclosure could start exploring more in breadth and depth because of their highly stressful life event, which in turn may change their identity status to one of achievement.

In this section, we have been considering the differences between normative development and PTG among children. However, we should also consider how PTG may apply to other developmental periods. Weiss (2014), for example, identified many similarities between PTG and gerotranscendence (e.g., domains of positive changes, correlates with wisdom, and leading to life satisfaction) and then suggested that PTG could be conceptualized as part of normative development toward self-transcendence. This viewpoint suggests the integration of the two paths: PTG and normative adult development. It is interesting to see that Weiss (2014) argued that the end goal is similar between PTG and gerotranscendence, and that PTG can be viewed as an accelerator allowing the young to glimpse the profound knowledge of self and the world (e.g., the world is less predictable, less controllable, or less simple than people could have imagined when they were young), and thus develop wisdom and come to appreciate small things. For example, a teenager who lost his father once said that he had to admit that other classmates sometimes sounded immature, compared to himself. He attributed his perspective to his traumatic experience, saying, "they are lucky, they don't know anything yet." But one remaining question is that some domains of PTG, such as new possibilities, are not necessarily fostered in the process of gerotranscendence or adult development; therefore, PTG and normative adult development may be overlapping but not identical.

## Similarities and Differences Between Children and Adults in PTG Processes

Studies have confirmed there are many similarities between children and adults with respect to the processes involved in the development of PTG. As Kilmer et al. (2014) summarized, traumatic events can shake a young person's basic assumptions about the self, others, and one's world; PTG can then be experienced through cognitive processing, such as productive and constructive rumination, just like the mechanisms depicted in the PTG model for adults (Calhoun, Cann, & Tedeschi, 2010). Meyerson et al. (2011) have offered a hypothesized model of PTG in children. Their model overlaps with the adult-focused model (Calhoun et al., 2010), in that trauma exposure leads to distress responses (posttraumatic stress and depressive symptoms; intrusive rumination), which are affected by a number of things, including the child's exposure to other stressful life experiences. As is seen in adults, processes involved in PTG include acceptance of the event/s, deliberate rumination regarding the experience, positive reappraisals, and contextual elements such as adequate provision of social support and/or religious/spiritual frameworks.

However, some differences between PTG in adults and children have been identified. The model of PTG in children (Cryder et al., 2006; Meyerson et al., 2011) has not been fully supported empirically. For instance, the relationships found between ruminative thinking and PTG in children are not as consistent as has been found in adults. Some studies have found no correlations (Wolchik, Coxe, Tein, Sandler, & Ayers, 2008) between rumination and PTG, whereas others have (Wilson et al., 2016). The role of challenges to core beliefs is also an example of the differences between PTG in children and in adults. Disruption of, or challenges to, core beliefs are assumed to be key in both children and adults. However, the core beliefs of children are likely to be different from those in adults. Most adults hold value systems that can guide them in their daily lives; and, to some extent, so do children. However, due to the limited experiences of most children, their beliefs may be more likely to be stereotypical or one-sided (e.g., "My mom is a good person, so she will get better soon. She is not going to die" or "If you do bad things, bad things will happen to you"). Because children's core beliefs are limited in their possibilities, children may react to highly stressful events in more physical or emotional ways, rather than being able to rely on cognitive processing. Even though the schemas of children may be less complex, and still in the process of being built from experience (Janoff-Bulman, 2006), Clay, Knibbs, and Joseph (2009) have suggested that because children's schemas are not yet well established, they may be more likely to accommodate positive and negative trauma-related narratives into schema that are yet to be established.

Another difference in the development of PTG in children and adults may be the significant role of parents or caregivers in PTG experiences. The presence of significant others plays an important role in PTG among adults as well (Nenova, DuHamel, Zemon, Rini, & Redd, 2013; Shakespeare-Finch & Enders, 2008); however, from a developmental perspective, researchers have emphasized a more critical role of families, caregivers, and other significant adults in the child's life in supporting the PTG processes (Kilmer & Gil-Rivas, 2010; Kilmer et al., 2014). For example, one study showed that the stronger relationships between family and oncologist, and parents' religious coping, were associated with children's PTG (Wilson et al., 2016). Wolchik et al. (2008) found that seeking support from parents was a significant predictor of PTG, illustrating the important role of supportive parents. McDiarmid and Taku (2017) found that experiencing PTG, in ways that adolescents feel their family would want them to experience it, is associated with higher self-esteem in both American and Japanese adolescents. This finding suggests that it is important for adolescents to know whether their experiences align with their families' values. For example, American adolescents were more likely than Japanese adolescents to believe that their parents want them to experience "having stronger religious faith" or be "more willing to express emotions," and if they experienced these types of growth, their self-esteem was rated higher. On the other hand, Japanese adolescents were more likely than American adolescents to believe that their parents want them to experience "greater appreciation for value of life" and "better appreciate each day"; experiencing changes in the appreciation of life domain of PTG was likely to foster the self-esteem of Japanese adolescents. So, the adolescents' perceptions of parents' expectation played a significant role. However, more studies are needed to examine the interactive relationships between children's PTG and their caregivers' role, because the literature has not yet provided enough consistent empirical findings. Several studies have shown that social support was not correlated with PTG (Cryder et al., 2006; Felix et al., 2015) in children, and scores on a measure of benefit-finding for children were not correlated with their parents' PTG in a study by Michel, Taylor, Absolom, and Eiser (2010).

Both parties may be affected when parents and children together experience a common set of traumatic circumstances. Parents may sometimes be experiencing traumatic reactions concurrently with their child that in turn can lead to PTG. For example, Barakat, Alderfer, and Kazak (2006) examined 150 families in which a child (7–16 years old at the time of the diagnosis and treatment) had experienced cancer and its associated treatments. Of the nine questions regarding positive change posed, at least one positive change was attributed to the illness and treatments by approximately 85% of the children, with a third of the sample reporting changes in four or more areas. Mothers' reporting of positive changes was higher than their child's, with 90% reporting one area of change and half of the mothers reporting positive change in four or more areas. Fathers' responses indicated slightly less frequency of growth compared to the children.

Another difference between PTG in adults and PTG in children may be due to the relatively high levels of resilience observed in children. Tillery, Sharp, Okado, Long, and Phipps (2016), for example, compared the level of benefit finding and PTSS in children and adolescents ranging in age from 8 to 17 years. They found that the overwhelming majority of youth showed a high level of resilience and that the experience of PTSS was not a necessary precursor to the development of PTG; 36% of participants demonstrated high levels of PTG with low levels of PTSS. The findings that most youth appear to be resilient and experience low levels of distress following an adverse event, and yet are able to find benefit, may indicate the growth mechanisms in children are not identical to those in adults.

The content or indicators of PTG may also differ between children and adults. Taku and McDiarmid (2015), for example, asked American adolescents (mean age = 15.75), the majority of whom were Christians, to indicate which items on the 21-item PTGI were personally important to them. Results showed that the item "I discovered that I am stronger than I thought I was" was most frequently rated as important, whereas the item of "I have a better understanding of spiritual matters" was reported as important by only 7.59% of the participants. The relative importance of the PTGI contents may reflect developmental characteristics, since adolescents are more likely to focus on becoming autonomous and independent from others at this life stage.

Laceulle and colleagues (2015) examined PTG in 1,290 children in the Netherlands who were between 8 and 12 years old. The children had experienced an event that was rated as very adverse or fulfilled the DSM criterion A1 for PTSD. Older children reported less growth than younger children, and girls were more likely to report PTG than boys. Children who identified as religious and/or children who had good support from peers had higher levels of PTG than non-religious children and those with lower levels of peer support. Time since the event was not predictive of total PTG scores. However, the authors also examined the dimensions of PTG and found some differences between sub-groups of the children. For example, if the experience was more than six months earlier, the children were more likely to report new possibilities than if the event was less than six months prior to data collection. These results are consistent with research conducted with adults.

It appears that, in spite of some differences, there are more similarities in the mechanisms for growth in children, adolescents, and adults. However, the ways in which PTG may manifest itself may differ with different developmental stages. Because of that, the ways in which therapists, parents, friends, or other caregivers may help to facilitate PTG are also likely to differ. For example, young children, especially traumatized children, may not have the capacity to use words to express the feelings associated with their experience, and other forms of expression, such as drawing, may be more useful for them to communicate as they negotiate their journey to healing and PTG.

# CHAPTER 13

# Posttraumatic Growth and Neurological and Biological Mechanisms

The vast majority of research on PTG uses either qualitative methods or self-report inventories completed by the person who has experienced trauma, or by a significant other. However, there is an emerging body of literature that is combining self-report approaches with methodologies assessing neural mechanisms that may be associated with PTG.

## Brain Function and PTG

In what may have been the first study combining brain function assessment with self-reported PTG data, a group of German researchers examined frontal brain asymmetry, positive and negative affect, and self-reported PTG in 82 people who had been in serious motor vehicle accidents (Rabe, Zöllner, Maercker, & Karl, 2006). The researchers hypothesized, based on previous findings, that the left anterior regions of the cortex would be associated with positive emotions and eudaimonic well-being and that there would be more relative left frontal activity in those who reported PTG. Baseline electroencephalogram (EEG) data was collected and then followed by an event-related potential and emotion induction experiment that included participants being exposed to traumatic images. Significant correlations were found between fronto-central asymmetry and all domains measured by the PTGI with the exception of the spiritual/religious dimension, even after controlling for dispositional positive affect. These results suggest that PTG is better explained by approach-related tendencies that are reflected by left frontal activity, and not explained merely by positive affect. Because the left frontal activity seems to reflect goal-directed approach tendencies, a self-enhancing coping style, and adaptive emotion regulation, the authors suggested that the more goal-directed domain of PTG (e.g., new possibilities) might be associated with anterior frontal brain asymmetry, whereas other domains (e.g., spiritual change) are unlikely to be related to approach tendencies, and perhaps that is why the spiritual domain was not correlated with fronto-central EEG asymmetry.

In a recent study by Anders et al. (2015), a quasi-experimental design was used to examine neural markers that might correlate with scores on the PTGI. Magnetoencephalography (MEG) is a neuroimaging technique that is noninvasive and maps brain activity (MEG is similar to EEG but can provide more accurate localization of neural activation). MEG was used in conjunction with diagnostic interviews, a trauma exposure measure, and the PTGI in two groups of veterans. The first group had PTSD ($N = 106$) and the second was a control group of veterans who did not have PTSD ($N = 193$). There were no significant differences in PTGI scores between the groups, but results demonstrated that global synchronous neural interactions (SNIs) significantly decreased in strength (decorrelation) as scores on the PTGI increased; however, this was only seen in the veterans who did not have PTSD. Neural network decorrelation can be interpreted as an indicator of availability for encoding new information, which was suggested by the results of a study showing this mechanism with resilience (James et al., 2013). This study showed that the decorrelation observed in the control group (those who were not diagnosed as having PTSD) could release neural space that can allow PTG to occur—such relationships were not found in those who were diagnosed as having PTSD. Although these results may show that decorrelated trauma and PTG are overlapping, they were observably different with left and right hemispheres involved in both. The effects were more conspicuous in the right hemisphere for the trauma group as opposed to the left hemisphere for PTG. The authors suggested that failures in the coding, expression, and inhibition of fear in people with PTSD may impact the integration and processing of traumatic memories, thereby leading to lowered changes of PTG. It may be that the processing and integration of traumatic memories, which decorrelate the neural networks, allow for more neural freedom to absorb other information, thereby providing the means to explore alternatives such as PTG. Although the results of this study may seem contradictory to the findings of coexistence of PTG and PTSD symptoms, it is important to note that PTG levels were not different between those with PTSD and those without PTSD in this study. Rather, these results may provide a possible reason why PTG could occur in those who have experienced a traumatic event but who do not report clinical levels of PTSD symptoms. This study suggests that having PTSD is not necessarily a prerequisite to the PTG experience, and that those with no PTSD can still experience PTG, just as some people with PTSD also report growth, because the neural network decorrelation seems more available for them.

Functional magnetic resonance imaging (fMRI) is another tool used in exploring brain function. Fujisawa and colleagues (2015) used resting-state fMRI to investigate the relationship between the strength of network connectivity in various areas of the brain and scores on the PTGI. Participants ($N = 33$) were screened to ensure they had no psychiatric disorders, drug or substance abuse, physical injury, etc. They completed several measures, including the nature of the highly stressful or traumatic event they had experienced, and the Japanese versions of the PTGI, the IES-R (Japanese language version of the Impact of Event Scale Revised; Asukai et al., 2002), and the Beck Depression Inventory (BDI; Beck, Steer, & Carbin, 1988). Sex and age were entered as covariates, as was the BDI because it was negatively correlated with scores on the PTGI, so its effect needed to be excluded. IES-R scores were not related to PTGI scores. Results demonstrated that there were two areas of the left central executive network (rostral prefrontal cortex and

superior parietal lobule) in which the strength of the activity was positively correlated with the PTGI. People with higher scores on the PTGI had stronger connectivity between the superior parietal lobule and the supramarginal gyrus, a region
known to be important in social functioning. The authors suggested that people
who have higher levels of PTG have stronger connections between memory and
social functioning. That is, PTG experiences may be provided by collaborative
efforts between memory function and social function, such as reasoning about
the beliefs, intentions, and desires of others, but the reverse may also be true. PTG
experiences, such as developing a good interpersonal relationship, may result in a
positive relationship between memory and social functioning.

Pagani and colleagues (2011) used EEG to search for preliminary evidence
regarding the mechanisms involved in EMDR as a therapeutic approach. These
researchers used a number of measures, including the Impact of Event Scale (IES;
Horowitz, Wilner, & Alvarez, 1979), the PTGI, the Beck Depression Inventory
(BDI; Beck et al., 1988), and the Symptom Checklist-90 Revised (SCL-90 R; Derogatis & Lazarus, 1994). There were no changes in PTG after EMDR, although large
changes in PTSD symptoms were reported.

## Brain Injury and PTG

There have been several studies on PTG in people with brain injuries. As Ownsworth and Fleming (2011) indicated, brain injury is one of the most life-altering
events a person can experience, and thus, it is critical to further study PTG so it can
be integrated into rehabilitation programs for those with a brain injury. However,
it is often assumed that survivors of brain injury are not likely to experience PTG
because of acquired impairments in general cognitive processing, potential problems in orienting to new goals, and/or having insufficient communicative or social
skills to maintain or develop a relationship (McGrath, 2011). It is therefore particularly interesting to see that several studies have confirmed that PTG can occur
in survivors of brain injury. Hawley and Joseph (2008), for example, conducted a
longitudinal study among people with a traumatic brain injury. In order to assess
positive psychological changes, they used the Changes in Outlook Questionnaire
(CiOQ: Joseph, Williams, & Yule, 1993). Over half of the sample indicated positive psychological growth resulting from the struggles with traumatic brain injury,
such as "I don't take life for granted any more" or "I value my relationships much
more now." In addition, there was a negative relationship between positive growth
and anxiety and depression at long-term follow-up.

Graff, Christensen, Poulsen, and Egerod (2018) used thematic analysis to
explore interview data gathered from 20 patients with a traumatic brain injury.
One of the three themes emerging from the data was labelled "A new life." This
theme contained sub-themes that revealed closer relationships with family,
greater appreciation of life, new beginnings, and changed priorities. Since it is
critical to study the effects of long-term follow-up after traumatic brain injury,
Powell, Ekin-Wood, and Collin (2007) compared early survivors (one to three
years post-injury) and late survivors (ten to 12 years post-injury) in the level
of PTG, as well as anxiety, depression, and life satisfaction. After confirming

that the two groups were well matched on the other relevant variables, such as age, sex, severity of injury, severity of disability, and activity levels, the authors found that overall PTG and all five domains of PTG were significantly higher in late survivors. No differences were found in anxiety, depression, or life satisfaction. Because the early survivors may still be going through the trauma of adjusting to life post-head injury (e.g., the early group did not report change in lifestyle as positive in their study), perhaps a longer time frame since the experience of head injury and being vulnerable might lead the late survivors to recognize PTG. Change in lifestyle was in fact noted by the late survivors group as the second most positive change after head injury (the first was appreciating people and life more) in the qualitative survey (Powell et al., 2007). The researchers also asked what advice they would give to a person who had a head injury. The two most common answers were "It takes time—you will improve. Time is a healer" and "Don't give up—have a positive attitude." The impact of time seems particularly important for brain injury survivors.

Another study compared the levels of PTG in those with acquired brain injury to those with myocardial infarction (heart attack) (Karagiorgou & Cullen, 2016). The authors chose these two groups because they both represent two common, often unexpected, and serious medical events, and yet, they differ because brain injury affects neurological functions such as cognition, sensation, and movement, whereas myocardial infarction typically does not. When they compared the PTGI scores between the two groups, they did not find any differences, except for the relating to others domain (those with acquired brain injury reported higher levels than those with myocardial infarction). Because being in a relationship was strongly associated to the domain of relating to others, it is possible that the impact of current relationships on PTG may be larger in those with acquired brain injury. However, the sample sizes were different for the two groups, so it was difficult to draw definite conclusions. This study did show that impairments in cognitive processing due to the brain injury are not likely to automatically impair the potential for PTG.

Predictors of PTG among those with a brain injury have also been identified. One study, for example, indicated that the level of subjective impairment at discharge predicted overall level of PTG at six-months' follow up in people with acquired brain injury (Silva, Ownsworth, Shields, & Fleming, 2011), indicating the importance of the subjective impact of the trauma on subsequent PTG. The authors concluded that patients who more aware of the functional consequences of their brain injury were more likely to derive positive meaning and experience growth. A recent meta-analytical study (Grace, Kinsella, Muldoon, & Fortune, 2015) indicated that growth is related to employment, longer education, subjective beliefs about change post-injury, relationship status, older age, lower levels of depression, and longer time since injury. The impact of time since the brain injury was also pointed out by McGrath (2011), who suggested that PTG is a possibility for people who have experienced a brain injury, but that the time taken to achieve or recognize PTG may be longer than it generally is in people who have experienced other kinds of trauma that has not necessarily, or obviously, physically impacted the brain.

## Physical Health, Cognitive Functioning and PTG

There is also some evidence that PTG is associated with biologically related measurements, such as physical health or cognitive functioning. For example, one study indicated that patients who perceived more benefits from their illness, such as cancer or lupus, reported less pain (Katz, Flasher, Cacciapaglia, & Nelson, 2001). In order to explain the mechanisms linking benefit finding to physical health outcomes, Bower, Moskowitz, and Epel (2009) suggested an integrative conceptual model that identifies psychological and physiological pathways through which benefit finding affects physical health. The model indicates that finding benefit from an illness is associated with the development of intrapersonal and interpersonal resources that promote more adaptive responses to future stressors, which leads to reduced activity in the body's stress response systems, which will in turn minimize the deleterious effects of excessive or prolonged exposure to stress hormones. The authors also suggest that benefit finding may reduce physiological arousal at rest by increasing activity in the body's restorative systems (e.g., parasympathetic nervous system, sleep).

Another study, conducted with people with HIV, used two clinical markers—HIV RNA viral load to measure the quantity of HIV in the blood, and CD4 counts, that is, a measure of T-helper cells that indicates the damage to the immune system—to examine their relationships with PTG (Milam, 2006). Results showed that the relationships depended on the ethnicity and personality of the participant. Overall, PTG was positively associated with CD4 counts, but only for Hispanic participants and those with low levels of optimism; PTG was beneficial in the physical adaptation to HIV, but only over time and only under certain circumstances.

In a study that assessed rumination and blood pressure reactivity, Ayduk and Kross (2008) provided some intriguing findings. In this study, the authors asked participants to recall an experience when they were angry, and then randomly assigned them to one of two conditions. In one, participants were asked to assume a self-immersed perspective, and in the other, participants were asked to assume a self-distanced perspective. Participants in the self-distanced group reported lower levels of emotional reactivity than those in the self-immersed group. Although this study did not include PTG, the shift of rumination from self-immersed to self-distance may overlap with the shift from intrusive rumination to deliberate rumination.

In a study of cognitive functions, Eren-Koçak and Kiliç (2014) tested the relationships between PTG and cognitive functions by using neuropsychological measurements in a group of earthquake survivors. They found that higher performance in visual recall, fewer errors in a short category test, and better verbal fluency performance in human names were all positively correlated with PTG in the combined domains of new possibilities and personal strength. Because the sample size was rather small, future studies are needed to assess the relationship between PTG and memory loss. One may speculate that PTG might potentially serve as a protective factor for a decline in reasoning or memory.

# CHAPTER 14

# Ideal Research Strategies for Posttraumatic Growth

## Cross-Sectional Approaches to the Study of PTG

Despite the limitations involved with cross-sectional research, this strategy has many advantages. The most obvious is that researchers can get a "snapshot" of the relationship between a number of variables in a cost-effective and timely fashion. Cross-sectional designs can be administered in person, by mail or email, or hosted on online platforms. Large data sets can be gathered from people in diverse geographical locations. It can take considerable time and money to create and to put participants through experimental research protocols. Depending on the type of data, various analytic techniques can be used to test hypotheses: for example, correlation, ANOVAs, regression, factor analysis, and structural equation modeling.

Cross-sectional qualitative research can be conducted (e.g., interviews, focus groups) to gather rich data sets from which we can learn much about the phenomena under study. This approach is useful when there is not much known about the topic or population of interest, or if the interest is in more detailed understanding of people's lives or an aspect of their lives. In PTG research, qualitative data can be used to understand the lived experiences of people who have endured various kinds of events, their responses to what happened, their ways of coping, and their ways of finding meaning in what has occurred. With people from cultures different from that of the researcher, dynamic and reflective qualitative methods can assist in knowing if the researcher and participants are accurately understanding each other, and if a seemingly identical construct is interpreted as such across cultural groups, as discussed in Part II, Chapter 11.

There is debate about combining quantitative and qualitative methods due to their ontological and epistemological differences, but there is also a call to go beyond the rhetoric around these different methodological perspectives (e.g., Venkatesh, Brown, & Bala, 2013); there are advantages to researchers in combining these approaches. The terms mixed methods and multimethods are sometimes used interchangeably in describing this combination of approaches, but they are different. Multimethods refers to using more than one method to gather data in a study. It may be using two or more methods to elicit quantitative data, like survey and experimental approaches, or that both are qualitative, such as interviews and observations. Mixed methods refers to using methods that view things through a different lens—combining qualitative and quantitative approaches. The approaches may be used sequentially or concurrently (Venkatesh et al., 2013).

Qualitative data can be useful to better understand quantitative data or to provide a foundation of information to inform the development of quantitative research protocols. For example, a researcher may have a goal to develop a scale to measure posttraumatic disclosure and, in addition to reviewing literature, they may initially use interviews or focus groups to explore a variety of experiences of disclosure and what the construct means to people. Following analysis of the data, items for a quantitative survey scale development project can be created and data gathered from a larger group of people. Alternatively, qualitative methods may be used to better understand the results of research that has used quantitative methods. Combining qualitative and quantitative approaches can go some way to ameliorating limitations associated with either approach.

Because cross-sectional designs examine the relationships between variables at a single point in time, it is not possible to determine cause and effect. For example, when we use a test battery comprising the CBI (Core Beliefs Inventory: Cann et al., 2010), the ERRI (Event-Related Rumination Inventory: Cann et al., 2011), and the PTGI (Posttraumatic Growth Inventory: Tedeschi & Calhoun, 1996), we usually assume that CBI and ERRI scores will affect the PTGI scores based on the PTG theoretical model and a mounting body of research (Calhoun, Cann, & Tedeschi, 2010). However, it is possible that the PTG experiences have affected the CBI or ERRI scores. Whether or not the participants received an opportunity to report their PTG experiences, if they do at the survey point, cognitive processing may have been affected by their current value systems, their general assumptions about the world and their place in it, and other people. Another reason causality can never be determined in cross-sectional research is the potential influence of third variables. For example, women may report higher levels of PTG than males in general, but the difference in reported levels of PTG might be explained by disclosure of the experience and the subsequent discussion of that experience in a safe and supportive environment.

Order effects can also be a problem in cross-sectional approaches. Even though data are collected at one point, there are always sequences involved in the method: the order in which inventories are administered, questions are asked, and items are presented all have the potential to affect the outcomes. Hafner-Fink and Uhan (2013) suggested other factors, such as the cognitive sophistication of the respondents or the content of the measured concept, should be taken into account. Where possible, counter-balancing or randomization of sequences can minimize the likelihood of order effects. Fatigue may play a part in results if assessments or procedures take a long time.

Another potential limitation of the cross-sectional study of PTG is that data are collected at a single point in time, which may limit the generalizability of results. In PTG research, one question to be considered is: How long we should wait until we ask a person about the possibility of experiencing PTG? Although it depends on the characteristics of participants (e.g., current symptoms of distress or disorder, age) and events (e.g., natural disaster, diagnosis of life-threatening illness), conducting a cross-sectional study at one month after the event may be considered to be too soon by some. Similarly, collecting data 50 years after the event may raise questions about the validity of such recall. For example, several studies have been conducted with Holocaust survivors (Lev-Wiesel & Amir, 2003; Lurie-Beck, Liossis, & Gow, 2008). Participants (62 years or older) were asked to complete the PTGI, focusing on Holocaust experiences that happened more than 60 years ago (some people were under the age of 5 when it happened). Their total PTGI scores were 43.21 (*SD* = 17.32) and 56.09 (*SD* = 27.94), respectively, indicating that participants in both studies perceived moderate levels of PTG even after 60 years. These studies are, without a doubt, highly valuable, because investigating the possibility of PTG in this population is getting more and more challenging as time goes by, for it has now been more than 70 years since the end of World War II. In addition, the fact that the war ended 70 years ago does not mean the lives of persons experiencing the war were immediately back to "normal" at that time. It is more than likely that they re-experienced their trauma for a long time and think of their Holocaust or war experiences as something that lasted for decades after the war ended (or it may not be "ended" for some survivors). Even with such intense and difficult circumstances, there is a need to take care in the interpretation of data about events that happened in the distant past.

Because cross-sectional designs allow for collection of data at one time, there may be some concern that findings, based on the retrospective recall of PTG, are invalid because PTG should reflect "changes" and accurate self-awareness of such changes. Coyne and Tennen (2010), for example, asserted that people cannot accurately perform the set of psychological tasks involved in reporting PTG, as they must

> (a) evaluate her/his current standing on the dimension described in the item, e.g., a sense of closeness to others; (b) recall her/his previous standing on the same dimension; (c) compare the current and previous standings; (d) assess the degree of change; and (e) determine how much of that change can be attributed to the stressful encounter.
>
> (Coyne & Tennen, 2010, p. 23)

However, this proposed sequence may not reflect daily cognitive processes. If the phenomenon of PTG is completely new to people, and thus they need to think about it after they are asked, then this cognitive sequence may actually occur as participants respond to the questions on PTG measures. However, PTG was observed in humans for a long time before the terminology was proposed (Tedeschi & Calhoun, 1995). Participants are likely to have experienced PTG without having articulated it; thus, the self-report inventory is only asking them to identify if the statements apply to them and if so, to what extent. Also, the sequence suggests these researchers view PTG as synonymous with physiological measurements, and thus expect respondents to compare and subtract to recognize changes. However, PTG is not identical to physiological measurements. It is an experience that cannot be free from an evaluative process.

One limitation in research may be the restricted variation within data; it can act to underestimate the strength of relationships between variables. On the other hand, some statistically significant results may not be psychologically significant. For example, if the sample size is large enough, almost any bivariate correlation is likely to produce a significant result as a function of the sample size. There are numerous articles that report significant correlations between variables with coefficients of around .20. However, a coefficient of .20 explains only 4% of variance and the question then becomes one of if this relationship is psychologically meaningful when obviously there are many other factors at play that are not included in the research measures. However, when a large body of research, undertaken in different places and at different times, provides very similar findings, one can be more confident in assuming that the reported relationships are reliable.

## Longitudinal Research in PTG

Longitudinal studies of PTG can overcome some of the limitations associated with cross-sectional designs (Helgeson, Reynolds, & Tomich, 2006). A strength of such designs is that participants act as their own controls, eliminating variance that can be created by individual differences. However, longitudinal research designs come with their own challenges and limitations. First, attrition is one major problem, which can limit generalizability of findings. For example, one of the relatively large longitudinal PTG studies was conducted with adolescents (Arpawong et al., 2015). The attrition rate was substantial (41.9%), just as in many other longitudinal studies. If data are available from the participants no longer continuing with the study and/or if the reasons for their discontinuation of the research is known, some analytical adjustments can be made (e.g., using multi-level modeling). Or, data collected until the point of attrition may be compared to those continuing in the study to ensure no systematic differences exist between people continuing in the study and those who did not.

Second, care must be taken with the timing of baseline, of follow-up intervals (Anusic & Yap, 2014), and with cohort effects. If the baseline data are collected several months, or more, after the event, there is a possibility that participants may have already fully experienced PTG (Bostock, Sheikh, & Barton, 2009). It is very challenging to obtain baseline data regarding participants' mental health prior to their experience of a traumatic event, but having that data can be important. The amount of time that has passed between data collection points may also play a role in practice effects in responding to questionnaires.

Third, care must be taken in the interpretation of changes in self-reported PTG. Because PTG experiences may involve changes in values, priorities, and principles, it is possible that the meaning of these variables, rather than their amount, changes. At one point, survivors may report, "I have changed a lot since then. I understand others' pain more than before." A year later, they may say, "I can now confidently say I understand others' pain more than before." And five years later, they may say, "Now I can say, I feel like I understand others' pain more than before." If these three statements were recorded in a numeric way, the subtracted changes might be shown as zero. However, that does not automatically mean that their PTG has not been changed. Upon closer examination of the explanations these participants may offer, they may point out that their understanding of the concept or the meaning of it has shifted, so that they now recognize these concepts as different from those they had assumed before.

This phenomenon of "response shift" (Howard, 1980) may need to be considered in PTG research. Schwartz et al. (2013) have been working in health-related quality of life research, and described three versions of the cognitive processing involved in pre-post change estimations of participants in longitudinal studies. These processes may also be involved in PTG measurement: scale recalibration, or changes in internal standards of measurement; reprioritization, or changes in values; and reconceptualization, or redefinition of the measured construct. It is easy to see how PTG may inherently involve these rather sophisticated cognitive activities. For example, what is seen as a great deal of change may itself change over time; or what is seen as an important change may change over time; or the understanding or meaning of an aspect of PTG may change over time, usually producing a deeper or more profound appreciation of the construct. Although a longitudinal design may be seen as superior to a cross-sectional method, it still may not fully and accurately capture the quality of PTG when the method relies only on standard quantitative instruments such as the PTGI. To appreciate nuances of change in the experience of PTG might require a careful qualitative approach that involves interviewing participants who may be able to articulate the evolution of their experience of over time, particularly if using a longitudinal qualitative design with multiple data collection points. Schwartz et al. (2013) also suggest that some statistical methods can be used to detect and address response shift in quantitative data.

Fourth, it is unlikely that researchers can control for the possible events that may occur between data collection time points, but mixed and multiple methods can assist. Researchers may choose to assess for such events, but it is unclear if it would be efficient to try to identify them all. Not only intervening events, but other significant life events, and the influences of other people, media exposure, and other experiences may be important in the development of PTG over time. Instead of thinking of these factors as contaminants of the data, it may be more useful to consider them as potential factors to be integrated into a model of the PTG process.

A multimethod longitudinal study in Taiwan used multiple time points and time between interviews in a study of 313 people who were in the final stages of terminal cancer, until their death (Tang et al., 2015). In addition to interview data, the researchers collected scores on the PTGI, with some minor modifications, to reflect the terminal stage of cancer participants were requested to reflect upon. Information about coping strategies, demographics, and social support were also measured, as well as time that had passed since the patient accepted that their cancer was terminal. Patients within 30 days of their death reported significantly lower PTGI scores ($M = 26.13$; $SD = 21.59$) than they had more than six months prior to their death ($M = 40.33$; $SD = 27.71$). The standard deviation at the final data collection point indicted considerable variation across participants. However, when entering other measurements into the regression equation, including time since recognition of terminal status and social support, significant differences were no longer evident. The number of variables and the interviews used and measured across time permitted quite a thorough investigation of PTG in terminally ill cancer patients. Tang and colleagues urge researchers and clinicians to work to develop programs or ways of supporting people in end of life care so that the experience of PTG is fostered, social support networks are built, and acceptance of their illness status be supported, rather than focusing on symptom reduction and suffering. They suggest that a PTG approach would be more likely to see the last stage of life as a positively transformative experience.

## Qualitative Methods

Some researchers using quantitative methods may assume that qualitative research is unreliable, easy to conduct, non-scientific, and not systematic. It would be a very poor piece of qualitative research that fit those assumptions. Systematic observations are scientific, and qualitative research strategies can teach us things we simply would not know without them. Ethnography, observations, case studies, interviews, focus groups, and other approaches provide an opportunity to explore the lived experiences of others. Varying forms of analysis permit different levels of depth extracted from the data, and the choice reflects the intention of the research (Levitt, Motulsky, Wertz, Morrow, & Ponterotto, 2017). For example, if researchers were interested in a broad understanding of a phenomenon, a thematic analysis of data may be appropriate. If researchers wanted to explore the lived experiences of a person or group of people, an interpretative phenomenological approach may suit. If there is very little or nothing known about something of interest, ethnography could be a good choice, and if there is limited or no theoretical basis about a construct or phenomena, grounded theory is likely to be a good option.

Thorough qualitative research can be arduous in analysis but rewarding in results. There are some limitations noted in the literature, but many of them are arguable. For example, replicability is more difficult to be achieved in qualitative methods than quantitative methods. Perhaps, by using the standardized rigorous methodologies, such as a grounded theory approach, researchers are able to demonstrate the credibility of their work (e.g., Shakespeare-Finch & Copping, 2006). However, a criticism due to replicability is not warranted, because it is not the goal of qualitative research and might not be possible to achieve even if it was. Qualitative research is dynamic and iterative—responding to the context and continuous streams of information available. Decisions are made constantly; for example, about what probes to use in interviews or when to move from one observational site to another. Interpretations of data are influenced by what the researcher brings to the research, hence the need for reflexivity and reflection. All of these elements mean that exact replication is not possible, because researchers could not define exactly what replication would be (Katz, 2015).

Second, sample selection may have a bigger impact on the findings in qualitative research than in quantitative research, because the sample size is usually small and is often identified within the reach of researchers. This may, therefore, limit the generalizability. For participants with cancer, for example, it is often necessary to exclude people who are extremely distressed during their regular consultation, because participation may be harmful for them (Horgan, Holcombe, &

Salmon, 2011). Because of the way participants are approached or recruited, the selected sample may not be a good representative of the population the researchers intended to study. However, these sample restrictions are not only applicable to qualitative research. Following the reading of an informed consent document, people likely to be distressed may not participate in quantitative research, either. Using convenience, purposive, or snowball sampling techniques to recruit a sample for qualitative research has no less bias than recruiting only university students in a quantitative study of trauma or highly challenging events.

Because in-depth approaches to data collection are commonly used in qualitative research, it is important to consider the impact of researcher-participant interactions on the participants' responses. That is why qualitative researchers should routinely engage in reflective and reflexive practices. There is a need for researchers to consider their position in relation to participants; for example, could there be a perceived power differential? If there is, what things can the researcher do to minimize that or to account for it? There are lots of techniques for reducing unwarranted influence in interview-based research and narrative inquiry, such as developing rapport before the interview and using a longitudinal qualitative design where a relationship between participant and researcher develops over time and instills trust to be open and honest (Berry, 2016). It is important that the researcher and participant understand their roles in their exchange and, in PTG research, it is especially important to be aware of the potential vulnerability of the participant. If a participant is experiencing difficulty reconciling their experience during the interview, a researcher needs to be careful not to slip into the role of therapist and, rather, step back from the research.

There are well known experiments in psychology that have clearly shown people change their behavior when being viewed (i.e., the Hawthorne effect), and this may also be the case in qualitative observational research if participants are aware of the observation taking place. One way to minimize those effects is engaging the researcher as a participant. There are many advantages to doing this; for example, being a participant can assist researchers in becoming more sensitized to the content of narratives under study. Probst (2016) described a project in which the researchers were also participants in a narrative inquiry. Analyzing transcripts, memos and journal reflections, three broad categories emerged about this dual role of being an interviewer and an interviewee. The first was *losing safety,* which referred to vulnerability when losing the relative safety afforded by the distance created when you are the researcher. Participant-researchers spoke of feeling shame and guilt at disclosing things about their families, feeling exposed and vulnerable. The vulnerability enhanced their capacity to put themselves in the shoes of the other non-researcher participants. The second theme was called *cracking the mirror* and reflected identifying with other interviewee narratives—how similar the stories were to their own lives was like looking into a mirror of their own lives. With this came the need to consciously put aside that feeling of similarity to listen for differences. The third theme was labelled *measuring the distance.* This theme arose well into the research when the participant researchers realized that their different ethnic backgrounds had influenced their interpretation of the data. One, who came from a Latino background, felt protective of participants and identified with their stories. Conversely, the Caucasian interviewers intellectualized and distanced themselves, retreating into the role of clinician when content was too familiar.

Depending on the way PTG is asked about, participants may feel the need to articulate positive changes, even when the researchers have made all possible efforts to develop non-leading questions. Investigators need to be careful about the way to ask about possible PTG. Questions can be framed in a "did anything help or hinder your journey negotiating the challenges you have faced" kind of way.

There are strengths and limitations in any research design; researchers need to be aware of them and do what they can to minimize error regardless of the methods used—for example, statistical error or error in interpretation of qualitative data. Combining approaches can have theoretical implications (e.g., deductive and inductive methods have different philosophical underpinnings), but can also go some way to overcoming the limitations associated with one particular approach. In PTG research, qualitative data has added depth to the understanding of growth and the pathways that are most likely to promote or thwart growth. Quantitative research has meant that hypotheses about many variables and their relationship to PTG have been systematically tested. Experimental designs are becoming more common and some provide physical measures of fundamental brain functioning that are beginning to help us unpack biological mechanisms that may be involved in PTG.

## Studying PTG Using Both Quantitative and Qualitative Methods

Prevalence rates, domains of PTG, predictors and outcomes, the mechanisms associated with PTG, and individual/cross-cultural differences in the level of PTG have been revealed by studying PTG in quantitative ways using standardized measurements. But the way PTG is experienced, fostered or suppressed, and expressed has been more deeply understood by studying PTG in qualitative ways. A fundamental premise of quantitative research is to be able to generalize research findings to the population of interest through inductive processes. Based on quantitative studies, the five broad domains of PTG have been observed in many different cultures and geographical regions. However, worldviews and PTG experiences can also be unique and specific to each person, and these nuances may be better understood through qualitative methods.

Something that should not be overlooked in the discussion of quantitative and qualitative approaches to research is the experience of the researchers. There are clinicians who conduct quantitative research whose research is based on years of clinical practice. In the discussion of evidence-based practice, we must not undersell the value of practiced-based evidence, especially in research on PTG, a construct that is so closely connected with the experiences of many who seek help from clinicians.

# PART III

# Application

# CHAPTER 15

# Facilitation of Posttraumatic Growth Through Expert Companionship

Since the first book on PTG in clinical work (Calhoun & Tedeschi, 1999), the emphasis has been on *facilitation*, not intervention, and on *integration* with existing models of trauma treatment, rather than on the introduction of a new type of therapy. It is important to remember that in most people, PTG occurs without professional intervention, and that there may be other people in the lives of trauma survivors who provide the kind of companionship that encourages PTG. Tedeschi and Calhoun (2006) have described their approach to facilitation of PTG as *expert companionship*.

The basic principles of expert companionship overlap, to some extent, with the principles of all good clinical practice as described broadly by Rogers (1957/2007) and the common factor theory (Weinberger, 2014). Beyond these basic foundations of therapeutic relating and listening (Tedeschi, 1990), there are specific emphases in therapeutic practice that are important in facilitating PTG through expert companionship (Calhoun & Tedeschi, 2013). Given that trauma survivors are often mystified and frightened by their own responses, expert companions must be able to understand and explain the common physiological and psychological responses to traumatic events. Because survivors often are ruminative, the expert companion must be willing to listen to repetitions of the story of the trauma. It can take substantial time to reconstruct challenged core beliefs, and hence expert companions must be patient and able to consider carefully the various philosophies of living that trauma survivors may find themselves exploring. In addition, because survivors have often experienced events that are excruciating for them and for listeners, the expert companion must be able to encourage disclosure and discussion of things that can be very uncomfortable. Given that all this may be done in an emotionally charged atmosphere, the expert companion must be able to offer ways to manage these emotions, and to manage their own emotional responses. The expert companion must also be guided by basic principles in the relationship with the trauma survivor. These have been articulated as

> respect for survivors that extends to being open to being changed by survivors; being the humble learner rather than the expert; highlighting how aspects of post-trauma experiences reported indicate developing areas of PTG; fashioning a narrative together with the trauma survivor that respects the horror of

trauma while at the same time opening areas of change and development; and encouraging an appreciation for the paradoxical in the trauma experience, so that vulnerability can be strength, and loss is a change that can also be positive.

(Tedeschi, 2011, p. 139).

With the confusing, frightening, and debilitating experiences of many people who have experienced traumatic events, including those with PTSD, clinicians are usually trained to focus on reducing those symptoms. Because of this long-standing practice, it is easy for clinicians to focus only on the amelioration of symptoms without considering the possibility of PTG. A person who shows these symptoms may not appear to be a good candidate for personal transformation, and this is another reason this focus can be overlooked. A good companion should be someone, whether trained professional or not, who is willing to explore the potential for PTG. This sounds straightforward, but in reality it may not be, perhaps due, in part, to the training that the typical clinician receives. In most clinical training programs in clinical psychology, for example, the focus is on diagnosis (e.g., DSM or ICD classifications), methods of obtaining information (e.g., clinical interview, diagnostic scales), and reducing symptoms that interfere with life in some way. Because the curricula of many clinical programs need to adhere to extensive accrediting standards, little room may be left for discussions of PTG.

The expert companion uses knowledge of PTG processes to guide the approach to the trauma survivor, recognizing where in the process that person may be and providing the kind of companionship that is suitable at any given point in time. Expert companions need to respect the client's pace and framework. They also need to be able to recognize when clients are ready to take steps on the path of transition; for example, the move from intrusive rumination to deliberate rumination, or from being overwhelmed by the shattered worldview to start rebuilding and restructuring worldview. The expert companion offers time to reflect on these processes as they appreciate that they are facilitating something that can occur naturally in the aftermath of trauma. Companions on the posttraumatic journey are often not trained clinicians—they are quite likely to be friends or family members (Tedeschi & Moore, 2016b).

## Potential Problems in Promoting PTG

The approach of expert companionship allows clinicians to avoid pitfalls in their work on PTG in trauma survivors. The respectful treatment of people will preclude mistakes that would otherwise be possible. These mistakes come from a heavy-handed approach where the clinician assumes the role of "expert" rather than that of expert companion. The clinician who presents only as an expert is intent on identifying what is problematical or pathological, and on prescribing the methods for getting better. The clinician who provides expert companionship, however, approaches the client as a person from whom they will learn, who is unique and different from other people they have listened to, and who has resources for healing and growth, and for possibilities of personal transformation. The clinician who is an expert companion works with a trauma survivor to facilitate PTG, but avoids a strong agenda that prescribes PTG, on one hand, or a skeptical attitude that treats PTG as an illusion, on the other.

As we discussed earlier, some researchers may attempt to distinguish "authentic" from "illusory" PTG. However, Calhoun and Tedeschi (1999) have emphasized that the expert companion must be willing to accept that some degree of positive illusions may be present in the PTG process or journey and that it is often difficult to predict how perspectives that appear illusory may lead people to life choices, behaviors, and identities that are developed over time. The clinician must create an appropriate clinical environment to foster PTG while, at the same time, respecting the survivor's own framework of understanding, beliefs, and story of the trauma and its aftermath. Because PTG involves rebuilding of a worldview that was challenged by trauma, reconstruction of narrative is an important component, and the co-authoring of the narrative is central to the process.

The processes involved in expert companionship may seem rather passive, in contrast to some standard trauma treatments such as exposure therapy or EMDR. However, the clinician who is focused on PTG is very alert to the strengths and changes in the trauma survivor, and is able to discuss paradox in ordinary language and encourage experiences that highlight positive changes. The work is subtle but active, while respecting and enlisting the natural processes of change that have been appreciated as inherent in self-change and psychotherapy (Norcross, Krebs, & Prochaska, 2011). The important point here is that effective therapy and providing an environment conducive to growth is about a client-centered approach where a therapist supports, nurtures, illuminates, and gets to know the client well enough to be able, in a more direct way, to gently challenge and encourage restructuring of the unhelpful narrative that brought the client to therapy in the first place. The simple recognition of the strength of traumatized people seeking help and "being in the room" may be a seed for PTG.

A study of a cohort of childhood sexual abuse (CSA) survivors who described effective and ineffective therapy provides an excellent illustration of the dangers of inappropriate trauma therapy, as opposed to the response of clients to expert companions. Vilenica, Shakespeare-Finch, and Obst (2014) studied 21 women and 11 men who had experienced CSA and had sought counseling, who spoke of what was important to them in finding a pathway to healing in therapy. The participants were also very clear about what did not help. A common negative experience reported was if the counselor insisted on hearing the details of the CSA, believing that the client had to relive the experience with the counselor to move forward. Another theme of negative experience was if the client wanted to speak in detail about what had happened, but the counselor did not want to hear about it or looked uncomfortable. Another theme was if the counselor was perceived as overly friendly, falsely sweet, or distanced. A fourth unhelpful therapy theme was not letting the client lead the process in their own time to their own goal, seeing the sexual assault as the only issue, and focusing too much on symptom reduction at the expense of gaining any real understanding of core issues. On the other hand, positive interactions and outcomes were related to the practitioner as a person—having a non-judgmental, supportive, gently challenging, accepting, and encouraging style. Having a place of safety and trust was important and could be developed by being consistent, reliable, and accessible. Providing hope was very important—promoting the belief that healing is possible and that the client was in control of the future. These positive attributes of the therapist and the context they create are likely to foster the potential for PTG.

## Introducing PTG Soon After a Traumatic Experience

The data about how time since the event and PTG are related provides mixed results when considering the question of the proper time to introduce the concept of PTG to trauma survivors. Sometimes PTG is associated with a longer time period since a trauma (Grace, Kinsella, Muldoon, & Fortune, 2015), whereas in other studies time has not been found to be a significant factor (Linley & Joseph, 2004; Prati & Pietrantoni, 2009)—and sometimes results are inconclusive (Bostock, Sheikh, & Barton, 2009). Clinicians should keep this variability in mind and tailor their approach to the individual client. Although the clinician should be open to the possibility of PTG, the timing, as well as the context or the type of event, may dictate very careful wording in discussions of PTG. For example, bereaved parents may take offense at any suggestion that the death of their child could result in anything positive (Tedeschi & Calhoun, 2004a). It is appropriate to make a mental note of indications of growth seen in a client early on, but not to steer a conversation in that way until a person has had a chance to express the emotions and thoughts they have connected to the event. That does not necessarily mean that every client needs to discuss the traumatic event in detail, as is done in exposure therapies. Clinicians should emphasize that no trauma is good in and of itself, but what will determine its effect on people's lives is the approach they take in the struggle with the aftermath of those events. It may be appropriate in some circumstances to educate people about the possibility of PTG early on in the process of intervention.

## The Expert Companion's Use of Language in PTG Facilitation

There is a large body of literature on the impact of language in interpersonal communication in general, and in clinical practice in particular (Wachtel, 2011). The importance of choosing the right words to communicate with clients about PTG also has been emphasized. For example, Calhoun and Tedeschi (2013) highlight the need for clinicians to focus on meaning associated with the struggle a person is engaged in rather than on the event they have experienced. Clinicians need to be very careful to take the lead from their client and not to impose labels, reflections, or the potential for PTG if that is not evident in the language the client is using.

One of the fundamental decisions for clinicians working with trauma survivors is the choice of words to use to refer to them. Some have given this much thought and are sensitive to these choices, while others have not considered this very much at all. Words like victim and survivor are often used as descriptors for people who have experienced a traumatic event, and the choice as to which, if either, of the words to use can shape the mutually constructed therapeutic space. For example, in an article examining the lived experiences of people with a history of childhood sexual abuse (CSA), participants made it clear they did not want to be referred to as "victims," but were comfortable to acknowledge they had been victims of a crime (Vilenica et al., 2014). The crime was in the past, but being perceived by others or having self-perceptions of themselves as victims seemed to give power to the abuser and to the perpetrator. The label of victim implied a person in a position without power. Many of the participants in this research did not want to be labeled as a survivor, either, and for the same reason. Each term, while important in the way people consider themselves at various times throughout recovery, suggests that the person is defined by the event. Being a person with a history of CSA refers to an event in the past and creates the sense of a future beyond the event/s. The cause of the difficulty is in the past. The impact of the experience may still be a source of psychological struggle, but a careful use of language can encourage persons not to be defined by their past. So, for many people, there may be a movement during therapy from being a victim, to a survivor, to a person who is no longer defined by the event. Sometimes PTG has been termed "thriving," and the term "thriver" might seem to be an appropriate label. But even this may be too limiting and have a cloying quality. Best might be a recognition of the individual person, without particular labels that imply the traumatic event has an active role in the present, because PTG is not about the event, but how a person lives in its aftermath.

The word "trauma" is usually not understood by the general population in the same way that it is by mental health professionals. Clinicians need to be careful in introducing this word. Sometimes clients apply the word trauma to situations that professionals and diagnostic manuals (e.g., the American DSM) would not deem traumatic, while other clients do not seem to perceive events as traumatic that clearly appear to be traumatic to the clinician. It is the subjective experience of the event that is important to understand and work with.

The term posttraumatic growth is unlikely to have been encountered by most people who are coming to clinicians for help, even those who clearly see themselves as having experienced a traumatic event. As mentioned above, it is important for the clinician to properly time the introduction of this word in order to maintain a strong alliance. Using this word, or simply introducing the concept, too early may imply that the clinician is giving short shrift to the depth and intensity of the event and the ways it still reverberates psychologically. If the term PTG is going to be used explicitly, there should be some discussion of what it means; *the term itself does not need to be used* in order to help clients appreciate their personal growth. Calhoun and Tedeschi (2013) caution about using the term posttraumatic growth. They do not suggest it never be used, but to be judicious about it. If a client is sharing elements of growth, describing positive changes they have made in their lives or in the way they view themselves and the world, it may be useful to introduce the term as a way of increasing understanding of such changes. However, a clinician can listen for and reflect elements of growth if they are raised without actually using any term, including PTG.

During the process of therapy that attends to the possibility of PTG, emotional regulation should also be addressed, and accurately labeling emotional experience is an important component (Constantinou, van den Houte, Bogaerts, van Diest, & van den Bergh, 2014; Tabibnia, Lieberman, & Craske, 2008). The way in which people bestow subjective meaning to an emotion affects their communication with themselves, with others, and ultimately their well-being. Meanings are important in therapy and especially in PTG-focused work. When clinicians are working with trauma survivors, emotional reactions, their meaning, and their regulation are important to address early in the process.

Let us consider how meaning can be given to an emotion by labeling and how this might function in a person who has a trauma history. Bob is in his mid-20s. He frequently has outbursts of rage seemingly triggered by the minor indiscretions of others—she looked at me wrong; he had a rude tone; she drove too close to me. In other words, Bob thinks the reason for his regular outbursts, which involve yelling, swearing, accusations about other people's motivations to annoy him, are because someone else is at fault; if his attributions are accurate, then his response can be seen as reasonable and understandable. But over a period of time, it became known that Bob experienced a number of episodes of physical abuse as a child and as a teenager by peers. The abuse left a legacy of great distress, and he was diagnosed with clinical depression when he was around 18. The depression was characterized by irritability and frequent outbursts of anger and verbal abuse toward members of his immediate family. From his perspective, it was their fault he was angry. This way of interacting with others became his way of being in the world. As he became more isolated from others, his anger intensified. With gentle confrontation, Bob came to learn that his anger and associated behaviors were not about others as much as about his deep distress, his self-loathing at the thought of himself as a victim, his inability as a child to fight back, and his self-blame. These emotions, which were hidden beneath the anger, were the real emotions Bob needed to deal with in order to move forward. His realization, with help, that this was driving his anger, assisted Bob in naming the emotions that were driving his behavior. He began to engage in effortful rumination and develop a new narrative where he accepted that he had been a victim during his early life, the abuse was not his fault, and nor was it the fault of the people currently around him. In order to accomplish this change, he had to learn how to label accurately the emotions he felt and the origins of these emotions. Now the emotions made sense in a different way, and the task became something more constructive than punishing others or defending against them. This can then allow for new ways to relate to others and a changed sense of self, as well as other changes that reflect domains of PTG. Careful use of language in the processing of the meaning of emotions is important in facilitating PTG. Tedeschi and Moore (2016a) recommend several exercises to help survivors name and understand their emotions, because putting a variety of feelings into words may be helpful in the PTG process.

# CHAPTER 16

# Intervention Models for Posttraumatic Growth

As Roepke (2015) has noted, there are still very few studies examining intervention programs that were specifically designed to foster PTG. This may reflect the distinctions between immediate needs of alleviating symptoms and longer-term PTG, or that fostering PTG involves adaptations to usual therapeutic interventions rather than the creation of a whole new intervention. For example, Tedeschi and McNally (2011) proposed a framework for PTG interventions that was developed for combat veterans. Their model includes five elements that are generally utilized in sequence, but that have a good deal of flexibility in the timing and the focus at different points in treatment. These elements overlap to a degree with what is found in standard therapies for trauma while representing a direct application of the theoretical model of PTG (Calhoun, Cann, & Tedeschi, 2010; Calhoun & Tedeschi, 2013; Tedeschi & Calhoun, 1995), with the important processes described in that model addressed in the interventions. Calhoun and Tedeschi (2013) devoted a book to describing the application of this approach to a variety of trauma survivors.

The first element of PTG intervention involves psycho-education in order to promote understanding of the trauma response. The physiological responses to trauma are normalized and the psychological responses, especially core belief disruption, are reviewed as they represent opportunities to reassess basic beliefs and ways to live one's life. The normalization of the responses to trauma allow the person to see that there is nothing wrong with them, that their reactions are understandable in the context of the event(s) they have encountered. This could be summed up in the motto, "it is not what's wrong, it's what happened." Understanding this can bring substantial relief to people who fear they are out of control, broken, or beyond hope.

The second part of the sequence involves the management of emotional distress. Posttraumatic distress, especially anxiety, insomnia, and intrusive rumination, are addressed so the person can begin to deliberately ruminate about the event in a constructive way. Following the theoretical model, it is clear that some degree of success in managing emotional distress is necessary so that the person is not so preoccupied with symptoms that they cannot focus on the possibility of PTG. In this step, the clinician can employ various calming techniques for reducing anxiety and intrusive rumination, such as relaxation techniques, mindfulness practices, physical exercise, recreation, and artistic expression.

The third element in the PTG facilitation sequence is constructive self-disclosure. Standard PTSD therapies vary in the degree to which they encourage disclosure about traumatic events, but such disclosure is central to exposure treatments and cognitive processing therapy. Exploration of intrusive rumination through self-disclosure helps to increase a sense of control over this thinking, and articulating those thoughts helps in the process of organizing thinking. Note that the exploration here is of the intrusive thoughts currently being experienced, not necessarily a deep exploration of the experience/s themselves. Some people may feel more comfortable expressing their thoughts and emotions with privately written words (e.g., a diary or poetry). Other people may be willing or be ready to disclose their experiences to trusted friends or family, which, if successful, can elicit emotional and instrumental support from others. But, of course, clinicians should use caution in encouraging their clients to disclose their experience to others; the response of others to that disclosure can have either a positive or negative consequence for the client, depending on the degree of support those responses offer. By talking to others, especially a trusted companion, clients may start developing a coherent narrative and be able to look at things from different perspectives. Participating in peer support can be a particularly powerful way to disclose as this can produce a reassuring bonding in an environment that allows people to tell their story while developing safe and warm relationships.

The fourth part of the sequence involves the development of a coherent narrative that integrates life before the traumatic event, the events themselves, and the aftermath of the event. The focus on the aftermath emphasizes the expression of the five domains of PTG, and an appreciation of the paradoxes involved in this recognition. The ability to appreciate paradox and to think dialectically is encouraged in this phase, as a revised life narrative is constructed that points to a meaningful future. When trauma survivors see that they can author narratives that will define their lives going forward, there is often an enthusiasm that develops that points to the final development in the PTG process.

In the fifth and final phase, the narrative that is being constructed leads to the articulation of new or revised life principles that can be robust to the challenges emanating from future traumatic events, and to the development of new meanings and missions in life. For example, the consolidation of PTG into daily living may include enhanced compassion for others who experience trauma, an altruistic goal of helping others, or simply in valuing how learning about how to create new pathways and opportunities has had a profound and positive impact on their lives (Tedeschi & McNally, 2011). By discussing how PTG experiences are now translated into everyday lives, expert companions can also help people who have experienced trauma to not only accept their identity, but to play an active role in the development of that identity.

## The Initial Implementation of a PTG Facilitation Program

A model for including PTG in interventions can be understood as something that guides perspectives, philosophy, interpretations, and attitudes of the expert companion, and not a mechanistic or formulaic specification of highly specific intervention techniques. It is an approach that arises out of a theoretical model and the research that tests and evolves that model, lending itself to empirical testing. A form of this PTG model of intervention has been applied in a group intervention program for combat veterans. This program, at Boulder Crest Retreat in Virginia, is not designed as a clinical intervention, but uses the five PTG domains in its design and expert companionship as the basis for its implementation, with military veterans filling many of the roles in the program. The combination of the PTG-based program, the people implementing it with an expert companionship focus with peer support, and the place itself, a quiet, rural setting where outdoor, physical, meditative activities are integrated into the experience, is perhaps an optimal approach to trauma survivors using a PTG model. The Boulder Crest program is the first fully implemented PTG intervention program and is therefore a true groundbreaking effort. Tedeschi and Moore (2016b) describe the specific advantages of this PTG-based program when it is combined with the most effective physical and interpersonal environment.

The Boulder Crest program demonstrates how the principles of PTG and its facilitation using the five phases are best implemented in a program that fits the life experiences and contexts of the persons attending. In the case of Boulder Crest, the activities are designed to connect with military history and experience, providing credibility and some familiarity for the veterans who attend. For example, archery, an ancient combat tool, is used to advance the ability to calm oneself in the manner necessary to shoot an arrow accurately. Other types of physical activities, such as working with horses, rock climbing, kayaking, and hiking, can have aspects that resonate with military service members. At the same time, they have aspects that are demanding yet meditative and involving; this dialectic can be appreciated from the perspective of PTG, while the activities themselves introduce emotional regulation processes that are important to master in order to allow for self-reflection and deliberate rumination that foster PTG. Program participants are introduced to a variety of physical, creative, and meditative activities for the clear purpose of facilitating the process of PTG. The activities are facilitative because they are introduced and guided in a way that facilitates emotional regulation, self-reflection, acceptance of help and mutual helping, and having fun in a constructive way. Although the program utilizes a variety of alternative therapeutic approaches, these are synthesized into a retreat experience that is constantly focused on facilitating PTG. The activities of the seven-day retreat are described in detail in a guide book, so that they will be faithfully executed with the proper understanding of how the activities foster PTG and how they are delivered with an expert companionship approach.

The success of the program is dependent on the qualities of expert companionship that are communicated by all staff, from the very start of their stay. The constant message conveyed is of respect and encouragement, and that this experience is for them. It is free, and the participants spend time in beautiful log cabins and do their training in a lovely log lodge on grounds where everything is finely maintained. The message of all this is how much the participants are valued to have this freely given. The program is called "training" and the participants are "students," so that from the first there is no indication that participants are seen as disordered or pathological. The motto is that they have come because of what happened and not because of what's wrong. Furthermore, what happened is not assumed to be combat-related. For some students it is, for others, not. More often than not, the struggles these students confront have more to do with what happened before combat—childhood struggles, or what has happened since military deployment—the struggles involved in reentering the civilian world and family life. Every person has a different story, and each is invited to share it in a respectful atmosphere.

This seven-day retreat is just the beginning of the commitment to the students who attend. They are followed for 18 months through video meetings with the other members of their team and a Boulder Crest guide who contacts them regularly to track their progress back home. A curriculum for this program is being developed that will be comparable to the detail seen in the seven-day retreat materials. An evaluation of the 18-month program is underway in order to quantitatively measure its long-term effects on PTG, symptoms, and healthy lifestyle, and to further develop the program. Boulder Crest Retreat has essentially become a laboratory for the design and implementation of PTG-based interventions. It is expected that these interventions will be designed for other groups besides veterans and military service members, using the experience of Boulder Crest and the PTG model as a foundation.

Other researchers and clinicians have added a PTG module to their intervention programs. For example, Shakespeare-Finch and colleagues (2014) included a module on PTG in an intervention conducted with newly recruited police officers. Using a longitudinal randomized controlled trial (RCT), PTG was seen to increase in those who received the intervention compared to recruits who received standard psycho-education training. Recently a similar intervention has been piloted for use with mental health nurses which showed very promising results for enhancing resilience and PTG (Foster, Shochet, Wurfl, Roche, Maybery, Shakespeare-Finch, & Furness, in press).

## PTG as Self-Help

PTG was originally investigated (Tedeschi & Calhoun, 1988; Calhoun & Tedeschi, 1989–90) as a naturally occurring response to trauma. People have found ways toward PTG without professional facilitation, and this is likely the case for the vast majority of people facing trauma. A combination of the naturally occurring PTG process facilitated by some accurate information provided through popular self-help methods rather than traditional therapy would seem to be quite an appropriate approach. At the same time, expert companionship, most often in the form of non-professionals, can foster PTG. Recognizing this, Tedeschi and Moore (2016a) have published a guide to the PTG process and expert companionship in a "workbook" format. The workbook utilizes the five elements of the PTG intervention model and includes modified versions of research measures utilized to encourage self-reflection. For some, this workbook approach may be most effective when combined with guidance and support from professional expert companions.

## PTG Integrated With Standard Trauma Therapies

Calhoun and Tedeschi (1999, 2013) have suggested ways that trauma therapists could integrate PTG into existing treatment approaches, recognizing that these are the foundations for accepted trauma treatment. The PTG intervention model utilizes familiar elements of these approaches, such as psycho-education, emotional regulation training, narrative development, and cognitive processing. They have been examining ways to integrate approaches to maximizing the potential for PTG to occur within existing intervention approaches that include these elements (Tedeschi & Calhoun, 2006). The goal is not to fine-tune these approaches, but to use PTG as a new foundation for intervention, and use appropriate elements of existing therapies in ways that better serve the particular circumstances and needs of each person who has encountered trauma. It is clear that our existing trauma treatments fall short, as reported in a review by Steenkamp, Litz, Hoge, and Marmar (2015), who found that traditional therapies such as prolonged exposure and cognitive processing have left those receiving treatment with significant clinical problems, and have high drop out rates. Perhaps more focus on relationship or common factors, and tailoring therapy more carefully to the needs of the clients, would advance the field (Bollinger, 2017). The PTG approach may provide an avenue for such an improvement of trauma therapy.

Examples of the use of the PTG concept in derivatives of other therapeutic modalities appear in the ideas of Nelson (2011) and Gregory (Gregory & Embrey, 2009; Gregory & Prana, 2013). Nelson's (2011) "posttraumatic growth path" is described as integrating cognitive, narrative, Jungian, and solution-focused approaches, and is divided into phases labeled "Deal, Feel, Heal, and Seal." Although it purports to be focused on PTG, almost all the work described is actually exposure therapy and cognitive processing. The process involves choosing a traumatic event of focus, writing a trauma event narrative, doing imaginal exposure and cognitive processing, and engaging in a PTG perspective on it.

Gregory and Embrey (2009) developed a trauma treatment program called "companion recovery" for former child soldiers in an attempt to address their catastrophic trauma and promote resilience. Although not derived from PTG theory, this model was later utilized by Gregory and Prana (2013) with refugees on the Ivory Coast using various trauma interventions along with a PTG focus. This companion recovery model emphasizes peer mutual support, with didactic work in three general areas: trauma impact reduction and education, resilience, and PTG. Peer support is specifically designed to utilize the expert companion approach to intervention, and a final "commencement" celebration marks a return to the community in a way that is designed to consolidate a new sense of a resilient self. PTGI data gathered in the program indicated that this approach was effective in fostering PTG in these refugees. This program shows great promise as a culturally sensitive approach to facilitate PTG in an essentially collectivist population that has suffered extreme trauma.

Cognitive Behavioral Therapy (CBT) and Exposure Therapy or Prolonged Exposure (PE) are frequently used in the treatment of people with posttraumatic symptoms. They are currently regarded as the "gold standard" of interventions for people diagnosed with PTSD (e.g., Phelps, Dell, & Forbes, 2013), yet there is little evidence that one approach is better than another. As discussed in an earlier section, what the therapist and client bring and the relationship they create is more important than a particular technique or framework. With a foundation of understanding the importance of interpersonal relationships in recovery from the impacts of trauma, Markowitz et al. (2015) conducted a randomized controlled trial of exposure therapy, interpersonal therapy (ITP), and relaxation therapy with 110 people who had CAPS scores greater than 50. Exclusion criteria were numerous, including: comorbid diagnoses of psychotic disorders, bipolar disorder, and alcohol or other drug dependence. Exposure therapy, an element of many other frameworks such as CBT, required participants to divulge increasingly detailed descriptions of the traumatic circumstances. Relaxation therapy involved progressive mental and muscle relaxation, coupled with homework listening to relaxation tapes. ITP involved no homework and rather than focusing on the trauma, the focus was on the aftermath and the way interpersonal relationships had changed, and that might have been challenged in the present. Following a 14-week treatment program, improvement was measured as CAPS scores with more than a 30% reduction. In the ITP group, 63% showed a 30% reduction in scores, 47% showed such reduction in the prolonged exposure group, and 38% in the relaxation group. Attrition was highest in the relaxation group (34%), followed by the prolonged exposure group (29%), with only 15% of those in the ITP group not completing the 14-week program.

Hagenaars and van Minnen (2010) reported that a standard prolonged exposure treatment produced PTG outcomes in the areas of new possibilities and personal strength, and that PTG was negatively related to PTSD symptoms. It is unclear what aspect of the therapy may have accounted for these gains, although a successful experience with prolonged exposure (i.e., reducing symptoms such as anxiety) could be seen to result in people feeling stronger and opening up to new possibilities for living their lives.

Although there have been many reports of PTG among military people (e.g., Bush, Skopp, McCann, & Luxton, 2011; Elder, Domino, Rentz, & Mata-Galán, 2017; McLean et al., 2013), only a few studies have assessed the effect of interventions. One study, designed to address combat stress injuries in active-duty military personnel, evaluated the effects of a novel exposure-based intervention (Gray et al., 2012). It addressed difficulties specific to the military, such as moral injury and traumatic loss. A total of 44 Marines enrolled in a program called Adaptive Disclosure. The main goal was to share and process memories of war zone experiences in a therapeutic manner. Therapy consisted of six 90-minute weekly sessions. PTGI was assessed pre- and post-intervention, and results showed an increase in PTG scores.

CBT is recommended by various treatment guidelines such as the National Institute for Clinical Excellence (see Kar, 2011, for review). More recently, the treatment effects of CBT on PTG have been examined, based on the part of the PTG model that indicates that cognitive restructuring strategies are likely to foster PTG (Roepke, 2015). One study, for example, tested the effects of an internet-based CBT intervention on PTG by randomly assigning traumatized participants to one of two groups—a treatment group and a wait-list control group (Knaevelsrud, Liedl, & Maercker, 2010). Those in the treatment group were given two weekly 45-minute writing assignments over a five-week period. Cognitive restructuring, such as directly questioning whether there was anything positive the participant might have learned from their traumatic experience, was the focus. Therapy consisted of three phases: self-confrontation (e.g., participants were instructed to describe the traumatic event thoroughly in the present tense to increase the effect of the exposure), cognitive reconstruction (e.g., participants were instructed to write a supportive letter to an imaginary friend who had been through the same experience), and social sharing (e.g., participants were asked to summarize what happened to them, reflect on the therapeutic process and describe how they will cope now and in the future). Comparison of pre-intervention and post-intervention data indicated a significant increase in PTG for the treatment group. In addition, changes in intrusions significantly predicted PTG at the end of treatment, indicating that reducing intrusions is likely to contribute to PTG.

Dolbier, Jaggars, and Steinhardt (2010) tested the effects of a resilience intervention program by randomly assigning participants to an intervention or to a wait-list control group. The program consisted of four weekly two-hour sessions, including CBT. Those who participated in the intervention showed greater increases in total PTGI compared with the control group. In addition, moderate effects of the intervention were found for the PTG domains of appreciation of life, personal strength, and new possibilities, whereas small effects were found for spiritual change and the relating to others domains. The authors suggested that their intervention facilitated cognitive and emotional processing, personal resources, and psychological functioning (e.g., resilience, self-leadership, self-esteem, and decrease in depressive symptoms), which in turn may have fostered PTG.

Wagner and her colleagues (2016) investigated the effects of Cognitive-Behavioral Conjoint Therapy (CBCT) in PTG among intimate couples (one partner in each couple had to meet diagnostic criteria for PTSD due to sexual assault, combat, and so on). CBCT consists of three phases with 15 sessions (Monson & Fredman, 2012). The first phase involves psycho-education about PTSD symptoms and relationships. The second phase involves improving communication, decreasing emotional numbing or avoidance, and increasing relationship satisfaction. The third phase includes making meaning of the traumatic event by reevaluating it to arrive at an adaptive interpretation of the event. Researchers examined longitudinal changes in PTG by comparing those who were in CBCT and those who were in waitlist. They found that participation in the CBCT led to a moderate effect size increase in PTG. Because only one member of the dyad had PTSD and thus responded to PTGI, we cannot know how the partner felt by participating in the CBCT. However, this study demonstrated that CBCT designed for PTSD could facilitate PTG despite the relatively brief direct focus on PTG.

Other studies have focused on the effects of CBT on benefit finding. Penedo et al. (2006) found that CBT fostered benefit finding and quality of life, mediated by the development of stress management skills. Bower and Segerstrom (2004) summarized the possible reasons why CBT or CBSM (Cognitive-Behavioral Stress Management) can foster benefit finding. They suggested that one important function of CBSM is to provide a supportive and structured context for cognitive processing that makes it more likely to resolve positively by fostering emotional expression and cognitive processing, and by training people in skills, such as how to enhance social support, promote a reconsideration of the direction of one's life, engage in meaningful activities, increase an ability to adjust to events that cannot be changed, cultivate positive change in self-view, and use effective coping strategies.

Overall, these studies have supported the positive effects of CBT on PTG. A meta-cognitive stance, where one is able to observe the process of thoughts while directly engaging in the process of thinking, seems to facilitate the dialectical thoughts that are important to develop PTG (Tedeschi & Blevins, 2015). Future research is needed to examine the conditions under which CBT is likely to foster PTG. For example, one study testing the effects of prolonged exposure therapy on PTG found that pre-treatment PTG in the domain of appreciation of life predicted better treatment outcomes after controlling for pre-treatment level of PTSD symptoms (Hagenaars & van Minnen, 2010). It is possible that pre-trauma characteristics and pre-intervention (i.e., soon after the traumatic experiences) characteristics may also impact the effects of CBT on PTG. A study with motor vehicle accident survivors, for instance, suggested that CBT was effective in reducing PTSD but not in promoting PTG (Zoellner, Rabe, Karl, & Maercker, 2010). However, because that data showed increases in two of the PTG domains (i.e., new possibilities and personal strength), the precise effect of intervention may vary depending on the domain of PTG. For example, the spiritual change domain may be less affected by CBT than the other PTG domains such as personal strength (Roepke, 2015). Kar (2011) pointed out that in spite of many reports of the efficacy of CBT on reduction of PTSD symptoms, non-response to CBT for PTSD can be as high as 50%.

Other forms of treatment in their "pure" version may also be expected to enhance PTG. Narrative therapy (Meichenbaum, 2006; Neimeyer, 2006) and logotherapy (Tedeschi & Riffle, 2016) focus on the development of new meanings, which is also central to the facilitation of PTG. Integration of cognitive, narrative, and existential approaches in the PTG intervention model may optimize the elements of the therapies that are most effective in trauma treatment, especially when they are offered in the spirit of expert companionship and in environments that allow persons who have experienced traumatic events to engage the PTG process in a concentrated, reflected fashion.

## PTG in Narrative Therapy and Expressive Therapy

The important role that narrative plays in the development of PTG has been emphasized since the beginning of work in this area. The description of events by the individual who has experienced them can help to identify PTG. Clinical interventions can be considered as an iterative process of narrative development that reveals new details and perspectives that allow for PTG (Calhoun & Tedeschi, 1999). Narrative and expressive therapies have been used to promote meaning reconstruction, support emotional and cognitive processing, generate insight, and foster PTG. Problem-saturated narratives are deconstructed with a therapist or expert companion and then co-authored or co-constructed in a manner in which the development of a new "sense of myself" is achieved. There are many layers to this therapeutic approach to working with people who have experienced chronic and multiple traumas that center around helping a person reconnect with or reconstruct that which they value in life and validating that person's values and goals for the future (White, 2004).

One study tested the effects of a brief three-session version of an approach to narrative therapy that included exposure in a sample of traumatized Iraqi refugees (Hijazi et al., 2014). The intervention was intended to enhance the construction of detailed life stories, but with a focus on the traumatic circumstances. Session 1 began with psycho-education. Participants met a therapist one-on-one in a private room and constructed a chronological narrative of his or her life, starting with highlights of childhood and then focusing on traumatic experiences they had during adulthood. They were encouraged to describe sensory, cognitive, and emotional experiences related to their trauma. While participants were narrating, the therapist handwrote the story and later fully transcribed it. In Session 2, participants revised or enhanced their transcribed narrative while the therapist was reading it aloud. The process of constructing the life narrative continued, focusing on processing traumatic experiences. Session 3 involved re-reading the narrative and discussing the participant's fears, goals, and hopes for the future. A hard copy of the narrative was given to the participant at the end. Results indicated that those who received narrative exposure therapy reported greater PTG at two-month and four-month follow-ups.

Emotional disclosure seems effective in facilitating PTG regardless of the different methods used. One study compared the level of PTG in four disclosure conditions (written, talking privately to a tape recorder, talking to a passive listener, talking to an active facilitator) and control conditions (Slavin-Spenny, Cohen, Oberleithner, & Lumley, 2011). All groups had one 30-minute session. After six weeks, those who participated in the disclosure groups showed higher PTG than those in controls; however, no differences were observed between the four disclosure groups. The effects of disclosure were evident in four (personal strength, new possibilities, relating to others, and appreciation of life) out of the five PTG domains. Another study using an internet-based expressive writing exercise confirmed that PTG was increased from baseline to an eight-week follow-up in the expressive writing group (Stockton, Joseph, & Hunt, 2014).

A study assessed the effects of expressive writing on PTG (Smyth, Hockemeyer, & Tulloch, 2008). This study included 25 people with a verified diagnosis of PTSD—11 men with PTSD resulting from war or combat experiences and 14 women with PTSD resulting from sexual assault. They were randomly assigned into either an expressive writing condition (they were instructed to write about their traumatic event) or to a placebo control condition (they were instructed to write about a neutral topic). Results indicated that there were no significant group differences in the two PTG domains, spiritual change and relating to others. However, differences were observed in the new possibilities, personal strength, and appreciation of life domains, with those in the expressive writing about their trauma condition scoring higher levels of PTG than those in the neutral condition.

It is important to note that the content, but not necessarily the procedure, of disclosure is likely to affect PTG. Ullrich and Lutgendorf (2002) compared growth among three groups—a group focusing on emotions related to a trauma, a group focusing on cognitions and emotions related to a trauma, and one in which they wrote factually about media events (control condition). Results indicated that growth was higher in those who focused on both cognitions and emotions related to trauma than in the other two conditions.

Narrative reconstruction has been shown to be effective in developing PTG in older traumatized persons who may suffer from memory problems. Knaevelsrud et al. (2014) developed integrative testimonial therapy, an internet-based, therapist-assisted CBT approach designed to obtain a detailed testimony of an individual's traumatic experience and integrate this testimony in a resource-oriented biographical narrative. The participants (65 to 85 years old), who had experienced World War II and also showed PTSD symptoms, were asked to complete two 45-minute writing assignments per week during a six-week period. Of a total of 11 essays completed, the first seven were based on the Erikson's psychosocial phases (e.g., childhood, puberty). To encourage narrative reconstruction, participants received historical memory cues and typical developmental experience cues. Of the remaining four essays, two were focused on traumatic events, and two were focused on writing a support letter to their younger self from their current perspective as a trauma survivor. At the post-intervention and at the three-month follow-up, PTGI scores were higher than baseline scores, indicating that the use of the biographical narrative reconstruction was helpful in fostering PTG.

A narrative intervention based on fairy tales was used in group therapy with 21 women who had been diagnosed with an adjustment disorder (Ruini, Masoni, Ottolini, & Ferrari, 2014). The researchers (clinicians) included the appreciation of life and personal strength items from the PTGI, which they administered pre- and post-therapy program. Both of these domains of PTG significantly increased, as did personal growth and self-acceptance, as measured by Ryff's Psychological Well-being Scale. Symptoms of anxiety also significantly decreased. Participants explained that the changes they reported were because they learned to accept that stress is part of life and that the stories they shared in the group normalized their experiences. They became aware of their strengths and capacity to deal with difficulty, and they developed a new sense of meaning.

Following the devastating earthquake in Haiti in 2010, when 230,000 people were killed, many people went to provide physical and psychological assistance to those who survived. Two clinicians and researchers developed "Trauma Narrative Treatment" (Lane, Myers, Hill, & Lane, 2016, p. 567), a treatment created to suit that specific cultural context. They delivered it in groups to local leaders. The authors understood the need to be cognizant of the possibility of PTG in the development of a new life story in order to promote growth as well as to reduce PTSD symptoms. One group of teachers and paraprofessionals agreed to participate in a pre- and post-test evaluation of the impact the approach had on symptoms of PTSD. Symptoms were reduced and feedback from participants indicated the intervention had helped them to develop a new and positive narrative, with themes akin to those of PTG. These studies have demonstrated that (re)constructing narratives can help lead to PTG experiences.

## Activity-Based Therapies and PTG

It is only recently that research has been undertaken to investigate the effects of activity-based therapies (e.g., art therapy, physical activity) on PTG. Art therapy has been used to manage stress symptoms and to facilitate the process of psychological readjustment after traumatic events (Wood, Molassiotis, & Payne, 2011). Art therapy is also related to self-disclosure and emotional expression, and it can allow expressions of non-verbal aspects of traumatic experiences or simply be an additional way to express and communicate internal experiences. Singer et al. (2012), for example, used art therapy over a period of 22 weeks with patients who had been diagnosed with hematological malignancies. Those who were assigned to the intervention condition were first asked to perform simple drawing tasks. Patients then started gradually exploring and expressing their feelings by drawing their current mood and by painting a self-portrait. In the final phase of the program, patients were encouraged to create a book containing, for example, their ideas about the disease and their coping processes. The Stress-Related Growth Scale was administered at pre- and post-intervention to assess the effects. Their results, however, did not yield a significant difference, providing no evidence for a positive effect of art therapy on growth although the authors had assumed that art therapy would foster positive changes. Since their hypotheses were not supported, they provided several possible reasons why their data did not yield significant results, including the following: non-randomized trial, sample differences between intervention and control groups at baseline, measurement issues, and a lack of assessment of psychological struggle that is key in PTG.

However, art therapy was found to be useful in a younger population. Mohr (2014) described an art-therapy intervention with a group of youth survivors who had experienced an earthquake in Peru, three years before the intervention. The art therapy included a nine-month intervention with the technique of photo elicitation, followed by art making and community sharing. Many participants noted that they had developed a stronger sense of life purpose from helping others and a heightened sense of empathy, as well as honoring the experience and developing a sense of freedom. It is important to note, however, that this study did not look at the "direct effects" of art therapy on PTG, because there was no control condition and no systematic pre/post interview.

The potential coexistence between "doing something new" and PTG can be found in a study investigating the perceived influence of an exercise intervention with cancer survivors (Hefferon, Grealy, & Mutrie, 2008). Participants reported that they viewed exercise as an integral part of their rehabilitation and PTG processes. The class helped the participants move away from self-pity and despair. It also seemed to foster support in a safe environment, exploring body functions, meeting new role models, and engaging in new health behaviors, which in turn fostered a sense of responsibility for their own health. This study did not have a control condition or pre- and post-assessment; thus, we cannot say attending the exercising program fostered PTG, but we know at least that their participants attributed much of their PTG to the experience of participating in group-based physical activity.

Another program for cancer patients compared a mindfulness stress reduction program with a creative arts program (Garland, Carlson, Cook, Lansdell, & Speca, 2007). There were 44 people in the creative arts program, which involved movement to music, creative writing, drawing, and journaling, and 60 people in the mindfulness program. The PTGI was included in a battery that was completed pre- and post- the respective programs. Significant differences in PTG were found between the time points in both programs. Total PTGI scores increased on the following factors: relating to others, personal strength, and new possibilities.

In a currently unpublished study using a rapid ethnographic methodology, an art therapy program (Art to Healing) was conducted with 27 young women (ages 13–22) who had been rescued from commercial sexual exploitation in Nepal (Volgin, Shakespeare-Finch, & Shochet, under review). The program focused on women's sexual health rather than on the extreme trauma the young women had experienced. This focus is particularly relevant in a cultural context where women and girls are generally regarded as second-class citizens. Throughout the six-week period, the ethnographer (Volgin) observed changes in the participants. While there were significant somatic complaints and visible intense distress initially, after the program the girls and women gained significant strength, shifted perceptions of self-worth, developed compassion for others, and demonstrated a positive future orientation. For example, one girl said, "I want to go to remote villages and teach women they are not weak and that they are strong" and another said, "I want to work with child's rights." Another participant said, "I had already forgotten what a laugh or smile is and it is me that has to understand it." What was concluded was that a strengths-based creative arts program, delivered in a safe group environment, can facilitate positive change, and such changes may foster PTG.

Following years of work with women who had been rescued from sex trafficking in Asia, Tan (2012) suggested that art and dance therapies can play an important role in facilitating PTG. In the model of PTG (Calhoun & Tedeschi, 2013) disclosure about trauma that is supported by others plays an important role. Alternative therapies, such as creating art and art therapy, can be effective in promoting PTG. Such activities can provide a way for a people to share their responses to traumatic events (Gantt & Tinnin, 2009). Bloom (1998) describes how art can be a vehicle to healing and change in communities and larger groups. Social change can be created through the voices of artists who are able to influence culture through their work.

As mentioned earlier in the description of the Boulder Crest Retreat program, activity-based therapies will likely be most effective in promoting PTG when they are integrated into a program that has the PTG model at its core. These therapies can then be utilized to advance particular aspects of the PTG process, such as emotion regulation, disclosure, or narrative development in a more effective sequencing. Using activity-based therapies alone and without a PTG-context, an expert companionship may limit their usefulness in facilitating growth.

## PTG Approaches to Cancer Care

As survival rates have continued to improve with advances in medical care, the need for a variety of psychosocial interventions, for both patients and their families, has received increasing attention (Fawzy, Fawzy, Arndt, & Pasnau, 1995; Gauthier & Gagliese, 2012). These interventions are designed to decrease or manage the negatives (e.g., a sense of helplessness, hopelessness, anxiety, depression, fatigue, pain) and increase the positives (e.g., a sense of increased support, self-care, self-efficacy, coping). The outcome measures used to evaluate the efficacy of such interventions include coping skills, affective state, quality of life, knowledge regarding disease and treatment, compliance, physical status, recurrence, and survival (Fawzy et al., 1995). A growing body of literature has also looked at PTG in the experience of cancer patients. For example, a recent study considered age, stress, and the negative effects of cancer on PTG in 175 women who had been newly diagnosed with breast cancer (Boyle, Stanton, Ganz, & Bower, 2017). Higher levels of negative cancer impacts and having undergone chemotherapy were both related to PTG, but only for older women when age was kept as a continuous variable. In younger women, PTG was predicted by greater use of approach-oriented coping strategies, and there was no association found between negative impacts of cancer and PTG. One recent study examined the relationships between distress and PTG in women with breast cancer across 5 time points over an 18-month period (Groarke, Curtis, Groarke, Hogan, Gibbons, & Kerin, 2017). The researchers demonstrated that the greater cancer-specific stress at diagnosis predicted higher PTG six months later, which in turn was associated with subsequent reduction in both cancer-specific stress and global stress. Thus, PTG can be an important factor in managing stress in the long run. Next, we discuss why it is important to integrate PTG into cancer care, recognizing rather common and useful experience of PTG in cancer patients without recommending that PTG itself should necessarily be set as a specific goal of such interventions.

First, PTG should be integrated because it closely connects with physiological elements and the immune system. Bower and Segerstrom (2004) summarized how the experience of finding benefit or meaning from a cancer experience may be translated into immune change. They suggested five psychological mechanisms as important to include in programs to support people with cancer and their families. These were: (1) changed perspectives of future stress from threat to challenge, (2) developing more intimate, stronger relationships or social support, (3) setting and engaging in more meaningful life goals, (4) increased positive emotions, and (5) education regarding the direct relationships between cognitive changes and physiological changes. Meta-analyses have shown (Sawyer, Ayers, & Field, 2010; Shand, Cowlishaw, Brooker, Burney, & Ricciardelli, 2015) that the role of PTG is not necessarily to directly alleviate symptoms of distress, but to guide people in understanding the wide variety of mediators, which in turn helps cancer survivors to integrate their illness into their new identity while managing the symptoms. Qualitative study also emphasizes the important role of body in PTG processes among cancer patients (Hefferon, Grealy, & Mutrie, 2010), because they reported having a new awareness of their body, a more positive relationship with their body, developing a novel ability to listen to their body, and being able to see one's body as a barometer to self-monitor while experiencing PTG. When the researchers asked cancer survivors who participated in a group intervention program during rehabilitation about body awareness, they attributed their PTG to the program (Hefferon et al., 2008), indicating the inseparable relationship between PTG and physical changes.

Second, PTG should be integrated into support programs because it can serve as a motivator for cancer survivors to continue commitment to future healthcare. Milam et al. (2015), for instance, assessed the factors associated with maintaining cancer-related follow-up care among childhood cancer survivors. They found that PTG was marginally associated with the previous receipt of follow-up care but, perhaps more importantly, PTG was associated with the intent to seek follow-up care. Follow-up care is critical for cancer survivors, so if PTG can be a resource for optimizing health behaviors and for making a long-term commitment, it should be integrated. As Milam et al. (2015) suggested, a brief strengths-based case-management intervention for cancer patients, aiming for self-efficacy and PTG, should be offered.

Third, PTG should be integrated because it can be fostered by interventions that are not designed explicitly to lead to PTG. For example, Antoni et al. (2001) assessed the effects of a ten-week group cognitive-behavioral stress management program for women diagnosed at stage II or below. The intervention was focused on stress reduction, effective coping strategies, emotional expression, and social support, however, the authors also included the possibility of benefit finding. Although the research was not originally focused on benefit finding, their results indicated that the intervention fostered benefit finding and the effect remained at a three-month follow-up. The authors suggested that their intervention fostered benefit finding because it resulted in "cognitive restructuring; anger management and assertion training, leading to better communication with significant others; and the positive experience of sharing difficulties and victories with other patients in a mutually supportive group environment" (Antoni et al., 2001, p. 28). Interestingly, benefit finding was also associated with emotional processing (i.e., being able to take time to figure out one's own feeling and emotions) in their study, which may also be important for cancer patients. If these researchers did not pay attention to the possibilities of positive outcomes, these findings might have been overlooked.

Fourth, PTG should be integrated into cancer support programs because cancer patients often show changes in their response to the disease and its treatment several months or years after treatment. A recent study identified four different post-cancer treatment adaptation profiles: distressed, resistant, constructive growth, and struggling growth, in a sample of female breast cancer patients (Pat-Horenczyk et al., 2016). Both types of growth were related to cognitive flexibility, so the distinction between struggling and constructive growth was made based on concurrent level of distress and types of coping. Constructive growth was characterized by lower levels of distress and lower endorsement of negative coping strategies, whereas struggling growth was characterized by higher level of distress and higher endorsement of negative coping strategies. Interestingly, the authors found that both distressed and resistant groups showed fairly stable trajectories, while the majority of transitions between these different adaptation profiles, particularly shifts toward PTG, occurred between 6 and 12 months after treatment. The authors concluded that during the first year after completing cancer treatment, women may be most open to change, and practitioners should carefully consider timing and other personal factors in promoting change.

A longitudinal study with 312 Taiwanese women who had surgery for breast cancer was conducted by Wang and colleagues (2017). These researchers collected data about PTG, distress, and vulnerability at five time points from day 1 to 24 months post-surgery. Results demonstrated a significant relationship over time, with increased levels of PTG being predictive of lower levels of distress. PTG was found to be a buffer against vulnerability that leads to distress, but this was only the case in women who had undergone a mastectomy. No interaction effect between PTG, vulnerability, and distress was found in women who had undergone a lumpectomy. PTGI scores remained stable across time, as did perceptions of vulnerability, whereas distress decreased somewhat. For many people, PTG may not be realized shortly after a highly challenging experience, but descriptive data provided in this study suggests that was not the case for some in this group of women with cancer, who were able to report PTG in the early phases of their cancer experience.

Morris et al. (2014) discussed the importance of language in peer support groups for people who have had cancer, and sought to identify influences on developing the identity of a "survivor," "victim," or other identities in relation to their cancer. These researchers conducted two studies—one with 514 men participating in a prostate cancer peer support program and the other with 160 women participating in an online breast cancer support group. In the prostate cancer group, measures included cancer identity, the PTGI, ERRI, CBI, threat appraisal, and peer support factors (connection and seeking cancer understanding through peers). More than half of the group saw themselves as people who have/had cancer and only 35% saw themselves as cancer survivors. In order to determine which factors were predictive of cancer identity, demographic variables and time since diagnosis were entered into step one of a stepwise logistic regression. None of these variables were significant predictors of identity. The remainder of the measures were entered into a step two. Understanding cancer through peers, lower levels of threat appraisal, and deliberate rumination were significant predictors of a survivor identity. Although PTG correlated with a survivor identity, it marginally failed to reach statistical significance in the regression ($p = .052$). In the second study, women who were within three years of a breast cancer diagnosis were randomly allocated into two conditions—there were six groups of approximately 14 women allocated to an online support group and another six groups to an enhanced prosocial online support group. Data collection methods used included pre- and post-intervention self-report measures and interviews. Half of the women in this study identified as survivors, or used other terms denoting a survivor mentality, such as sur-thriver and cancer warrior. Similar to the men with prostate cancer, neither time since diagnosis, age, nor cancer stage were related to survivor identity. Seeing oneself as a survivor was related to feelings of connection and emotional belonging to the group, and to cognitive growth. These findings suggest that although a survivor identity was related to positive aspects of peer support and to PTG, less than half of these participants wanted to identify themselves as a cancer survivor; using such terms with cancer patients should thus be done only with careful consideration. McGrath and Holewa (2012) interviewed 50 people who had a diagnosis of hematological malignancy. The majority of people in their study actively disliked the term survivor. As one person said, "survivor is an adjective, not a person" (p. 3290).

Peer support groups aimed at enhancing well-being are usually in the form of discussions in person or online. But Morris, Campbell, Dwyer, Dunn, and Chambers (2011) sought to explore if a challenge-oriented peer support group could enhance well-being and PTG. The Amazon Heart Thunder group was devised to offer an alternative to discussion-based peer support groups for women who had experienced breast cancer. In this case, 27 women from around the world took a ten-day ride on Harley-Davidson motorcycles in Australia, the USA, and/or the UK. An online discussion group was set up six months prior to the ride/s to allow the women to connect with each other and share experiences. Analyzing interview transcripts from before and after the rides using a phenomenological framework, PTG was evident in the transcripts of all women following the ride. Changes were reported in enhanced positive perceptions of themselves, new meaningful relationships, a new appreciation for (living) life, and in a future orientation that was characterized by seizing new opportunities. For example, one woman said, "I can ride a Harley on the Sydney Harbour Bridge, I can do that. There's not much I can't do now," and another said, "it [cancer] changes your perspective about what is important in life" (p. 670). These results are consistent with those found in breast cancer survivors ($N = 20$) who participated in a dragon boat racing program (Sabiston, McDonough, & Crocker, 2007). All of the participants reported PTG experiences to some degree predominantly in personal strength (89%), new and closer relationships (75%), new possibilities (75%) and appreciation of life (65%).

Ramos and colleagues (2017) designed a support group specifically based on the PTG process model in order to determine if such an approach could enhance PTG in breast cancer survivors. This structured group experience included sessions that followed the PTG model and educated the participants about PTG. The PTG groups were offered to 58 women, while 147 women participated in support groups that did not follow the PTG model. Compared to the control group, the PTG intervention group reported more PTG with core beliefs challenged and intrusive rumination acting as moderators.

Again, it is important to emphasize that we are not recommending that PTG should be added as the sole goal of the intervention. It is possible to use cancer diagnosis and treatment as a "teachable moment" for promoting health behavior change (Jacobsen & Andrykowski, 2015), and integrating PTG into the existing cancer care programs seems desirable. On the other hand, support groups may not be indicated for all patients. For example, Matsui and Taku (2016) pointed out that we often assume regardless of cultural background or personality that cancer survivors will receive benefit from actively interacting with others initiated by help-seeking behaviors; however, it may not be effective for patients with high social inhibition or introverted personality, as well as collectivistic cultural characteristics.

## PTG in Crisis Intervention

PTG can be facilitated in both proactive and reactive ways. For example, for those who work in roles that expose them to crisis and potentially traumatic events commonly (e.g., police, paramedics, firefighters), psycho-education, using a strengths-based approach can be beneficial in helping identify strategies and resources for self-care; learning about signs and symptoms of distress, common responses to trauma, and other highly challenging events; and identifying personal strengths and resources that are likely to help negotiate post-exposure paths. However, when proactive approaches to trauma are considered, we may be intervening to build resilience rather than to allow for the development of PTG. If people are better able to adapt to future trauma, they will be less likely to experience challenge to core beliefs and PTG. However, both may be possible to facilitate in a pre-trauma training program, where strategies for responding to trauma are enhanced in a way that allows for the kind of perspective-taking and deliberate rumination that allows for PTG. People might be encouraged to respond in ways that optimize positive change, placing them at the top of the inverted U-shaped curve that may characterize the distress–PTG relationship.

An example of a hybrid resilience–PTG intervention was described by Shochet et al. (2011). Using a randomized control design to test the effectiveness of a resilience building intervention designed for newly recruited police officers, these researchers explicitly included a module about PTG in their seven-week program. The module used a number of techniques, including video of an interview with an experienced officer, workbook exercises (e.g., identifying PTG themes in the video), and self-reflection regarding previous successful ways the recruits had dealt with challenging events. Data from three time points (pre-program, post-program, and six months post-baseline) was analyzed using linear mixed models. Significant differences were found between participants in the intervention group compared to the psycho-education as usual group, with increases in total PTGI scores and in all five PTGI factors (Shakespeare-Finch, Schweitzer, King, & Brough, 2014). Other emergency service organizations have adopted psycho-education programs and crisis response interventions that are very comprehensive and include activities and discussions about PTG. According to Scully (2011), such an approach has increased mental health and decreased psychological injury in paramedics.

In the above situations, the potential stressors associated with crisis work are usually known, and the people who work in high risk occupations have self-selected for the role. However, for most people, traumatic events and crises are not expected. Consider the experience of a natural disaster: an earthquake or flood. Disasters impact individuals and entire communities. The way in which a community, its leaders, such as politicians, and the media respond can impact the way people negotiate the crisis at the time and in the aftermath. Maximizing the potential for resilience and PTG involves practical, cognitive, and emotional responses. Many governing bodies have guidelines that involve effective communication (people can deal better with bad news than not knowing the state of things), practical and emotional support, validation of emotional expression, identifying coping strategies and resources, and providing information about and access to resources (e.g., Emergency Management Australia, 2004).

Keogh, Apan, Mushtaq, King, and Thomas (2011) conducted a quantitative and qualitative study ($N = 91$) in an area that had experienced devastating floods. The researchers found the participants to be extremely resilient. Factors that fostered the presence of mental health were a sense of belonging in the community, community and organizational cooperation, strong social networks, and a sense of responsibility for preparedness and response to the disasters. These factors that promoted mental health have also been found to be important in promoting PTG. The common thread is involvement in the community: participating in the disaster response. Karanci and Acarturk (2005) conducted research with 200 people who experienced the magnitude 7.4 earthquake that shook Marmara, Turkey and took more than 17,000 lives. The sample comprised two groups: 100 people were volunteer responders to the earthquake and the other 100 were not. All people were residents of the impact zone. PTG was predicted by optimistic and problem-solving approaches, perceived social support, and a fatalistic coping style. People from the worst hit areas reported significantly more growth than those in lighter hit areas. After controlling for distress, severity of exposure, and coping strategies, being a member of the volunteer response team was also a significant predictor of growth.

Peer supporters, whether fellow firefighters (e.g., Armstrong, Shakespeare-Finch, & Shochet, 2014), people from refugee backgrounds (e.g., Shakespeare-Finch & Wickham, 2010), the partner of a person with cancer (e.g., Weiss, 2002), or emergency medical personnel (Scully, 2011) have elevated levels of mental health when compared to non-peer supporter counterparts, and are viewed by others as important to psychological well-being.

Public media also has an important role to play as a conduit for information during a disaster but also in connecting people and setting the tone for the way in which the broader community responds to the crisis. Taylor, Wells, Howell, and Raphael (2012) conducted an online research project about social media use during a number of natural disasters and ways in which social media platforms may assist in the promotion of mental health in a context of crisis. Participants ($N = 1146$) reported using both social media and more traditional outlets to remain informed, but used them in different ways. For example, social media often acted as a conduit for official information to reach a broader audience, but it had a much more profound impact on mental health through generating a sense of community in the virtual space, connections with others, a feeling of support and of supporting others, usefulness, and empowerment.

# CHAPTER 17

# Posttraumatic Growth Beyond the Individual

Although PTG has been studied primarily as an experience of individuals, there have been a number of studies that indicate that PTG experienced in an individual can affect the experience of close others. Some kind of transmission of PTG by the influence of those experiencing it may even extend beyond close others to larger groups or social systems, particularly when PTG has initiated an active motivation to exert social influence.

## Partners of Trauma Survivors and PTG

There have been many reports of PTG experiences by the partners of cancer survivors. Weiss (2002), for example, examined PTG among husbands whose wives were diagnosed with breast cancer. The results, using open-ended questions, indicated that 88% of husbands (and 98% of the wives) reported significant, long-lasting positive changes in their lives (e.g., "no longer taking life and health for granted"). Weiss (2002) also used the PTGI by modifying the instruction so the crisis was defined as "your wife's breast cancer." The total PTGI score was 46.00 ($SD = 22.83$) for husbands, and 60.21 ($SD = 18.81$) for wives. Therefore, the degree of PTG was not as high as their wives' PTG; however, partners of breast cancer survivors did report PTG. The same patterns have been found in a longitudinal study (Manne, Ostroff, Winkel, Goldstein, Fox, & Grana, 2004). Manne and colleagues examined PTG among female breast cancer survivors and their partners at three time points spaced nine months apart. On average, partners' PTG increased significantly over time; however, their PTG level was not as high as their partners' (female breast cancer survivors') PTG.

Similar findings have been reported when looking at a wider variety of cancer survivors and their partners. Zwahlen, Hagenbuch, Carley, Jenewein, and Buchi (2010) examined the levels of PTG in male cancer patients and their female partners, as well as in female cancer patients and their male partners, to take biological sex into consideration. Their results indicated that male partners did experience PTG; however, the level was significantly lower than their partners, that is, female cancer patients. This tendency was observed in females whose partners (i.e., male patients) were diagnosed with cancer, but only in one PTG domain (i.e., new possibilities). In the other four domains, there were no differences between male patients and their female partners. This is consistent with a study examining PTG in male patients who were treated for prostate cancer and the perspectives of their female partners (Thornton & Perez, 2006). In this study, there were no differences in the level of PTG (total and five subscales) between male patients and their female partners. From these studies, it appears that cancer patients' partners do experience PTG in all five domains. However, if partners are males, their PTG level is not as high as their female partners (cancer survivors)' PTG. If partners are females, their PTG level is as high as their male partners (cancer survivors)' PTG, suggesting a fundamental sex difference in PTG levels. However, many more controlled designs are required before drawing a conclusion about biological sex and the likelihood of experiencing PTG. The best statistical solutions to predicting the potential for PTG are complex and beyond the attribution of one individual difference factor.

Elliot, Scott, Monsour, and Nuwayhid (2015) conducted a mixed method investigation of six couples in which the male partner had been undergoing treatment for advanced prostate cancer. Data included video of couple interaction, interviews, and survey measures. While there were myriad stressors reported, as would be expected, the majority of couples reported high levels of satisfaction with their life and intimate relationship, as well as resilience. Satisfaction was related to coping strategies, having faith in the medical profession, relationship closeness, and having negotiated past experiences of cancer. This latter factor could be taken to indicate that previous experiences had established dyadic ways of coping with cancer and associated treatments and perhaps a sense of personal strength in their capacity to cope, having had those earlier experiences.

In what was proposed to be the first couples-based intervention with a focus on promoting PTG in women with breast cancer and their partners, a pilot study with 14 couples was conducted to assess the impact of a couples-based intervention aimed at relationship enhancement (Baucom et al., 2009). Couples were assigned to the intervention tailored to the population or a treatment as usual condition that comprised providing information about community resources available for people with breast cancer. Amongst a battery of tests, the PTGI, a measure of marital satisfaction, and measures of distress, self-image, and pain were used pre- and post- interventions and at a one-year follow-up. Although there were no significant differences in PTGI scores between the intervention groups, scores were significantly higher post-intervention and were higher in the women than in their male partners. For example, women had PTGI scores with a mean of 50.13 prior to the tailored intervention ($SD = 31.45$), and 65.29 post-intervention ($SD = 26.98$), whereas the male partners' scores provided a mean of 43.88 ($SD = 21.58$) before the intervention and 49.00 ($SD = 18.93$) and 52.86 ($SD = 20.46$) post-intervention. PTGI scores for both partners dipped slightly at the one-year follow-up. It is interesting to note that changes in women's scores in the treatment as usual condition were not as dramatic as the tailored intervention and that baseline measures in the intervention group were a lot lower than baseline in the control group ($M = 50.13$ vs 61.00).

Heinrichs, Zimmerman, Huber, Herschbach, and Russell (2012) conducted a randomized controlled trial of a cancer adaptation program for couples in

Germany with 72 couples in which the woman had breast or gynecological cancer. The primary difference between the control and intervention groups was the intervention group specifically included teaching dyadic skills. Psychological distress, relationship satisfaction, communication, and PTG were measured pre- and post-intervention. Consistent with other research in this area and in PTG more broadly, all couples experienced PTG, but women's scores were higher than their male partners. While PTGI scores increased for both partners in the intervention group with a dyadic focus, women in the control group showed a slight decrease in scores in the short term. However, at the 16-month follow-up intervention differences disappeared, with continued increases in PTG across groups. This study has implications for interventions, including a question about if left to their own devices, couples would recover from the high levels of distress initially identified in the participants in this study. Results did demonstrate short-term increases in functioning, which may have value in itself.

## Relationships Between Siblings' PTG Scores

As Picoraro, Womer, Kazak, and Feudtner (2014) pointed out, PTG in siblings and other family members has not been well studied. However, there is evidence in the literature that siblings of children experiencing traumatic circumstances do experience PTG. Sanders and Szymanski (2013) investigated PTG for siblings of people who were diagnosed with a mental disorder. They found that siblings experienced all five domains of PTG. Moreover, the PTG levels among siblings were higher than people in a control group who were asked to reflect on a potentially traumatic event. Kamibeppu et al. (2010) assessed PTG in young adult childhood cancer survivors and their siblings by using the PTGI. Their results showed that siblings reported PTG but not as high as their siblings who were diagnosed with cancer, regardless of gender. They also compared the levels of PTG between siblings and people in a control group (i.e., those with no history of childhood cancer or siblings with any history of cancer), who were asked to reflect on a major stressful life event. Results indicated that, regardless of gender, scores in the appreciation of life domain of the PTGI was higher in siblings of cancer survivors than people in the control group. And, when focusing on females, the total PTGI score and relating to others subscale of the PTGI were also higher in siblings than people in the control group.

Most recently D'Urso, Mastroyannopoulou, and Kirby (2017) conducted interviews with six siblings of children diagnosed with cancer. They couched their research within a PTG framework. Using a thematic analysis approach to the data, both positive and negative experiences were reported. Results indicated three themes: difficulty with emotions, personal development, and strengthened relationships. Difficulty with emotion varied depending on the time since diagnosis and in treatment that was being referred to. For example, the siblings spoke of shock, fear, numbness, and sadness at the time of diagnosis, but for most those feelings eased or changed over the course of treatment. Some children spoke about being jealous of the number of gifts their ill sibling received, or questioning why it was their sibling who was ill and not them. The second theme highlighted increased closeness in the relationships in the family, both with their ill sibling and with their parents and other siblings. The children also spoke about the importance of relationships with people outside the family: with friends, a school counselor, or a mental health professional. The third theme was about increased personal strength; for example, one child said, "I am more confident I think," and another said, "I guess, even though I try to forget about that year, it was the year that made me" (p. 309). Four participants spoke about changed values and future orientations, such as developing an interest in charity work and in helping others in need more generally.

In a study focusing on PTG, coping, and psychological functioning in adolescent cancer patients ($N = 31$), those same variables were assessed in the parents and siblings of the patient (Turner-Sack, Menna, Setchell, Maan, & Cataudella, 2016). The main focus was on PTG, psychological functioning, and coping. The psychological distress scores of both parents and siblings were similar to that of the adolescent cancer survivor. However, PTGI scores were similar in parents and the adolescent who had experienced cancer. Although parent and survivor scores were not significantly different to each other, they were significantly higher than the PTG reported by siblings. There were no significant differences in other measures, including active and avoidant coping and life satisfaction. Neither parent nor sibling PTG was associated with any of the other study variables measured. The coping strategies used by siblings and survivors were similar. The results demonstrated that even younger siblings reported PTG in relation to their brother or sister's cancer diagnosis and treatment. The research also highlighted a need to include the whole family when assessing PTG in adolescents and children in order to gain some insight into aspects of the family system and relationships likely to promote the opportunity to realize PTG. The interaction among elements of the family system is apparent in a study by Stephenson and colleagues (2017). They conducted a longitudinal study across four years with 70 children from 58 different families in which at least one child had a progressive and non-curable genetic, metabolic, or neurological health condition. Over two of those time points, 52 siblings from 43 families completed the PTGI in addition to their mothers. The new possibilities factor of the PTGI completed by mothers was the only dimension associated with higher levels of PTG found to significantly relate to less externalizing and problem behaviors in siblings, but not with internalizing behavior in those children.

## Forgiveness and PTG in Couples

Forgiveness has been identified as a relevant factor to PTG in individuals. Currier, Mallot, Martinez, Sandy, and Neimeyer (2013) assessed forgiveness in three aspects—self-forgiveness, forgiveness of others, and perceived forgiveness from God—and showed that the level of forgiveness was positively correlated with PTG. Especially after experiencing a significant interpersonal transgression, forgiveness may play an important role in PTG. Interpersonal forgiveness is the process through which an individual who has been hurt or wronged by another person releases negative sentiments (e.g., anger, hurt, bitterness, revenge, avoidance) and may adopt more positive or prosocial responses (e.g., empathy, benevolence) toward the offender (Schultz, Tallman, & Altmaier, 2010). In its literal translation, forgiveness is something you *give* to others. This transformational process from unforgiveness into forgiveness may overlap with PTG processes, especially in the domain of relating to others. In continuing relationships where blaming, hurting, and increased hostility might have occurred, a couple may experience PTG by forgiving each other. But it is also possible that a couple decides to take a different path, not necessarily because they do not forgive each other but because they realize that will be the best decision for them, which may also lead to PTG.

There is at least one study that investigated the role of forgiveness in PTG among people who are in continuing relationships. Heintzelman, Murdock, Krycak, and Seay (2014) examined the relationships between forgiveness and PTG in a sample of people who remained in a relationship in which infidelity had occurred longer ago than six months prior. Given that the couples were still together in their study, forgiveness was the only factor that significantly predicted PTG; that is, those who were able to forgive their partners for the infidelity experienced more growth. In this case, the process of forgiving seemed to parallel the process of PTG.

It is important to note, however, that the act of forgiving and PTG are distinct. Although forgiveness is overall considered beneficial to the well-being of the forgiver, in certain contexts, such as abusive relationships, forgiveness may be harmful (Lomas & Ivtzan, 2016). Because there is no absolute criteria for what can be forgiven, what should be forgiven, or who should be forgiven, across contexts, it is possible for people to choose not to forgive because they experience PTG (e.g., realization of what is important). Cobb, Tedeschi, Calhoun, and Cann (2006), for example, have shown that leaving an abusive relationship was positively related to PTG. Thus, this theme can provide another reason why PTG should not be exclusively measured as overt behavior (forgive or not), because the meaning of action will depend on the context. Exemplifying this point further, Laufer, Raz-Hamama, Levine, and Solomon (2009) investigated the role of forgiveness and religiosity as it related to PTG in a sample of 1,482 16-year-olds in Israel. In the youth who identified as secular, PTG was positively related to not forgiving, whereas in the youth who identified as religious, forgiveness was positively related to PTG.

## Research Approaches to Dyad-Level PTG

Some studies have qualitatively investigated PTG at a dyad-level. Mosher and her colleagues (2017) conducted semi-structured interviews with 23 cancer patients and their caregivers and analyzed the data by using thematic analysis. Results produced five overarching themes that reflected the factors of the PTGI, with the exception of the personal strength factor, which was not forthcoming in the interview data, however, increased compassion for others was. Changes in health behaviors were also reported. This is a finding that consistently comes out of the literature when the population under study has experienced a diagnosis of cancer and its associated treatments (e.g., Morris et al., 2012; Sears, Stanton, & Danoff-Burg, 2003). Only a minority of the participants reported no positive changes. When examining dyad-level data, about half of the patients and caregivers reported at least one positive change common to them both. The most common divergence between reports was the patient reporting no positive change in the caregiver whilst the caregiver reported positive changes in themselves. Obviously much of the change people perceive is cognitive and/or emotional, which may not easily be observed in others.

Dyadic perspectives about PTG have also been investigated using quantitative methods. For example, Weiss (2002) examined correlations between the PTGI scores of women who had been diagnosed and treated for breast cancer and their partners' PTGI scores during the same timeframe. Moderate positive correlations between patient and partner scores were documented. Showing similar results of positive and moderate correlations between cancer patients' PTG and their caregivers' own PTG, Moore and her colleagues (2011) provided several explanations. They suggested a possible hypothesis that duration and the proximity of the relationships between patients and caregivers would predict a significant correlation in PTG reports. Alternatively, they suggested that people who experience PTG may be more likely to partner with people likely to experience PTG after a potentially traumatic life event. Moore et al. also considered that the patient or the caregiver may influence others' levels of PTG after a potentially traumatic life event; thus, the research design is confounded and, of course, causal explanations cannot be made using correlational designs. Given the idea that processes involved with developing PTG may be of mutual benefit, several other studies have investigated dyad-level PTG.

There is no consensus regarding how to analyze couple-level data, and researchers have used different analytical methods. Manne et al. (2004), for example, considered two approaches: a mean score approach that averages couples' PTGI scores, and a discrepancy score approach. They used a discrepancy approach where differences between a person's PTGI scores and their partners' PTGI scores were the dependent variable. In this approach, predictors such as a person's intrusion and their partners' intrusion remain at the individual level. In addition to evidence suggesting positive correlations between patients' PTG and their partners' PTG, researchers also found that the discrepancies between patients' and partners' PTG decreased over time if partners used more positive reappraisal. In addition, the patients' PTG exceeded that of the partner if the patient reported fewer physical impairments, whereas patients' PTG was more similar to their partners' PTG if the patient reported more physical impairment. The patients' PTG exceeded that of the partner over time if the partner reported higher emotional expressiveness, whereas patients and partners' PTG became more similar over time if the partner reported less emotional expressiveness. These findings suggest that patients' PTG is not solely an intrapersonal activity, and this more interpersonal aspect is also a core component of the PTG model. Relationships matter. Patients report higher PTG when their partners disclose their own feelings about the experience they are sharing, albeit from different vantage points.

Another study (Zwahlen et al., 2010) used the linear mixed-effect model and a Likelihood Ratio test to assess the random effects of a dyad when considering the gender and role (patient versus partner) of each pair. They found that patients and partners were likely to experience parallel PTG, but the association of PTG in male patients and their female partners was slightly stronger than the association of PTG in female patients and their male partners. This may be a reflection of a frequent finding that females are more likely to report higher levels of PTG than males.

Similarly, Ávila, Coimbra, Park, and Matos (2017) used the dyadic actor-partner interdependence model (APIM) to examine the role in couples of attachment in PTG resulting from breast cancer. By using the APIM, researchers can assess the actor effect (e.g., effects of a person's own attachment on his/her own PTG) and the partner effect (e.g., effects of a person's attachment on his/her partner's PTG) simultaneously. They found that couple-secure emotional exchanges played an important role in predicting PTG—that is, only the partner's security and not his/her own security predicts PTG, regardless of being the patient or the healthy partner. It is interesting to see a greater impact of one's partner's attachment than one's own attachment on PTG, suggesting that the PTG experiences among married and cohabiting couples will largely depend on their partners and thus may require more than his/her own individual cognitive efforts.

## Mutually Enhancing PTG in Couples

Some literature suggests that PTG may be a two-way street of shared experiences (Zwahlen et al., 2010). Patients' PTG may be enhanced by their partners' emotional expression and positive appraisals (Manne et al., 2004). Weiss (2004) assessed PTG in female breast cancer survivors and their husbands and demonstrated that husbands' PTG was significantly predicted by wives' PTG. Weiss interpreted this result as an example of a more positive manifestation of the well-documented stress contagion phenomenon—that is, exposure to a wife who makes positive interpretations of her cancer experience is "contagious"—or that there is transmission of PTG between marital partners, supporting the mutually enhancing nature of PTG experiences. Büchi et al. (2009) studied PTG among couples who lost their premature baby two to six years prior to the survey using the German translated version of the PTGI. They found that the quality of a couple's grief process affected both fathers' and mothers' PTG. Couples were divided into two groups depending on their grief scores: a concordant group and a discordant group. In concordant couples, both partners were more likely to share the PTG processes, whereas in discordant couples, the PTG processes were less likely to be connected, so that the loss of the baby triggered processes that separated the individual world of both partners and appeared to result in low satisfaction with the relationship, suggesting the important role of a shared grief process in PTG. These findings have been supported by other qualitative studies (e.g., Black & Sandelowski, 2010).

There is little dyadic research examining either positive or negative changes in intimate relationships in the context of traumatic experiences. Cohan, Cole, and Schoen (2009) used longitudinal data of divorces rates (month papers were filed) pre- and post-terrorist attacks in New York City and in an additional four counties that varied in distance from New York. The interest in this multiple site investigation was if proximal or psychological variables were predictive of divorce rates. In other words, did divorce rates change, and if so, was it due to the social and economic disruption caused by the attacks or to psychological aspects, such as the extent to which people perceived risk? Using a time series analytic strategy, these researchers found the monthly rates of filing for divorce (a measure of marital instability) significantly decreased in New York in 2002, the year following the 9/11 attacks, before returning to a more usual rate in subsequent years. Not wanting to assume the reason for the decline was due to psychological factors rather than civil disruptions to infrastructure, they looked at the counties close by, where many of the dead had resided. Despite no civil disruption in these counties, they too showed significant decreases in divorce applications filed. Declines in places like Los Angeles and Philadelphia were hypothesized to be due to becoming closer with an intimate partner in the face of perceived threat, a proposal consistent with terror management theory. Berger (2015) cites a conference paper presented by Shamai in Jerusalem in 2012. Shamai examined marital relationships in the context of shared experiences of terror in communities on the Gaza border. Her results showed that some couples reported increased anxiety and tension, and that intimacy levels had decreased. Conversely, other couples said the shared experience of being subject to rocket attacks and terror created a closer bond between them and enhanced their coping strategies. Such positive changes in couple relationships are also evident in clinical practice. When people struggle together to overcome a significant adversity, they can subsequently report their relationship to have become strengthened, their love for each other grown, and the development of team-like strategies for dealing with difficulty (Berger, 2015).

There is some evidence that perceptions of PTG in a partner may have a significant effect on relationship quality and personal well-being. For example, in a study of 61 couples who had experienced a natural disaster, Canevello, Michels, and Hilaire (2016) examined the way PTG affected relationship quality over time. These couples completed measures on two occasions six months apart after having been flooded out of their homes in a small US Midwestern town. Canevello et al. reported that when people perceived that their partners' PTG had increased over time, relationship quality was reported to have increased, and psychological distress decreased. These results were the same for men and women. Furthermore, the results hold no matter the level of the person's PTG who is reporting on relationship quality. That is, people derive benefits from their partner's PTG even when they do not report PTG themselves. The authors point out that these data suggest that perceptions of PTG in partners can have a powerful effect on relationships, and on psychological well-being over time.

Such results indicating enhanced relationships have been found in couples where the female partner had been diagnosed and treated for breast cancer. Ávila, Coimbra, Park, and Matos (2017) examined PTG, time since diagnosis, and attachment in 84 married heterosexual couples and used path analysis to examine the relationship between variables. Results indicated that there was no impact of time on PTG or differences between the sexes. An individual's attachment was not predictive of growth. However, the partner's attachment was an important predictor of PTG in both members of the couple. Similarly, partner's expressions of negotiating grief following the loss of their child and drawing on each other for support predicted PTG in a sample of 197 parents (Albuquerque, Narciso, & Pereira, 2017). Results demonstrated the importance of positive dyadic coping and cautioned clinicians to be sensitive in their approach to investigating the potential for growth following bereavement and ensuring appropriate validation of distress, as some people will not experience positive changes attributed to the struggle with their loss.

## PTG in Families

PTG can occur not only at an individual level but also at a group level. Family is the first group to which many belong. Some traumatic experiences occur at a "group-level" in nature, such as a fire or earthquake, and other experiences, such as a traffic accident, can involve multiple people in the family. Hafstad, Gil-Rivas, Kilmer, and Raeder (2010), for example, investigated PTG in a child and parent dyad who had been directly exposed to the 2004 tsunami in Thailand. They found that the parents' self-reported PTG was a significant predictor of PTG in their children, indicating each of the family members' PTG experiences are likely to be correlated when they all experienced the same trauma. But other traumatic experiences may directly occur at an "individual-level," such as a diagnosis of life-threatening illness; however, because family members are often interdependent, many traumatic experiences can challenge family well-being, family functioning, and family dynamics. The role of family in this sense is beyond that of the support provider. For instance, Colville and Cream (2009) demonstrated how parents experienced PTG after their child's admission to intensive care treatment. Kissil, Nino, Jacobs, Davey, and Tubbs (2010), on the other hand, demonstrated how adolescents experienced PTG after their parent's cancer. Moore et al. (2011) showed how family caregivers experienced PTG after their family member's diagnosis of advanced cancer. Thus, there are many reports that have investigated how a family member recognized or developed PTG as a result of the other family member's traumatic experience. Qualitative studies have also indicated that PTG is a shared experience for many family members, including patient-family caregiver dyads (Mosher et al., 2017). However, there have been few reports directly trying to assess family-level PTG by applying or modifying the PTGI that was originally designed to capture an individual-level of PTG.

A few studies have, instead, investigated the relationships between one of the family member's PTG and the other family members' characteristics or perceptions. Wilson et al. (2016), for example, examined the predictors for PTG in childhood cancer survivors by considering the psychosocial factors of the patient, family, and health care team. They found that the pediatric cancer survivors' PTG was predicted by their own stress symptoms, parents' religious coping, and stronger relationships between family and the treating oncologist. Although this study did not directly assess family-level PTG, we may be able to speculate on the parallel relationships between children's PTG experiences and the family's experiences of positive changes by getting involved in treatment processes and building a good relationship with healthcare professionals.

Felix et al. (2015) studied PTG and family functioning in parent-youth dyads who had been evacuated from multiple wildfires. Interestingly, there were no correlations between family functioning and PTG in either youth or parents. Based on the descriptive statistics, youth and parents equally reported a moderate level of PTG assessed by PTGI-SF; however, it seems that an individual-level PTG did not automatically lead to healthier family functioning. The authors found that the set of predictors they had (demographic variables, perceived severity of the stress, recovery environment such as social support, mental health, and coping) did not predict the parents' reported family functioning; however, the model at least predicted the children's reported family functioning. Younger age was associated with more positive views of family functioning after the disaster. The authors proposed that the developmental changes that adolescents often experience may lead them to view their family life more critically than their younger counterparts, suggesting that each member's developmental stage is important to consider when studying family functioning. In addition, they found that positive reappraisal was a significant predictor of PTG and healthy family functioning among youth. However, given that there were no relationships between family functioning and PTG, the sum of each member's individual PTG may not be the best way to predict family functioning or family-level PTG.

As indicated in a family resilience framework by Walsh (2003), families may be empowered by overcoming prolonged adversity. The key processes involve three domains: family belief systems (e.g., healthy families may approach adversity as a shared challenge), organizational patterns (e.g., families may be able to construct a new sense of normality as they reorganize patterns of interaction to fit new conditions), and communication/problem-solving (e.g., creative brainstorming and resourcefulness may open new possibilities for healing and growth). Berger and Weiss (2009) also looked at the family as a unit that can experience PTG, suggesting family-system PTG (i.e., positive changes in the family's identity and legacy, members' relationships with each other and with extended family and friends, and the family's belief system and priorities in life) that may occur as a parallel to the three PTG broad dimensions reported at an individual level (i.e., changes in perception of self, relating to others, and philosophy of life). In addition, Duran (2013) reviewed a total of 35 published studies that reported the positive effects of negotiating a cancer journey by the survivors and their families and identified five themes: meaning-making, appreciation of life, self-awareness, closeness and family togetherness (i.e., enhanced family relationships and harmony, including emotional bonds and family attachments), and a desire to pay back society. As Duran pointed out, data for fathers' and siblings' experiences were very scarce, and most of the studies have focused on mother-child relationships or husband-wife relationships. Although challenging, developing systematic assessments to investigate family-level PTG, clarifying the relationships between family-level PTG and each member's individual PTG, and assisting a family to experience PTG warrants further investigation. It is important to note that these studies of PTG within families are generally examined in terms of correlations between one particular family member's PTG with another's. Essentially, this approach is an extension of studying PTG in individuals, but families are systems that are more complex than the sum of the individuals within it. Most studies do not account for ethnic differences in families or for an increasing array of structures that comprise family systems. For example, we could find no research that specifically examined PTG in families with same-sex parents, although there are some studies that acknowledge same sex-led families were included in their research (e.g., Manne et al., 2004).

Figley and Burnette (2017) discuss the complexities of work in this area with a focus on resilience rather than PTG, but as discussed earlier, these concepts do have some conceptual overlaps. The points made about studying diverse families as systems can apply to both areas as well as others: for example, the intergenerational transmission of trauma. There are a number of key points made in this article. One such point is that when families are exposed to trauma as a unit or through shared experiences among some of its members (e.g., natural disasters), the shared experience can act to create closer bonds and commitment within the family unit. In order for positive post-trauma changes to occur at a family or systems level, strengths within the family must not only be present but also able to be mobilized at a time of crisis. Another point was the difficulty of quantitative research to really be able to unpack what is happening in families in this area of work. The authors discuss the value of qualitative approaches such as ethnography. In the area of family research, ethnographic techniques may include the use of taping video interactions within families to detect non-verbal cues, interviews, and other approaches that rely largely on naturalistic observations, note taking, and journaling. Therapeutically, assisting families in effectively coping with trauma exposure and realizing the potential for growth as a unit involves building capacity and strength within and between family members and reducing risk factors. There are many proposed frameworks for such interventions, but limited research capable of concluding a best-practice approach. This is particularly concerning for the ever-growing number of ethnically diverse families in what were once predominantly Caucasian contexts, such as the US. Ethnic minorities generally have higher levels of struggles with mental health following trauma, for many reasons (e.g., history of severe trauma such as that experienced by many refugees and asylum seekers; migration—forced or not—that breaks continuations of relationships and, hence, a reduction in social networks, low SES). Although the elements of a family systems approach may be useful when taken together, practitioners must be increasingly mindful that approaches seen to be effective in one cultural group may not be applicable to another. Narrative approaches are ideal in these populations, as they are in any group or with any individual, because they position the person or family in focus, keenly attending to the historical context as well as the current state and future orientations. Indeed, the expert companion model is similar, with a focus on empowerment, re-narration of traumatic stories, encouragement of multiple perspectives and reflections of strength, and capacity to move forward. Within a family therapy situation, approaches like these encourage meaning making through the narratives of individual members' trauma experience, which are sometimes quite disparate despite being an objectively shared event. Each person's narrative is unpacked with a goal toward creating a merged or shared family narrative that includes meaning and goals for the future (Saltzman, Pynoos, Lester, Layne, & Beardslee, 2013). Of course, a family's capacity to achieve this goal depends on numerous factors. For example, a parent generally needs to be able to assist children in expressing their narrative, through verbal and/or non-verbal expression (art, play). A parent who is struggling themselves may not have the available emotional resources to co-construct a coherent and structured narrative that can help a child develop skills for dealing with current or future difficulties. Research has demonstrated that a parent's degree of resolution regarding trauma impacts their capacity to successfully co-create new meaningful narratives with their child. Research has also demonstrated that a child's capacity for emotional and behavioral regulation, and their ability to co-construct an emotionally well-structured narrative with their mother, is important in affective meaning making, particularly in populations of traumatized children and families (Oppenheim, Nir, Warren, & Emde, 1997; Oppenheim, 2006; Saltzman et al., 2013).

## PTG in Organizations

Just as individuals can be stronger as a result of struggling with a potentially traumatic life event, both public and private organizations can be stronger (e.g., more sustainable, connected, productive) as a result of their crises, which may provide more opportunities to improve the work environment, foster work engagement, and build stronger relationships with community or other organizations. Powley (2009) reported an organization's capacity to recover after an unexpected organizational crisis (i.e., a shooting and standoff in a business school). Based on interviews, three social mechanisms were identified: (1) liminal suspension, that is, the alteration of relational structures and the emergence of new relational patterns as a result of crisis, (2) compassionate witnessing that involved noticing and feeling empathy for others, and (3) relational redundancy, which refers to how interpersonal connections intersect and span beyond immediate social reference groups. It is the effect of individual action on larger social entities, such as building a security task force, connecting to the community, and attending a celebration at City Hall to honor the police officers involved, that was important in the promotion of positive mental health outcomes.

In order to study PTG in organization-level, it is critical to identify the set of criteria and indicators that can be interpreted as "positive" changes from a long-term perspective. Showing more respect for past achievements and history can be considered as "growth" for some organizations, whereas other organizations may prioritize future development or current tangible products (e.g., advance technology, increase in the number of employees, productivity, building stronger relationships with other associations or within the organizations, building a stronger leadership, and developing interconnected structures). What constitutes "growth" is also influenced by cultural values and visions. Findings about the vision attributes that have been studied in the area of business may be helpful, such as brevity, clarity, abstractness, challenge, future orientation, stability, and desirability or ability to inspire, to investigate organizational PTG (Haque, TitiAmayah, & Liu, 2016).

There are proactive and reactive ways in which an organization can promote resilience, well-being, and PTG. Although multiple approaches can be put in place by any organization, a comprehensive approach to staff support and organizational connectedness is especially important in organizations in which exposure to relatively high levels of potential trauma is part of the workplace daily activity. Such work settings include prisons; police, ambulance, and fire services; child protection; and the military. For example, Scully (2011) describes a comprehensive proactive and reactive program in a paramedical organization. Over a period of 20 years (at the time of publication), this organization has been committed to research, reflection, and education, in a conscious effort to provide the best possible program for staff and their families. While they initially put in place programs to identify people potentially at risk for mental ill-health—for example due to exposure to what may have been regarded as an objectively traumatic event like attending to multiple vehicular fatalities or attending to a case of sudden infant death syndrome—research quickly revealed that a focus on such incidents failed to capture the array of potential staff stress and trauma. Stigma associated with mental ill-health was a barrier for employees who considered themselves hardier that the average person to access help even if they thought it was needed. The organization's approach began to incorporate a focus on the positive promotion of mental health and on resilience and PTG. Educational materials developed over time to explicitly include the model of PTG, case studies of employees' struggles with trauma and pathways to growth, and, importantly, assessment of employees' understanding of these concepts through assessment modules for new recruits. In addition to assessment models about stress, trauma, coping, and PTG, newly recruited personnel are required to complete a reflective journal reexamining their narratives around a particular event, and to identify the most useful strategies they have for coping, reconciling, and moving forward. Internal and external counselors are brought together annually for a two-day workshop where external experts in this area are engaged to provide the latest information about trauma interventions, including PTG.

Geiger (2016) conducted in-depth interviews with a sample of 11 male Israeli police officers and subjected her data to content analysis to explore how they dealt with the aftermath of attending to terrorist events. As has been found in other groups, effectively compartmentalizing their emotions at the time in order to execute their work roles effectively was the primary strategy employed, followed by a post-incident period of trying to relieve the inevitable tension that such experiences likely instill. A reliance on black humor was evident in the officers, and sharing of such humor was conductive to developing bonds between colleagues— a vital component to promoting PTG that has been found in other emergency service workers (e.g., in firefighters; Armstrong, Shakespeare-Finch, & Shochet, 2016). In the Israeli police officers, the most important component influencing mental health was a belief they were doing the work of a higher power—that they were connected to a higher power. It was through this belief that meaning was made, purpose was reconfirmed, a sense of coherence was realized, and ultimately transformative PTG occurred, which in turn strengthened their resolution to continue doing the best they could in their life-saving roles. In doing so, they did not forget the intrusive thoughts regarding the events—for example,

> The events stay engraved in your head. If anyone says that he is used to this type of event he is not speaking the truth. These incidents stay with you. You go to sleep with them and you wake up with them.
>
> (p. 423)

Recognition that PTG does not preclude ongoing distress for some people is a strength of the model. People generally do not "get over" traumatic experiences as such. They can learn to weave the experience of trauma into the narrative of their life, learn lessons from it and develop wisdom, use it as a reminder to appreciate today and the people that matter. As discussed earlier, distress and growth are not mutually exclusive or at opposite ends of a continuum.

## Facilitating PTG at the Level of Groups, Communities, and Societies

Several studies have developed psycho-educational intervention programs in a school setting and assessed their effects. Steele, Kuban, and Raider (2009) reported the follow-up results of children (6 to 12 years old) who participated in a school-based trauma intervention program called "I Feel Better Now!" that was conducted after school. Their ten-week program included a series of sensory-based activities that are related to the major experiences of trauma in order to support cognitive processes to enhance survivor/thriver thinking rather than victim thinking. Although the details of the program were not available, at the six-month follow-up, children, parents, and social workers participated in the focus group and reported PTG experiences as an outcome of the intervention. Taku, Cann, Tedeschi, and Calhoun (2017) implemented a brief psycho-educational intervention program for high school students in Japan. The program involved a 20- to 25-minute interactive presentation that contained discussion as well as questions and answers. Seven topics were covered: (1) introduction of stressful life events that the students might have experienced, such as earthquake, car accident, death of a family member, or relationships conflicts, (2) psychological, emotional, and behavioral immediate reactions, such as feeling shocked, anger, being in denial, and crying, (3) psychological distress that may also occur after the stressful life event, such as intrusive rumination or avoidance, (4) potentially positive personal changes or PTG, such as being more compassionate and having new opportunities, (5) various forms of PTG, via introducing the five domains of PTG, (6) known predictors and mechanisms of PTG, such as core beliefs challenged, rumination, and social support, and (7) individual differences likely to affect PTG, such as personality traits and a person's pre-trauma history. By comparing with the baseline PTG, students who participated in the PTG-focused psycho-educational intervention program reported greater PTG three weeks after the intervention. In this study, another group of students received a psycho-educational program focusing on negative changes or PTSD and they reported a lower level of PTG after the program than those who participated in a PTG-focused program. These results suggest that learning only about negative reactions caused by stressful experiences are likely to reinforce students' existing beliefs, because more people are familiar with negative changes, which may encourage them to focus on the negative aspects of trauma, whereas learning about positive changes might have encouraged students to take a broader perspective, which can foster PTG perceptions.

These studies suggest that educating children in the possibility of PTG in addition to normal stress reactions and coping mechanisms is beneficial and should be integrated into general health education. Children who receive this education may transfer their knowledge and experiences to the rest of their family members as well as find benefits themselves. Also, people still may absorb more information about negative changes resulting from trauma, and this schema-consistent information is likely to be retained, which may suppress PTG experiences. Therefore, developing a psycho-educational program that can broaden perceptions of trauma response is important.

There have been recent studies that incorporate psycho-education intervention programs, focusing on PTG in various groups, such as ex-offenders in an offender rehabilitation program (Mapham & Hefferon, 2012), or focusing on resilience among college students (Dolbier, Jaggars, & Steinhardt, 2010). Berger (2015) discusses the value of group-based trauma interventions and highlights the school environment as a particularly useful context for such activities when facilitated by appropriately qualified professionals. Berger suggests working in this way helps to essentially normalize reactions to a shared experience, mobilizes a network of support and helps children learn they are not alone in their struggles and that the difficulties they are experiencing are not isolated only to them. One example of a program that has been run for some years now in a school that specifically caters for children from refugee backgrounds is the Tree of Life (e .g, Schweitzer, Vromans, Ranke, & Griffin, 2014). This manualized narrative arts-based program is designed to help children and adolescents to re-narrate their traumatic experiences and current difficulties to identify strengths within themselves and the networks around them. Over seven 80-minute weekly sessions, the children are encouraged to draw a picture of their tree, the roots, the ground, trunk, branches, leaves, which are woven into a story of past and present that includes concepts of strength, hope, and dreams. Metaphors, such as a storm, facilitate discussion of challenges and potential dangers. In a case study of a 14-year-old girl from Liberia (randomly selected from a group of students participating in the program, all from Liberia), Schweitzer and colleagues provided an in-depth analysis of how each component of the program was interpreted by their case study participant, "Miriam." A key finding was giving permission for her to view her future in a positive light—such permission came from facilitators modeling such dreams and positive future orientations and hearing stories from peers about their considerations of the future. In this way, a safe space was created for Miriam to explore her future aspirations. Consistent with other research, meaning making was important in attaining perceptions of growth and in overcoming hardships. The program helped Miriam to develop her own meaning about the past, present, and future in the "adoption of preferred self-narratives, and the development of a capacity for reflective functioning, using a focused creative approach" (Schweitzer et al., 2014, p. 105).

## PTG at a Broad Social Level

In the literature on PTG, the metaphor of an earthquake has been used to describe the process that is a precursor to growth. Just as earthquakes can damage everything that has been built and produce a significant threat to existing structures, seismic events can challenge our existing beliefs at an individual level. After earthquakes, the remains of old structures that collapsed need to be removed. This work is usually done by a group of people in the community, as well as volunteers from outside of the community, so new, stronger, and earthquake-resistant systems can be built, which in turn strengthen connectedness within the community. So, the notion of group-level PTG was identified at the very beginning of PTG research (Tedeschi, Park, & Calhoun, 1998). Groups, communities, and societies go through PTG transformation that is similar to individual PTG by building new norms, strengthening bonds, and providing new opportunities. Leadership is important to promote community growth, as is the framing of media coverage.

Based on the indices of peace culture as proposed by UNESCO (i.e., rejection of human rights violations and political participation), Rimé, Páez, Basabe, and Martínez (2010) developed items that can assess benefits of PTG that have a more macro-social or collective nature. Sample items related to collective growth were: "reinforced political participation and engagement," "reinforced sensibility towards human rights violations in this country," and "reinforced awareness of human rights violations in the world." By using these items, Wlodarczyk et al. (2016) assessed PTG among people who were affected by natural disasters in Spain, Chile, and Colombia at individual, community, and society levels. They found that individual-level and communal- or social-level PTG were positively correlated with each other, and that all levels of PTG were higher in more collectivistic countries such as Chile and Colombia than the more individualistic country, Spain. These results may overlap with the findings at the individual level, where PTG tends to be higher for people who value and have access to social support; this could be another indication of the parallel relationships between individual PTG and group PTG. However, this study also shows us how challenging it is to measure community- or group-level PTG.

Williamson (2014) wrote an interesting paper about collective PTG that she extracted from the testimonials of 18 female survivors of the genocide that took place in Rwanda. She explained that PTG changes at an individual level are largely cognitive in nature, but that socially shared ideological changes can be seen as collective PTG. Using discourse analysis, Williamson established that some of the testimonials included changes in philosophy of life and the making of new meaning and that PTG at a collective level is about agency and communion. Williamson also raised an important question regarding what constitutes collective PTG. For example, an increase in group cohesion and collective identity may appear positive from one side but may be seen as unfavorable for outgroup members. The balance between autonomy (freedom) and relatedness (reconciliation) is suggested as a key element.

Perhaps, as an example of relatedness at the community level, Prioleau and her colleagues (2016) reported community outreach in disaster-affected societies in Japan and the US. Specifically, they designed an international exchange program between 3/11 Fukushima Japan earthquake/tsunami/nuclear power plant disaster survivors and 9/11 survivors in New York. Impacts of these survivor exchange trips were assessed by interview and the survey. The PTGI was used with both the

3/11 recipient community and the 9/11 donor community. Participants included survivors, mental health professionals, students, and children. Although PTGI scores were not associated with their interactions with trip members, PTGI scores were associated with continuing involvement in the relief effort. At the interviews, survivors underscored the importance of direct outreach, through person-to-person contact and repetitive visits, so they were able to share their experiences. Even though many of the survivors were not bilingual, participants noted that their common disaster experiences helped mitigate cultural and language barriers.

At an even broader distal level, disasters have changed societies. Sixteen years before the 3/11 earthquake/tsunami that happened in Japan, there was another large earthquake in Kobe. Prior to the earthquake, Kobe was considered one of the most earthquake-prepared cities in Japan; however, this belief was wrong, and over 6,000 people were reported dead. As Williams, Baker, and Williams (1999) reflected, the Japanese national and local governments, including emergency services, have publicly accepted that the disaster response to Kobe was poorly handled. However, perhaps ironically thanks to the initial inefficient services, the community had to accept volunteers to fill in the gap. "Prior to the use of volunteers in this disaster, there was no history of volunteerism or 'volunteer culture' to guide the Japanese" (Williams et al., 1999, p. 113). It has been 22 years, but the date of the Kobe earthquake, January 17, is now called Disaster Prevention and Volunteer Day, and many events (e.g., evacuation practice, trial of volunteers) are annually held. In addition, the aftermath of the disaster made clear that there were emotional responses that could be better addressed by mental health services that had often been seen as a Western phenomenon (Williams et al., 1999). The awareness and understanding of PTSD spread around Japan as well. This kind of social awareness can pave the way for a recognition and promotion of PTG. Bonanno, Romero, and Klein (2015) proposed that the resilient outcomes for communities that were exposed to acute stressful life events would likely be manifest as stable healthy population wellness, with a good level of community economic development, disaster management, institutional vitality, and availability as well as maintenance of resources and assets. If so, community-level PTG would include something beyond population wellness. There may be community versions of the domains of PTG such as an increased sense of connectedness among community groups, new opportunities that would not have been available without the crisis (e.g., memorial/appreciation events, community centers for evacuation, and new network services), and a sense of trust or confidence in the capability of the community.

Tedeschi (1999) explained how positive developments have occurred within many social systems in the aftermath of violence. Examples may include changes in drunk driving laws in the United States after consciousness-raising by bereaved parents. Tedeschi identified three aspects to consider in the coincidence of personal and social transformation: (1) the role of leaders, (2) the credibility of the trauma survivors, and (3) mutual leadership. Traumas can have an important impact on the social fabric, creating an enduring need to revisit, heal, and learn from these experiences. Tedeschi cites Ground Zero in Hiroshima, the Anne Frank House in Amsterdam, and the Vietnam Veterans Memorial in Washington as powerful reminders of the suffering that violence produces. Although such memorials are usually erected because they are needed for individual healing, they may be maintained to keep societies vigilant for the repetition of the mistakes of the past. These all can be considered as examples of society-level PTG. Therefore, it may be surprisingly easy to identify group-based PTG in human history; however, what is challenging, perhaps, is how to measure it using the common research methods used in social science area.

# CHAPTER 18

# Vicarious and Secondary
# Posttraumatic Growth

The terms *secondary* and *vicarious trauma* are often used interchangeably. Both terms refer to the impact of indirect exposure to trauma. Such exposure can be in the form of hearing the narrative of another person's trauma, as is the case with therapists who work with traumatized clients, or witnessing the trauma of others, as is the case for people working in emergency services and the military. However, there are differences in the definition of these terms. Secondary trauma refers to symptoms of PTSD experienced as a result of hearing or seeing the trauma of others. Vicarious trauma refers to internal changes such as shifts in cognition. These shifts in cognition are a result of empathic engagement with another person. When PTG occurs in people with indirect exposure to trauma, vicarious PTG is the preferred term.

Vicarious PTG (VPTG) can manifest itself in the same ways PTG does; the difference is that the person reporting PTG did not directly experience the traumatic event. However, when family members report VPTG, the boundary between VPTG and PTG may not always be clear. In these cases, there may be a mixture of direct emotional impact from living in an intimate relationship with a traumatized person, and also learning the lessons of post-trauma life from observations and interactions with that person. For instance, McCormack, Hagger, and Joseph (2011) examined VPTG by conducting interviews with wives of veterans, because wives were exposed vicariously to the combat distress that their husbands directly experienced. Likewise, Zerach (2015) found that children of Israeli prisoners of war, 40 years after the war, reported more PTG than children of veterans who were not POWs. Zerach describes this as "secondary PTG" to indicate that there are a variety of continuing influences that accrue from life with a trauma survivor. Greene, Lahav, Kanat-Maymon, and Solomon (2015) also found higher secondary PTG in wives of former POWs with PTSD, compared to those without and to controls. Other researchers such as Dekel (2007) examined PTG in the wives of prisoners of war, but without considering this PTG to be "vicarious." In another study, Dekel, Mandl, and Solomon (2013) seemed to extend the notion of vicarious PTG as they investigated the transgenerational transmission of trauma by assessing PTG and PTSS, longitudinally, among second-generation Holocaust survivors. They found that second-generation veterans reported less PTG than veterans who were not second generation, indicating that transmission of trauma

(Nazi Holocaust) from one generation to the next may be implicated in the off-spring's PTG following subsequent trauma (combat). Although more studies are needed, the notion of transgenerational transmission of trauma provides an interesting insight for further understanding of PTG processes. If it is possible for people to experience vicarious PTG, it may be plausible for people to experience PTG by deriving meaning from the most severe and painful events that happened before they were born. It may also be possible to facilitate empathy as a form of vicarious experience of trauma. Matz, Vogel, Matter, and Montenegro (2015) conducted a novel trial using dialogue groups that comprised the adult children of at least one parent who had survived the Holocaust with adult children of members of the Third Reich—a member of the Nazi party. A phenomenological analysis of transcribed interviews showed that the adult children of Holocaust survivors reported a sense of connection with the children of the Third Reich as the experience humanized them. They developed empathy and compassion hearing about the challenges and the struggles of the Third Reich children through the war and currently as a result of the shame and guilt they felt and still feel. As one participant said, "what could she do? She could not change her family history" (p. 197). Results demonstrated a reduction in prejudice and a sense of healing.

## Vicarious PTG in Health Care Professionals

Because VPTG may involve varying degrees of direct and indirect trauma exposure, we consider PTG specifically in professionals, such as physicians, nurses, social workers, and emergency workers as VPTG. These professionals observe others going through traumatic circumstances but, at the same time, are often directly affected by the same traumatic circumstances. The concept of vicarious resilience seems related to VPTG in the same way that resilience is related to PTG. Engstrom, Hernandez, and Gangsei (2008) reported that vicarious resilience does not show a higher level of functioning in therapists who are otherwise positively affected by the resilience of their clients. The content of VPTG includes unique dimensions, such as becoming a better professional and developing greater awareness of an involvement in social justice (Cohen & Collens, 2013).

Manning-Jones, de Terte, and Stephens (2015) conducted a systematic review of VPTG in 28 articles that used both quantitative and qualitative designs in a variety of populations (e.g., therapists, nurses, funeral directors, general population). Accounts of VPTG were very similar to PTG, but that there were also subtle differences. For example, those working with traumatized people reported broadening their spiritual views in an existential way and marveled at the resilience they saw in people. Another difference was that VPTG included positive changes in the worker's sense of competence and an enhanced sense of professional identity (Brockhouse, Msetfi, Cohen, & Joseph, 2011).

Professionals working with trauma survivors may also experience PTG as a result of their observations of others who demonstrate PTG as well as those who do not. In the latter case, we would expect professionals to report they are determined to live better than others had been living, and to respond better to trauma than what they observed in others. In either case, the experience of PTG is catalyzed by a challenge to core beliefs that occurs as the professional considers the reactions of others to traumatic circumstances. Beck, Morgan-Eaton and Gable (2017) investigated PTG and the role of core beliefs in 467 nurses who had experienced delivery and labor associated with women's traumatic births. The quantitative data indicated appreciation of life as the most endorsed domain of PTG, whereas qualitative data indicated positive changes in relationships had occurred most frequently as an outcome of their exposure to the trauma of others through their work role. There was a lot of variability in the data, with some nurses reporting low levels of growth and others extremely high levels of transformative change. Cohen and Collens (2013) suggested that the challenge to beliefs can occur in relation to either the patient's or client's traumatic experiences or to observing their PTG.

VPTG has been examined quantitatively and qualitatively in various populations of professionals. One of the first published studies to explicitly examine VPTG was a qualitative study of 21 psychotherapists in the US (Arnold, Calhoun, Tedeschi, & Cann, 2005). Using a naturalistic interview design and content analysis to extract themes, Arnold et al. found that in addition to experiencing some negative consequences of working with traumatized clients, including intrusive thoughts, sadness, anger, and self-doubt, all participants had positive reports of ways in which they had changed because of the nature of their work. The positive changes reported included deeper spiritual understanding, a greater appreciation for their own lives, increased compassion, and a sense that they had learned about themselves through their clients' journeys and through witnessing their clients' PTG. Hyatt-Burkhart (2014) conducted interviews and focus groups with 12 mental health professionals who specialized in trauma work. All of the clinicians in the sample said they had experienced VPTG as a result of witnessing PTG in the children that they counseled. They reported changes in their philosophy of life, in perceptions of themselves, appreciation of life, new possibilities, and their relationships. For example, watching children learn how to have meaningful relationships inspired the therapists to examine their own relationships; seeing them grow prompted explorations regarding their own potential for new possibilities and an optimistic orientation in expecting positive outcomes.

Studies of mental health professionals who work with severely traumatized persons provide a good test of the relationship of other factors to VPTG. Samios, Rodzik, and Abel (2012) sampled 61 therapists who work with sexual violence survivors and found that PTG moderated the effects of secondary traumatic stress, operating as a protective factor. Ben-Porat (2015) conducted a quantitative study with 143 therapists who worked with people who had experienced domestic violence and a comparison group of 71 therapists who worked for a social service and reported not having worked with traumatized clients in the preceding week. In addition to other measures, Ben-Porat administered the PTGI. Therapists who worked for the social service reported higher rates of PTG than the therapists who worked with clients who experienced domestic violence. However, such a comparison can be confounded by the therapists' own experiences of trauma. When the sample was split according to therapists' experiences of trauma, rather than workrole, there was significantly more PTG in those who had experienced trauma. And significant linear and curvilinear relationships between PTG and reports of secondary traumatic stress were found. It is difficult to distinguish between growth resulting from personal trauma and VPTG, since they often seem to interact with each other.

Barrington and Shakespeare-Finch (2014) conducted a longitudinal qualitative study in Australia in which they interviewed clinicians who specialized in working with people who had arrived as refugees or as asylum seekers and who were survivors of trauma and torture. Consistent with Arnold et al. (2005), the majority of clinicians reported both positive and negative changes in themselves as a result of their work. Those changes were consistent over one year. Using Interpretive Phenomenological Analysis, five superordinate themes were revealed, including VPTG. The five constituent themes that comprised the VPTG superordinate theme were the same as the five factors measured by the PTGI. Cosden, Sanford, Koch, and Lepore (2016) investigated VPTG and vicarious trauma (VT) in 51 counselors specializing in treating people with substance abuse issues. They found a positive linear relationship between VT and VPTG; a curvilinear solution did not significantly add to their predictions. Counselors who had a history of substance abuse themselves were more likely to report both VT and VPTG. Consistent with other work cited in this section, results also demonstrated significantly higher growth in those with a personal history of trauma. These studies suggest that the therapists' personal traumatic experiences may increase psychological preparedness to experience VPTG while working with their clients. Perhaps personal traumatic experiences may make them more sensitive rather than more vulnerable, or possibly make them more empathic, because an empathic engagement with traumatized clients seems to play an important role in promoting VPTG (Cohen & Collens, 2013).

Brockhouse et al. (2011) studied VPTG in 118 therapists. Organizational support was not related to growth, but empathy was a positive predictor. In addition to empathetic engagement, experiencing VPTG was also related to optimism and to positive affect. A few studies have examined the differences in the level of VPTG depending on occupation or professional role. For example, nurses have reported more PTG than social workers (Lev-Wiesel, Goldblatt, Eisikovits, & Admi, 2009), social workers more than psychologists (Manning-Jones et al., 2016), and body handlers reported more PTG than rehabilitation workers (Shiri, Wexler, Alkalay, Meiner, & Kreitler, 2008). Yet staff in pediatric intensive care units reported similar degrees of VPTG as noncritical pediatric staff (Rodríguez-Rey et al., 2017).

## PTG or VPTG in Emergency Workers

The first study that explicitly examined PTG in emergency service workers was published in 2003 (Shakespeare-Finch, Smith, Gow, Embelton, & Baird). In that research, 526 operational ambulance personnel completed the PTGI and results demonstrated that 98.6% reported some level of PTG, with mean scores indicating moderate changes. Half of the sample reported PTG in the moderate range, with a further quarter of the group reporting changes to a "great" or "very great" degree. As traumatic events can happen in one's personal life, as well as in the course of their employ, the researchers compared PTG between those officers who had experienced trauma in both work and personal lives with those who had experienced work-related trauma exposure only. There was a significant difference between the groups, with those who experienced trauma in both lives reporting higher levels of PTG than those who had only experienced vicarious trauma. Although some personality traits have been found to relate to PTG in ambulance officers (e.g., extraversion, openness to experience), coping strategies and resources have been shown to account for more variance and largely mediate the relationship between personality and PTG (Shakespeare-Finch, Gow, & Smith, 2005).

PTG was also evident in a longitudinal study of police officers (Burke & Shakespeare-Finch, 2011). Officers were surveyed when they first joined the academy and followed until they had been operational police officers for 12 months. Those officers who had experienced trauma prior to joining the force, or who had experienced trauma prior to joining and had been exposed to vicarious trauma through operational duties, had higher scores on most dimensions of the PTGI than those who had either not experienced trauma prior to joining or those that had only experienced operational trauma. It may be that the successful negotiation of an earlier traumatic experience increased the officers' capacity to negotiate future potentially traumatizing events, consistent with the results found with counselors and therapists (Cosden et al., 2016). PTG has also been found to be related to better physical health in police officers (Pole, Kulkarni, Bernstein, & Kaufmann, 2006).

Armstrong, Shakespeare-Finch, and Shochet (2014) examined predictors of VPTG and PTSD in a sample of 218 firefighters. Results were consistent with those cited above in that experiencing trauma from multiple sources and the use of self-care coping strategies were predictive of growth. Organizational stress was predictive of distress but not of VPTG. This latter result is consistent with that of Boermans and colleagues (2014), who found that although team cohesion and organizational constraints were related to symptoms of fatigue in 971 Dutch peacekeepers on military deployment, they were not related to VPTG. Kehl, Knuth, Holubová, Hulse, and Schmidt (2014, 2015) conducted a large study ($N = 1916$) of firefighters from eight European countries. Multiple types of events (e.g., house fire, terrorist attack, traffic accident) were categorized, and although event type was not predictive of distress, natural disaster exposure was predictive of VPTG. Czech and Turkish firefighters reported higher levels of growth than those in the UK, Italy, and Poland. The number of potentially traumatizing events to which firefighters were exposed was predictive of distress, but not of VPTG, consistent with Chopko's (2010) findings with 183 American police officers. As Chopko indicated, police officers are often exposed to many different types of traumatic events during their careers. But it is important to remember that the total number of traumatic events does not seem to predict VPTG in emergency workers. Rather than these situational factors, perhaps subjective cognitive factors or social support may play an important role, as was the case with VPTG among healthcare professionals. For instance, one study focused on the role of internal factors in PTG, such as gratitude, social support, and satisfaction with life, in addition to the number of stressful life events experienced among police officers ($N = 113$) working in the New Orleans area following Hurricane Katrina (Leppma et al., 2017). They found that these internal factors moderated the relationships between stressful life events and PTG. That is, the expression of appreciation for people or things in life, support, and a sense of satisfaction were associated with PTG, especially in those who experienced a greater magnitude of stressful life events. Authors also suggested that the police officers might have overall habituated to stressful life events over time due to the stress inoculation effects, and if so, the way they perceive and cope with stressful life events should be different from general population.

Using structural equation modeling, Armstrong, Shakespeare-Finch, and Shochet (2016) sought to identify factors that were predictive of VPTG and of symptoms of PTSD in a sample of 250 firefighters. This research aimed to identify potentially modifiable factors that may promote VPTG and buffer against symptoms of PTSD. Operational stress (e.g., attending to fires or car accidents) was directly related to increased symptoms of PTSD, whereas organizational stress (e.g., paperwork, relationship with superiors) was not. Organizational stress was not directly related to VPTG but was mediated by workplace belongingness or connectedness. Workplace belonging measures the extent to which a person feels connected with, valued, and respected by peers and supervisors. An encouraging thing about this finding is that belongingness can be modified through changes in organizational behavior and attitudes rather than the common focus on individual difference variables that are deemed the responsibility of the individual to change.

Emergency Medical Dispatchers (EMDs) are the first point of contact for people in crisis who call emergency hotlines (e.g., 911 in the USA; 000 in Australia). Although they are not physically on the scene, it is a time-critical role that requires the use of verbal and audio skills to identify the nature of the medical emergency, the location of the patient, deployment of crews, and try to calm callers so they can be instrumentally useful within a context that is often highly stressful or traumatic for them. VPTG has recently been examined both quantitatively and qualitatively in EMDs. For example, self-efficacy, and giving and receiving social support, were examined as predictors of VPTG, eudaimonic well-being, and PTSD symptoms in a sample of 60 EMDs (Shakespeare-Finch, Rees, & Armstrong, 2015). Both self-efficacy and receiving social support positively predicted VPTG and well-being, and were negatively related to PTSD symptoms. There was also a moderate correlation between well-being and VPTG. Adams, Shakespeare-Finch, and Armstrong (2015) conducted a qualitative study of the lived experiences of 15 EMDs. Three superordinate themes emerged from the data: operational stress and trauma, organizational stress, and VPTG. All participants discussed how they had to challenge their cognitions and perceptions of the world early in their career in order to be able to deal with the constant distress of others, but that they had found ways to find enrichment and positive transformative changes as a result of their work. A number of strategies for enhancing the possibility of VPTG in this cohort were identified, such as cognitive strategies, self-care, acceptance, the use of humor, and support. For example, one participant said, "It [the job] just makes you realize how short a life can be, and to just make the most of it while you have it" (p. 440). Another said "when you talk to other people about it, you've shared with someone. You've heard what they think, they've heard what you think . . . lightening the load" (p. 441). An optimistic outlook toward the future has also been reported to be associated with PTG in other trauma workers. Shiri, Wexler, and Kreitler (2010) pointed out that beliefs about future goals may carry more weight than beliefs about the self among those who face trauma frequently in their work.

## The Relationship Between PTG and Professional Burnout

Unlike vicarious and secondary trauma, burnout is a chronic condition that is usually associated with a person's employment and is characterized by a gradual depletion of resources, and loss of motivation and commitment to the role. Burnout suggests that a person becomes increasingly exhausted. Taku (2014) sampled 289 physicians investigating determinants of VPTG and burnout, including family support, dispositional resilience, marital status, and age. Higher levels of resilience, growth, and family support were inversely related to burnout. Taku suggested that for those physicians who did not have much family support, or were not inherently resilient, VPTG experiences are important in buffering the potential for burnout. Gibbons, Murphy, and Joseph (2011) examined a number of factors influencing the mental health of 61 social workers, including PTG and burnout. They found that the social workers reported high levels of burnout and moderate levels of PTG, and that there was a significant negative relationship between PTG and burnout ($r = -.30$). The factor that seemed to account for higher levels of growth and lower levels of burnout was the extent to which the social workers valued themselves and perceived themselves to be valued by others. Linley and Joseph (2007) examined burnout, compassion satisfaction, compassion fatigue, and PTG in a sample of 156 therapists; a number of factors were predicted to influence these states, including the type of training that they had and their current practice orientation. Therapists who had transpersonal therapy training and used that approach in their practice reported greater PTG, whereas burnout was more likely in those who were trained in and practiced cognitive behavioral therapy (CBT). In addition, therapists with a history of trauma reported more personal growth.

The relationships between VPTG and burnout should receive more attention, because it is sometimes hard to draw the line between personal life and professional life. Bauwens and Tosone (2010), for instance, investigated PTG in clinicians who were in Manhattan in September 2001 during the terrorist attacks on the World Trade Center. These participants were clinicians but at the same time victims, and their reports included both pain and growth. They reported personal vulnerability, but also profound growth and professional skill development. The authors identified "blurred roles" as one important theme (e.g., "I mean that my patients and myself were 'in the soup' together, so to speak and both my patients and myself talked together about our experiences, thoughts, and feelings," p. 508), making it challenging to distinguish VPTG from PTG. Burnout can occur if healthcare professionals themselves experience trauma and yet keep maintaining their professional work without receiving supervision, personal therapy, consultation, or other support.

Ying, Wang, Lin, and Chen (2016) applied the concept of burnout to adolescents and their academic pursuits. They examined academic burnout, PTG, and trait resilience in adolescents before and after the Wenchuan earthquake in China.

There was a weak, but significant, negative relationship between burnout and PTG, and quite a substantial relationship between PTG and resilience ($r = .56$) at Time 1. Controlling for age, gender, and burnout at Time 1 regression analysis revealed that PTG and resilience at Time 1 were not associated with burnout scores 24 months later, but that there was an interaction effect. PTG at Time 1 was significantly and positively correlated with burnout in those who had low levels of trait resilience, but there was no such relationship in those who had high trait resilience scores. It appears that the earthquake may have affected students with low trait resilience more significantly, resulting in greater PTG.

## PTG in Healthcare Professionals and the Effect on PTG in Patients

It is possible that PTG in healthcare professionals may have a positive impact on their patients or clients, just as clients' PTG experiences may have a positive impact on healthcare professionals (Brockhouse et al., 2011; Hyatt-Burkhart, 2014). However, there is almost no research about how professionals' PTG may affect PTG in their patients or clients. VPTG may affect the work of professionals through the way they interact with clients (e.g., non-verbal behavior, responses, attitudes, etc.), but the professionals may not directly disclose their own VPTG to their clients; clients may not know about the experiences or perspectives of the people helping them.

# CHAPTER 19

# Non-Posttraumatic Growth

PTG was originally identified among traumatized people and communities; however, as more studies have been conducted and the PTG theoretical model has been elaborated, we have come to realize that other events can be potentially "seismic" enough to challenge people's assumptive world. Naturally, most of the triggering events in PTG literature are potentially traumatic in nature, because the initial emotional, cognitive, and physical reactions are so painful and overwhelming that they elicit the cognitive processing that plays an important role in PTG processes. However, the question arises as to whether other events that may not lead to such negative reactions can still foster personal growth.

## Positive Events and Growth

Roepke (2013), for example, studied how people experience positive changes as a result of experiencing positive events and categorized them into five areas: positive emotions (e.g., "I was invited by a close friend to attend the Academy Awards ceremony"), engagement (e.g., "taking my first solo vacation and learning to surf"), relationships (e.g., "falling in love for the first time"), meaning (e.g., "the day I got saved/baptized"), and accomplishment (e.g., "writing the final words of the first draft of my first, yet-to-be-sold novel"). In order to assess growth after positive experiences, Roepke developed an inventory that has 19 items, with a four-factor structure: meaning in life (e.g., "I have a new role in life"), spiritual change (e.g., "I have a better understanding of spiritual matters"), relationship (e.g., "I became more open"), and self-esteem (e.g., "I like myself more"). These changes are named as post-ecstatic growth (PEG), compared to PTG, although the items are very similar to those on the PTGI and the factors are very similar to new possibilities, spiritual-existential change, relating to others, and personal strength, respectively. Roepke proposed that "positive events are actually critical catalysts for lasting psychological growth, and can powerfully shape our character, values and outlook" (Roepke, 2013, p. 280). Roepke concluded there is substantial overlap between the positive changes people report after the negative and positive experiences of their lives. However, there appear to be some distinctions from PTG. For example, we know that for many people there is lasting distress related to their trauma in those who report PTG. After the death of a child, natural disaster, or loss of your family in civil war prior to fleeing from your home, there will be days or times in some days when those feelings of despair return. Such feelings do not negate reports of growth but, rather, provide a more accurate picture of the complexity of the human condition. Mangelsdorf and Eid (2015) also attempted to unify the concepts of PTG and PEG by conducting surveys in the US and India. They suggested the Thriver Model, which is based on the assumption that people who are more likely to experience PTG are also more likely to experience PEG and vice versa. According to this model, it is not the quality of a triggering event, but the way it is processed (e.g., meaning making, supportive relationships, and positive emotions) that is critical for the occurrence of post-event growth. They found that the negative events were perceived as more impactful than positive ones in the US, whereas the reverse was found in India. In addition, they found that PTG and PEG were highly related to each other, making them conclude that growth can occur after turning points in life, regardless of positive or negative valence.

It seems, however, still controversial to conclude that PTG and PEG overlap, because one key element for PTG lies in processes that involve psychological struggle, not the outcome, as well as the subtle differences between positive change and the transformative change of PTG. However, the boundaries between PTG and PEG would become more blurred if people reported that positive experiences challenged what they used to believe, made them ruminate about the experiences, perhaps talked about it with other people who are close to them, and recognized their own changes as personal growth. In addition, people sometimes hold not just negative memories but positive ones, even when they reflect on their most traumatic life events. Veterans who belonged to the Danish Contingent of the International Security Assistance Force 7 in Afghanistan, for example, reported negative (e.g., witnessing explosion) and positive memories (e.g., being accepted by the platoons there) several months after deployment (Staugaard, Johannessen, Thomsen, Bertelsen, & Berntsen, 2015). These researchers found that the centrality of highly emotional memories from deployment, whether positive or negative, predicted PTG in their longitudinal study. This study suggests that

> it may not be only the nature of the event itself (i.e., that it is traumatic) that promotes growth, but rather growth might be related to a psychological propensity to assign centrality to highly emotional events regardless of their valence. This could lead to an emotionally balanced, realistic view of the period of deployment with both good and bad memories being considered important in the aftermath.
>
> (Staugaard et al., 2015, p. 374)

Another perspective on the process of positive change is offered by Pluess and Belsky (2013). They explain that we all vary in developmental plasticity and that these differences may be a basis for differences in what they call *vantage sensitivity* (p. 901). In this article, Pluess and Belsky discuss vantage sensitivity in response to positive experiences and review evidence that suggests this tendency for some people to be more positively responsive to their environment is due to genetic factors (e.g., dopamine DRD4 & serotonin 5-HTTPLR, p. 907) and environmental factors (e.g., attachment, supportive networks). People who essentially remain or return to a pre-positive event level of functioning are said to be *vantage resistant*, resembling resilience to negative experiences. Those people proposed to have vantage sensitivity tend to grow from previous levels of functioning following positive experiences, much in the way we depict PTG following highly challenging and traumatic events.

## Self-Initiated Growth

Similarly, we can consider whether self-initiated challenges can lead to PTG. One element of trauma is unpredictability. People do not generally seek to experience trauma in order to experience personal growth. However, there are some experiences people are willing to initiate, although highly stressful, because they have some mission to complete or desire to challenge themselves. To some extent, volunteering for military service has some elements of initiating at least the possibility of confronting trauma. Another example is spaceflight. Ihle, Ritsher, and Kanas (2006) investigated the positive effects of being in space among astronauts and cosmonauts by using the PTGI as well as developing a new set of items that are unique to spaceflight (e.g., "I gained a stronger appreciation of the Earth's beauty" and "I gained a stronger sense of wonder about the universe"). They found that the participants gained a stronger appreciation for the beauty and fragility of the Earth, as well as more common PTG (e.g., "new opportunities are available which wouldn't have been otherwise" was highly endorsed). Yaden et al. (2016) described the "overview effect"—the effect that some who observe Earth from space report that they have felt overcome with emotion, have come to see themselves and their world differently, and have returned to Earth with a renewed sense of purpose. Their reports of (1) appreciation and perception of beauty, (2) unexpected and even overwhelming emotion, and (3) an increased sense of connection to other people and the Earth as a whole, seem really close to what the PTG model has suggested. Some domains of PTG, such as spiritual change (Suedfeld, Legkaia, & Brcic, 2010), may be particularly implicated in spaceflight experiences, and some, such as new possibilities, were reported at even higher in cosmonauts (veterans of the Soviet/Russian space program) than first-time mothers or those who had experienced various forms of trauma (Suedfeld, Brcic, Johnson, & Gushin, 2012).

Similar experiences may be observed in those who initiated quests and pilgrimages, such as Appalachian Trail hikers in the US or the Shikoku pilgrimage in Japan (i.e., they visit 88 Buddhist temples in the island, often by foot). In addition, there are some "reality" TV programs that provide challenges, where contestants are excited to be challenging themselves to withstand physical and psychological difficulties associated with limited food, shelter, comfort, etc. Contestants generally report feeling a stronger sense of self and a future-oriented *can do* mentality. By studying the commonalities and differences in growth in the aftermath of traumatic and positive experiences, and those initiated or less predictably experienced, we will be able to advance our understanding of how people grow and experience positive changes as a result of experiencing positive major life events.

## PTG Through Parenting Experiences

There are several reports of PTG after childbirth or from parenting a child (Sawyer & Ayers, 2009). Taubman-Ben-Ari, Shlomo, Sivan, and Dolizki (2009), for example, investigated PTG related to the transition to motherhood. They conducted a longitudinal study among first-time mothers during the third trimester of their pregnancy (Time 1) and two months after giving birth (Time 2). Growth scores that included the five domains of the PTGI were significantly higher at Time 2. They also found that in addition to a measurably better marital relationship, higher appraisal of motherhood as a challenge contributed to a greater sense of growth. "Having experienced a critical life transition, the appraisal of the situation as less threatening may therefore lead to higher well-being, but in order to experience growth, the situation must be assessed as a challenge" (Taubman-Ben-Ari et al., 2009, pp. 964–965), being consistent with the PTG model.

The significant role of perceptions of challenges or severity of the triggering event in PTG has also been demonstrated in a study comparing first-time parents of preterm babies and those of full-term babies (Spielman & Taubman-Ben-Ari, 2009). One month after the birth of their child, parents participated in completion of a survey that included the PTGI. Results showed that PTG was higher in parents of premature infants than those of full-term infants, and that PTG was higher in mothers than in fathers. The authors suggested that giving birth to a baby who is born prematurely is likely to create a crisis type of event, as most often a pregnant woman would expect their baby to be full-term, and there can be more risks associated with premature births for both the mother and the child when compared to births that occur in the expected timeframe. Hence, the premature birth may give rise to core belief disruption in a way that a full-term birth may not, laying a foundation for the potential for PTG (Spielman & Taubman-Ben-Ari, 2009). These researchers, in fact, have conducted many more studies regarding personal growth following childbirth with a wider age range of parents and even grandparents, and confirmed the content validity as well as the factorial validity of the PTGI (Taubman-Ben-Ari, Findler, & Sharon, 2011; Taubman-Ben-ari, Shlomo, & Findler, 2012).

Other studies have focused on parenting a child with special needs or a child who has acquired life-altering disabilities (Konrad, 2006). Phelps, McCammon, Wuensch, and Golden (2009), for example, assessed growth among parents raising a child with an autism spectrum disorder. They hypothesized that the potential for traumatic losses, such as the realization that a child will not develop typically, may lead parents to find new insights in life and develop a greater sense of spirituality and strength. They used the PTGI by changing the original instruction of "as a result of the crisis" to "as a result of having a child with an autism spectrum disorder." The mean score of the PTGI yielded a moderate to high level of growth ($M = 67.47$, $SD = 20.65$). Their results also showed that PTG was not correlated with stress or the symptom severity of their child, consistent with the notion that stress and growth are not the opposite ends of a single spectrum. Zhang, Yan, Barriball, White, and Liu (2015) also studied PTG in mothers of children with autism in China in order to consider the possible effects of an Asian cultural context. They conducted semi-structured interviews with 11 mothers and found that the majority of them spontaneously reported PTG, especially a greater sense of personal strength and enhancement of relationships with others. The authors highlighted that PTG was found despite the achievement-oriented focus of Chinese culture, the one-child policy that was observed in China for many years, and a context in which autism spectrum disorder is not as understood across the community as it is in some other cultural contexts. Caring for someone with an autism spectrum disorder or other form of special need is in many instances a lifelong experience. There may be a distinction between PTG that occurs in parents who have a premature baby or child with a special need from growth processes that generally occur in any parents as their child develops, since they do not experience any major event that has a clear separation from before to after. However, for many parents, the time of diagnosis of autism or other congenital disorders is traumatic or at least highly stressful. They may have to wait for a diagnosis, suspecting something is not the way they expect but not knowing for certain. Parents may struggle to have their child's difference recognized within the school system, or gain access to supports needed by the child and his or her parents.

## Is It Possible to Experience PTG as a Result of Daily Hassles?

It is probably true that PTG would be over-reported if it is observed not only after a traumatic event, but also in those who have experienced daily hassles such as "I was late because I could not find a key," "I am stressed out because there are too many things to do," or "I need to fulfill obligations but I do not really want to." However, personal change can emerge from a series of small doses of hassles or stress. For example, O'Brien and Klein (2017) asserted that everyday fluctuations that are often caused by small events create ambiguity regarding when they reflect substantive shifts versus mere noise. They designed a series of studies to assess a handful of poor grades, bad games of sport, and gained pounds that led participants to report that intellect, athleticism, and health officially changed in a negative way. Yet corresponding positive signs were dismissed as fickle flukes, suggesting a negative bias in reporting the data. Even so, the opposite may be possible, too. The accumulation of daily hassles could, one day, add up at some point, and provide an opportunity for reflection about where a person is in their lives and where they want to be, prioritizing new goals, realizing their own capabilities, and/or shifting in which priorities in life are most important to them.

It remains likely, however, that PTG is distinctive from changes that occur after experiences that require little challenge to core beliefs, and to one's emotional life. PTG, by definition, reflects transformative changes that can occur for people as the result of the struggle they engage in following an experience that was so confronting, it disintegrated their schemas about the world and their place in it. Coping strategies and resources were overwhelmed by the event, unlike the stress from daily hassles or positive events (e.g., a wedding, a new baby). PTG is a transformative change that requires work; effortful rumination; challenging self-perceptions; reconfiguring life; and reassessing relationships, personal philosophy, and meaning making, and does not deny that some distress often remains to varying degrees. Sought challenges may be indicators that people are already questioning and seeking new ways to understand themselves and their lives before taking on the challenges themselves, so in some cases there may be PTG-like processes at work and PTG-like outcomes. To the degree that daily hassles pile up to an extent that they become major challenges, there may be an initiation of the processes that lead to PTG. To the degree that positive events challenge core beliefs, there may be PTG-like outcomes. However, in each case, the events must exert enough power to produce a transformative effect, which is distinctive from mere change and maturational development.

# CHAPTER 20

# Final Considerations

## PTG and Implications for the Life Philosophy

When the phenomenon of PTG appeared in the psychological literature in the 1990s, its primary purpose was to make people aware of the potential for positive post-trauma change and to encourage clinicians and researchers to have a well-balanced view of traumatized people's experiences, because past studies often focused only on negative aspects and how to alleviate the symptoms of pathology. Even at the very beginning of PTG history, it was conceptualized as a phenomenon distinct from the recovery process or decreased states of stress (Tedeschi & Calhoun, 1995). And yet, PTG caught considerable attention from many researchers and clinicians, not only because they in fact observed the phenomenon (so they understood the essence of PTG), but also because some were perhaps hoping that PTG could help in alleviating the negative symptoms they saw in their clients. However, as studies have accumulated, researchers have come to realize what Tedeschi and Calhoun originally meant—that is, experiencing PTG and PTSD are not contradictory and can coexist. However, for people who tend to take dichotomous perspectives, the coexistence of positives and negatives perhaps elicited some questions—if PTG does not always result in the alleviation of symptoms of distress, what good would PTG do for people?

First, PTG involves a reexamination of our own beliefs and attitudes, especially related to binary or dichotomous thinking such as good versus bad, positives versus negatives, all versus nothing, and justice versus injustice. According to Janoff-Bulman (1992), the assumptive world is a basic conceptual system that we develop over time, and it provides us with expectations about ourselves and the world so that we might function effectively. These core beliefs include views of human nature (benevolence and malevolence of people), the world (benevolence and malevolence of the world), the determination of the course of our lives (largely determined by chance or our control of outcomes), and other basic concepts that guide our ways of living. People hold various versions of these core beliefs, although the strength and importance of them varies. But striving for PTG following an event that led to challenging such schema forces us to reexamine what we believe. Perhaps there is growth in the realization and acceptance that bad things happen to good people, that sometimes bad people do well in life despite hurting others, that the world is not always fair and just, and that natural and manmade disasters both destroy lives. Just as there is no answer for what constitutes the right beliefs, there is probably no answer for what constitutes "positive" change that is applicable to all. Internalizing a PTG framework can help us to continuously reexamine our lives. PTG is not meant to be a Pollyanna view of the world. It does not deny extreme pain and distress or the difficulty of recovery, let alone the work involved in truly transformative change. In developing a system of core beliefs that is robust to future challenges, people become more comfortable with dialectical thinking that allows them to hold apparently opposing viewpoints simultaneously. The dialectic may be a more accurate view of people, the life course, and the world. One aspect of dialectical thinking that can emerge from PTG is the fact that we can only live here and now, and yet we constantly change. Change and the stress that can accompany it are inevitable in the human condition, and yet with change there is the opportunity for growth.

Experiencing PTG helps to create a meaningful experience out of the misery of trauma. As the existentialists have pointed out, suffering is an inescapable part of living, but creating a meaningful way to live through it brings a degree of comfort. With meaning there is hope and the ability to manage distress and even symptoms of PTSD. In the face of distress, the PTG process may allow people to seek the support of family and friends, proceed with humor (Veselka, Schermer, Martin, & Vernon, 2010) and positive emotions (Hutchinson & Pretelt, 2010), stay active (Bell, 2008), and so become more resilient.

Since core beliefs are implicated in the PTG process, PTG consistently poses ultimate questions of how and why we live. Many PTG researchers face the question of "so what" if people report growth? Does PTG lead to greater understanding of how to live life well? People may believe the goal in life is to have a good death, a lack of disease, a high level of well-being, happiness, and so on, and these ideas can be outcome variables in their studies. However, there are cultural differences in how we think about the ultimate goal of life (Joshanloo, 2014). Therefore, we need to be careful in making decisions about measuring quality of life in relation to PTG in various cultures and populations.

## The Role of PTG in Our Understanding of Trauma Response and Trauma Treatment

Perhaps, someday, PTG can become the usual way to think about trauma. Currently, PTG still tends to be perceived as "optional." Patients and survivors are considered to have had successful outcomes if symptoms have been reduced. In our work on PTG, we hope that the lens on trauma response has been widened to include the commonplace experiences of people who sincerely describe and live out the new perspectives that make their suffering tolerable and sometimes worthwhile. The work on PTG therefore moves us past the medical model of symptomology to a broader conception of trauma response. It is unclear if the PTG perspective will ever find a place in the DSM, but it will increasingly find a place in clinical practice and, even more importantly, the general public's understanding of what trauma survivorship entails.

There are important implications of the PTG focus for clinical work. Seeing PTG as a possible and common process for trauma survivors means that clinicians will be more focused on the definition of trauma from the point of view of the individual's core beliefs or assumptive world, and the degree to which these are challenged. Clinicians will be more willing to be expert companions, rather than to assume expertise about another person's experiences. Clinicians will also be more aware of the domains of PTG that may be emerging in the people they work with, and to bring these changes out into the open and focus on them. Clinicians will also be more focused on the aftermath of trauma, rather than on the trauma itself. And clinicians will be aware that PTG leads to ways for the people they work with to become equipped to be expert companions for others. The focus on PTG can be integrated into other standard trauma treatments, but will also change them to a degree.

At a broader social level, an understanding of PTG will produce a greater respect for people who have endured traumatic events. They will be appreciated as people who have been on the hero's journey and have something to offer the rest of us who only dimly perceive what they clearly see (Tedeschi & McNally, 2011). They can challenge the status quo, build social movements, and ultimately change societies (Bloom, 1998; Tedeschi, 1999).

In order to further these advances to clinical work and to the role of trauma survivors in our culture, research on PTG will continue to provide understanding of the processes involved. As we conduct this research, we must continue to be aware that there are subtle individual differences in the PTG process and that the experiences people have in the aftermath of trauma cannot be managed in a mechanical way. Instead, we need to know more about expert companionship, drawing on the rich literatures of interpersonal relationships and psychotherapy processes. PTG research has already shown us that there are various domains of PTG and various trajectories of PTG over time. There is more to learn by reaching down to the individual level of experience as well as using the group level analyses that we have referred to many times in this volume.

Finally, as all of us writing this book are involved in academics, we are aware that there is typically little focus on PTG in clinical training. We believe that this needs to change, and that students must be made more aware of how common trauma experiences are in people's lives, and consider how these experiences can be mined for ways to enhance the meanings and purposes people use to guide their life choices and everyday behavior. In a time where clinicians have become preoccupied with treatment manuals and empirically based interventions, we hope that practices arising out of PTG research will also be recognized as empirically based while at the same time representing the importance of a close connection to and respect for people seeking help that is clearly found in humanistic, existential, narrative, and constructivist approaches to therapy.

Over the years, we have heard from many people who have survived various kinds of trauma, who have encountered our work, most often by chance but also sometimes in talkback radio situations. What is most gratifying is when they tell us "that is exactly what I have been going through; I didn't realize there was a name for it!" This is the personally important validation that leads us to continue to pursue work in PTG research and clinical practice, and we hope our readers will likewise be motivated to pursue ways to contribute to this field.

# References

Aboelela, S. W., Larson, E., Bakken, S., Carrasquillo, O., Formicola, A., Glied, S. A., . . . Gebbie, K. M. (2007). Defining interdisciplinary research: Conclusions from a critical review of the literature. *Health Services Research, 42*, 329–346. doi: 10.1111/j.1475-6773.2006.00621.x

Abraído-Lanza, A. F., Guier, C., & Colón, R. M. (1998). Psychological thriving among Latinas with chronic illness. *Journal of Social Issues, 54*, 405–424. doi: 10.1111/j.1540-4560.1887.tb01227.x

Abu-Raiya, H., Pargament, K. I., & Mahoney, A. (2011). Examining coping methods with stressful interpersonal events experienced by Muslims living in the United States following the 9/11 attacks. *Psychology of Religion and Spirituality, 3*, 1–14. doi: 10.1037/a0020034

Adams, H. L. (2015). Insights into processes of posttraumatic growth through narrative analysis of chronic illness stories. *Qualitative Psychology, 2*, 111–129. doi: 10.1037/qup0000025

Adams, K., Shakespeare-Finch, J., & Armstrong, D. (2015). An interpretative phenomenological analysis of stress and well-being in Emergency Medical Dispatchers. *Journal of Loss and Trauma, 20*, 443–448. doi: 10.1080/15325024.2014.949141

Affleck, G., & Tennen, H. (1996). Construing benefits from adversity: Adaptational significance and dispositional underpinnings. *Journal of Personality, 64*, 899–922. doi: 10.1111/j.1467-6494.1996.tb00948.x

Ai, A. L., Hall, D., Pargament, K., & Tice, T. N. (2013). Posttraumatic growth in patients who survived cardiac surgery: The predictive and mediating roles of faith-based factors. *Journal of Behavior Medicine, 36*, 186–198. doi: 10.1007/s10865-012-9412-6

Albuquerque, S., Narciso, I., & Pereira, M. (2018). Posttraumatic growth in bereaved parents: A multidimensional model of associated factors. *Psychological Trauma: Theory, Research, Practice, and Policy, 10*(2), 199–207. doi:10.1037/tra0000305

Alisic, E., van der Schoot, T. A. W., van Ginkel, J. R., & Kleber, R. J. (2008). Looking beyond posttraumatic stress disorder in children: Posttraumatic stress reactions, posttraumatic growth, and quality of life in a general population sample. *Journal of Clinical Psychiatry*, *69*, 1455–1461.

Allbaugh, L. J., Wright, M. O., & Folger, S. F. (2016). The role of repetitive thought in determining posttraumatic growth and distress following interpersonal trauma. *Anxiety, Stress, & Coping, 29*, 21–37. doi: 10.1080/10615806.2015.1015422

Aloni, N. (1989). The three pedagogical dimensions of Nietzsche's philosophy. *Educational Theory, 39*, 301–306. doi: 10.1111/j.1741-5446.1989.00301.x

American Psychiatric Association. (1980). *Diagnostic and statistical manual of mental disorders* (3rd ed.). Washington, DC: Author.

American Psychiatric Association. (1994). *Diagnostic and statistical manual of mental disorders* (4th ed.). Washington, DC: Author.

American Psychiatric Association. (2013). *Diagnostic and statistical manual of mental disorders* (5th ed.). Washington, DC: Author.

Anders, A. L., Peterson, C. K., James, L. M., Engdahl, B., Leuthold, A. C., & Georgopoulos, A. P. (2015). Neural communication in posttraumatic growth. *Experimental Brain Research, 233*, 2013–2020. doi: 10.1007/s00221-015-4272-2

Anderson, D., Prioleau, P., Taku, K., Naruse, Y., Sekine, H., Maeda, M., . . . Yanagisawa, R. (2016). Post-traumatic stress and growth among medical student volunteers after the March 2011 disaster in Fukushima, Japan: Implications for student involvement with future disasters. *Psychiatric Quarterly, 87*, 241–251. doi: 10.1007/s11126-015-9381-3

Andrades, M., García, F. E., Reyes-Reyes, A., Martínez-Arias, R., & Calonge, I. (2016). Psychometric properties of the Posttraumatic Growth Inventory for Children in Chilean population affected by the earthquake of 2010. *American Journal of Orthopsychiatry, 86*, 686–692. doi: 10.1037/ort0000182

Antoni, M. H., Lehman, J. M., Kilbourn, K. M., Boyers, A. E., Culver, J. L., Alferi, S. M., . . . Carver, C. S. (2001). Cognitive-behavioral stress management intervention decreases the prevalence of depression and enhances benefit finding among women under treatment for early-stage breast cancer. *Health Psychology, 20*, 20–32. doi: 10.1037/0278-6133.20.1.20

Antonovsky, A. (1987). *Unraveling the mystery of health: How people manage stress and stay well*. San Francisco, CA: Jossey-Bass.

Antonovsky, H., & Sagy, S. (1986). The development of a sense of coherence and its impact on responses to stress situations. *The Journal of Social Psychology, 126*, 213–225.

Anusic, I., & Yap, S. C. Y. (2014). Using longitudinal studies to understand post-traumatic growth. *European Journal of Personality, 28*, 332–333. doi: 10.1002/per.1970

Arënliu, A., & Landsman, M. S. (2010). Thriving in postwar Kosova. In R. Berger & T. Weiss (Eds.), *Posttraumatic growth and culturally competent practice: Lessons learned from around the globe* (pp. 65–72). Hoboken, NJ: John Wiley & Sons.

Arikan, G., Stopa, L., Carnelley, K., & Karl, A. (2016). The associations between adult attachment, posttraumatic symptoms, and posttraumatic growth. *Anxiety, Stress, & Coping, 29*, 1–20. doi: 10.1080/10615806.2015.1009833

Armeli, S., Gunthert, K., & Cohen, L. (2001). Stressor appraisals, coping, and post-event outcomes: The dimensionality and antecedents of stress-related growth. *Journal of Social & Clinical Psychology, 20*, 366–395. doi: 10.1521/jscp.20.3.366.22304

Armstrong, D., Shakespeare-Finch, J., & Shochet, I. (2014). Predicting posttraumatic growth and posttraumatic stress in fire-fighters. *Australian Journal of Psychology, 66*, 38–46. doi: 10.1111/ajpy.12032

Armstrong, D., Shakespeare-Finch, J., & Shochet, I. (2016). Organisational belongingness mediates the relationship between sources of stress and post-trauma outcomes in fire-fighters. *Psychological Trauma: Research, Theory Practice & Policy, 8*, 343–347. doi: 10.1037/tra0000083

Arnold, D., Calhoun, L. G., Tedeschi, R., & Cann, A. (2005). Vicarious posttraumatic growth in psychotherapy. *Journal of Humanistic Psychology, 45*, 239–263. doi: 10.1177/0022167805274729

Aronson, K. R., Kyler, S. J., Morgan, N. R., Perkins, D. F., & Love, L. (2017). Spouse and family functioning before and after a Marine's suicide: Comparisons to deaths by accident and in combat. *Military Psychology, 29*, 294–306. doi: 10.1037/mil0000156

Arpawong, T. E., Sussman, S., Milam, J. E., Unger, J. B., Land, H., Sun, P., & Rohrbach, L. A. (2015). Post-traumatic growth, stressful life events, and relationships with substance use behaviors among alternative high school students: A prospective study. *Psychology & Health, 30*, 475–494. doi: 10.1080/08870446.2014.979171

Aspinwall, L. G., & Tedeschi, R. G. (2010). The value of positive psychology for health psychology: Progress and pitfalls in examining the relation of positive phenomena to health. *Annals of Behavioral Medicine, 39*, 4–15. doi: 10.1007/s12160-009-9153-0

Asukai, N., Kato, H., Kawamura, N., Kim, Y., Yamamoto, K., Kishimoto, J., . . . Nishizono-Maher, A. (2002). Reliability and validity of the Japanese-language version of the Impact of Event Scale-Revised (IES-R-J): Four studies of different traumatic events. *Journal of Nervous and Mental Disease, 190*, 175–182. doi: 10.1097/00005053-200203000-00066

Ávila, M., Coimbra, J. L., Park, C. L., & Matos, P. M. (2017). Attachment and posttraumatic growth after breast cancer: A dyadic approach. *Psycho-Oncology, 26*, 1929–1935. doi: 10.1002/pon.4409

Ayduk, Ö., & Kross, E. (2008). Enhancing the pace of recovery: Self-distanced analysis of negative experiences reduces blood pressure reactivity. *Psychological Science, 19*, 229–231. doi: 10.1111/j.1467-9280.2008.02073.x

Baer, R. A., Smith, G. T., Hopkins, J., Krietemeyer, J., & Toney, L. (2006). Using self-report assessment methods to explore facets of mindfulness. *Assessment, 13*(1), 27–45. doi: 10.1177/1073191105283504

Baker, J. M., Kelly, C., Calhoun, L. G., Cann, A., & Tedeschi, R. G. (2008). An examination of posttraumatic growth and posttraumatic depreciation: Two exploratory studies. *Journal of Loss and Trauma, 13*, 450–465. doi: 10.1080/15325020802171367

Baltes, P. B. (1987). Theoretical propositions of life-span developmental psychology: On the dynamics between growth and decline. *Developmental Psychology, 23*, 611–626. doi: 10.1037/0012-1649.23.5.611

Bangen, K. J., Meeks, T. W., & Jeste, D. V. (2013). Defining and assessing wisdom: A review of the literature. *American Journal of Geriatric Psychiatry, 21*, 1254–1266. doi: 10.1016/j.jagp.2012.11.020

Banth, S., & Talwar, C. (2012). Anasakti, the Hindu ideal, and its relationship to well-being and orientations to happiness. *Journal of Religion and Health, 51*, 934–946. doi: 10.1007/s10943-010-9402-3

Barakat, L. P., Alderfer, M. A., & Kazak, A. E. (2006). Posttraumatic growth in adolescent survivors of cancer and their mothers and fathers. *Journal of Pediatric Psychology, 31*, 413–419. doi: 10.1093/jpepsy/jsj058

Barrington, A., & Shakespeare-Finch, J. (2013). Posttraumatic growth and posttraumatic depreciation as predictors of psychological adjustment. *Journal of Loss and Trauma, 18*, 429–443. doi: 10.1080/15325024.2012.714210

Barrington, A., & Shakespeare-Finch, J. (2014). Giving voice to service providers who work with survivors of torture and trauma. *Qualitative Health Research, 24*, 1686–1699. doi: 10.1177/1049732314549023

Bates, G. W., Trajstman, S. E. A., & Jackson, C. A. (2004). Internal consistency, test-retest reliability and sex differences on the Posttraumatic Growth Inventory in an Australian sample with trauma. *Psychological Reports, 94*, 793–794. doi: 10.2466/PR0.94.3.793-794

Baucom, D. H., Porter, S., Kirby, J. S., Gremore, T. M., Wiesenthal, N., Aldridge, W., . . . Keefe, F. J. (2009). A couple-based intervention for female breast cancer. *Psycho-Oncology, 18,* 276–283. doi: 10.1002/pon.1395

Bauwens, J., & Tosone, C. (2010). Professional posttraumatic growth after a shared traumatic experience: Manhattan clinicians' perspectives on post-9/11 practice. *Journal of Loss and Trauma, 15,* 498–517. doi: 10.1080/15325024.2010.519267

Bayer-Topilsky, T., Itzhaky, H., Dekel, R., & Marmor, Y. N. (2013). Mental health and posttraumatic growth in civilians exposed to ongoing terror. *Journal of Loss and Trauma, 18,* 227–247. doi: 10.1080/15325024.2012.687325

Beck, A. T., Steer, R. A., & Carbin, M. G. (1988). Psychometric properties of the Beck Depression Inventory: Twenty-five years of evaluation. *Clinical Psychology Review, 8,* 77–100. doi: 10.1016/0272-7358(88)90050-5

Beck, C., Morgan-Eaton, C., & Gable, K. (2017). Vicarious posttraumatic growth in labor and delivery nurses. *Journal of Obstetric, Gynecologic & Neonatal Nursing, 43,* S43. doi: 10.1016/j.jogn.2017.04.123

Behr, S. K., Murphy, D. L., & Summers, J. A. (1991). *Kansas inventory of parental perceptions.* Lawrence: University of Kansas.

Bell, C. C. (2008). Asian martial arts and resiliency. *Ethnicity and Inequalities in Health and Social Care, 1,* 11–17. doi: 10.1108/17570980200800016

Bellizzi, K. M., Smith, A. W., Reeve, B. B., Alfano, C. M., Bernstein, L., Meeske, K., . . . Ballard-Barbash, R. R. (2009). Posttraumatic growth and health-related quality of life in a racially diverse cohort of breast cancer survivors. *Journal of Health Psychology, 15,* 615–626. doi: 10.1177/1359105309356364

Ben-Porat, A. (2015). Vicarious posttraumatic growth: Domestic violence therapists versus social service department therapists in Israel. *Journal of Family Violence, 30,* 923–933. doi: 10.1007/s10896-015-9714-x

Bensimon, M. (2012). Elaboration on the association between trauma, PTSD and posttraumatic growth: The role of trait resilience. *Personality and Individual Differences, 52,* 782–787. doi: 10.1016/j.paid.2012.01.011

Berger, R. (2015). *Stress, trauma and posttraumatic growth: Social context, environment and identities.* New York, NY: Routledge.

Berger, R., & Weiss, T. (2009). The posttraumatic growth model: An expansion to the family system. *Traumatology, 15,* 63–74. doi: 10.1177/1534765608323499

Berntsen, D., & Rubin, D. C. (2006). The centrality of event scale: A measure of integrating a trauma into one's identity and its relation to post-traumatic stress disorder symptoms. *Behaviour Research and Therapy, 44,* 219–231. doi: 10.1016/j.brat.2005.01.009

Berry, L. E. (2016). The research relationship in narrative enquiry. *Nurse Researcher, 24,* 10–14. doi: 10.7748/nr.2016.e1430

Bhushan, N. (2008). Toward an anatomy of mourning: Discipline, devotion and liberation in a Freudian-Buddhist framework. *Sophia, 47,* 57–69. doi: 10.1007/s11841-008-0048-5

Black, B., & Sandelowski, M. (2010). Personal growth after severe fetal diagnosis. *Western Journal of Nursing Research, 32,* 1011–1030. doi: 10.1177/0193945910371215

Blackie, L. E. R., Jayawickreme, E., Helzer, E.G., Forgeard, M. J. C., & Roepke, A. M. (2015). Investigating the veracity of self-perceived posttraumatic growth: A profile analysis approach to corroboration. *Social Psychological and Personality Science, 6,* 788–796. doi: 10.1177/1948550615587986

Bloom, S. L. (1998). By the crowd they have been broken, by the crowd they shall be healed: The social transformation of trauma. In R. G. Tedeschi, C. L. Park, & L. G. Calhoun (Eds.), *Posttraumatic growth: Positive changes in the aftermath of crisis* (pp. 179–213). Mahwah, NJ: Lawrence Erlbaum Associates, Inc.

Boals, A. (2010). Events that have become central to identity: Gender differences in the Centrality of Events Scale for positive and negative events. *Applied Cognitive Psychology*, *24*, 107–121. doi: 10.1002/acp.1548

Boermans, S., Kamphuis, W., Delahaij, R., van den Berg, C., & Euwema, M. (2014). Team spirit makes the difference: The interactive effects of team work engagement and organizational constraints during a military operation on psychological outcomes afterwards. *Stress and Health*, *30*, 386–396. doi: 10.1002/smi.2621

Bollinger, J. W. (2017). Evidence of absence: Proposals for improving the treatment of combat-related PTSD. *The Military Psychologist*, *32*, 11–14.

Bonanno, G. A., Mancini, A., Horton, J., Powell, T., Leardmann, C., Boyko, E., . . . Smith, T. (2012). Trajectories of trauma symptoms and resilience in deployed US military service members: Prospective cohort study. *The British Journal of Psychiatry*, *200*, 317–323. doi: 10.1192/bjp.bp.111.096552

Bonanno, G. A., Romero, S. A., & Klein, S. I. (2015). The temporal elements of psychological resilience: An integrative framework for the study of individuals, families, and communities. *Psychological Inquiry*, *26*, 139–169. doi: 10.1080/1047840X.2015.992677

Bostock, L., Sheikh, A. I., & Barton, S. (2009). Posttraumatic growth and optimism in health-related trauma: A systematic review. *Journal of Clinical Psychology in Medical Settings*, *16*, 281–296. doi: 10.1007/s10880-009-9175-6

Bower, J. E., Kemeny, M. E., Taylor, S. E., & Fahey, J. L. (1998). Cognitive processing, discovery of meaning, CD 4 decline, and AIDS-related mortality among bereaved HIV-seropositive men. *Journal of Consulting and Clinical Psychology*, *66*, 979–986.

Bower, J. E., Moskowitz, J. T., & Epel, E. (2009). Is benefit finding good for your health? Pathways linking positive life changes after stress and physical health outcomes. *Current Directions in Psychological Science*, *18*, 337–341.

Bower, J. E., & Segerstrom, S. C. (2004). Stress management, finding benefit, and immune function: Positive mechanisms for intervention effects on physiology. *Journal of Psychosomatic Research*, *56*, 9–11. doi: 10.1016/S0022-3999(03)00120-X

Boyle, C. C., Stanton, A. L., Ganz, P. A., & Bower, J. E. (2017). Posttraumatic growth in breast cancer survivors: Does age matter? Age and posttraumatic growth after cancer. *Psycho-Oncology*, *26*, 800–807. doi: 10.1002/pon.4091

Bozo, Ö., Gündoğdu, E., & Büyükaşik-çolak, C. (2009). The moderating role of different sources of perceived social support on the dispositional optimism: Posttraumatic growth relationship in postoperative breast cancer patients. *Journal of Health Psychology*, *14*, 1009–1020. doi: 10.1177/1359105309342295

Britt, T. W., & Jex, S. M. (2015). *Thriving under stress: Harnessing demands in the workplace*. New York, NY: Oxford University Press.

Brockhouse, R., Msetfi, R. M., Cohen, K., & Joseph, S. (2011). Vicarious exposure to trauma and growth in Therapists: The moderating effects of sense of coherence, organizational support, and empathy. *Journal of Traumatic Stress*, *24*, 735–742. doi: 10.1002/jts.20704

Brooks, M., Graham-Kevan, M., Lowe, M., & Robinson, S. (2017). Rumination, event centrality, and perceived control as predictors of post-traumatic growth and distress: The Cognitive Growth and Stress model. *British Journal of Clinical Psychology*, *56*, 286–302. doi: 10.1111/bjc.12138

Brown, E. (2016). Plato on well-being. In G. Fletcher (Ed.), *The Routledge handbook of philosophy of well-being* (pp. 9–19). New York, NY: Routledge. doi: 10.4324/9781315682266

Brown, L. (2015). *Not the price of admission: Healthy relationships after childhood trauma*. Seattle, WA: Createspace Independent Publishing Platform.

Brunet, J., McDonough, M. H., Hadd, V., Crocker, P. R. E., & Sabiston, C. M. (2010). The Posttraumatic Growth Inventory: An examination of the factor structure and invariance among breast cancer survivors. *Psycho-Oncology, 19*, 830–838. doi: 10.1002/pon.1640

Bryan, C. J., Ray-Sannerud, B., Morrow, C. E., & Etienne, N. (2013). Guilt is more strongly associated with suicidal ideation among military personnel with direct combat exposure. *Journal of Affective Disorders, 148*, 37–41. doi: 10.1016/j.jad.2012.11.044

Büchi, S., Mörgeli, H., Schnyder, U., Jenewein, J., Glaser, A., Fauchère, J. C., . . . Sensky, T. (2009). Shared or discordant grief in couples 2–6 years after the death of their premature baby: Effects on suffering and posttraumatic growth. *Psychosomatics, 50*, 123–130.

Burke, K. J., & Shakespeare-Finch, J. (2011). Markers of resilience in new police officers: Appraisal of potentially traumatising events. *Traumatology, 17*, 52–60.

Bush, N. E., Skopp, N. A., McCann, R., & Luxton, D. D. (2011). Posttraumatic growth as protection against suicidal ideation after deployment and combat exposure. *Military Medicine, 176*(11), 1215–1222. doi:10.7205/MILMED-D-11-00018

Buswell, R. E., & Lopez, D. S. (2013). *The Princeton dictionary of Buddhism*. Princeton, NJ: Princeton University Press.

Cacciatore, J., & Flint, M. (2012). Attend: Toward a mindfulness-based bereavement care model. *Death Studies, 36*, 61–82. doi: 10.1080/07481187.2011.59.1275

Cadell, S., Regehr, C., & Hemsworth, D. (2003). Factors contributing to posttraumatic growth: A proposed structural equation model. *American Journal of Orthopsychiatry, 73*, 279–287. doi: 10.1037/0002-9432.73.3.279

Calhoun, L. G., Cann, A., & Tedeschi, R. G. (2010). The posttraumatic growth model: Sociocultural considerations. In T. Weiss & R. Berger (Eds.), *Posttraumatic growth and culturally competent practice: Lessons learned from around the globe* (pp. 1–14). Hoboken, NJ: John Wiley & Sons, Inc.

Calhoun, L. G., Cann, A., Tedeschi, R. G., & McMillan, J. (2000). A correlational test of the relationship between posttraumatic growth, religion, and cognitive processing. *Journal of Traumatic Stress, 13*, 521–527. doi: 10.1023/A:1007745627077

Calhoun, L. G., & Tedeschi, R. G. (1989-1990). Positive aspects of critical life problems: Recollections of grief. *Omega, 20*, 265–272.

Calhoun, L. G., & Tedeschi, R. G. (1991). Perceiving benefits in traumatic events: Some issues for practicing psychologists. *The Journal of Training and Practice in Professional Psychology, 5*, 45–52.

Calhoun, L. G., & Tedeschi, R. G. (1998a). Beyond recovery from trauma: Implication for clinical practice and research. *Journal of Social Issues, 54*, 357–371. doi: 10.1111/j.1540-4560.1998.tb01223.x

Calhoun, L. G., & Tedeschi, R. G. (1998b). Posttraumatic growth: Future directions. In R. G. Tedeschi, C. L. Park, & L. G. Calhoun (Eds.), *Posttraumatic growth: Positive changes in the aftermath of crisis* (pp. 215–238). Mahwah, NJ: Lawrence Erlbaum Associates, Inc.

Calhoun, L. G., & Tedeschi, R. G. (1999). *Facilitating posttraumatic growth: A clinician's guide*. Mahwah, NJ: Lawrence Erlbaum Associates, Inc.

Calhoun, L. G., & Tedeschi, R. G. (2004). The foundations of posttraumatic growth: New considerations. *Psychological Inquiry, 15*, 93–102.

Calhoun, L. G., & Tedeschi, R. G. (2006). The foundations of posttraumatic growth: An expanded framework. In L. G. Calhoun & R. G. Tedeschi (Eds.), *Handbook of posttraumatic growth: Research and practice* (pp. 3–23). Mahwah, NJ: Lawrence Erlbaum Associates, Inc.

Calhoun, L. G., & Tedeschi, R. G. (2013). *Posttraumatic growth in clinical practice*. New York and London: Routledge.

Calhoun, L. G., Tedeschi, R. G., Cann, A., & Hanks, E. A. (2010). Positive outcomes following bereavement: Paths to posttraumatic growth. *Psychologica Belgica, 50*(1&2), 125–143.

Canevello, A., Michels, V., & Hilaire, N. (2016). Posttraumatic growth: Spouses' relationship quality and psychological distress. *Journal of Loss and Trauma, 21*(6), 548–559. doi: 10.1080/15325024.2016.1159112

Cann, A., Calhoun, L. G., Tedeschi, R. G., Kilmer, R. P., Gil-Rivas, V., Vishnevsky, T., & Danhauer, S. C. (2010). The Core Beliefs Inventory: A brief measure of disruption in the assumptive world. *Anxiety, Stress, & Coping, 23*, 19–34. doi: 10.1080/10615800802573013

Cann, A., Calhoun, L. G., Tedeschi, R. G., & Solomon, D. T. (2010). Posttraumatic growth and depreciation as independent experiences and predictors of well-being. *Journal of Loss and Trauma, 15*, 151–166. doi: 10.1080/15325020903375826

Cann, A., Calhoun, L. G., Tedeschi, R. G., Taku, K., Vishnevsky, T., Triplett, K. N., & Danhauer, S. C. (2010). A short form of the Posttraumatic Growth Inventory. *Anxiety, Stress, & Coping, 23*, 127–137. doi: 10.1080/10615800903094273

Cann, A., Calhoun, L. G., Tedeschi, R. G., Triplett, K. N., Vishnevsky, T., & Lindstrom, C. M. (2011). Assessing posttraumatic cognitive processes: The Event Related Rumination Inventory. *Anxiety, Stress, & Coping, 24*, 137–156. doi: 10.1080/10615806.2010.529901

Carlson, R. (2006). *You can be happy no matter what: Five principles for keeping life in perspective.* Novato, CA: New World Library.

Carver, C. S. (1998). Resilience and thriving: Issues, models, and linkages. *Journal of Social Issues, 54*(2), 245–266. doi: 10.1111/0022-4537.641998064

Caspi, A., Roberts, B. W., & Shiner, R. L. (2005). Personality development: Stability and change. *Annual Review of Psychology, 56*, 453–484. doi: 10.1146/annurev.psych.55.090902.141913

Chan, C. S., & Rhodes, J. E. (2013). Religious coping, posttraumatic stress, psychological distress, and posttraumatic growth among female survivors four years after Hurricane Katrina. *Journal of Traumatic Stress, 26*, 257–265. doi: 10.1002/jts.21801

Cheng, C. H. K., Ho, S. M. Y., & Rochelle, T. L. (2017). Examining the psychometric properties of the Chinese Post-Traumatic Growth Inventory for patients suffering from chronic diseases. *Journal of Health Psychology, 22*, 874–885. doi: 10.1177/1359105315617330

Chopko, B. A. (2010). Posttraumatic distress and growth: An empirical study of police officers. *American Journal of Psychotherapy, 64*, 55–72.

Chun, S., & Lee, Y. (2008). The experience of posttraumatic growth for people with spinal cord injury. *Qualitative Health Research, 18*, 877–890. doi: 10.1177/1049732308318028

Chun, S., & Lee, Y. (2010). The role of leisure in the experience of posttraumatic growth for people with spinal cord injury. *Journal of Leisure Research, 42*, 393–415.

Cieslak, R., Benight, C., Schmidt, N., Luszczynska, A., Curtin, E., Clark, R. A., & Kissinger, P. (2009). Predicting posttraumatic growth among Hurricane Katrina survivors living with HIV: The role of self-efficacy, social support, and PTSD. *Anxiety, Stress, & Coping, 22*, 449–463. doi: 10.1080/10615800802403815

Clay, R., Knibbs, J., & Joseph, S. (2009). Measurement of posttraumatic growth in young people: A review. *Clinical Child Psychology and Psychiatry, 14*, 411–422. doi: 10.1177/1359104509104049

Cobb, A. R., Tedeschi, R. G., Calhoun, L. G., & Cann, A. (2006). Correlates of posttraumatic growth in survivors of intimate partner violence. *Journal of Traumatic Stress, 19*, 895–903. doi: 10.1002/jts.20171

Cockshaw, W., & Shochet, I. (2010). The link between belongingness and depressive symptoms: An exploration in the workplace interpersonal context. *Australian Psychologist, 45*, 283–289. doi: 10 .1080/00050061003752418

Cohan, C. L., Cole, S. W., & Schoen, R. (2009). Divorce following the September 11 terrorist attacks. *Journal of Social and Personal Relationships, 26*, 512–530. doi: 10.1177/0265407509351043

Cohen, K., & Collens, P. (2013). The impact of trauma work on trauma workers: A metasynthesis on vicarious trauma and vicarious posttraumatic growth. *Psychological Trauma: Theory, Research, Practice, and Policy, 5*, 570–580. doi: 10.1037/a0030388

Cohen, L. H., Cimbolie, K., Armeli, S. R., & Hettler, T. R. (1998). Quantitative assessment of thriving. *Journal of Social Issues, 54*, 323–335. doi: 10.1111/0022-4537.681998068

Cohen, L. H., Hettler, T. R., & Pane, N. (1998). Assessment of posttraumatic growth. In R. G. Tedeschi, C. L. Park, & L. G. Calhoun (Eds.), *Posttraumatic growth: Positive changes in the aftermath of crisis* (pp. 23–42). Mahwah, NJ: Erlbaum.

Cohen, M., & Numa, M. (2011). Posttraumatic growth in breast cancer survivors: A comparison of volunteers and non-volunteers. *Psycho-Oncology, 20*, 69–76. doi: 10.1002/pon.1709

Collicutt McGrath, J. (2006). Posttraumatic growth and the origins of early Christianity. *Mental Health, Religion, & Culture, 9*, 291–306.

Collins, R. L., Taylor, S. E., & Skokan, L. A. (1990). A better world or a shattered vision? Changes in life perspectives following victimization. *Social Cognition, 8*, 263–285. doi: 10.1521/soco.1990.8.3.263

Colville, G., & Cream, P. (2009). Post-traumatic growth in parents after a child's admission to intensive care: Maybe Nietzsche was right? *Intensive Care Medicine, 35*, 919–923. doi: 10.1007/s00134-009-1444-1

Constantinou, E., van den Houte, M., Bogaerts, K., van Diest, I., & van den Bergh, O. (2014). Can words heal? Using affect labeling to reduce the effects of unpleasant cues on symptom reporting. *Frontiers in Psychology, 22*. doi: 10.3389/fpsyg.2014.00807

Copping, A. (2010). *The role of distal and proximate culture on post-trauma outcomes: African and Australian populations.* Unpublished PhD manuscript. University of Tasmania, Tasmania.

Copping, A., & Shakespeare-Finch, J. (2013). Trauma and survival in African humanitarian entrants to Australia. In K. M. Gow & M. Celenski (Eds.), *Mass trauma: Impact and recovery issues* (pp. 331–348). New York: Nova Science.

Copping, A., Shakespeare-Finch, J., & Paton, D. (2010). Towards a culturally appropriate mental health system: Sudanese- Australians' experiences with trauma. *Journal of Pacific Rim Psychology, 4*(1), 53–60. doi: 10.1375/prp.4.1.53

Cosden, M., Sanford, A., Koch, L. M., & Lepore, C. (2016). Vicarious trauma and vicarious posttraumatic growth among substance abuse treatment providers. *Substance Abuse, 37*, 619–624. doi: 10.1080/08897077.2016.1181695

Costa, R. V., & Pakenham, K. I. (2012). Association between benefit finding and adjustment outcomes in thyroid cancer. *Psycho-Oncology, 21*, 734–744. doi: 10.1002/pon.1960

Cox, N., Dewaele, A., van Houtte, M., & Vincke, J. (2011). Stress-related growth, coming out, and internalized homonegativity in lesbian, gay, and bisexual youth: An examination of stress-related growth within the minority stress model. *Journal of Homosexuality, 58*(1), 117–137. doi: 10.1080/00918369.2011.533631

Coyne, J. C., & Tennen, H. (2010). Positive psychology in cancer care: Bad science, exaggerated claims, and unproven medicine. *Annals of Behavioral Medicine, 39*, 16–26. doi: 10.1007/s12160-009-9154-z

Cozzolino, P. J., Staples, A. D., Meyers, L. S., & Samboceti, J. (2004). Greed, death, and values: From terror management to transcendence management theory. *Personality and Social Psychology Bulletin, 30*, 278–292. doi: 10.1177/0146167203260716

Cryder, C. H., Kilmer, R. P., Tedeschi, R. G., & Calhoun, L. G. (2006). An exploratory study of posttraumatic growth in children following a natural disaster. *American Journal of Orthopsychiatry, 76*, 65–69. doi: 10.1037/0002-9432.76.1.65

Currier, J. M., Hermes, S., & Phipps, S. (2009). Brief report: Children's response to serious illness: Perceptions of benefit and burden in a pediatric cancer population. *Journal of Pediatric Psychology, 34,* 1129–1134. doi: 10.1093/jpepsy/jsp021

Currier, J. M., Mallot, J., Martinez, T. E., Sandy, C., & Neimeyer, R. A. (2013). Bereavement, religion, and posttraumatic growth: A matched control group investigation. *Psychology or Religion and Spirituality, 5,* 69–77. doi: 10.1037/a0027708

Dabrowski, K. (1964). *Positive disintegration.* Oxford, UK: Little, Brown.

Danhauer, S. C., Russell, G. B., Case, L. D., Sohl, S. J., Tedeschi, R. G., Addington, E. L., . . . Avis, N. E. (2015). Trajectories of posttraumatic growth and associated characteristics in women with breast cancer. *Annals of Behavioral Medicine, 49*(5), 650–659. doi: 10.1007/s12160-015-9696-1

Danhauer, S. C., Russell, G. B., Tedeschi, R. G., Jesse, M. T., Vishnevsky, T., . . . Powell, B. L. (2013). A longitudinal investigation of posttraumatic growth in adult patients undergoing treatment for acute leukemia. *Journal of Clinical Psychology in Medical Settings, 20,* 13–24. doi: 10.1007/s10880-012-9304-5

Davis, C. G., & McKearney, J. M. (2003). How do people grow from their experience with trauma or loss? *Journal of Social and Clinical Psychology, 22,* 477–492. doi: 10.1521/jscp.22.5.477.22928

Day, M. C., & Wadey, R. (2016). Narratives of trauma, recovery, and growth: The complex role of sport following permanent acquired disability. *Psychology of Sport and Exercise, 22,* 131–138. doi: 10.1016/j.psychsport.2015.07.004

Dekel, R. (2007). Posttraumatic distress and growth among wives of prisoners of war: The contribution of husbands' posttraumatic stress disorder and wives' own attachment. *American Journal of Orthopsychiatry, 77,* 419–426. doi: 10.1037/0002-9432.77.3.419

Dekel, S., Hankin, I. T., Pratt, J. A., Hackler, D. R., & Lanman, O. N. (2016). Posttraumatic growth in trauma recollections of 9/11 survivors: A narrative approach. *Journal of Loss and Trauma, 21*(4), 315–324. doi:10.1080/15325024.2015.1108791

Dekel, S., Mamon, D., Solomon, Z., Lanman, O., & Dishy, G. (2016). Can guilt lead to psychological growth following trauma exposure? *Psychiatry Research, 236,* 196–198. doi: 10.1016/j.psychres.2016.01.011

Dekel, S., Mandl, C., & Solomon, Z. (2013). Is the Holocaust implicated in posttraumatic growth in second-generation Holocaust survivors? A prospective study. *Journal of Traumatic Stress, 26,* 530–533. doi: 10.1002/jts.21836

Delle Fave, A., Brdar, I., Wissing, M. P., Araujo, U., Castro Solano, A., Freire, T., . . . Soosai-Nathan, L. (2016). Lay definitions of happiness across nations: The primacy of inner harmony and relational connectedness. *Frontiers in Psychology, 7,* 30. doi: 10.3389/fpsyg.2016.00030

Denney, R. M., Aten, J. D., & Leavell, K. (2011). Posttraumatic spiritual growth: A phenomenological study of cancer survivors. *Mental Healthy Religion & Culture, 14,* 371–391. doi: 10.1080/13674671003758667

Derogatis, L. R., & Lazarus, L. (1994). SCL-90—R, Brief Symptom Inventory, and matching clinical rating scales. In M. E. Maruish (Ed.), *The use of psychological testing for treatment planning and outcome assessment* (pp. 217–248). Hillsdale, NJ: Lawrence Erlbaum Associates.

Devine, K. A., Reed-Knight, B., Loiselle, K. A., Fenton, N., & Blount, R. L. (2010). Posttraumatic growth in young adults who experienced serious childhood illness: A mixed-methods approach. *Journal of Clinical Psychology in Medical Settings, 17,* 340–348. doi: 10.1007/s10880-010-9210-7

DeViva, J. C., Sheerin, C. M., Southwick, S. M., Roy, A. M., Pietrzak, R. H., & Harpaz-Rotem, I. (2016). Correlates of VA mental health treatment utilization among OEF/OIF/

OND veterans: Resilience, stigma, social support, personality, and beliefs about treatment. *Psychological Trauma: Theory, Research, Practice, and Policy, 8*, 310–318. doi: 10.1037/tra0000075

Diener, E., Emmons, R. A., Larsen, R. J., & Griffin, S. (1985). The satisfaction with life scale. *Journal of Personality Assessment, 49*, 71–75.

Diener, E., Wirtz, D., Tov, W., Kim-Prieto, C., Choi, D., Oishi, S., & Biswas-Diener, R. (2010). New well-being measures: Short scales to assess flourishing and positive and negative feelings. *Social Indicators Research, 97*(2), 143–156. doi:10.1007/s11205-009-9493-y

Dirik, G., & Karanci, A. N. (2008). Variables related to posttraumatic growth in Turkish rheumatoid arthritis patients. *Journal of Clinical Psychology in Medical Settings, 15*, 193–203. doi: 10.1007/s10880-008-9115-x

Dolbier, C. L., Jaggars, S. S., & Steinhardt, M. A. (2010). Stress-related growth: Pre-intervention correlates and change following a resilience intervention. *Stress and Health, 26*, 135–147. doi: 10.1002/smi.1275

Dong, C., Gong, S., Jiang, L., Deng, G., & Lui, X. (2015). Posttraumatic growth within the first three months after accidental injury in China: The role of self-disclosure, cognitive processing, and psychosocial resources. *Psychology, Health, & Medicine, 20*, 154–164. doi: 10.1080/13548506.2014.913795

Dong, X., Guopeng, L., Lui, C., Kong, L., Fang, Y., Kang, X., & Li, P. (2017). The mediating role of resilience in the relationship between social support and posttraumatic growth among colorectal cancer survivors with permanent intestinal ostomies: A structural equation model analysis. *European Journal of Oncology Nursing, 29*, 47–52. doi: 10.1016/j.ejon.2017.04.007

Doron-LaMarca, S., Vogt, D. S., King, D. W., King, L. A., & Saxe, G. N. (2010). Pretrauma problems, prior stress exposure, and gender as predictors of change in posttraumatic stress symptoms among physically injured children and adolescents. *Journal of Consulting and Clinical Psychology, 78*, 781–793. doi: 10.1037/a0021529

Dunkel, C. S., & Sefcek, J. A. (2009). Eriksonian lifespan theory and life history theory: An integration using the example of identity formation. *Review of General Psychology, 13*, 13–23. doi: 10.1037/a0013687

Duran, B. (2013). Posttraumatic growth as experienced by childhood cancer survivors and their families: A narrative synthesis of qualitative and quantitative research. *Journal of Pediatric Oncology Nursing, 30*, 179–197. doi: 10.1177/104345421387433

Durkin, J., & Joseph, S. (2009). Growth following adversity and its relation with subjective well-being and psychological well-being. *Journal of Loss and Trauma, 14*, 228–234. doi: 10.1080/15325020802540561

D'Urso, A., Mastroyannopoulou, K., & Kirby, A. (2017). Experiences of posttraumatic growth in siblings of children with cancer. *Clinical Child Psychology and Psychiatry, 22*, 301–317. doi: 10.1177/1359104516660749

Elder, W. B., Domino, J. L., Rentz, T. O., & Mata-Galán, E. L. (2017). Conceptual model of male military sexual trauma. *Psychological Trauma: Theory, Research, Practice and Policy, 9*(Suppl 1), 59–66. doi:10.1037/tra0000194

Elliot, K. J., Scott, J. L., Monsour, M., & Nuwayhid, F. (2015). Profiles of dyadic adjustment for advanced prostate cancer to inform couple-based intervention. *Psychology and Health, 30*, 1257–1273. doi: 10.1080/08870446.2015.1043301

Emergency Management Australia. (2004). *Manual 10 recovery*. Australian Emergency Manual Series. Edited and published by the Australian Institute for Disaster Resilience, on behalf of the Australian Government Attorney-General's Department. East Melbourne, Victoria, Australia.

Emerson, M., Mirola, W., & Monahan, S. (2016). *What sociology teaches us about religion in our world.* New York, NY: Routledge.

Engstrom, D., Hernandez, P., & Gangsei, D. (2008). Vicarious resilience: A qualitative investigation into its description. *Traumatology, 14,* 13–21. doi: 10.1177/1534765608319323

Epstein, S. (1990). Cognitive-experiential self-theory. In L. A. Pervin (Ed.), *Handbook of personality: Theory and research* (pp. 165–192). New York, NY: Guilford Press.

Eren-Koçak, E., & Kiliç, C. (2014). Posttraumatic growth after earthquake trauma is predicted by executive functions: A pilot study. *Journal of Nervous and Mental Disease, 202,* 859–863. doi: 10.1097/NMD.0000000000000211

Erikson, E. H. (1968). *Identity: Youth and crisis.* New York: Norton.

Erikson, E. H. (1984). Reflections on the last stage: And the first. *The Psychoanalytic Study of the Child, 39,* 155–165.

Exenberger, S., Ramalingam, P., & Höfer, S. (2016). Exploring posttraumatic growth in Tamil children affected by the Indian Ocean Tsunami in 2004. *International Journal of Psychology.* doi: 10.1002/ijop.12395

Falb, M. D., & Pargament, K. I. (2013). Buddhist coping predicts psychological outcomes among end-of-life caregivers. *Psychology of Religion and Spirituality, 5,* 252–262. doi: 10.1037/a0032653

Fardella, J. A. (2008). The recovery model: Discourse ethics and the retrieval of the self. *Journal of Medical Humanities, 29,* 111–126. doi: 10.1007/s10912-008-9054-4

Fawzy, F. I., Fawzy, N. W., Arndt, L. A., & Pasnau, R. O. (1995). Critical review of psychosocial interventions in cancer care. *Archives of General Psychiatry, 52*(2), 100–113. doi:10.1001/archpsyc.1995.03950140018003

Felix, E., Afifi, T., Kia-Keating, M., Brown, L., Afifi, W., & Reyes, G. (2015). Family functioning and posttraumatic growth among parents and youth following wildfire disasters. *American Journal of Orthopsychiatry, 85,* 191–200. doi: 10.1037/ort0000054

Figley, C. R., & Burnette, C. E. (2017). Building bridges: Connecting systemic trauma and family resilience in the study and treatment of diverse traumatized families. *Traumatology, 23,* 95–131. doi: 10.1037/trm0000089

Finkel, N. J. (1974). Stress and traumas: An attempt at categorization. *American Journal of Community Psychology, 2,* 265–273.

Finkel, N. J. (1975). Strens, traumas and trauma resolution. *American Journal of Community Psychology, 3,* 173–178.

Fleeson, W. (2014). Four ways of (not) being real and whether they are essential for post-traumatic growth. *European Journal of Personality, 28,* 336–337. doi: 10.1002/per.1970

Forgeard, M. J. C. (2013). Perceiving benefits after adversity: The relationship between self-reported posttraumatic growth and creativity. *Psychology of Aesthetics, Creativity, and the Arts, 7,* 245–264. doi: 10.1037/a0031223

Foster, K., Shochet, I., Wurfl, A., Roche, M., Maybery, D., Shakespeare-Finch, J., & Furness, T. (in press). On PAR: A feasibility study of the Promoting Adult Resilience program with mental health nurses. *International Journal of Mental Health Nursing.*

Frankl, V. E. (1963). *Man's search for meaning: An introduction to logotherapy.* New York: Washington Square Press.

Frankl, V. E. (1965). *The doctor and the soul: From psychotherapy to logotherapy.* New York: Bantam Books (Original work published 1946).

Frattaroli, J. (2006). Experimental disclosure and its moderators: A meta-analysis. *Psychological Bulletin, 132,* 823–865. doi: 10.1037/0033-2909.132.6.823

Frazier, P., Tennen, H., Gavian, M., Park, C., Tomich, P., & Tashiro, T. (2009). Does self-reported posttraumatic growth reflect genuine positive change? *Psychological Science, 20,* 912–919. doi: 10.1111/j.1467-9280.2009.02381.x

Fredrickson, B. L. (2001). The role of positive emotions in positive psychology: The broaden-and-build theory of positive emotions. *American Psychologist, 56,* 218–226. doi: 10.1037/0003-066X.56.3.218

Frese III, S. J., Stanley, J., Kress, K., & Vogel-Scibilia, S. (2001). Integrating evidence-based practice and the recovery model. *Psychiatric Services, 52,* 1462–1468. doi: 10.1176/appi.ps.52.11.1462

Frisina, P. G., Borod, J. C., & Lepore, S. J. (2004). A meta-analysis of the effects of written emotional disclosure on the health outcomes of clinical populations. *The Journal of Nervous and Mental Disease, 192,* 629–634. doi: 10.1097/01.nmd.0000138317.30764.63

Froh, J. J. (2004). The history of positive psychology: Truth be told. *NYS Psychologist, 16,* 18–20.

Fujisawa, T. X., Jung, M., Kojima, M., Saito, D. N., Kosaka, H., & Tomoda, A. (2015). Neural basis of psychological growth following adverse experiences: A resting state functional MRI study. *Plos One, 10*(8), e0136427. doi: 10.1371/journal.pone.0136427

Gangstad, B., Norman, P., & Barton, J. (2009). Cognitive processing and posttraumatic growth after stroke. *Rehabilitation Psychology, 54,* 69–75. doi: 10.1037/a0014639

Gantt, L., & Tinnin, L. W. (2009). Support for a neurobiological view of trauma with implications for art therapy. *The Arts in Psychotherapy, 36,* 148–153. doi: 10.1016/j.aip.2008.12.005

Gao, J., & Qian, M. (2010). The revision and preliminary application of Chinese version of Posttraumatic Growth Inventory in a sample of adolescents who experienced the 5.12 earthquake. *Chinese Mental Health Journal, 2,* 126–130.

García, F. E., & Wlodarczyk, A. (2016). Psychometric properties of the Posttraumatic Growth Inventory: Short form among Chilean adults. *Journal of Loss and Trauma, 21,* 303–314. doi: 10.1080/15325024.2015.1108788

Garland, E. L., Farb, N. A., Goldin, P. R., & Fredrickson, B. L. (2015). The mindfulness-to-meaning theory: Extensions, applications, and challenges at the attention–appraisal–emotion interface. *Psychological Inquiry, 26*(4), 377–387. doi: 10.1080/1047840X.2015.1092493

Garland, S. N., Carlson, L. E., Cook, S., Lansdell, L., & Speca, M. (2007). A non-randomized comparison of mindfulness-based stress reduction and healing arts programs for facilitating post-traumatic growth and spirituality in cancer outpatients. *Support Care Cancer, 15*(8), 949–961.

Gauthier, L. R., & Gagliese, L. (2012). Bereavement interventions, end-of-life cancer care, and spousal well-being: A systematic review. *Clinical Psychology: Science and Practice, 19*(1), 72–92. doi:10.1111/j.1468-2850.2012.01275.x

Geiger, B. (2016). An inside look at Israeli police critical incident first responders. *Contemporary Social Science, 11,* 414–431. doi: 10.1080/21582041.2016.1228012

Gerber, M. M., Boals, A., & Schuettler, D. (2011). The unique contributions of positive and negative religious coping to posttraumatic growth and PTSD. *Psychology of Religion and Spirituality, 3,* 298–307. doi: 10.1037/a0023016

Gibbons, S., Murphy, D., & Joseph, S. (2011). Countertransference and positive growth in social workers. *Journal of Social Work Practice, 25,* 17–30. doi: 10.1080/02650530903579246

Gibson, B., & Sanbonmatsu, D. M. (2004). Optimism, pessimism, and gambling: The downside of optimism. *Personality and Social Psychology Bulletin, 30,* 149–160. doi: 10.1177/0146167203259929

Gil, S. (2005). Evaluation of premorbid personality factors and pre-event posttraumatic stress symptoms in the development of posttraumatic stress symptoms associated with a bus explosion in Israel. *Journal of Traumatic Stress, 18,* 563–567. doi: 10.1002/jts.20065

Glad, K. A., Jensen, T. K., Holt, T., & Ormhaug, S. M. (2013). Exploring self-perceived growth in a clinical sample of severely traumatized youth. *Child Abuse & Neglect, 37,* 331–342. doi: 10.1016/j.chiabu.2013.02.007

Grace, J. J., Kinsella, E. L., Muldoon, O. T., & Fortune, D. G. (2015). Post-traumatic growth following acquired brain injury: A systematic review and meta-analysis. *Frontiers in Psychology, 6,* 1162. doi: 10.3389/fpsyg.2015.01162

Graff, H. J., Christensen, U., Poulsen, I., & Egerod, I. (2018). Patient perspectives on navigating the field of traumatic brain injury rehabilitation: A qualitative thematic analysis. *Disability and Rehabilitation, 40,*926–934. doi: 10.1080/09638288.2017.1280542

Gray, M. J., Schorr, Y., Nash, W., Lebowitz, L., Amidon, A., Lansing, A., . . . Litz, B. T. (2012). Adaptive disclosure: An open trial of a novel exposure-based intervention for service members with combat-related psychological stress injuries. *Behavior Therapy, 43*(2), 407–415. doi:10.1016/j.beth.2011.09.001

Greenberg, J., Pyszczynski, T., & Solomon, S. (1986). The causes and consequences of a need for self-esteem: A Terror management theory. In R. F. Baumeister (Ed.), *Public self and private self.* New York: Springer. doi: 10.1007/978-1-4613-9564-5_10

Greene, T., Lahav, Y., Kanat-Maymon, Y., & Solomon, Z. (2015). A longitudinal study of secondary posttraumatic growth in wives of ex-POWs. *Psychiatry: Interpersonal and Biological Processes, 78*(2), 186–197.

Gregory, J. L., & Embrey, D. G. (2009). Companion recovery model to reduce the effects of profound catastrophic trauma for former child soldiers in Ganta, Liberia. *Traumatology, 15*(1), 40–51. doi: 10.1177/1534765608326178

Gregory, J. L., & Prana, H. (2013). Posttraumatic growth in Côte d'Ivoire refugees using the companion recovery model. *Traumatology, 19,* 223–232. doi: 10.1177/1534765612471146

Groarke, A., Curtis, R., Groarke, J., Hogan, M. J., Gibbons, A., & Kerin, M. (2017). Posttraumatic growth in breast cancer: How and when do distress and stress contribute? *Psycho-Oncology, 26,* 967–974. doi: 10.1002/pon.4243

Groleau, J. M., Calhoun, L. G., Cann, A., & Tedeschi, R. G. (2013). The role of centrality of events in posttraumatic distress and posttraumatic growth. *Psychological Trauma: Theory, Research, Practice, and Policy, 5*(5), 477–483. doi: 10.1037/a0028809

Gul, E., & Karanci, N. (2017). What determines posttraumatic stress and growth following various traumatic events? A study in a Turkish community sample. *Journal of Traumatic Stress, 30,* 54–62. doi: 10.1002/jts.22161

Guse, T., & Hudson, D. (2014). Psychological strengths and posttraumatic growth in the successful reintegration of South African ex-offenders. *International Journal of Offender Therapy and Comparative Criminology, 58,* 1449–1465. doi: 10.1177/0306624X113502299

Haas, M. (2015). *Bouncing forward: Transforming bad breaks into breakthroughs.* New York, NY: Enliven.

Hafner-Fink, M., & Uhan, S. (2013). Bipolarity and/or duality of social survey measurement scales and the question-order effect. *Quality & Quantity: International Journal of Methodology, 47,* 839–852. doi: 10.1007/s11135-011-9569-z

Hafstad, G. S., Gil-Rivas, V., Kilmer, R. P., & Raeder, S. (2010). Parental adjustment, family functioning, and posttraumatic growth among Norwegian children and adolescents following a natural disaster. *American Journal of Orthopsychiatry, 80,* 248–257. doi: 10.1111/j.1939-0025.2010.01028.x

Hagenaars, M. A., & van Minnen, A. (2010). Posttraumatic growth in exposure therapy for PTSD. *Journal of Traumatic Stress, 23,* 504–508. doi: 10.1002/jts.20551

Hall, B. J., Hobfoll, S. E., Palmieri, P. A., Canetti-Nisim, D., Shapira, O., Johnson, R. J., & Galea, S. (2008). The psychological impact of impending forced settler disengagement in Gaza: Trauma and posttraumatic growth. *Journal of Traumatic Stress, 21*, 22–29. doi: 10.1002/jts.20301

Hall, B. J., Rattigan, S., Walter, K. H., & Hobfoll, S. E. (2006). Conservation of resources theory and trauma: An evaluation of new and existing principles. In P. Buchwald (Ed.), *Stress and anxiety: Application to health, community, work place, and education* (pp. 230–250). Newcastle Upon Tyne, UK: Cambridge Scholar Press Ltd.

Hall, J. M., Roman, M. W., Thomas, S. P., Travis, C. B., Powell, J., Tennison, C. R., . . . McArthur, P. M. (2009). Thriving as becoming resolute in narratives of women surviving childhood maltreatment. *American Journal of Orthopsychiatry, 79*, 375–386. doi: 10.1037/a0016531

Hall, M. E. L., Lunger, R., & McMartin, J. (2010). The role of suffering in human flourishing: Contributions from positive psychology, theology, and philosophy. *Journal of Psychology and Theology, 38*, 111–121.

Hanley, A. W., Garland, E. L., & Tedeschi, R. G. (2017). Relating dispositional mindfulness, contemplative practice, and positive reappraisal with posttraumatic cognitive coping, stress, and growth. *Psychological Trauma: Theory, Research, Practice, and Policy, 9*, 526–536.

Haque, M. D., TitiAmayah, A., & Liu, L. (2016). The role of vision in organizational readiness for change and growth. *Leadership & Organization Development Journal, 37*, 983–999. doi: 10.1108/LODJ-01-2015-0003

Harmon-Jones, E., Simon, L., Greenberg, J., Pyszczynski, T., Solomon, S., & McGregor, H. (1997). Terror management theory and self-esteem: Evidence that increased self-esteem reduces mortality salience effects. *Journal of Personality and Social Psychology, 72*, 24–36. doi: 10.1177/01461672982411008

Harris, J. I., Erbes, C. R., Engdahl, B. E., Tedeschi, R. G., Olson, R. H., Winskowski, A. M. M., & McMahill, J. (2010). Coping functions of prayer and posttraumatic growth. *The International Journal for the Psychology of Religion, 20*, 26–38. doi: 10.1080/10508610903418103

Harter, S., & Buddin, B. J. (1987). Children's understanding of the simultaneity of two emotions: A five-stage developmental acquisition sequence. *Developmental Psychology, 23*(3), 388–399. doi: 10.1037/0012-1649.23.3.388

Hawley, C. A., & Joseph, S. (2008). Predictors of positive growth after traumatic brain injury: A longitudinal study. *Brain Injury, 22*, 427–435. doi: 10.1080/02699050802064607

Hays, P. A. (1996). Culturally responsive assessment with diverse older clients. *Professional Psychology: Research and Practice, 27*, 188–193. doi: 10.1037/0735-7028.27.2.188

Hazlett, A., Molden, D. C., & Sackett, A. M. (2011). Hoping for the best or preparing for the worst? Regulatory focus and preferences for optimism and pessimism in predicting personal outcomes. *Social Cognition, 29*, 74–96.

Hefferon, K. (2013). *Positive psychology and the body: The somato-psychic side to flourishing.* Maidenhead, England: Open University Press.

Hefferon, K., Grealy, M., & Mutrie, N. (2008). The perceived influence of an exercise class intervention on the process and outcomes of post-traumatic growth. *Mental Health and Physical Activity, 1*, 32–39. doi: 10.1016/j.mhpa.2008.06.003

Hefferon, K., Grealy, M., & Mutrie, N. (2009). Post-traumatic growth and life threatening physical illness: A systematic review of the qualitative literature. *British Journal of Health Psychology, 14*, 343–378. doi: 10.1348/135910708X332936

Hefferon, K., Grealy, M., & Mutrie, N. (2010). Transforming from cocoon to butterfly: The potential role of the body in the process of posttraumatic growth. *Journal of Humanistic Psychology, 50*, 224–247. doi: 10.1177/0022167809341996

Heinrichs, N., Zimmerman, T., Huber, B., Herschbach, P., & Russell, D. (2012). Cancer distress reduction with couple-based skills training: A randomized controlled trial. *Annals of Behavioral Medicine, 43,* 239–252. doi: 10.1007/s12160-011-9314-9

Heintzelman, A., Murdock, N. L., Krycak, R. C., & Seay, L. (2014). Recovery from infidelity: Differentiation of self, trauma, forgiveness, and posttraumatic growth among couples in continuing relationships. *Couple and Family Psychology: Research and Practice, 3,* 13–29. doi: 10.1037/cfp0000016

Helgeson, V. S., Reynolds, K. A., & Tomich, P. L. (2006). A meta-analytic review of benefit finding and growth. *Journal of Consulting and Clinical Psychology, 74,* 797–816. doi: 10.1037/0022-006X.74.5.797

Hemenover, S. H. (2003). The good, the bad, and the healthy: Impacts of emotional disclosure of trauma on resilient self-concept and psychological distress. *Personality and Social Psychology Bulletin, 29,* 1236–1244. doi: 10.1177/0146167203255228

Hijazi, A. M., Lumley, M. A., Ziadni, M. S., Haddad, L., Rapport, L. J., & Arnetz, B. B. (2014). Brief narrative exposure therapy for posttraumatic stress in Iraqi refugees: A preliminary randomized clinical trial. *Journal of Traumatic Stress, 27,* 314–322. doi: 10.1002/jts.21922

Hipolito-Delgado, C. P., & Lee, C. C. (2007). Empowerment theory for the professional school counselor: A manifesto for what really matters. *Professional School Counseling, 10,* 327–332.

Ho, S. M. Y., Chan, C. L. W., & Ho, R. T. H. (2004). Posttraumatic growth in Chinese cancer survivors. *Psycho-Oncology, 13,* 377–389. doi: 10.1002/pon.758

Ho, S. M. Y., Chu, K. W., & Yiu, J. (2008). The relationship between explanatory style and posttraumatic growth after bereavement in a non-clinical sample. *Death Studies, 32,* 461–478. doi: 10.1080/07481180801974760

Ho, S. M. Y., Law, L. S. C., Wang, G. L., Shih, S. M., Hsu, S. H., & Hou, Y. C. (2013). Psychometric analysis of the Chinese version of the Posttraumatic Growth Inventory with cancer patients in Hong Kong and Taiwan. *Psycho-Oncology, 22,* 715–719. doi: 10.1002/pon.3024

Hobfoll, S. E. (1989). Conservation of resources: A new attempt at conceptualizing stress. *American Psychologist, 44,* 513–524. doi: 10.1037/0003-066X.44.3.513

Hobfoll, S. E., Hall, B. J., Canetti-Nisim, D., Galea, S., Johnson, R. J., & Palmieri, P. A. (2007). Refining our understanding of traumatic growth in the face of terrorism: Moving from meaning cognitions to doing what is meaningful. *Applied Psychology: An International Review, 56,* 345–366. doi: 10.1111/j.1464-0597.2007.00292.x

Holt, S. A., & Austad, C. S. (2013). A comparison of rational emotive therapy and Tibetan Buddhism: Albert Ellis and the Dalai Lama. *International Journal of Behavioral Consultation and Therapy, 7,* 8–11. doi: 10.1037/h0100959

Holtmaat, K., van der Spek, N., Cuijpers, P., Leemans, C. R., & Verdonck-de Leeuw, I. M. (2016). Posttraumatic growth among head and neck cancer survivors with psychological distress. *Psycho-Oncology, 26,* 96–101. doi: 10.1002/pon.4106

Hooper, L. M., Marotta, S. A., & Lanthier, R. P. (2008). Predictors of growth and distress following childhood parentification: A retrospective exploratory study. *Journal of Child and Family Studies, 17,* 693–705. doi: 10.1007/s10826-007-9184-8

Horgan, O., Holcombe, C., & Salmon, P. (2011). Experiencing positive change after a diagnosis of breast cancer: A grounded theory analysis. *Psycho-Oncology, 20,* 1116–1125. doi: 10.1002/pon.1825

Horowitz, M. J., Wilner, N., & Alvarez, W. (1979). Impact of Event Scale: A measure of subjective stress. *Psychosomatic Medicine, 41*(3), 209–218. doi:10.1097/00006842-197905000-00004

Howard, G. S. (1980). Response-shift bias: A problem in evaluating interventions with pre/post self-reports. *Evaluation Review, 4*(1), 93–106. doi: 10.1177/0193841X8000400105

Huppert, F., & So, T. (2013). Flourishing across Europe: Application of a new conceptual framework for defining well-being. *Social Indicators Research, 110,* 837–861. doi: 10.1007/s11205-011-9966-7

Husson, O., Zebrack, B., Block, R., Embry, L., Aguilar, C., Hayes-Lattin, B., & Cole, S. (2017). Posttraumatic growth and well-being among adolescents and young adults (AYAs) with cancer: A longitudinal study. *Support Care Cancer, 25,* 2881–2890. doi: 10.1007/s00520-017-3707-7

Hutchinson, J., & Pretelt, V. (2010). Building resources and resilience: Why we should think about positive emotions when working with children, their families and their schools. *Counselling Psychology Review, 25,* 20–27.

Hyatt-Burkhart, D. (2014). The experience of vicarious posttraumatic growth in mental health workers. *Journal of Loss and Trauma, 19,* 452–461. doi: 10.1080/15325024.2013.797268

Ickovics, J. R., Meade, C. S., Kershaw, T. S., Milan, S., Lewis, J. B., & Ethier, K. A. (2006). Urban teens: Trauma, posttraumatic growth, and emotional distress among female adolescents. *Journal of Consulting and Clinical Psychology, 74,* 841–850. doi: 10.1037/0022-006X.74.5.841

Ihle, E. C., Ritsher, J. B., & Kanas, N. (2006). Positive psychological outcomes of spaceflight: An empirical study. *Aviation, Space, and Environmental Medicine, 77,* 93–101.

Jaarsma, T. A., Pool, G., Sanderman, R., & Ranchor, A. V. (2006). Psychometric properties of the Dutch version of the Posttraumatic Growth Inventory among cancer patients. *Psycho-Oncology, 15,* 911–920. doi: 10.1002/pon.1026

Jacobsen, P. B., & Andrykowski, M. A. (2015). Tertiary prevention in cancer care: Understanding and addressing the psychological dimensions of cancer during the active treatment period. *American Psychologist, 70,* 134–145. doi: 10.1037/a0036513

James, L. M., Engdahl, B. E., Leuthold, A. C., Lewis, S. M., van Kampen, E., & Georgopoulos, A. P. (2013). Neural network modulation by trauma as a marker of resilience: Differences between veterans with posttraumatic stress disorder and resilient controls. *JAMA Psychiatry, 70,* 410–418. doi: 10.1001/jamapsychiatry,2013.878

Janoff-Bulman, R. (1992). *Shattered assumptions: Towards a new psychology of trauma.* New York, NY: Free Press.

Janoff-Bulman, R. (2004). Posttraumatic growth: Three explanatory models. *Psychological Inquiry, 15,* 30–34. doi: 10.1207/s15327965pli1501_02

Janoff-Bulman, R. (2006). Schema-change perspectives on posttraumatic growth. In L. G. Calhoun & R. G. Tedeschi (Eds.), *Handbook of posttraumatic growth: Research and Practice* (pp. 81–99). Mahwah, NJ: Lawrence Erlbaum Associates, Inc.

January, A. M., Zebracki, K., Chlan, K. M., & Vogel, L. C. (2015). Understanding posttraumatic growth following pediatric-onset spinal cord injury: The critical role of coping strategies for facilitating positive psychological outcomes. *Developmental Medicine & Child Neurology, 57,* 1143–1149. doi: 10.1111/dmcn.12820

Jayawickreme, E., & Blackie, L. E. R. (2014). Post-traumatic growth as positive personality change: Evidence, controversies and future directions. *European Journal of Personality, 28,* 312–331. doi: 10.1002/per.1963

Jin, Y., Xu, J., & Liu, D. (2014). The relationship between post traumatic stress disorder and post traumatic growth: Gender differences in PTG and PTSD subgroups. *Social Psychiatry and Psychiatric Epidemiology, 49,* 1903. doi: 10.1007/s00127-014-0865-5

Johnson, H., Thompson, A., & Downs, M. (2009). Non-Western interpreters' experiences of trauma: The protective role of culture following exposure to oppression. *Ethnicity & Health, 14,* 407–418. doi: 10.1080/13557850802621449

Johnson, R. J., Canetti, D., Palmieri, P. A., Galea, S., Varley, J., & Hobfoll, S. E. (2009). A prospective study of risk and resilience factors associated with posttraumatic stress symptoms and depression symptoms among Jews and Arabs exposed to repeated acts of terrorism in Israel. *Psychological Trauma: Theory, Research, Practice, and Policy, 1,* 291–311. doi: 10.1037/a0017586

Johnson, S. F., & Boals, A. (2015). Refining our ability to measure posttraumatic growth. *Psychological Trauma: Theory, Research, Practice, and Policy, 7,* 422–429. doi: 10.1037/tra0000013

Joseph, S. (2009). Growth following adversity: Positive psychological perspectives on posttraumatic stress. *Psychological Topics, 18,* 335–344.

Joseph, S. (2011a). Religiosity and posttraumatic growth: A note concerning the problems of confounding in their measurement and the inclusion of religiosity within the definition of posttraumatic growth. *Mental Health, Religion & Culture, 14,* 843–845. doi: 10.1080/13674676.2011.609162

Joseph, S. (2011b). *What doesn't kill us: The new psychology of posttraumatic growth.* New York: Basic Books.

Joseph, S. (2012). Religiosity and posttraumatic growth: A note concerning the problems of confounding in their measurement and the inclusion of religiosity within the definition of posttraumatic growth. *Mental Health, Religion & Culture, 14,* 843–845. doi: 10.1080/13674676.2011.609162

Joseph, S. (2014). Assessment of post-traumatic growth. *European Journal of Personality, 28,* 340–341. doi: 10.1002/per.1970

Joseph, S., & Hefferon, K. (2013). Post-traumatic growth: Eudaimonic happiness in the aftermath of adversity. In I. Boniwell, S. A. David, & A. Conly Ayers (Eds.), *Oxford handbook of happiness.* Oxford, UK: Oxford University Press. doi: 10.1093/oxfordhb/9780199557257.013.0069

Joseph, S., Linley, A., Andrews, L., Harris, G., Howle, B., Woodward, C., & Sheylin, M. (2005). Assessing positive and negative changes in the aftermath of adversity: Psychometric evaluation of the changes in outlook questionnaire. *Psychological Assessment, 17,* 70–80. doi: 10.1037/t00057-000

Joseph, S., & Linley, P. A. (2008). Psychological assessment of growth following adversity: A review. In S. Joseph & P. A. Linley (Eds.), *Trauma, recovery, and growth: Positive psychological perspectives on posttraumatic stress* (pp. 21–36). Hoboken, NJ: John Wiley & Sons, Inc. doi: 10.1002/9781118269718.ch2

Joseph, S., Maltby, J., Wood, A. M., Stockton, H., Hunt, N., & Regel, S. (2012). The Psychological Well-Being—Post-Traumatic Changes Questionnaire (PWB-PTCQ): Reliability and validity. *Psychological Trauma: Theory, Research, Practice, and Policy, 4,* 420–428. doi: 10.1037/a0024740

Joseph, S., & Murphy, D. (2014). Trauma: A unifying concept for social work. *British Journal of Social Work, 44,* 1094–1109. doi: 10.1093/bjsw/bcs207

Joseph, S., Williams, R., & Yule, W. (1993). Changes in outlook following disaster: The preliminary development of a measure to assess positive and negative responses. *Journal of Traumatic Stress, 6,* 271–279. doi: 10.1002/jts.2490060209

Joshanloo, M. (2014). Eastern conceptualizations of happiness: Fundamental differences with western views. *Journal of Happiness Studies, 15,* 475–493. doi:10.1007/s10902-013-9431-1

Kaler, M. E., Erbes, C. R., Tedeschi, R. G., Arbisi, P. A., & Polusny, M. A. (2011). Factor structure and concurrent validity of the Posttraumatic Growth Inventory: Short form among veterans from the Iraq war. *Journal of Traumatic Stress, 24,* 200–207. doi: 10.1002/jts.20623

Kamibeppu, K., Sato, I., Honda, M., Ozono, S., Sakamoto, N., Iwai, T., . . . Ishida, Y. (2010). Mental health among young adult survivors of childhood cancer and their siblings including posttraumatic growth. *Journal of Cancer Survivorship, 4,* 303–312. doi: 19.1007/s11764-010-0124-z

Kampman, H., Hefferon, K., Wilson, M., & Beale, J. (2015). "I can do things now that people thought were impossible, actually, things that I thought were impossible": A meta-synthesis of the qualitative findings on posttraumatic growth and severe physical injury. *Canadian Psychology, 56,* 283–294. doi: 10.1037/cap0000031

Kar, N. (2011). Cognitive behavioral therapy for the treatment of post-traumatic stress disorder: A review. *Neuropsychiatric Disease and Treatment, 7,* 167–181. doi: 10.2147/NDT. S10389

Karagiorgou, O., & Cullen, B. (2016). A comparison of posttraumatic growth after acquired brain injury or myocardial infarction. *Journal of Loss and Trauma, 21,* 589–600. doi: 10.1080/15325024.2016.1161427

Karanci, A. N., Işıklı, S., Aker, A. T., Gül, E. I., Erkan, B. B., Özkol, H., & Güzel, H. Y. (2012). Personality, posttraumatic stress and trauma type: Factors contributing to posttraumatic growth and its domains in a Turkish community sample. *European Journal of Psychotraumatology, 3.* doi: 10.3402/ejpt.v3i0.17303

Karanci, N. A., & Acarturk, C. (2005). Post-traumatic growth among Marmara earthquake survivors involved in disaster preparedness as volunteers. *Traumatology, 11,* 307–323. doi: 10.1177/153476560501100409

Kastenmüller, A., Greitemeyer, T., Epp, D., Frey, D., & Fischer, P. (2012). Posttraumatic growth: Why do people grow from their trauma? *Anxiety, Stress, & Coping, 25,* 477–489. doi: 10.1080/10615806.2011.571770

Katz, J. (2015). A theory of qualitative methodology: The social system of analytic fieldwork, méthod(e)s. *African Review of Social Sciences Methodology, 1,* 131–146. doi: 10.1080/23754745.2015.1017282

Katz, R. C., Flasher, L., Cacciapaglia, H., & Nelson, S. (2001). The psychosocial impact of cancer and lupus: A cross validation study that extends the generality of "benefit-finding" in patients with chronic disease. *Journal of Behavioral Medicine, 24,* 561–571. doi: 10.1023/A:1012939310459

Kausar, R., & Saghir, S. (2010). Posttraumatic growth and marital satisfaction after breast cancer: Patient and spouse perspective. *Pakistan Journal of Social and Clinical Psychology, 8,* 3–17.

Kayser, K., Wind, L., & Shanker, A. (2008). Disaster relief within a collectivist context: Supporting resilience after the tsunami in South India. *Journal of Social Service Research, 34,* 87–98. doi: 10.1080/01488370802086526

Kehl, D., Knuth, D., Holubová, M., Hulse, L., & Schmidt, S. (2014). Relationships between firefighters' postevent distress and growth at different times after distressing incidents. *Traumatology, 20*(4), 253–261. doi: 10.1037/h0099832

Kehl, D., Knuth, D., Hulse, L., & Schmidt, S. (2015). Predictors of postevent distress and growth among firefighters after work-related emergencies: A cross-national study. *Psychological Trauma: Theory, Research, Practice, and Policy, 7,* 203–211. doi: 10.1037/a0037954

Kelly, G. A. (1955). *The psychology of personal constructs, Vol. 1: A theory of personality.* Oxford, England: W. W. Norton.

Kent, E. E., Alfano, C. M., Smith, A. W., Bernstein, L., McTiernan, A., Baumgartner, K. B., & Ballard-Barbash, R. (2013). The roles of support seeking and race/ethnicity in posttraumatic growth among breast cancer survivors. *Journal of Psychosocial Oncology, 31,* 393–412. doi: 10.1080/07347332.2013.798759

Keogh, D. U., Apan, A., Mushtaq, S., King, D., & Thomas, M. (2011). Resilience, vulnerability and adaptive capacity of an inland rural town prone to flooding: A climate change adaptation case study of Charleville, Queensland, Australia. *Natural Hazards, 59*, 699–723. doi: 10.1007/s11069-011-9791-y

Khawaja, N. G., White, K. M., Schweitzer, R., & Greenslade, J. (2008). Difficulties and coping strategies of Sudanese refugees: A qualitative approach. *Transcultural Psychiatry, 45*, 489–512. doi: 10.1177/1363461508094678

Khechuashvili, L. (2016). Investigation of psychometric properties of the Georgian version of Posttraumatic Growth Inventory. *Journal of Loss and Trauma, 21*, 522–532. doi: 10.1080/15325024.2016.1157409

Kilic, C., & Ulsoy, M. (2003). Psychological effects of the November 1999 earthquake in Turkey: An epidemiological study. *Acta Psychiatrica Scandinavica, 108*, 232–238. doi: 10.1034/j.1600-0447.2003.00119.x

Kilmer, R. P., & Gil-Rivas, V. (2010). Exploring posttraumatic growth in children impacted by Hurricane Katrina: Correlates of the phenomenon and developmental considerations. *Child Development, 81*, 1211–1227. doi: 10.1111/j.1467-8624.2010.01463.x

Kilmer, R. P., Gil-Rivas, V., Griese, B., Hardy, S. J., Hafstad, G. S., & Alisic, E. (2014). Posttraumatic growth in children and youth: Clinical implications of an emerging research literature. *American Journal of Orthopsychiatry, 84*, 506–518. doi: 10.1037/ort0000016

Kilmer, R. P., Gil-Rivas, V., Tedeschi, R. G., Cann, A., Calhoun, L. G., Buchanan, T., & Taku, K. (2009). Use of the revised Posttraumatic Growth Inventory for children. *Journal of Traumatic Stress, 22*, 248–253. doi: 10.1002/jts.20410

Kim, J., Kim, M., & Park, S. H. (2016). Exploring the relationship among posttraumatic growth, life satisfaction, and happiness among Korean individuals with physical disabilities. *Psychological Reports, 119*, 312–327. doi: 10.1177/0033294116653954

Kim, Y., Schulz, R., & Carver, C. (2007). Benefit finding in the cancer caregiving experience. *Psychosomatic Medicine, 69*, 283–291. doi: 10.1097/PSY.0b013e3180417cf4

Kira, I. A., Aboumediene, S., Ashby, J. S., Odenat, L., Mohanesh, J., & Alamia, H. (2013). The dynamics of posttraumatic growth across different trauma types in a Palestinian sample. *Journal of Loss and Trauma, 18*, 120–139. doi: 10.1080/15325024.2012.679129

Kissil, K., Nino, A., Jacobs, S., Davey, M., & Tubbs, C. Y. (2010). "It has been a good growing experience for me": Growth experiences among African American youth coping with parental cancer. *Families, Systems, & Health, 28*, 274–289. doi: 10.1037/a0020001

Kjærgaard, A., Leon, G. R., & Venables, N. C. (2015). The "right stuff" for a solo sailboat circumnavigation of the globe. *Environment and Behavior, 47*(10), 1147–1171.

Kjærgaard, A., Leon, G. R., Venables, N. C., & Fink, B. A. (2013). Personality, personal values and growth in military special unit patrol teams operating in a polar environment. *Military Psychology, 25*(1), 13–22.

Kleim, B., & Ehlers, A. (2009). Evidence for a curvilinear relationship between posttraumatic growth and posttrauma depression and PTSD in assault survivors. *Journal of Traumatic Stress, 22*, 45–52. doi: 10.1002/jts.20378

Knaevelsrud, C., Böttche, M., Pietrzak, R. H., Freyberger, H. J., Renneberg, B., & Kuwert, P. (2014). Integrative testimonial therapy: An internet-based, therapist-assisted therapy for German elderly survivors of the World War II with posttraumatic stress symptoms. *The Journal of Nervous and Mental Disease, 202*, 651–658. doi: 10.1097/NMD.0000000000000178

Knaevelsrud, C., Liedl, A., & Maercker, A. (2010). Posttraumatic growth, optimism and openness as outcomes of a cognitive-behavioural intervention for posttraumatic stress reactions. *Journal of Health Psychology, 15*, 1030–1038. doi: 10.1177/1359105309360073

Konrad, S. C. (2006). Posttraumatic growth in mothers of children with acquired disabilities. *Journal of Loss and Trauma, 11*, 103–113. doi: 10.1080/15325020500358274

Kraut, R. (2016). Aristotle on well-being. In G. Fletcher (Ed.), *The Routledge handbook of philosophy of well-being* (pp. 20–28). New York, NY: Routledge. doi: 10.4324/9781315682266

Kroger, J., Martinussen, M., & Marcia, J. E. (2010). Identity status change during adolescence and young adulthood: A meta-analysis. *Journal of Adolescence, 33*, 683–698. doi: 10.1016/j.adolescence.2009.11.002

Kroo, A., & Nagy, H. (2011). Posttraumatic growth among traumatized Somali refugees in Hungary. *Journal of Loss and Trauma, 16*, 440–458. doi: 10.1080/15325024.2011.575705

Krosch, D. J., & Shakespeare-Finch, J. (2016). Grief, traumatic stress, and posttraumatic growth in women who have experienced pregnancy loss. *Psychological Trauma: Theory, Research, Practice, and Policy*. doi: 10.1037/tra0000183

Krutiš, J., Mareš, J., & Ježek, S. (2011). Posttraumatický rozvoj u vojáků ačr po návratu ze zahraniční mise. [Post-traumatic growth in soldiers of the Army of the Czech Republic after return from foreign mission]. *Československá Psychologie: Časopis Pro Psychologickou Teorii A Praxi, 55*, 245–256. Retrieved from http://cspsych.psu.cas.cz/result.php?from=710&to=710

Kuenemund, A., Zwick, S., Rief, W., & Exner, C. (2016). (Re-)defining the self-enhanced posttraumatic growth and event centrality in stroke survivors: A mixed-method approach and control comparison study. *Journal of Health Psychology, 21*, 679–689. doi: 10.1177/1359105314535457

Kunst, M. J. J., Winkel, F. W., & Bogaerts, S. (2010). Posttraumatic growth moderates the association between violent revictimization and persisting PTSD symptoms in victims of interpersonal violence: A six-month follow-up study. *Journal of Social and Clinical Psychology, 29*, 527–545. doi: 10.1521/jscp.2010.29.5.527

Laceulle, O. M., Kleber, R. J., & Alisic, E. (2015). Children's experience of posttraumatic growth: Distinguishing general from domain-specific correlates. *PLoS One, 10*, e0145736.

Lahav, Y., Solomon, Z., & Levin, Y. (2016). Posttraumatic growth and perceived health: The role of posttraumatic stress symptoms. *American Journal of Orthopsychiatry, 86*, 693–703. doi: 10.1037/ort0000155

Lamela, D., Figueiredo, B., Bastos, A., & Martins, H. (2014). Psychometric properties of the Portuguese version of the Posttraumatic Growth Inventory: Short form among divorced adults. *European Journal of Psychological Assessment, 30*, 3–14. doi: 10.1027/1015-5759/a000161

Lancaster, S. L., Klein, K. P., & Heifner, A. (2015). The validity of self-reported growth after expressive writing. *Traumatology, 21*, 293–298. doi: 10.1037/trm0000052

Lane, W. D., Myers, K. J., Hill, M. C., & Lane, D. E. (2016). Utilizing narrative methodology in trauma treatment with Haitian earthquake survivors. *Journal of Loss and Trauma, 21*(6), 560–574. doi:10.1080/15325024.2016.1159113

Laufer, A., & Solomon, Z. (2006). Posttraumatic stress symptoms and posttraumatic growth among Israeli youth exposed to terror incidents. *Journal of Social & Clinical Psychology, 25*, 429–447.

Laufer, L., Raz-Hamama, Y., Levine, S. Z., & Solomon, Z. (2009). Posttraumatic growth in adolescence: The role of religiosity, distress, and forgiveness. *Journal of Social and Clinical Psychology, 28*, 862–880. doi: 10.1521/jscp.2009.28.7.862

Lazarus, R. S., & Folkman, S. (1984). *Stress, appraisal, and coping.* New York: Springer.

Lee, J. A., Luxton, D. D., Reger, G. M., & Gahm, G. A. (2010). Confirmatory factor analysis of the Posttraumatic Growth Inventory with a sample of soldiers previously deployed in support of the Iraq and Afghanistan wars. *Journal of Clinical Psychology, 66*, 813–810. doi: 10.1002/jclp.20692

Leippe, M. R., Bergold, A. N., & Eisenstadt, D. (2017). Prejudice and terror management at trial: Effects of defendant race/ethnicity and mortality salience on mock-jurors' verdict judgments. *Journal of Social Psychology, 157,* 279–294. doi: 10.1080/00224545.2016.1184128

Lelorain, S., Bonnaud-Antignac, A., & Florin, A. (2010). Long term posttraumatic growth after breast cancer: Prevalence, predictors and relationships with psychological health. *Journal of Clinical Psychology in Medical Settings, 17,* 14–22. doi: 10.1007/s10880-009-9183-6

Leppma, M., Mnatsakanova, A., Sarkisian, K., Scott, O., Adjeroh, L., Andrew, M. E., . . . McCanlies, E. C. (2017). Stressful life events and posttraumatic growth among police officers: A cross-sectional study. *Stress and Health.* doi: 10.1002/smi.2772

Levine, S. Z., Laufer, A., Stein, E., Hamama-Raz, Y., & Solomon, Z. (2009). Examining the relationship between resilience and posttraumatic growth. *Journal of Traumatic Stress, 22,* 282–286. doi: 10.1002/jts.20409

Levitt, H. M., Motulsky, S. L., Wertz, F. J., Morrow, S. L., & Ponterotto, J. G. (2017). Recommendations for designing and reviewing qualitative research in psychology: Promoting methodological integrity. *Qualitative Psychology, 4*(1), 2–22. doi: 10.1037/qup0000082

Lev-Wiesel, R., & Amir, M. (2003). Posttraumatic growth among Holocaust child survivors. *Journal of Loss and Trauma, 8,* 229–237. doi: 10.1080/15325020305884

Lev-Wiesel, R., Goldblatt, H., Eisikovits, Z., & Admi, H. (2009). Growth in the shadow of war: The case of social workers and nurses working in a shared war reality. *British Journal of Social Work, 39,* 1154–1174. doi: 10.1093/bjsw/bcn021

Li, W. J., Miao, M., Gan, Y. Q., Zhang, Z. J., & Cheng, G. (2016). The relationships between meaning discrepancy and emotional distress among patients with cancer: The role of posttraumatic growth in a collectivistic culture. *European Journal of Cancer Care, 25,* 491–501. doi: 10.1111/ecc.12298

Linley, P. A., Andrews, L., & Joseph, S. (2007). Confirmatory factor analysis of the Posttraumatic Growth Inventory. *Journal of Loss and Trauma, 12,* 321–332. doi: 10.1080/15325020601162823

Linley, P. A., & Joseph, S. (2004). Positive change following trauma and adversity: A review. *Journal of Traumatic Stress, 17,* 11–21. doi: 10.1023/B:JOTS.0000014671.27856.7e

Linley, P. A., & Joseph, S. (2007). Therapy work and therapist's positive and negative well-being. *Journal of Social and Clinical Psychology, 26,* 385–403. doi: 10.1521/jscp.2007.26.3.385

Linley, P. A., & Joseph, S. (2011). Meaning in life and posttraumatic growth. *Journal of Loss and Trauma, 16,* 150–159. doi: 10.1080/15325024.2010.519287

Lomas, T., & Ivtzan, I. (2016). Second wave positive psychology: Exploring the positive-negative dialectics of wellbeing. *Journal of Happiness Studies, 17,* 1753–1768. doi: 10.1007/s10902-015-9668-y

López, J., Camilli, C., & Noriega, C. (2015). Posttraumatic growth in widowed and non-widowed older adults: Religiosity and sense of coherence. *Journal of Religion and Health, 54,* 1612–1628. doi: 10.1007/s10943-014-9876-5

Losavio, S. T., Cohen, L. H., Laurenceau, J. P., Dasch, K. B., & Parrish, B. P., & Park, C. L. (2011). Reports of stress-related growth from daily negative events. *Journal of Social and Clinical Psychology, 30,* 760–785. doi: 10.1521/jscp.2011.30.7.760

Lurie-Beck, J. K., Liossis, P., & Gow, K. (2008). Relationships between psychopathological and demographic variables and posttraumatic growth among Holocaust survivors. *Traumatology, 14,* 28–39. doi: 10.1177/1534765608320338

Luszczynska, A., Durawa, A. B., Dudzinska, M., Kwiatkowska, M., Knysz, B., & Knoll, N. (2012). The effects of mortality reminders on posttraumatic growth and finding benefits among patients with life-threatening illness and their caregivers. *Psychology & Health, 27,* 1227–1243. doi: 10.1080/08870446.2012.665055

Lykins, E. L. B., Segerstrom, S. C., Averill, A. J., Evans, D. R., & Kemeny, M. E. (2007). Goal shifts following reminders of mortality: Reconciling posttraumatic growth and terror management theory. *Personality and Social Psychology Bulletin, 33,* 1088–1099. doi: 10.1177/0146167207303015

Lyubomirsky, S., & Lepper, H. S. (1999). A measure of subjective happiness: Preliminary reliability and construct validation. *Social Indicators Research, 46,* 137–155. doi: 10.1023/A:1006824100041

Ma, K. K., Niño, A., Jacobs, S., Davey, M., & Tubbs, C. Y. (2010). "It has been a good growing experience for me": Growth experiences among African American youth coping with parental cancer. *Families, Systems, & Health, 28,* 274–289. doi: 10.1037/a0020001

Maercker, A., & Langner, R. (2001). Posttraumatic personal growth: Validation of German versions of two questionnaires. *Diagnostica, 47,* 153–162. doi: 10.1026// 0012-1924.47.3.153

Maercker, A., & Zoellner, T. (2004). The Janus face of self-perceived growth: Toward a two-component model of posttraumatic growth. *Psychological Inquiry, 15,* 41–48. doi: 10.1207/s15327965pli1501_02

Mangelsdorf, J., & Eid, M. (2015). What makes a thriver? Unifying the concepts of posttraumatic and postecstatic growth. *Frontiers in Psychology, 6,* 813. doi: 10.3389/ fpsyg.2015.00813

Manne, S., Ostroff, J., Winkel, G., Goldstein, L., Fox, K., & Grana, G. (2004). Posttraumatic growth after breast cancer: Patient, partner, and couple perspectives. *Psychosomatic Medicine, 66,* 442–454.

Manning-Jones, S., de Terte, I., & Stephens, C. (2015). Vicarious posttraumatic growth: A systematic literature review. *International Journal of Wellbeing, 5,* 125–139. doi: 10.5502/ ijw.v5i2.8

Manning-Jones, S., de Terte, I., & Stephens, C. (2016). Secondary traumatic stress, vicarious posttraumatic growth, and coping among health professionals: A comparison study. *New Zealand Journal of Psychology, 45*(1), 20–29.

Mapham, A., & Hefferon, K. (2012). "I used to be an offender: Now I'm a defender": Positive psychology approaches in the facilitation of posttraumatic growth in offenders. *Journal of Offender Rehabilitation, 51,* 389–413. doi: 10.1080/10509674.2012.683239

Mareš, J. (2009). Posttraumatický rozvoj: výzkum, diagnostika, intervence. [Posttraumatic growth: Research, diagnostics, intervention]. *Československá psychologie, 53,* 271–290. Retrieved from http://cspsych.psu.cas.cz/result.php?from=619&to=619

Markowitz, J. C., Petkova, E., Neria, Y., Van Meter, P. E., Yihong, Z., Hembree, E., . . . Marshall, R. D. (2015). Is exposure necessary? A randomized clinical trial of interpersonal psychotherapy for PTSD. *The American Journal of Psychiatry, 172,* 430–440. doi: 10.1176/ appi.ajp.2014.14070908

Marshall, E. M., Frazier, P., Frankfurt, S., & Kuijer, R. G. (2015). Trajectories of posttraumatic growth and depreciation after two major earthquakes. *Psychological Trauma: Theory, Research, Practice, and Policy, 7,* 112–121. doi: 10.1037/tra0000005

Maslow, A. H. (1970). *Motivation and personality.* New York: Harper & Row.

Matsui, T., & Taku, K. (2016). A review of posttraumatic growth and help-seeking behavior in cancer survivors: Effects of distal and proximate culture. *Japanese Psychological Research, 58,* 142–162. doi: 10.1111/jpr.12105

Matsumoto, D., & Juang, L. (2008). *Culture and psychology* (4th ed.). Belmont, CA: Thomson Wadsworth.

Matz, D., Vogel, E. B., Matter, S., & Montenegro, H. (2015). Interrupting intergenerational trauma: Children of holocaust survivors and the Third Reich. *Journal of Phenomenological Psychology, 46,* 185–205. doi: 10.1163/15691624-12341295

McAdams, D. P. (1993). *The stories we live by: Personal myths and the making of the self.* New York, NY: William Morrow & Co.

McBride, O., Dunwoody, L., Lowe-Strong, A., & Kennedy, S. M. (2008). Examining adversarial growth in illness: The factor structure of the silver lining questionnaire SLQ-38. *Psychology and Health, 23*, 661–678. doi: 10.1080/14768320701356540

McCann, I. L., & Pearlman, L. A. (1990). *Psychological trauma and the adult survivor: Theory, therapy, and transformation.* Philadelphia, PA: Brunner/Mazel.

McCormack, L., Hagger, M. S., & Joseph, S. (2011). Vicarious growth in wives of Vietnam veterans: A phenomenological investigation into decades of "lived" experience. *Journal of Humanistic Psychology, 51*, 273–290. doi: 10.1177/0022167810377506

McCrae, R. R. (1984). Situational determinants of coping responses: Loss, threat, and challenge. *Journal of Personality and Social Psychology, 46*, 919–928. doi: 10.1037/0022-3514.46.4.919

McDiarmid, L., & Taku, K. (2017). Family valued and personally important posttraumatic growth in American and Japanese adolescents. *Journal of Child and Family Studies, 26*, 357–369. doi: 10.1007/s10826-016-0565-8

McDonough, M. H., Sabiston, C. M., & Wrosch, C. (2014). Predicting changes in posttraumatic growth and subjective well-being among breast cancer survivors: The role of social support and stress. *Psycho-Oncology, 23*, 114–120. doi:10.1002/pon.3380

McGrath, J. C. (2011). Posttraumatic growth and spirituality after brain injury. *Brain Impairment, 12*, 82–92. doi: 10.1375/brim.12.2.82

McGrath, P., & Holewa, H. (2012). What does the term "survivor" mean to individuals diagnosed with a haematological malignancy? Findings from Australia. *Supportive Care in Cancer, 20*, 3287–3295. doi: 10.1007/s00520-012-1453-4

McLean, C. P., Handa, S., Dickstein, B. D., Benson, T. A., Baker, M. T., Isler, W. C., . . . Litz, B. T. (2013). Posttraumatic growth and posttraumatic stress among military medical personnel. *Psychological Trauma: Theory, Research, Practice, and Policy, 5*(1), 62–68. doi:10.1037/a0022949

McLean, K. C., & Pratt, M. W. (2006). Life's little (and big) lessons: Identity statuses and meaning-making in the turning point narratives of emerging adults. *Developmental Psychology, 42*, 714–722. doi: 10.1037/0012-1649.42.4.714

McMillen, C., Howard, M. O., Nower, L., & Chung, S. (2001). Positive by-products of the struggle with chemical dependency. *Journal of Substance Abuse Treatment, 20*, 69–79.

McMillen, C., Zuravin, S., & Rideout, G. (1995). Perceived benefit from child abuse. *Journal of Consulting and Clinical Psychology, 63*, 1037–1043.

McMillen, J. C., & Fisher, R. H. (1998). The perceived benefit scales: Measuring perceived positive life changes after negative events. *Social Work Research, 22*, 173–187. doi: 10.1093/swr/22.3.173

Meeus, W. (2011). The study of adolescent identity formation 2000–2010: A review of longitudinal research. *Journal of Research on Adolescence, 21*, 75–94. doi: 10.1111/j.1532-7795.2010.00716.x

Meichenbaum, D. (2006). Resilience and posttraumatic growth: A constructive narrative perspective. In L. G. Calhoun & R. G. Tedeschi (Eds.), *Handbook of posttraumatic growth: Research & practice* (pp. 355–367). Mahwah, NJ: Lawrence Erlbaum Associates, Inc.

Meyerson, D. A., Grant, K. E., Carter, J. S., & Kilmer, R. P. (2011). Posttraumatic growth among children and adolescents: A systematic review. *Clinical Psychology Review, 31*, 949–964. doi: 10.1016/j.cpr.2011.06.003

Michel, G., Taylor, N., Absolom, K., & Eiser, C. (2010). Benefit finding in survivors of childhood cancer and their parents: Further empirical support for the Benefit Finding Scale for Children. *Child: Care, Health and Development, 36*, 123–129. doi: 10.1111/j.1365-2214.2009.01034.x

Michélsen, H., Therup-Svedenlöf, C., Backheden, M., & Schulman, A. (2017). Posttraumatic growth and depreciation six years after the 2004 tsunami. *European Journal of Psychotraumatology, 8*, 1302691. doi: 10.1080/20008198.2017.1302691

Milam, J. E. (2006). Posttraumatic growth and HIV disease progression. *Journal of Consulting and Clinical Psychology, 74*, 817–827. doi: 10.1037/0022-006X.74.5.817

Milam, J. E., Meeske, K., Slaughter, R. I., Sherman-Bien, S., Ritt-Olson, A., Kuperberg, A., . . . Hamilton, A. S. (2015). Cancer-related follow-up care among Hispanic and non-Hispanic childhood cancer survivors: The project forward study. *Cancer, 121*, 605–613. doi: 10.1002/cncr.29105

Milam, J. E., Ritt-Olson, A., Tan, S., Unger, J., & Nezami, E. (2005). The September 11th 2001 terrorist attacks and reports of posttraumatic growth among a multi-ethnic sample of adolescents. *Traumatology, 11*, 233–246. doi: 10.1177/153476560501100404

Milam, J. E., Ritt-Olson, A., & Unger, J. B. (2004). Posttraumatic growth among adolescents. *Journal of Adolescent Research, 19*, 192–204. doi: 10.1177/0743558403258273

Miller, W. R. (2004). The phenomenon of quantum change. *Journal of Clinical Psychology, 60*(5), 453–460. doi: 10.1002/jclp.20000

Mohr, E. (2014). Posttraumatic growth in youth survivors of a disaster: An arts-based research project. *Art Therapy, 31*(4), 155–162. doi:10.1080/07421656.2015.963487

Monson, C. M., & Fredman, S. J. (2012). *Cognitive-behavioral conjoint therapy for posttraumatic stress disorder: Therapist's manual.* New York, NY: Guildford Press.

Moore, A. M., Gamblin, T. C., Geller, D. A., Youssef, M. N., Hoffman, K. E., Gemmell, L., . . . Steel, J. L. (2011). A prospective study of posttraumatic growth as assessed by self-report and family caregiver in the context of advanced cancer. *Psycho-Oncology, 20*, 479–487. doi: 10.1002/pon.1746

Morgan, J. K., & Desmarais, S. L. (2017). Associations between time since event and posttraumatic growth among military veterans. *Military Psychology,* Advance online publication. doi: 10.1037/mil0000170

Morris, B. A., Campbell, M., Dwyer, M., Dunn, J., & Chambers, S. K. (2011). Survivor identity and post-traumatic growth after participating in challenge based peer support programmes. *British Journal of Health Psychology, 16*, 660–674. doi: 10.1348/2044-8287.002004

Morris, B. A., Lepore, S. J., Wilson, B., Lieberman, M. A., Dunn, J., & Chambers, S. K. (2014). Adopting a survivor identity after cancer in a peer support context. *Journal of Cancer Survivorship, 8*, 427–436. doi: 10.1007/s11764-014-0355-5

Morris, B. A., & Shakespeare-Finch, J. (2011). Rumination, post-traumatic growth, and distress: Structural equation modelling with cancer survivors. *Psycho-Oncology, 20*, 1176–1183. doi: 10.1002/pon.1827

Morris, B. A., Shakespeare-Finch, J., Rieck, M., & Newbery, J. (2005). Multidimensional nature of posttraumatic growth in an Australian population. *Journal of Traumatic Stress, 18*, 575–585. doi: 10.1002/jts.20067

Morris, B. A., Shakespeare-Finch, J., & Scott, J. L. (2012). Posttraumatic growth after cancer: The importance of health-related benefits and new found compassion for others. *Supportive Care in Cancer, 20*, 749–756. doi: 10.1007/s00520-011-1143-7

Morris, B. A., Wilson, B., & Chambers, S. K. (2013). Newfound compassion after prostate cancer: A psychometric evaluation of additional items in the Posttraumatic Growth Inventory. *Supportive Care in Cancer, 21*, 3371–3378. doi: 10.1007/s00520-013-1903-7

Mosher, C. E., Adams, R. N., Helft, P. R., O'Neil, B. H., Shahda, S., Rattray, N. A., & Champion, V. L. (2017). Positive changes among patients with advanced colorectal cancer and their family caregivers: A qualitative analysis. *Psychology & Health, 32*, 94–109. doi: 10.1080/08870446.2016.1247839

Mugisha, I. R. (2012, July 2). Rwanda a model of reconstruction: Soyinka. *The New Times*. Retrieved from www.newtimes.co.rw/section/article/2012-07-02/54592/

Munetz, M. R., & Frese, F. J. (2001). Getting ready for recovery: Reconciling mandatory treatment with the recovery vision. *Psychiatric Rehabilitation Journal, 25*, 35–42. doi: 10.1037/h0095052

Mystakidou, K., Tsilika, E., Parpa, E., Galanos, A., & Vlahos, L. (2008). Post-traumatic growth in advanced cancer patients receiving palliative care. *British Journal of Health Psychology, 13*, 633–646. doi: 10.1348/135910707X246177

Neimeyer, R. A. (1993). An appraisal of constructivist psychotherapies. *Journal of Consulting and Clinical Psychology, 61*(2), 221–234. doi: 10.1037/0022-006X.61.2.221

Neimeyer, R. A. (2006). Re-storying loss: Fostering growth in the posttraumatic narrative. In L. G. Calhoun & R. G. Tedeschi (Eds.), *Handbook of posttraumatic growth: Research and practice* (pp. 3–23). Mahwah, NJ: Lawrence Erlbaum Associates, Inc.

Nelson, S. D. (2011). The posttraumatic growth path: An emerging model for prevention and treatment of trauma-related behavioral health conditions. *Journal of Psychotherapy Integration, 21*(1), 1–42. doi: 10.1037/a0022908

Nenova, M., DuHamel, K., Zemon, V., Rini, C., & Redd, W. H. (2013). Posttraumatic growth, social support, and social constraint in hematopoietic stem cell transplant survivors. *Psycho-Oncology, 22*, 195–202. doi: 10.1002/pon.2073

Nietzsche, F. (1889/1990). *Twilight of the idols*. New York, NY: Penguin Classics.

Nolen-Hoeksema, S., & Davis, C. G. (2004). Theoretical and methodological issues in the assessment and interpretation of posttraumatic growth. *Psychological Inquiry, 15*, 60–64. doi: 10.1207/s15327965pli1501_02

Nolen-Hoeksema, S., & Morrow, J. (1991). A prospective study of depression and posttraumatic stress symptoms after a natural disaster: The 1989 Loma Prieta earthquake. *Journal of Personality and Social Psychology, 61*(1), 115–121. doi: 10.1037/0022-3514.61.1.115

Norcross, J. C., Krebs, P. M., & Prochaska, J. O. (2011). Stages of change. *Journal of Clinical Psychology, 67*(2), 143–154. doi: 10.1002/jclp.20758

Norlander, T., Von Schedvin, H., & Archer, T. (2005). Thriving as a function of affective personality: Relation to personality factors, coping strategies and stress. *Anxiety, Stress & Coping: An International Journal, 18*, 105–116. doi: 10.1080/10615800500093777

O'Brien, E., & Klein, N. (2017). The tipping point of perceived change: Asymmetric thresholds in diagnosing improvement versus decline. *Journal of Personality and Social Psychology, 112*, 161–185. doi: 10.1037/pspa0000070

Ogińska-Bulik, N. (2015). The relationship between resiliency and posttraumatic growth following the death of someone close. *Omega: Journal of Death and Dying, 71*, 233–244. doi: 10.1177/0030222815575502

Oishi, S., Graham, J., Kesebir, S., & Galinha, I. C. (2013). Concepts of happiness across time and cultures. *Personality and Social Psychology Bulletin, 39*, 559–577. doi: 10.1177/0146167213480042

O'Keefe, T. (2016). Hedonistic theories of well-being in antiquity. In G. Fletcher (Ed.), *The Routledge handbook of philosophy of well-being* (pp. 20–28). New York, NY: Routledge. doi: 10.4324/9781315682266

O'Leary, V. E., Alday, C. S., & Ickovics, J. R. (1998). Life change and posttraumatic growth. In R. G. Tedeschi, C. R. Park, & L. G. Calhoun (Eds.), *Posttraumatic growth: Positive changes in the aftermath of suffering* (pp. 127–151). Mahwah, NJ: Lawrence Erlbaum Associates, Inc.

O'Leary, V. E., & Ickovics, J. R. (1995). Resilience and thriving in response to challenge: An opportunity for a paradigm shift in women's health. *Women's Health: Research on Gender, Behavior, and Policy, 1*, 121–142.

Oppenheim, D. (2006). Child, parent, and parent-child emotion narratives: Implications for developmental psychopathology. *Development and Psychopathology, 18,* 771–790. doi: 10.1017/S095457940606038X

Oppenheim, D., Nir, A., Warren, S., & Emde, R. N. (1997). Emotion regulation in mother-child narrative co-construction: Associations with children's narrative and adaptation. *Developmental Psychology, 33,* 284–294. doi: 10.1037/0012-1649.33.2.284

Ownsworth, T., & Fleming, J. (2011). Growth through loss after brain injury. *Brain Impairment, 12*(2), 79–81. doi: 10.1375/brim.12.2.79

Pagani, M., Di Lorenzo, G., Monaco, L., Niolu, C., Siracusano, A., Verardo, A., . . . Ammaniti, M. (2011). Pretreatment, intratreatment, and posttreatment EEG imaging of EMDR: Methodology and preliminary results from a single case. *Journal of EMDR Practice and Research, 5,* 42–56. doi: 10.1891/1933-3196.5.2.42

Pakenham, K. I., & Cox, S. (2009). The dimensional structure of benefit finding in multiple sclerosis and relations with positive and negative adjustment: A longitudinal study. *Psychology and Health, 24,* 373–393. doi: 10.1080/08870440701832592

Pargament, K. I. (1996). Religious methods of coping: Resources for the conservation and transformation of significance. In E. P. Shafranske (Ed.), *Religion and the clinical practice of psychology* (pp. 215–240). Washington, DC: American Psychological Association.

Pargament, K. I., Magyar, G. M., Benore, E., & Mahoney, A. (2005). Sacrilege: A study of sacred loss and desecration and their implications for health and well-being in a community sample. *Journal for the Scientific Study of Religion, 44,* 59–78. doi: 10.1111/j.1468-5906.2005.00265.x

Pargament, K. I., Smith, B. W., Koenig, H. G., & Perez, L. (1998). Patterns of positive and negative religious coping with major life stressors. *Journal for the Scientific Study of Religion, 37,* 710–724. doi: 10.2307/1388152

Park, C. L., Aldwin, C. M., Fenster, J. R., & Snyder, L. B. (2008). Pathways to posttraumatic growth versus posttraumatic stress: Coping and emotional reactions following the September 11, 2001, terrorist attacks. *American Journal of Orthopsychiatry, 78,* 300–312. doi: 10.1037/a0014054

Park, C. L., & Blumberg, C. J. (2002). Disclosing trauma through writing: Testing the meaning-making hypothesis. *Cognitive Therapy and Research, 26,* 597–616. doi: 10.1023/A:1020353109229

Park, C. L., Cohen, L. H., & Murch, R. L. (1996). Assessment and prediction of stress-related growth. *Journal of Personality, 64,* 71–105. doi: 10.1111/j.1467-6494.1996.tb00815.x

Park, C. L., & Fenster, J. R. (2004). Stress-related growth: Predictors of occurrence and correlates with psychological adjustment. *Journal of Social and Clinical Psychology, 23,* 195–215. doi: 10.1521/jscp.23.2.195.31019

Park, C. L., & Lechner, S. (2006). Measurement issues in assessing growth following stressful life experiences. In L. G. Calhoun & R. G. Tedeschi (Eds.), *Handbook of posttraumatic growth: Research and practice* (pp. 47–67). Mahwah, NJ: Erlbaum.

Pat-Horenczyk, R., Perry, S., Hamama-Raz, Y., Ziv, Y., Schramm-Yavin, S., & Stemmer, S. M. (2015). Posttraumatic growth in breast cancer survivors: Constructive and illusory aspects. *Journal of Traumatic Stress, 28,* 214–222. doi: 10.1002/jts.22014

Pat-Horenczyk, R., Saltzman, L. Y., Hamama-Raz, Y., Perry, S., Ziv, Y., Ginat-Frolich, R., & Stemmer, S. M. (2016). Stability and transitions in posttraumatic growth trajectories among cancer patients: LCA and LTA analyses. *Psychological Trauma: Theory, Research, Practice, and Policy, 8,* 541–549. doi: 10.1037/tra0000094

Penedo, F. J., Molton, I., Dahn, J. R., Shen, B. J., Kinsinger, D., Traeger, L., . . . Antoni, M. (2006). A randomized clinical trial of group-based cognitive-behavioral stress management in localized prostate cancer: Development of stress management skills improves quality of life and benefit finding. *Annals of Behavioral Medicine, 31,* 261–270. doi: 10.1207/s15324796abm3103_8

Pennebaker, J. W. (1999). The effects of traumatic disclosure on physical and mental health: The values of writing and talking about upsetting events. *International Journal of Emergency Mental Health, 1,* 9–18.

Peterson, C., Park, N., Pole, N., D'Andrea, W., & Seligman, M. (2008). Strengths of character and posttraumatic growth. *Journal of Traumatic Stress, 21,* 214–217. doi: 10.1002/jts.20332

Petrie, K. J., Booth, R. J., Pennebaker, J. W., Davison, K. P., & Thomas, M. G. (1995). Disclosure of trauma and immune response to a hepatitis B vaccination program. *Journal of Consulting and Clinical Psychology, 63,* 787–792. doi: 10.1037/0022-006X.63.5.787

Phelps, A., Dell, L., & Forbes, D. (2013). New guidelines for treatment of acute stress disorder and posttraumatic stress disorder: Update for psychologists [online]. *InPsych: The Bulletin of the Australian Psychological Society Ltd, 35*(6), 32–33. Retrieved March 26, 2017, from http://search.informit.com.au.ezp01.library.qut.edu.au/documentSummary; dn=667343996028164;res=IELAPA ISSN: 1441-8754

Phelps, K. W., McCammon, S. L., Wuensch, K. L., & Golden, J. A. (2009). Enrichment, stress, and growth from parenting an individual with an autism spectrum disorder. *Journal of Intellectual & Developmental Disability, 34,* 133–141. doi: 10.1080/13668250902845236

Phipps, S., Long, A. M., & Ogden, J. (2007). Benefit finding scale for children: Preliminary findings from a childhood cancer population. *Journal of Pediatric Psychology, 32,* 1264–1271. doi: 10.1093/jpepsy/jsl052

Picoraro, J. A., Womer, J. W., Kazak, A. E., & Feudtner, C. (2014). Posttraumatic growth in parents and pediatric patients. *Journal of Palliative Medicine, 17,* 209–218. doi: 10.1089/jpm.2013.0280

Pietrzak, R. H., Goldstein, M. B., Malley, J. C., Rivers, A. J., Johnson, D. C., Morgan III, C. A., & Southwick, S. M. (2010). Posttraumatic growth in veterans of operations enduring freedom and Iraqi freedom. *Journal of Affective Disorders, 126,* 230–235. doi: 10.1016/j.jad.2010.03.021

Pluess, M., & Belsky, J. (2013). Vantage sensitivity: Individual differences in response to positive experiences. *Psychological Bulletin, 139,* 901–916. doi: 10.1037/a0030196

Pole, N., Kulkarni, M., Bernstein, A., & Kaufmann, G. (2006). Resilience in retired police officers. *Traumatology, 12,* 207–216. doi: 10.1177/1534765606294993

Powell, S., Rosner, R., Butollo, W., Tedeschi, R. G., & Calhoun, L. G. (2003). Posttraumatic growth after war: A study with former refugees and displaced people in Sarajevo. *Journal of Clinical Psychology, 59,* 71–83. doi: 10.1002/jclp.10117

Powell, T., Ekin-Wood, A., & Collin, C. (2007). Post-traumatic growth after head injury: A long-term follow-up. *Brain Injury, 21,* 31–38. doi: 10.1080/02699050601106245

Powley, E. H. (2009). Reclaiming resilience and safety: Resilience activation in the critical period of crisis. *Human Relations, 62,* 1289–1326. doi: 10.1177/18726709334881

Prati, G., & Pietrantoni, L. (2009). Optimism, social support, and coping strategies as factors contributing to posttraumatic growth: A meta-analysis. *Journal of Loss and Trauma, 14,* 364–388. doi: 10.1080/15325020902724271

Prati, G., & Pietrantoni, L. (2014). Italian adaptation and confirmatory factor analysis of the full and the short form of the Posttraumatic Growth Inventory. *Journal of Loss and Trauma, 19,* 12–22. doi: 10.1080/15325024.2012.734203

Prioleau, P., Pham, T., Anderson, D., Yanagisawa, R., Taku, K., Lobel, M., & Katz, C. (2016). 3/11 and 9/11: A multi-faceted investigation of a survivor exchange program. In J. Shigemura & R. K. Chhem (Eds.), *Mental health and social issues following a nuclear accident: The case of Fukushima* (pp. 83–97). New York: Springer.

Probst, B. (2016). Both/and: Researcher as participant in qualitative enquiry. *Qualitative Research Journal, 16,* 149–158. doi: 10.1108/QRJ-06-2015-0038

Proffitt, D., Cann, A., Calhoun, L. G., & Tedeschi, R. G. (2007). Judeo-Christian clergy and personal crisis: Religion, posttraumatic growth, and wellbeing. *Journal of Religion and Health, 46*, 219–231. doi: 10.1007/s10943-006-9074-1

Punamäki, R. L. (2010). Posttraumatic growth in a Middle Eastern context: Expression and determinants of PTG among Palestinians. In T. Weiss & R. Berger (Eds.), *Posttraumatic growth and culturally competent practice: Lessons learned from around the globe* (pp. 31–48). Hoboken, NJ: John Wiley & Sons, Inc.

Rabe, S., Zöllner, T., Maercker, A., & Karl, A. (2006). Neural correlates of posttraumatic growth after severe motor vehicle accidents. *Journal of Consulting and Clinical Psychology, 74*, 880–886. doi: 10.1037/0022-006X.74.5.880

Ramos, C., Costa, P. A., Rudnicki, T., Marôco, A. L., Leal, I., Guimarães, R., . . . Tedeschi, R. G. (2017). The effectiveness of a group intervention to facilitate posttraumatic growth among women with breast cancer. *Psycho-Oncology.* doi: 10.1002/pon.4501

Ramos, C., Leal, I., Marôco, A. L., & Tedeschi, R. G. (2016). The Posttraumatic Growth Inventory: Factor structure and invariance in a sample of breast cancer patients and in a non-clinical sample. *The Spanish Journal of Psychology, 19.* doi: 10.1017/sjp.2016.65

Ren, H., Yunlu, D., Shaffer, M., & Fodchuk, K. (2015). Expatriate success and thriving: The influence of job deprivation and emotional stability. *Journal of World Business, 50*, 69–78. doi: 10.1016/j.jwb.2014.01.007

Resnick, S. G., & Rosenheck, R. A. (2006). Recovery and positive psychology: Parallel themes and potential synergies. *Psychiatric Services, 57*, 120–122. doi: 10.1176/appi. ps.57.1.120

Riddle, J. P., Smith, H. E., & Jones, C. J. (2016). Does written emotional disclosure improve the psychological and physical health of caregivers? A systematic review and meta-analysis. *Behaviour Research and Therapy, 80*, 23–32. doi: 10.1016/j.brat.2016.03.004

Rimé, B., Páez, D., Basabe, N., & Martínez, F. (2010). Social sharing of emotion, posttraumatic growth, and emotional climate: Follow-up of Spanish citizen's response to the collective trauma of March 11th terrorist attacks in Madrid. *European Journal of Social Psychology, 40*, 1029–1045. doi: 10.1002/ejsp.700

Ristvedt, S. L., & Trinkaus, K. M. (2009). Trait anxiety as an independent predictor of poor health-related quality of life and post-traumatic stress symptoms in rectal cancer. *British Journal of Health Psychology, 14*, 701–715. doi: 10.1348/135910708X400462

Rodríguez-Rey, R., Palacios, A., Alonso-Tapia, J., Pérez, E., Álvarez, E., Coca, A., . . . Belda, S. (2017). Posttraumatic growth in pediatric intensive care personnel: Dependence on resilience and coping strategies. *Psychological Trauma: Theory, Research, Practice, and Policy, 9*, 407–415. doi: 10.1037/tra0000211

Roepke, A. M. (2013). Gains without pains? Growth after positive events. *Journal of Positive Psychology, 8*, 280–291. doi: 10.1080/17439760.2013.791715

Roepke, A. M. (2015). Psychosocial interventions and posttraumatic growth: A meta-analysis. *Journal of Consulting and Clinical Psychology, 83*, 129–142. doi: 10.1037/ a0036872

Roepke, A. M., Forgeard, M. J. C., & Elstein, J. G. (2014). Providing context for behaviour: Cognitive change matters for post-traumatic growth. *European Journal of Personality, 28*, 347–348. doi: 10.1002/per.1970

Rogers, C. R. (1957/2007). The necessary and sufficient conditions of therapeutic personality change. *Psychotherapy: Theory, Research, Practice, Training, 44*, 240–248.

Rogers, C. R. (1961). *On becoming a person: A therapist's view of psychotherapy.* Boston: Houghton Mifflin Company.

Routledge, C., Ostafin, B., Juhl, J., Sedikides, C., Cathey, C., & Liao, J. (2010). Adjusting to death: The effects of mortality salience and self-esteem on psychological well-being, growth motivation, and maladaptive behavior. *Journal of Personality and Social Psychology, 99,* 897–916. doi: 10.1037/a0021431

Ruini, C., Masoni, L., Ottolini, F., & Ferrari, S. (2014). Positive narrative group psychotherapy: The use of traditional fairy tales to enhance psychological well-being and growth. *Psychological Well Being, 4,* 13. doi: 10.1186/s13612-013-0013-0

Rutter, M. (1985). Resilience in the face of adversity: Protective factors and resistance to psychiatric disorder. *The British Journal of Psychiatry, 147,* 598–611. doi: 10.1192/bjp.147.6.598

Ryff, C. D. (1989). Happiness is everything, or is it? Explorations on the meaning of psychological wellbeing. *Journal of Personality & Social Psychology, 57,* 1069–1081. doi: 10.1037/0022-3514.57.6.1069

Ryff, C. D. (2013). Eudaimonic well-being and health: Mapping consequences of self-realization. In A. S. Waterman & A. S. Waterman (Eds.), *The best within us: Positive psychology perspectives on eudaimonia* (pp. 77–98). Washington, DC: American Psychological Association. doi:10.1037/14092-005

Ryff, C. D., & Singer, B. H. (1998). The role of purpose in life and personal growth in positive human health. In P. T. P. Wong & P. S. Fry (Eds.), *The human quest for meaning: A handbook of psychological research and clinical applications* (pp. 213–235). Mahwah, NJ: Lawrence Erlbaum Associates, Inc.

Ryff, C. D., & Singer, B. H. (2008). Know thyself and become what you are: A eudaimonic approach to psychological well-being. *Journal of Happiness Studies, 9,* 13–39. doi: 10.1007/s10902-006-9019-0

Sabiston, C. M., McDonough, M. H., & Crocker, P. R. E. (2007). Psychological experiences of breast cancer survivors involved in dragon boat program: Exploring links to positive psychological growth. *Journal of Sport and Exercise Psychology, 29,* 419–438. doi: org. ezp01.library.qut.edu.au/10.1123/jsep.29.4.419

Saccinto, E., Prati, G., Pietrantoni, L., & Pérez-Testor, C. (2013). Posttraumatic stress symptoms and posttraumatic growth among Italian survivors of emergency situations. *Journal of Loss and Trauma, 18,* 210–226. doi: 10.1080/15325024.2012.687321

Salick, E. C., & Auerbach, C. F. (2006). From devastation to integration: Adjusting to and growing from medical trauma. *Qualitative Health Research, 16,* 1021–1037. doi: 10.1177/1049732306292166

Salo, J. A., Qouta, S., & Punamäki, R. L. (2005). Adult attachment, posttraumatic growth and negative emotions among former political prisoners. *Anxiety, Stress, and Coping, 18,* 361–378. doi: 10.1080/10615800500289524

Saltzman, W. R., Pynoos, R. S., Lester, P., Layne, C. M., & Beardslee, W. R. (2013). Enhancing family resilience through family narrative co-construction. *Clinical Child and Family Psychology Review, 16,* 294–310. doi: 10.1007/s10567-013-0142-2

Samios, C., Rodzik, A. K., & Abel, L. M. (2012). Secondary traumatic stress and adjustment in therapists who work with sexual violence survivors: The moderating role of posttraumatic growth. *British Journal of Guidance & Counselling, 40*(4), 341–356. doi: 10.1080/03069885.2012.691463

Sanders, A., & Szymanski, K. (2013). Siblings of people diagnosed with a mental disorder and posttraumatic growth. *Community Mental Health Journal, 49,* 554–559. doi: 10.1007/s10597-012-9498-x

Sarkar, M., & Fletcher, D. (2014). Ordinary magic, extraordinary performance: Psychological resilience and thriving in high achievers. *Sport, Exercise, and Performance Psychology, 3,* 46–60. doi: 10.1037/spy0000003

Sarkar, M., & Fletcher, D. (2017). Adversity-related experiences *are* essential for Olympic success: Additional evidence and considerations. *Progress in Brain Research, 232,* 169–165. doi: 10.1016/bs.pbr.2016.11.009

Sattler, D., Boyd, B., & Kirsch, J. (2014). Trauma-exposed firefighters: Relationships among posttraumatic growth, posttraumatic stress, resource availability, coping and critical incident stress debriefing experience. *Stress & Health, 30,* 356–365. doi: 10.1002/smi.2608

Sawyer, A., & Ayers, S. (2009). Post-traumatic growth in women after childbirth. *Psychology & Health, 24,* 457–471. doi: 10.1080/08870440701864520

Sawyer, A., Ayers, S., & Field, A. P. (2010). Posttraumatic growth and adjustment among individuals with cancer or HIV/AIDS: A meta-analysis. *Clinical Psychology Review, 30,* 436–447. doi: 10.1016/j.cpr.2010.02.004

Schaefer, J. A., & Moos, R. H. (1992). Life crises and personal growth. In B. Carpenter (Ed.), *Personal coping: Theory, research, and application* (pp. 149–170). Westport, CT: Praeger.

Scheier, M. F., & Carver, C. S. (1985). Optimism, coping, and health: Assessment and implications of generalized outcome expectancies. *Health Psychology, 4,* 219–247. doi: 10.1037/0278-6133.4.3.219

Scheier, M. F., Weintraub, J. K., & Carver, C. S. (1986). Coping with stress: Divergent strategies of optimists and pessimists. *Journal of Personality and Social Psychology, 51,* 1257–1264.

Schmidt, S. D., Blank, T. O., Bellizzi, K. M., & Park, C. L. (2012). The relationship of coping strategies, social support, and attachment style with posttraumatic growth in cancer survivors. *Journal of Health Psychology, 17,* 1033–1040. doi: 10.1177/1359105311429203

Schmidt, S. D., Blank, T. O., Bellizzi, K. M., & Park, C. L. (advanced online view, 2017). Posttraumatic growth reported by emerging adults: A multigroup analysis of the roles of attachment, support, and coping. *Current Psychology.* Retrieved from https://link.springer.com/article/10.1007/s12144-017-9670-0

Schroevers, M. J., Helgeson, V. S., Sanderman, R., & Ranchor, A. V. (2010). Type of social support matters for prediction of posttraumatic growth among cancer survivors. *Psycho-oncology, 19,* 46–53. doi: 10.1002/pon.1501

Schroevers, M. J., & Teo, I. (2008). The report of posttraumatic growth in Malaysian cancer patients: Relationships with psychological distress and coping strategies. *Psycho-Oncology, 17,* 1239–1246. doi: 10.1002/pon.1366

Schultz, J. M., Tallman, B. A., & Altmaier, E. M. (2010). Pathways to posttraumatic growth: The contributions of forgiveness and importance of religion and spirituality. *Psychology of Religion and Spirituality, 2,* 104–114. doi: 10.1037/a0018454

Schulz, A. J., Israel, B. A., Zimmerman, M. A., & Checkoway, B. N. (1995). Empowerment as a multi-level construct: Perceived control at the individual, organizational and community levels. *Health Education Research: Theory & Practice, 10,* 309–327. doi: 10.1093/her/10.3.309

Schwartz, C. E., Ahmed, S., Sawatzky, R., Sajobi, T., Mayo, N., Finkelstein, J., . . . Sprangers, M. G. (2013). Guidelines for secondary analysis in search of response shift. *Quality of Life Research: An International Journal of Quality of Life Aspects of Treatment, Care & Rehabilitation, 22*(10), 2663–2673. doi: 10.1007/s11136-013-0402-0

Schweitzer, R. D., Vromans, L., Ranke, G., & Griffin, J. (2014). Narratives of healing: A case study of a young Liberian refugee. *The Arts in Psychotherapy, 41,* 98–106. doi: 10.1016/j.aip.2013.10.006

Scully, P. J. (2011). Taking care of staff: A comprehensive model of support for paramedics and emergency medical dispatchers. *Traumatology, 17,* 35–42. doi: 10.1177/1534765611430129

Sears, S. R., Stanton, A. L., & Danoff-Burg, S. (2003). The yellow brick road and the emerald city: Benefit finding, positive reappraisal coping, and posttraumatic growth in women with early-stage breast cancer. *Health Psychology, 22,* 487–497. doi: 10.1037/0278-6133.22.5.487

Seligman, M. E. P., & Csikszentmihalyi, M. (2000). Positive psychology: An introduction. *American Psychologist, 55*, 5–14. doi: 10.1037/0003-066X.55.1.5

Şenol-Durak, E., & Ayvaşik, H. B. (2010). Factors associated with posttraumatic growth among the spouses of myocardial infarction patients. *Journal of Health Psychology, 15,* 85–95. doi: 10.1177/1359105309342472

Shakespeare-Finch, J. (2009). *The Victorian bush fires: Survivors and supporters sharing trauma.* Poster presented at the 25th annual meeting of the International Society for Traumatic Stress Studies, Atlanta, Georgia.

Shakespeare-Finch, J., & Armstrong, D. (2010). Trauma type and post-trauma outcomes: Differences between survivors of motor vehicle accidents, sexual assault, and bereavement. *Journal of Loss and Trauma, 15*, 69–82. doi: 10.1080/15325020903373151

Shakespeare-Finch, J., & Barrington, A. J. (2012). Behavioural changes add validity to the construct of posttraumatic growth. *Journal of Traumatic Stress, 25*, 433–439. doi: 10.1002/jts.21730

Shakespeare-Finch, J., & Copping, A. (2006). A grounded theory approach to understanding cultural differences in posttraumatic growth. *Journal of Loss and Trauma, 11*, 355–371. doi: 10.1080/15325020600671949

Shakespeare-Finch, J., & Daley, E. (2017). Workplace belongingness, psychological distress and resilience in emergency service workers. *Psychological Trauma: Research, Theory Practice & Policy, 9*, 32–35. doi: 10.1037/tra0000108

Shakespeare-Finch, J., & de Dassel, T. (2009). The impact of child sexual abuse on victims/ survivors. *Journal of Child Sexual Abuse, 18*, 623–640. doi: 10.1080/10538710903317224

Shakespeare-Finch, J., & Enders, T. (2008). Corroborating evidence of posttraumatic growth. *Journal of Traumatic Stress, 21*, 421–424. doi: 10.1002/jts.20347

Shakespeare-Finch, J., Gow, K., & Smith, S. (2005). Personality, coping and posttraumatic growth in emergency ambulance personnel. *Traumatology, 11*, 325–334. doi: 10.1177/153476560501100410

Shakespeare-Finch, J., & Lurie-Beck, J. (2014). A meta-analytic clarification of the relationship between posttraumatic growth and symptoms of posttraumatic distress disorder. *Journal of Anxiety Disorders, 28*, 223–229. doi: 10.1016/j.janxdis.2013.10.005

Shakespeare-Finch, J., Martinek, E., Tedeschi, R. G., & Calhoun, L. G. (2013). A qualitative approach to assessing the validity of the posttraumatic growth inventory. *Journal of Loss and Trauma, 18*, 572–591. doi: 10.1080/15325024.2012.734207

Shakespeare-Finch, J., & Morris, B. A. (2010). Posttraumatic growth in Australian populations. In T. Weiss & R. Berger (Eds.), *Posttraumatic growth and culturally competent practice: Lessons learned from around the globe* (pp. 157–186). New York: John Wiley & Sons.

Shakespeare-Finch, J., Rees, A., & Armstrong, D. (2015). Social support, self-efficacy, trauma and well-being in emergency medical dispatchers. *Social Indicators Research, 123*, 549–565. doi: 10.1007/s11205-014-0749-9

Shakespeare-Finch, J. E., Schweitzer, R., King, J., & Brough, M. (2014). Distress, coping and posttraumatic growth in refugees from Burma. *Journal of Immigrant and Refugee Studies, 12*, 311–330. Retrieved from www.tandfonline.com/doi/full/10.1080/15562948.2013.844876

Shakespeare-Finch, J. E., Shochet, I., Roos, C., Craig, C., Young, R., Wurfl, A., & Armstrong, D. (2014). *Promoting posttraumatic growth in police recruits: Preliminary results of a randomised control trial of a resilience intervention.* Proceedings of the Australia & New Zealand Disaster & Emergency Conference, Gold Coast (QLD), 5th–7th May 2014.

Shakespeare-Finch, J. E., Smith, S. G., Gow, K. M., Embelton, G., & Baird, L. (2003). The prevalence of posttraumatic growth in emergency ambulance personnel. *Traumatology, 9*, 58–70. doi: 10.1177/153476560300900104

Shakespeare-Finch, J., & Wickham, K. (2010). Adaptation of Sudanese refugees in an Australian context: Investigating helps and hindrances. *International Migration, 48,* 23–46. doi: 10.1111/j.1468-2435.2009.00561.x

Shand, L. K., Cowlishaw, S., Brooker, J. E., Burney, S., & Ricciardelli, L. A. (2015). Correlates of post-traumatic stress symptoms and growth in cancer patients: A systematic review and meta-analysis. *Psycho-Oncology, 24,* 624–634. doi: 10.1002/pon.3719

Shaw, A., Joseph, S., & Linley, P. A. (2005). Religion, spirituality, and posttraumatic growth: A systematic review. *Mental Health, Religion, & Culture, 8,* 1–11. doi: 10.1080/1367467032000157981

Sheikh, A. I. (2004). Posttraumatic growth in the context of heart disease. *Journal of Clinical Psychology in Medical Settings, 11,* 265–273. doi: 10.1023/B:JOCS.0000045346.76242.73

Sheldon, C. (2016). Thriving in adversity: Psychotherapeutic experiences in a Bone Marrow transplant unit. *Cambridge Quarterly of Healthcare Ethics, 25,* 113–120. doi: 10.1017/S0963180115000365

Sherman, R. A., Nave, C. S., & Funder, D. C. (2009). The apparent objectivity of behaviour is illusory. *European Journal of Personality, 23,* 430–433. doi: 10.1002/per.725

Shiri, S., Wexler, I. D., Alkalay, Y., Meiner, Z., & Kreitler, S. (2008). Positive and negative psychological impact after secondary exposure to politically motivated violence among body handlers and rehabilitation workers. *Journal of Nervous and Mental Disease, 196*(12), 906–911. doi: 10.1097/NMD.0b013e31818ec80b

Shiri, S., Wexler, I. D., & Kreitler, S. (2010). Cognitive orientation is predictive of posttraumatic growth after secondary exposure to trauma. *Traumatology, 16*(1), 42–48. doi: 10.1177/1534765609348243

Shochet, I. M., Dadds, M., Ham, D., & Montague, R. (2006). School connectedness is an underemphasized parameter in adolescent mental health: Results of a community prediction study. *Journal of Clinical Child and Adolescent Psychology, 35,* 170–179. doi: 10.1207/s15374424jccp3502_1

Shochet, I. M., Shakespeare-Finch, J., Young, R., Brough, P., Craig, C., & Roos, C., ... Hodge, R. (2011). The development of the Promoting Resilience Officers (PRO) program. *Traumatology, 17,* 43–51. doi: 10.1177/1534765611429080

Shuwiekh, H., Kira, I. A., & Ashby, J. S. (2017). What are the personality and trauma dynamics that contribute to posttraumatic growth? *International Journal of Stress Management.* doi: 10.1037/str0000054

Siegel, K., Schrimshaw, E. W., & Pretter, S. (2005). Stress-related growth among women living with HIV/AIDS: Examination of an explanatory model. *Journal of Behavioral Medicine, 28,* 403–414. doi: 10.1007/s10865-005-9015-6

Silva, J., Ownsworth, T., Shields, C., & Fleming, J. (2011). Enhanced appreciation of life following acquired brain injury: Posttraumatic growth at 6 months postdischarge. *Brain Impairment, 12,* 93–104. doi: 10.1375/brim.12.2.93

Silva, S. M., Moreira, H. C., Pinto, S. M. de A., & Canavarro, M. C. (2009). Cancro da mama e desenvolvimento pessoal e relacional: Estudo das características psicométricas do inventário de desenvolvimento pós-traumático numa amostra de mulheres da população Portuguesa [Breast cancer and personal and relational growth: Psychometric characteristics of the Portuguese version of the Posttraumatic Growth Inventory in a sample of Portuguese women]. *Revista Iberoamericana de Diagnóstico e Avaliação Psicológica, 28,* 105–133. Retrieved from www.researchgate.net/publication/234164878

Silverstein, M. W., Lee, D. J., Witte, T. K., & Weathers, F. W. (2017). Is posttraumatic growth trauma-specific? Invariance across trauma- and stressor-exposed groups. *Psychological Trauma: Theory, Research, Practice, and Policy, 9*(5), 553–560. doi: 10.1037/tra0000236

Singer, S., Götze, H., Buttstädt, M., Ziegler, C., Richter, R., Brown, A., . . . Geue, K. (2012). A non-randomized trial of an art therapy intervention for patients with haematological malignancies to support post-traumatic growth. *Journal of Health Psychology, 18*, 939–949. doi: 10.1177/1359105312458332

Siqveland, J., Hafstad, G. S., & Tedeschi, R. G. (2012). Posttraumatic growth in parents after a natural disaster. *Journal of Loss and Trauma, 17*, 536–544. doi: 10.1080/15325024.2012.678778

Slavin-Spenny, O. M., Cohen, J. L., Oberleithner, L. M., & Lumley, M. A. (2011). The effects of different methods of emotional disclosure: Differentiating post-traumatic growth from stress symptoms. *Journal of Clinical Psychology, 67*, 993–1007. doi: 10.1002/jclp.20750

Smith, H., & Novak, P. (2003). *Buddhism: A concise introduction.* San Francisco, CA: Harper Collins.

Smyth, J. M., Hockemeyer, J. R., & Tulloch, H. (2008). Expressive writing and post-traumatic stress disorder: Effects on trauma symptoms, mood states, and cortisol reactivity. *British Journal of Health Psychology, 13*(1), 85–93. doi:10.1348/135910707X250866

Sodergren, S. C., & Hyland, M. E. (2000). What are the positive consequences of illness? *Psychology and Health, 15*, 85–97. doi: 10.1080/08870440008400290

Solomon, D., McAbee, J., Åsberg, K., & McGee, A. (2015). Coming out and the potential for growth in sexual minorities: The role of social reactions and internalized homonegativity. *Journal of Homosexuality, 62*(11), 1512–1538. doi: 10.1080/00918369.2015.1073032

Spielman, V., & Taubman-Ben-Ari, O. (2009). Parental self-efficacy and stress-related growth in the transition to parenthood: A comparison between parents of pre- and full-term babies. *Health & Social Work, 34*, 201–212. doi: 10.1093/hsw/34.3.201

Splevins, K., Cohen, K., Bowley, J., & Joseph, S. (2010). Theories of posttraumatic growth: Cross-cultural perspectives. *Journal of Loss and Trauma, 15*, 259–277. doi: 10.1080/15325020903382111

Staugaard, S. R., Johannessen, K. B., Thomsen, Y. D., Bertelsen, M., & Berntsen, D. (2015). Centrality of positive and negative deployment memories predicts posttraumatic growth in Danish veterans. *Journal of Clinical Psychology, 71*, 362–377. doi: 10.1002/jclp.22142

Steger, M. F., Frazier, P. A., & Zacchanini, J. L. (2008). Terrorism in two cultures: Stress and growth following September 11 and the Madrid train bombings. *Journal of Loss and Trauma, 13*, 511–527. doi: 10.1080/15325020802173660

Steele, W., Kuban, C., & Raider, M. C. (2009). Connections, continuity, dignity, opportunities model: Follow-up of children who completed the I Feel Better Now! Trauma intervention program. *School Social Work Journal, 33*, 89–110.

Steenkamp, M. M., Litz, B. T., Hoge, C. W., & Marmar, C. R. (2015). Psychotherapy for military-related PTSD: A review of randomized clinical trials. *Journal of the American Medical Association, 31*(4), 489–500. doi: 10.1001/jama.2015.8370

Stephenson, E., DeLongis, A., Steele, R., Cadell, S., Andrews, G. A., Berg, C. A., . . . Holmbeck, G. H. (2017). Siblings of children with a complex chronic health condition: Maternal posttraumatic growth as a predictor of changes in child behavior problems. *Journal of Pediatric Psychology, 42*, 104–113. doi: 10.1093/jpepsy/jsw053

Stockton, H., Joseph, S., & Hunt, N. (2014). Expressive writing and posttraumatic growth: An internet-based study. *Traumatology: An International Journal, 20*, 75–83. doi: 10.1037/h0099377

Strickland, B. R. (1989). Internal-external control expectancies: From contingency to creativity. *American Psychologist, 44*(1), 1–12. doi: 10.1037/0003-066X.44.1.1

Stutts, L. A., Bills, S. E., Erwin, S. R., & Good, J. J. (2015). Coping and posttraumatic growth in women with limb amputations. *Psychology, Health & Medicine, 20*, 742–752. doi: 10.1080/13548506.2015.1009379

Su, Y. J., & Chen, S. H. (2015). Emerging posttraumatic growth: A prospective study with pre- and posttrauma psychological predictors. *Psychological Trauma: Theory, Research, Practice, and Policy, 7,* 103–111. doi: 10.1037/tra0000008

Subandi, M. A., Achmad, T., Kurniati, H., & Febri, R. (2014). Spirituality, gratitude, hope and post-traumatic growth among the survivors of the 2010 eruption of Mount Merapi in Java, Indonesia. *Australian Journal of Disaster and Trauma Studies, 18,* 19–26. Retrieved from www.massey.ac.nz/~trauma/issues/2014-1/AJDTS_18-1_Subandi.pdf

Suedfeld, P., Brcic, J., Johnson, P. J., & Gushin, V. (2012). Personal growth following long-duration spaceflight. *Acta Astronautica, 79,* 118–123. doi: 10.1016/j.actaastro.2012.04.039

Suedfeld, P., Legkaia, K., & Brcic, J. (2010). Changes in the hierarchy of value references associated with flying in space. *Journal of Personality, 78,* 1411–1136.

Sumalla, E. C., Ochoa, C., & Blanco, I. (2009). Posttraumatic growth in cancer: Reality or illusion. *Clinical Psychology Review, 29,* 24–33. doi: 10.1016/j.cpr.2008.09.006

Tabibnia, G., Lieberman, M. D., & Craske, M. G. (2008). The lasting effect of words on feelings: Words may facilitate exposure effects to threatening images. *Emotion, 8,* 307–317. doi: 10.1037/t11558-000

Taku, K. (2010). Posttraumatic growth in Japan: A path toward better understanding of culture-constant and culture-specific aspects. In T. Weiss & R. Berger (Eds.), *Posttraumatic growth and culturally competent practice: Lessons learned from around the globe* (pp. 146–163). Hoboken, NJ: John Wiley & Sons, Inc.

Taku, K. (2011). Commonly-defined and individually-defined posttraumatic growth in the US and Japan. *Personality and Individual Differences, 51,* 188–193. doi: 10.1016/j.paid.2011.04.002

Taku, K. (2013). Posttraumatic growth in American and Japanese men: Comparing levels of growth and perceptions of indicators of growth. *Psychology of Men and Masculinity, 14,* 423–432. doi: 10.1037/a0029582

Taku, K. (2014). Relationships among perceived psychological growth, resilience and burn-out in physicians. *Personality and Individual Differences, 59,* 120–123. doi: 10.1016/j.paid.2013.11.003

Taku, K., Calhoun, L. G., Cann, A., & Tedeschi, R. G. (2008). The role of rumination in the coexistence of distress and posttraumatic growth among bereaved Japanese university students. *Death Studies, 32,* 428–444.

Taku, K., Calhoun, L. G., Tedeschi, R. G., Gil-Rivas, V., Kilmer, R. P., & Cann, A. (2007). Examining posttraumatic growth among Japanese university students. *Anxiety, Stress, & Coping, 20,* 353–367. doi: 10.1080/10615800701295007

Taku, K., & Cann, A. (2014). Cross-national and religious relationships with posttraumatic growth: The role of individual differences and perceptions of the triggering event. *Journal of Cross-Cultural Psychology, 45,* 601–617. doi: 10.1177/0022022113520074

Taku, K., Cann, A., Calhoun, L. G., & Tedeschi, R. G. (2008). The factor structure of the posttraumatic growth inventory: A comparison of five models using confirmatory factor analysis. *Journal of Traumatic Stress, 21,* 158–164.

Taku, K., Cann, A., Tedeschi, R. G., & Calhoun, L. G. (2009). Intrusive versus deliberate rumination in posttraumatic growth across U.S. and Japanese samples. *Anxiety, Stress, & Coping, 22,* 129–136. doi: 10.1080/10615800802317841

Taku, K., Cann, A., Tedeschi, R. G., & Calhoun, L. G. (2015). Core beliefs shaken by an earthquake correlate with posttraumatic growth. *Psychological Trauma: Theory, Research, Practice, and Policy, 7,* 563–569. doi: 10.1037/tra0000054

Taku, K., Cann, A., Tedeschi, R. G., & Calhoun, L. G. (2017). Psychoeducational intervention program about posttraumatic growth for Japanese high school students. *Journal of Loss and Trauma, 22,* 271–282. doi: 10.1080/15325024.2017.1284504

Taku, K., Kilmer, R. P., Cann, A., Tedeschi, R. G., & Calhoun, L. G. (2012). Exploring post-traumatic growth in Japanese youth. *Psychological Trauma: Theory, Research, Practice, and Policy, 4*, 411–419. doi: 10.1037/a0024363

Taku, K., & McDiarmid, L. (2015). Personally important posttraumatic growth in adolescents: The effect on self-esteem beyond commonly defined posttraumatic growth. *Journal of Adolescence, 44*, 224–231. doi: 10.1016/j.adolescence.2015.08.001

Taku, K., & Oshio, A. (2015). An item-level analysis of the posttraumatic growth inventory: Relationships with an examination of core beliefs and deliberate rumination. *Personality and Individual Differences, 86*, 156–160. doi: 10.1016/j.paid.2015.06.025

Taku, K., Tedeschi, R. G., & Cann, A. (2015). Relationships of posttraumatic growth and stress responses in bereaved young adults. *Journal of Loss and Trauma, 20*, 56–71. doi: 10.1080/15325024.2013.824306

Taku, K., Tedeschi, R. G., Cann, A., & Calhoun, L. G. (2009). The culture of disclosure: Effects of perceived reactions to disclosure on posttraumatic growth and distress in Japan. *Journal of Social and Clinical Psychology, 29*, 1226–1243. doi: 10.1521/jscp.2009.28.10.1226

Tallman, B., Shaw, K., Schultz, J., & Altmaier, E. (2010). Well-being and posttraumatic growth in unrelated donor marrow transplant survivors: A nine-year longitudinal study. *Rehabilitation Psychology, 55*, 204–210. doi: 10.1037/a0019541

Tan, L. A. (2012). Art therapy with trafficked women. *Therapy Today, 23*, 26–31.

Tan, S. Y. (2013). Resilience and posttraumatic growth: Empirical evidence and clinical applications from a Christian perspective. *Journal of Psychology and Christianity, 32*, 358–364.

Tang, C. S. (2006). Positive and negative postdisaster psychological adjustment among adult survivors of the Southeast Asian earthquake-tsunami. *Journal of Psychosomatic Research, 61*, 699–705. doi: 10.1016/j.jpsychores.2006.07.014

Tang, S. T., Lin, K. C., Chen, J. S., Chang, W. C., Hsieh, C. H., & Chou, W. C. (2015). Threatened with death but growing: Changes in and determinants of posttraumatic growth over the dying process for Taiwanese terminally ill cancer patients. *Psycho-Oncology, 24*, 147–154. doi: 10.1002/pon.3616

Tangney, J. P., Stuewig, J., & Martinez, A. G. (2014). Two faces of shame: The roles of shame and guilt in predicting recidivism. *Psychological Science, 25*, 799–805. doi: 10.1177/0956797613508790

Tanyi, Z., Szluha, K., Nemes, L., Kovács, S., & Bugán, A. (2014). Health-related quality of life, fatigue, and posttraumatic growth of cancer patients undergoing radiation therapy: A longitudinal study. *Applied Research in Quality of Life, 9*(3), 617–630. doi: 10.1007/s11482-013-9261-7

Tarakeshwar, N., Pargament, K. I., & Mahoney, A. (2003). Measures of Hindu pathways: Development and preliminary evidence of reliability and validity. *Cultural Diversity and Ethnic Minority Psychology, 9*, 316–332. doi: 10.1037/1099-9809.9.4.316

Taubman-Ben-Ari, O., Findler, L., & Sharon, N. (2011). Personal growth in mothers: Examination of the suitability of the posttraumatic growth inventory as a measurement tool. *Women & Health, 51*, 604–622. doi: 10.1080/03630242.2011.614324

Taubman-Ben-Ari, O., Shlomo, S. B., & Findler, L. (2012). Personal growth and meaning in life among first-time mothers and grandmothers. *Journal of Happiness Studies, 13*, 801–820. doi: 10.1007/s10902-011-9291-5

Taubman-Ben-Ari, O., Shlomo, S. B., Sivan, E., & Dolizki, M. (2009). The transition to motherhood: A time for growth. *Journal of Social and Clinical Psychology, 28*, 943–970.

Taylor, M., Wells, G., Howell, G., & Raphael, B. (2012). The role of social media as psychological first aid as a support to community resilience building. *Australian Journal of*

*Emergency Management, 27,* 20–26. Retrieved from https://search.informit.com.au/docu mentSummary;dn=046721101149317;res=IELAPA

Taylor, S. C. (2011). *Social Death and Sexual Violence.* Melbourne, Australia: Spinifex Press.

Taylor, S. E. (1983). Adjustment to threatening events: A theory of cognitive adaptation. *American Psychologist, 38,* 1161–1173. doi: 10.1037/00003-066X.38.11.1161

Taylor, S. E., & Brown. J. D. (1988). Illusion and well-being: A social psychological perspective on mental health. *Psychological Bulletin, 103,* 193–210.

Taylor, S. E., Lerner, J. S., Sherman, D. K., Sage, R. M., & McDowell, N. K. (2003). Are self-enhancing cognitions associated with healthy or unhealthy biological profiles? *Journal of Personality and Social Psychology, 85,* 605–615. doi: 10.1037/0022-3514.85.4.605

Tedeschi, R. G. (1990). Therapeutic listening. In G. McGregor & R. S. White (Eds.), *Reception and response: Hearer creativity and the analysis of spoken and written texts* (pp. 37–51). London: Routledge.

Tedeschi, R. G. (1999). Violence transformed: Posttraumatic growth in survivors and their societies. *Aggression and Violent Behavior, 4,* 319–341.

Tedeschi, R. G. (2011). Posttraumatic growth in combat veterans. *Journal of Clinical Psychology in Medical Settings, 18,* 137–144. doi: 10.1007/s10880-011-9255-2

Tedeschi, R. G., & Blevins, C. L. (2015). From mindfulness to meaning: Implications for the theory of posttraumatic growth. *Psychological Inquiry, 26*(4), 373–376. doi: 10.1080/1047840X.2015.1075354

Tedeschi, R. G., & Blevins, C. L. (2017). Posttraumatic growth: A pathway to resilience. In U. Kumar & U. Kumar (Eds.), *The Routledge international handbook of psychosocial resilience* (pp. 324–333). New York, NY: Routledge/Taylor & Francis Group.

Tedeschi, R. G., & Calhoun, L. G. (1988). *Perceived benefits in coping with physical handicaps.* Paper presented at the annual meeting of the American Psychological Association, Atlanta.

Tedeschi, R. G., & Calhoun, L. G. (1994). *The perceived benefits scale: Assessing the positive side of trauma.* Paper presented at the annual meeting of the Southeastern Psychological Association, New Orleans.

Tedeschi, R. G., & Calhoun, L. G. (1995). *Trauma and transformation: Growing in the aftermath of suffering.* Thousand Oaks, CA: Sage.

Tedeschi, R. G., & Calhoun, L. G. (1996). The Posttraumatic Growth Inventory: Measuring the positive legacy of trauma. *Journal of Traumatic Stress, 9,* 455–471. doi: 10.1007/ BF02103658

Tedeschi, R. G., & Calhoun, L. G. (2004a). *Helping bereaved parents: A clinician's guide.* New York and Hove: Brunner-Routledge.

Tedeschi, R. G., & Calhoun, L. G. (2004b). Posttraumatic growth: Conceptual foundations and empirical evidence. *Psychological Inquiry, 15,* 1–18. doi: 10.1207/ s15327965pli1501_01

Tedeschi, R. G., & Calhoun, L. G. (2006). Expert companions: Posttraumatic growth in clinical practice. In L. G. Calhoun & R. G. Tedeschi (Eds.), *Handbook of posttraumatic growth: Research and practice* (pp. 291–310). Mahwah, NJ: Lawrence Erlbaum Associates.

Tedeschi, R. G., & Calhoun, L. G. (2008). Beyond the concept of recovery: Growth and the experience of loss. *Death Studies, 32,* 27–39. doi: 10.1080/07481180701741251

Tedeschi, R. G., & Calhoun, L. G. (2012). Pathways to personal transformation: Theoretical and empirical developments. In P. T. P. Wong (Ed.), *The human quest for meaning: Theories, research, and applications* (2nd ed., pp. 559–572). New York, London: Routledge.

Tedeschi, R. G., Calhoun, L. G., & Cann, A. (2007). Evaluating resource gain: Understanding and misunderstanding posttraumatic growth. *Applied Psychology: An International Review, 56*, 396–406. doi: 10.1111/j.1464-0597.2007.00299.x

Tedeschi, R. G., Calhoun, L. G., Morrell, R. W., & Johnson, K. A. (1984). *Bereavement: From grief to psychological development.* Paper presented at the annual meeting of the American Psychological Association, Toronto.

Tedeschi, R. G., Cann, A., Taku, K., Senol-Durak, E., & Calhoun, L. G. (2017). The posttraumatic growth inventory: A revision integrating existential and spiritual change. *Journal of Traumatic Stress, 30(1)*, 11–18. doi: 10.1002/jts.22155

Tedeschi, R. G., & McNally, R. J. (2011). Can we facilitate posttraumatic growth in combat veterans? *American Psychologist, 66*, 19–24. doi: 10.1037/a0021896

Tedeschi, R. G., & Moore, B. A. (2016a). *The posttraumatic growth workbook: Coming through trauma wiser, stronger, and more resilient.* Oakland, CA: New Harbinger Publications, Inc.

Tedeschi, R. G., & Moore, B. A. (2016b). A model for developing community-based, grass roots laboratories for postdeployment adjustment. *The Military Psychologist, 31*(2), 6–10.

Tedeschi, R. G., Park, C. L., & Calhoun, L. G. (1998). Posttraumatic growth: Conceptual issues. In R. G. Tedeschi, C. L. Park, & L. G. Calhoun (Eds.), *Posttraumatic growth: Positive changes in the aftermath of crisis* (pp. 1–22). Mahwah, NJ: Lawrence Erlbaum Associates.

Tedeschi, R. G., & Riffle, O. M. (2016). Posttraumatic growth and logotherapy: Finding meaning in trauma. *International Forum for Logotherapy, 39*(1), 40–47.

Teixeira, R. J., & Pereira, G. (2013). Growth and the cancer caregiving experience: Psychometric properties of the Portuguese posttraumatic growth inventory. *Families, Systems, & Health, 31*, 382–395. doi: 10.1037/a0032004

Tennen, H., Affleck, G., Urrows, S., Higgins, P., & Mendola, R. (1992). Perceiving control, construing benefits, and daily processes in rheumatoid arthritis. *Canadian Journal of Behavioral Science, 24*, 186–203.

Thombre, A., Sherman, A. C., & Simonton, S. (2010). Religious coping and posttraumatic growth among family caregivers of cancer patients in India. *Journal of Psychosocial Oncology, 28*, 173–188. doi: 10.1080/07347330903570537

Thornton, A. A., & Perez, M. A. (2006). Posttraumatic growth in prostate cancer survivors and their partners. *Psycho-Oncology, 15*, 285–296. doi: 10.1002/pon.953

Thrombre, A., Sherman, A., & Simonton, S. (2010). Posttraumatic growth amongst cancer patients in India. *Journal of Behavioral Medicine, 33*, 15–23. doi: 10.1007/s10865-009-9229-0

Tillery, R., Sharp, K. M. H., Okado, Y., Long, A., & Phipps, S. (2016). Profiles of resilience and growth in youth with cancer and healthy comparisons. *Journal of Pediatric Psychology*, 290–297. doi: 10.1093/jpepsy/jsv091

Tomich, P. L., & Helgeson, V. S. (2004). Is finding something good in the bad always good? Benefit finding among women with breast cancer. *Health Psychology, 23*, 16–23. doi: 10.1037/0278-6133.23.1.16

Triplett, K. N., Tedeschi, R. G., Cann, A., Calhoun, L. G., & Reeve, C. L. (2012). Posttraumatic growth, meaning in life, and life satisfaction in response to trauma. *Psychological Trauma: Theory, Research, Practice, and Policy, 4*, 400–410. doi: 10.1037/a0024204

Trull, T. J., & Widiger, T. A. (2015). Personality disorders and personality. In M. Mikulincer, P. R. Shaver, M. L. Cooper, & R. J. Larsen (Eds.), *APA handbook of personality and social psychology, volume 4: Personality processes and individual differences* (pp. 601–618). Washington, DC: American Psychological Association.

Tsai, J., Sippel, L. M., Mota, N., Southwick, S., & Pietrzak, R. (2015). Longitudinal course of posttraumatic growth among U.S. military veterans: Results from the national health and resilience in veterans' study. *Depression and Anxiety*, *33*, 9–18. doi: 10.1002/da.22371

Turner, S. G., & Maschi, T. M. (2015). Feminist and empowerment theory and social work practice. *Journal of Social Work Practice*, *29*, 151–162. doi: 10.1080/02650533.2014.941282

Turner-Sack, A. M., Menna, R., Setchell, S. R., Maan, C., & Cataudella, D. (2016). Psychological functioning, post-traumatic growth, and coping in parents and siblings of adolescent cancer survivors. *Oncology Nursing Forum*, *43*, 48–56. doi: 10.1188/16.ONF.48-56

Ullrich, P. M., & Lutgendorf, S. K. (2002). Journaling about stressful events: Effects of cognitive processing and emotional expression. *Annals of Behavioral Medicine*, *24*, 244–250. doi: 10.1207/S15324796ABM2403_10

Vanhooren, S., Leijssen, M., & Dezutter, J. (2015). Posttraumatic growth in sex offenders: A pilot study with a mixed-method design. *International Journal of Offender Therapy and Comparative Criminology*, 1–20. doi: 10.1177/0306624X15590834

Vaughn, A., Roesch, S., & Aldridge, A. (2009). Stress-related growth in racial/ethnic minority adolescents: Measurement, structure and validity. *Educational and Psychological Measurement*, *69*, 131–145. doi: 10.1177/0013164408318775

Vaughan, M. D., & Waehler, C. A. (2010). Coming out growth: Conceptualizing and measuring stress-related growth associated with coming out to others as a sexual minority. *Journal of Adult Development*, *17*, 94–109. doi: 10.1007/s10804-009-9084-9

Vázquez, C., & Páez, D. (2010). Posttraumatic growth in Spain. In T. Weiss & R. Berger (Eds.), *Posttraumatic growth and culturally competent practice: Lessons learned from around the globe* (pp. 97–112). Hoboken, NJ: John Wiley & Sons, Inc.

Venkatesh, V., Brown, S., & Bala, H. (2013). Bridging the qualitative—quantitative divide: Guidelines for conducting mixed methods research in information systems. *MIS Quarterly*, *37*, 21–54.

Veselka, L., Schermer, J. A., Martin, R. A., & Vernon, P. A. (2010). Laughter and resiliency: A behavioral genetic study of humor styles and mental toughness. *Twin Research and Human Genetics*, *13*, 442–449. doi: 10.1375/twin.13.5.442

Vilenica, S., & Shakespeare-Finch, J. (2012). A salutogenic approach to healing following child sexual assault. In E. Kalfoğlu & R. Faikoğlu (Eds.), *Sexual abuse: Breaking the silence* (pp. 33–56). Rijeka, Croatia: InTech. doi: 10.5772/28709

Vilenica, S., Shakespeare-Finch, J., & Obst. P. (2014). The role of counselling in healing from sexual assault in childhood from the phenomenological perspective of men and women. *Psychotherapy in Australia*, *20*. Retrieved from www.psychotherapy.com.au/journal/archive-and-search/

Vishnevsky, T., Cann, A., Calhoun, L. G., Tedeschi, R. G., & Demakis, G. J. (2010). Gender differences in self-reported posttraumatic growth: A meta-analysis. *Psychology of Women Quarterly*, *34*, 110–120. doi: 10.1111/j.1471-6402.2009.01546.x

Vloet, A., Simons, M., Vloet, T. D., Sander, M., Herpertz-Dahlmann, B., & Konrad, K. (2014). Long-term symptoms and posttraumatic growth in traumatized adolescents: Findings from a specialized outpatient clinic. *Journal of Traumatic Stress*, *27*, 622–625. doi: 10.1002/jts.21955

Volgin, R. N., Shakespeare-Finch, J., & Shochet, I. M. (under review). Posttraumatic distress, hope and growth in survivors of commercial sexual exploitation in Nepal. *Child Maltreatment*.

Vollhardt, J. R., & Staub, E. (2011). Inclusive altruism born of suffering: The relationship between adversity and prosocial attitudes and behavior toward disadvantaged outgroups. *American Journal of Orthopsychiatry*, *81*(3), 307–315. doi: 10.1111/j.1939-0025.2011.01099.x

Wachtel, P. L. (2011). *Therapeutic communication, knowing what to say when* (2nd ed.). New York, NY: Guilford Press.

Wada, K., & Park, J. (2009). Integrating Buddhist psychology into grief counseling. *Death Studies, 33*, 657–683. doi: 10.1080/07481180903012006

Wagner, A. C., Torbit, L., Jenzer, T., Landy, M. S. H., Pukay-Martin, N. D., Macdonald, A., . . . Monson, C. M. (2016). The role of posttraumatic growth in a randomized controlled trial of cognitive-behavioral conjoint therapy for PTSD. *Journal of Traumatic Stress, 29*, 379–383. doi: 10.1002/jts.22122

Wagner, B., Forstmeier, S., & Maercker, A. (2007). Posttraumatic growth as a cognitive process with behavioral components: A commentary of Hobfoll et al. (2007). *Applied Psychology: An International Review, 56*, 407–416. doi: 10.1111/j.1464-0597.2007.00295.x

Wakefield, J. C. (2016). Diagnostic issues and controversies in DSM-5: Return of the false positives problem. *Annual Review of Clinical Psychology*, 12105–12132. doi:10.1146/annurev-clinpsy-032814-112800

Wallace, B. A., & Shapiro, S. L. (2006). Mental balance and well-being: Building bridges between Buddhism and Western psychology. *American Psychologist, 61*, 690–701. doi: 10.1037/0003-066X.61.7.690

Walsh, F. (2003). Family resilience: A framework for clinical practice. *Family Process, 42*, 1–18. doi: 10.1111/j.1545-5300.2003.00001.x

Walsh, R. (2015). What is wisdom? Cross-cultural and cross-disciplinary syntheses. *Review of General Psychology, 19*, 278–293. doi: 10.1037/gpr0000045

Wang, A. W.-T., Chang, C.-S., Chen, S.-T., Chen, D.-R., Fan, F., Carver, C. S., & Hsu, W.-Y. (2017). Buffering and direct effect of posttraumatic growth in predicting distress following cancer. *Health Psychology, 36*, 549–559. doi: 10.1037/hea0000490

Wang, J., Chen, Y., Wang, Y. B., & Liu, X. H. (2011). Revision of the posttraumatic growth inventory and testing its reliability and validity. *Chinese Journal of Nursing Science, 26*, 26–28.

Wang, K., Rendina, H. J., & Pachankis, J. E. (2016). Looking on the bright side of stigma: How stress-related growth facilitates adaptive coping among gay and bisexual men. *Journal of Gay & Lesbian Mental Health, 20*(4), 363–375. doi: 10.1080/19359705.2016.1175396

Weathers, F. W., & Keane, T. M. (2007). The Criterion A problem revisited: Controversies and challenges in defining and measuring psychological trauma. *Journal of Traumatic Stress, 20*(2), 107–121. doi:10.1002/jts.20210

Weaver, K. E., Llabre, M. M., Lechner, S. C., Penedo, F., & Antoni, M. H. (2008). Comparing unidimensional and multidimensional models of benefit finding in breast and prostate cancer. *Quality of Life Research, 17*, 771–781. doi: 10.1007/s11136-008-9348-z

Webb, L. (2011). The recovery model and complex health needs: What health psychology can learn from mental health and substance misuse service provision. *Journal of Health Psychology, 17*, 731–741. doi: 10.1177/1359105311425276

Webster, J. D., & Deng, X. C. (2015). Paths from trauma to intrapersonal strength: Worldview, posttraumatic growth, and wisdom. *Journal of Loss and Trauma, 20*, 253–266. doi: 10.1080/15325024.2014.932207

Weinberger, J. (2014). Common factors are not so common and specific factors are not so specified: Toward an inclusive integration of psychotherapy research. *Psychotherapy, 51*, 514–518.

Weinrib, A. Z., Rothrock, N. E., Johnsen, E. L., & Lutgendorf, S. K. (2006). The assessment and validity of stress-related growth in a community-based sample. *Journal of Consulting and Clinical Psychology, 74*, 851–858. doi: 10.1037/0022-006X.74.5.851

Weiss, D. S., & Marmar, C. R. (1997). The impact of event scale: Revised. In J. P. Wilson & T. M. Keane (Eds.), *Assessing psychological trauma and PTSD* (pp. 399–411). New York: Guildford Press.

Weiss, T. (2002). Posttraumatic growth in women with breast cancer and their husbands: An intersubjective validation study. *Journal of Psychosocial Oncology, 20*, 65–80. doi: 10.1300/J077v20n02_04

Weiss, T. (2004). Correlates of posttraumatic growth in husbands of breast cancer survivors. *Psycho-Oncology, 13*, 260–268. doi: 10.1002/pon.735

Weiss, T. (2014). Personal transformation: Posttraumatic growth and gerotranscendence. *Journal of Humanistic Psychology, 54*, 203–226. doi: 10.1177/0022167813492388

Weiss, T., & Berger, R. (2006). Reliability and validity of a Spanish version of the posttraumatic growth inventory. *Research on Social Work Practice, 16*, 191–199. doi: 10.1177/1049731505281374

Weiss, T., & Berger, R. (2010). Posttraumatic growth around the world: Research findings and practice implications. In T. Weiss & R. Berger (Eds.), *Posttraumatic growth and culturally competent practice: Lessons learned from around the globe* (pp. 188–195). Hoboken, NJ: John Wiley & Sons, Inc.

Westphal, M., & Bonanno, G. A. (2007). Posttraumatic growth and resilience to trauma: Different sides of the same coin or different coins? *Applied Psychology: An International Review, 56*, 417–427.

Weststrate, N. M., & Glück, J. (2017). Hard-earned wisdom: Exploratory processing of difficult life experience is positively associated with wisdom. *Developmental Psychology, 53*, 800–814. doi: 10.1037/dev0000286

White, M. (2004). Working with people who are suffering the consequences of multiple trauma: A narrative perspective. *International Journal of Narrative Therapy & Community Work, 1*, 45–76.

Williams, M. B., Baker, G. R., & Williams, T. (1999). The great Hanshin-Awaji earthquake: Adapted strategies for survival. In E. S. Zinner & M. B. Williams (Eds.), *When a community weeps: Case studies in group survivorship* (pp. 102–116). Philadelphia, PA: Brunner/Mazel.

Williamson, C. (2014). Towards a theory of collective posttraumatic growth in Rwanda: The pursuit of agency and communion. *Traumatology, 20*, 91–102. doi: 10.1037/h0099393

Wilson, B., Morris, B. A., & Chambers, S. (2014). A structural equation model of posttraumatic growth after prostate cancer. *Psycho-Oncology, 23*, 1212–1219. doi: 10.1002/pon.3546

Wilson, J. Z., Marin, D., Maxwell, K., Cumming, J., Berger, R., Saini, S., . . . Chibnall, J. T. (2016). Association of posttraumatic growth and illness-related burden with psychosocial factors of patient, family, and provider in pediatric cancer survivors. *Journal of Traumatic Stress, 29*, 448–456. doi: 10.1002/jts.22123

Wlodarczyk, A., Basabe, N., Páez, D., Reyes, C., Villagrán, L., Madariaga, C., . . . Martínez, F. (2016). Communal coping and posttraumatic growth in a context of natural disasters in Spain, Chile, and Columbia. *Cross-Cultural Research, 50*, 325–355. doi: 10.1177/1069397116663857

Wolchik, S. A., Coxe, S., Tein, J. Y., Sandler, I. N., & Ayers, T. S. (2008). Six-year longitudinal predictors of posttraumatic growth in parentally bereaved adolescents and young adults. *Omega, 58*, 107–128. doi: 10.2190/OM.58.2.b

Woo, I. M. H., Chan, C. L. W., Chow, A. Y. M., & Ho, R. T. H. (2007). Chinese widower's self-perception of growth: An exploratory study. *Journal of Social Work in End-of-Life & Palliative Care, 3*, 47–67. doi: 10.1080/15524250802003422

Wood, M. M., Molassiotis, A., & Payne, S. (2011). What research evidence is there for the use of art therapy in the management of symptoms in adults with cancer? A systematic review. *Psycho-Oncology, 20*(2), 135–145. doi:10.1002/pon.1722

Xu, J., & Liao, Q. (2011). Prevalence and predictors of posttraumatic growth among adult survivors one year following 2008 Sichuan earthquake. *Journal of Affective Disorders, 133*, 274–280. doi: 10.1016/j.jad.2011.03.034

Yaden, D. B., Iwry, J., Slack, K. J., Eichstaedt, J. C., Zhao, Y., Vaillant, G. E., & Newberg, A. B. (2016). The overview effect: Awe and self-transcendent experience in space flight. *Psychology of Consciousness: Theory, Research, and Practice, 3*, 1–11. doi: 10.1037/cns0000086

Yalom, I. D., & Lieberman, M. A. (1991). Bereavement and heightened existential awareness. *Psychiatry, 54*, 334–345. doi: 10.1521/00332747.1991.11024563

Yanez, B. R., Edmondson, D., Stanton, A. L., Park, C. L., Kwan, L., Ganz, P. A., & Blank, T. O. (2009). Facets of spirituality as predictors of adjustment to cancer: Relative contributions of having faith and finding meaning. *Journal of Consulting and Clinical Psychology, 77*, 730–741. doi: 10.1037/a0015820

Yanez, B. R., Stanton, A. L., Hoyt, M. A., Tennen, H., & Lechner, S. (2011). Understanding perceptions of benefit following adversity: How do distinct assessments of growth relate to coping and adjustment to stressful events? *Journal of Social and Clinical Psychology, 30*, 699–721. doi: 10.1521/jscp.2011.30.7.699

Ying, L., Wang, Y., Lin, C., & Chen, C. (2016). Trait resilience moderated the relationship between PTG and academic adolescent burnout in a post-disaster context. *Personality and Individual Differences, 90*, 108–112. doi: 10.1016/j.paid.2015.10.048

Yu, N. X., Chen, L., Ye, Z., Li, X., & Lin, D. (2016). Impacts of making sense of adversity on depression, posttraumatic stress disorder, and posttraumatic growth among a sample of mainly newly diagnosed HIV positive Chinese young homosexual men: The mediating role of resilience. *AIDS Care, 29*. doi: 10.1080/09540121.2016.1210073

Yu, X., Lau, J. T. F., Zhang, J., Mak, W. W. S., Choi, K. C., Lui, W. W. S., . . . Chan, E. Y. Y. (2010). Posttraumatic growth and reduced suicidal ideation among adolescents at month 1 after the Sichuan earthquake. *Journal of Affective Disorders, 123*, 327–331. doi: 10.1016/j.jad.2009.09.019

Yu, Y., Peng, L., Chen, L., Long, L., He, W., Li, M., & Wang, T. (2014). Resilience and social support promote posttraumatic growth of women with infertility: The mediating role of positive coping. *Psychiatry Research, 215*, 401–405. doi: 10.1016/j.psychres.2013.10.032

Zerach, G. (2015). Secondary growth among former prisoners of war's adult children: The result of exposure to stress, secondary traumatization, or personality traits? *Psychological Trauma: Theory, Research, Practice, and Policy, 7*, 313–323. doi: 10.1037/tra0000009

Zerach, G., Solomon, Z., Cohen, A., & Ein-Dor, T. (2013). PTSD, resilience and posttraumatic growth among ex-prisoners of war and combat veterans. *Israel Journal of Psychiatry and Related Sciences, 50*, 91–99.

Zernicke, K., Campbell, T. S., Speca, M., McCabe Ruff, K., Flowers, S., Tamagawa, R., & Carlson, L. (2016). The eCALM trial: eTherapy for cancer applying mindfulness: Exploratory analyses of the associations between online mindfulness-based cancer recovery participation and changes in mood, stress symptoms, mindfulness, posttraumatic growth, and spirituality. *Mindfulness, 7*, 1071–1081. doi: 10.1007/s12671-016-0545-5

Zhang, W., Yan, T. T., Barriball, K. L., White, A. E., & Liu, X. H. (2015). Post-traumatic growth in mothers of children with autism: A phenomenological study. *Autism, 19*, 29–37. doi: 10.1177/1362361313509732

Zheng, P., & Gray, M. J. (2015). Posttraumatic coping and distress: An evaluation of Western conceptualization of trauma and its applicability to Chinese culture. *Journal of Cross-Cultural Psychology, 46*, 723–736. doi: 10.1177/0022022115580848

Zimmerman, M. A. (1995). Psychological empowerment: Issues and illustrations. *American Journal of Community Psychology, 23,* 581–598. doi: 10.1007/BF02506983

Zoellner, T., & Maercker, A. (2006). Posttraumatic growth in clinical psychology: A critical review and introduction of a two component model. *Clinical Psychology Review, 26,* 626–653. doi: 10.1016/j.cpr.2006.01.008

Zoellner, T., Rabe, S., Karl, A., & Maercker, A. (2008). Posttraumatic growth in accident survivors: Openness and optimism as predictors of its constructive or illusory sides. *Journal of Clinical Psychology, 64,* 245–263. doi: 10.1002/jclp.20441

Zoellner, T., Rabe, S., Karl, A., & Maercker, A. (2010). Post-traumatic growth as outcome of a cognitive-behavioural therapy trial for motor vehicle accident survivors with PTSD. *Psychology and Psychotherapy: Theory, Research and Practice, 84,* 201–213. doi: 10.1348/147608310X520157

Zwahlen, D., Hagenbuch, N., Carley, M. I., Jenewein, J., & Buchi, S. (2010). Posttraumatic growth in cancer patients and partners—effects of role, gender and the dyad on couples' posttraumatic growth experience. *Psycho-Oncology, 19,* 12–20. doi: 10.1002/pon.1486

# Index

Made in the USA
Middletown, DE
16 May 2019